FINANCIAL
ECONOMICS

FINANCIAL TIMES

Prentice Hall

In an increasingly competitive world, it is quality
of thinking that gives an edge. An idea that opens new
doors, a technique that solves a problem, or an insight
that simply helps make sense of it all.

We work with leading authors in the fields of
management and finance to bring cutting-edge thinking
and best learning practice to a global market.

Under a range of leading imprints, including
Financial Times Prentice Hall, we create world-class
print publications and electronic products giving readers
knowledge and understanding which can then be
applied, whether studying or at work.

To find out more about our business and professional
products you can visit us at www.financialminds.com

For other Pearson Education publications, visit
www.pearsoned-ema.com

Pearson
Education

FINANCIAL ECONOMICS

Making sense of information
in financial markets

BRIAN KETTELL

An imprint of **Pearson Education**

London · New York · San Francisco · Toronto · Sydney
Tokyo · Singapore · Hong Kong · Cape Town · Madrid
Paris · Milan · Munich · Amsterdam

PEARSON EDUCATION LIMITED

Head Office:
Edinburgh Gate
Harlow CM20 2JE
Tel: +44 (0)1279 623623
Fax: +44 (0)1279 431059

London Office:
128 Long Acre
London WC2E 9AN
Tel: +44 (0)20 7447 2000
Fax: +44 (0)20 7240 5771
Website: www.financialminds.com

First published in Great Britain in 2001

ISBN 0 273 63073 3

British Library Cataloguing in Publication Data
A CIP catalogue record for this book can be obtained from the British Library

Transferred to digital print on demand, 2006

Typeset by Pantek Arts Ltd, Maidstone, Kent
Printed and bound by Antony Rowe Ltd, Eastbourne

The Publishers' policy is to use paper manufactured from sustainable forests.

ABOUT THE AUTHOR

Brian Kettell (MSc, BSc Econ) has many years experience working in financial markets and banking. A graduate of the London School of Economics, he has worked for Citibank, American Express, Arab Banking Corporation (Vice President) and Shearson Lehman (Vice President). He has delivered training courses on the markets for a variety of organizations including Chase Manhattan Bank, Nomura, Morgan Stanley, Kleinwort Benson, Banque Indosuez and The Euromoney Institute of Finance. Formerly Senior Lecturer at London University and a visiting Professor of Finance at several French Business Schools he is currently Economic Advisor to the Central Bank of Bahrain.

He has published widely (over 80 articles) in numerous journals including *Central Banking*, *The Banker*, *Euromoney* and *The Securities Journal*, and his previous books include, *What Drives Financial Markets*, *What Drives Currency Markets*, *Fed Watching*, *The International Debt Game* (with George Magnus, Chief Economist UBS Warburg), *Businessman's Guide to the Foreign Exchange Market*, *Monetary Economics*, *The Finance of International Business*, *Gold* and *The Foreign Exchange Handbook* (with Steve Bell, Chief Economist Deutsche Bank). In addition he has published a large number of case studies on financial markets.

The author would like to dedicate this book to his wife Nadia, without whose support it would not have been written, and to his sister Pat without whom it would not have been typed.

ACKNOWLEDGEMENTS

Chapters 16, 17 and 18 were originally written by Professor John Cochrane, a consultant at the Federal Reserve Bank of Chicago and published in Economic Perspectives. The views expressed in those articles are those of the author, John Cochrane, and do not necessarily represent the views of the Federal Reserve Bank of Chicago or the Federal Reserve System. I would like to take this opportunity to thank both Professor John Cochrane and The Federal Reserve Bank of Chicago for permission to reprint these articles.

Appendix 7.1 was reprinted from the Lombard Street Research Monthly Economic Review, September 1999, with the permission of Professor Tim Congdon.

CONTENTS

INTRODUCTION

The announcement that the Nobel Prize for Economics had been awarded to Merton Miller, William Sharpe and Harry Markowitz, in 1990, finally acknowledges that financial economics is a genuine science, in the same league as the physical sciences. Defining what is financial economics is not straightforward as it is a subject which overlaps with both economics, finance and also with statistics. However, for the purposes of this book, we will use the term to refer to those aspects of economics, finance and investment management which involve the study of financial markets. More precisely, we will be using the term *financial economics* to mean a subject which concerns itself with the building of models of asset price determination for investors seeking to build portfolios in a world of uncertainty.

Finance itself, as a subject for serious academic study in its own right, is relatively new, having grown out of applied economics over the past 50 years or so. Financial economics is even more recent. Notwithstanding its short life, the empirical research and theoretical developments in financial economics have been immense, with the USA dominating the subject for most of the period.

The last 20 years have seen a revolution in the way financial economists understand the world around us. It was once thought that stock market and bond market returns were essentially unpredictable. Now it is recognized that stock and bond market returns have a substantial predictable component at long horizons. It was once thought that the capital asset pricing model (CAPM) provided a good description of why average returns on some stocks, portfolios, funds or strategies were higher than others. Now it is recognized that the average returns of many investment opportunities cannot be explained by the CAPM, and so-called 'multifactor models' have supplanted the CAPM to explain them. It was once thought that long-term interest rates reflected expectations of future short-term rates and that interest rate differentials across countries reflected expectations of exchange-rate depreciation. Now we can see what are known as time-varying risk premiums in bond and foreign exchange markets as well as in stock markets.

The build up to these ideas are developed throughout the text providing a comprehensive review of all the key issues in this exciting new subject: financial economics.

Brian Kettell

CHAPTER 1

What is financial economics?

- Background
- Setting the picture – valuation models
- Taking risk into account: the capital asset pricing model
- How do you design an efficient investment portfolio?
- Efficient markets: hypothesis or reality?
- The theory of options
- Term structure of interest rates
- Old finance, modern finance and the new finance

BACKGROUND

The announcement that the Nobel Prize for Economics had been awarded to Merton Miller, William Sharpe and Harry Markowitz, in 1990, finally acknowledges that financial economics is a genuine science, in the same league as the physical sciences. Coming up with a definiton of financial economics is not simple, as it is a subject which overlaps with both economics and finance and also with statistics. However, for the purposes of this book, we will use the term financial economics to refer to those aspects of economics, finance and investment management which involve the study of financial markets. More precisely we will be using the term financial economics as being a subject which concerns itself with the building of models of asset price determination for investors seeking to build portfolios in a world of uncertainty.

A key aspect of financial economics is how to value both individual securities and portfolios of securities.

Finance itself, as a subject for serious academic study in its own right, is relatively new, having grown out of applied economics over the past 50 years or so. Financial economics is even newer. Notwithstanding its short life, the empirical research and theoretical developments in financial economics have been immense, with the USA dominating the subject for most of the period.

The last 20 years have seen a revolution in the way financial economists understand the world around us. It was once thought that stock market and bond market returns were essentially unpredictable. Now it is recognized that stock and bond market returns have a substantial predictable component at long horizons. It was once thought that the capital asset pricing model (CAPM) provided a good description of why average returns on some stocks, portfolios, funds or strategies were higher than others. Now it is recognized that the average returns of many investment opportunities cannot be explained by the CAPM, and so called 'multifactor models' have supplanted the CAPM to explain them. It was once thought that long-term interest rates reflected expectations of future short-term rates and that interest rate differentials across countries reflected expectations of exchange-rate depreciation. Now we can see what are known as time-varying risk premiums in bond and foreign exchange markets as well as in stock markets. But we are getting ahead of ourselves here. These ideas are discussed in later chapters, particularly Chapters 16, 17 and 18. At this stage it is essential to run through some of the standard theory before moving on to the most recent developments.

SETTING THE PICTURE – VALUATION MODELS

There are several basic valuation models which can be applied to value shares in a company but, in reality, these all represent different ways of assessing the same future expected returns from the company. Thus a share's value is determined by the present value of the future dividend stream, the present value of the free cash flow per share, or the current earnings per share multiplied by the appropriate price earnings multiple.

All these valuation models require the use of an appropriate discount rate to bring expected future returns back to their present values. This discount rate must be set in the context of the risk associated with the investment. However, the risk of any company can be split into two components: its unique, diversifiable, unsystematic risk and its market or systematic risk. The *capital asset pricing model* argues that investors can diversify away the unique risk of any company by operating an efficient investment portfolio. Hence they should only be compensated, through increased expected returns, for the market risk of the company. This systematic risk, measured by the company's beta, represents the degree to which the company's return is affected by changes in the market return as a whole.

An alternative model, *the arbitrage pricing theory*, allows for more variables to be used to determine the overall expected return on the particular investment. Indeed, the specifically relevant variables are not identified in the theory, but later empirical tests have highlighted some not surprising factors which appear to influence expected returns.

These theories depend upon the efficiency of financial markets and this area has been the subject of massive empirical research. Relative definitions of market efficiency have been very neatly broken down into three categories:

1 the weak form (markets have no memory);

2 the semi-strong form (prices already incorporate all publicly available information);

3 the strong form (prices already reflect all information, whether public or private).

A recent area of concentrated work by financial economists has been in option pricing models. In most cases, options represent a way of either hedging risks or of speculating on an investment. But both strategies require valuation models, which turn out to be mathematically quite complex. Although the theoretical models suffer from conceptual flaws, they can be and are, used to generate real option prices to support the vast volumes of options on shares which are traded each day.

Interest rates underpin an appreciation of financial economics because all risky returns are calculated by reference to the risk-related premium required over a risk-free interest rate. Interest has to compensate for the time value of money (the real interest rate) and the potential lost purchasing power caused by inflation (giving us a nominal interest rate which is the product of the real return and the expected rate of inflation).

Some general points should be made before going on to consider financial economics in more detail. Most of the valuation theories apply to the financial markets in general rather than a single specific company at a particular point in time. Thus the theory can describe how shares are valued but the theory does not necessarily indicate whether any specific share is currently under-valued or over-valued.

There are some key problems appreciation of which is important to properly understand several of the theories considered below. Most theories are tested for their practical applicability by reference to actual market data. By definition this actual data is historic and hence the theory is applied retrospectively to try to see how well it explains actual events. Unfortunately most of the theory and all practical investment decisions are really based on *expected or anticipated* future returns, rather than on the actual return which is achieved. Thus the investor may be more or less than satisfied by the actual financial outcome, but it may be difficult to build this level of satisfaction into the financial analysis of actual historic out-turns.

The valuation of bonds

Before the basic valuation models for company shares are highlighted it is useful to review the appropriate logic for valuing bonds and other interest-yielding investments. The rationale for this type of investment is that the investor receives a known, relatively certain, annual return during the life of the investment and then, at the end of this life, receives back the face value of the bond or similar security. The value of this terminal receipt is not necessarily exactly equal to the initial purchase price of the investment as it is in the case of a bank deposit where interest is received during the life of the deposit and the principal is repaid at the end of the deposit period. In the case of a bond, the investor will calculate an initial purchase price for the bond so that the total return received over the life of the investment is acceptable considering alternative returns in investments with a similar risk profile. Thus if the annual interest rate payable on this particular bond is below similar market rates, the investor would only be willing to buy the bond at a discount to its full face value. Since the bond will ultimately be redeemed at its full face value, the resulting capital appreciation over the life of the investment increases the total annualized return to an acceptable level, normally known as the yield to maturity of the bond. Mathematically the yield to maturity is equivalent to the internal rate of return of the bond, as is illustrated in the numerical example given in Figure 1.1. Conversely, if the rate of interest payable on the bond is above prevailing similar risk market yields, the investor would be prepared to pay a premium over its face value to buy the bond, even though this results in an inevitable capital loss over the life of the bond.

(a) A €1 million five-year bond offers a 7% rate of interest payable annually in arrears. The current required market rate of return for this type of investment is 8%.

(b) Two years later, a general reduction in interest rates reduces the required market rate of return for this bond to 5%.

How are the bonds valued?

(a) An investor buying the bond will receive annual interest payments of €70,000 for five years and a principal repayment at the end of the five-year term of €1 million. These cash flows are discounted back to their present values, using the required rate of return of 8%, which represents the valid current purchase price of the bond.

Years	Cash flow	Discount factor at 8%	Present value
1–5	€70,000 p.a.	3.993	€279,500
5	€1,000,000	0.681	€681,000
Current acceptable purchase price of bond			€960,500

(b) If interest rates have fallen, the fixed future cash flows to be received from the bond have increased in value. This increase is shown by using the appropriate lower discount rate of 5% to calculate the present value of the remaining cash flows.

Years	Cash flow	Discount factor at 5%	Present value
1–3	€70,000 p.a.	2.673	€187,100
3	€1,000,000	0.864	€864,000
Acceptable purchase price of bond at end of year 2			€1,051,100

Conclusion
Initially this bond would have to be sold at a discount to its face value because its nominal yield is below that required by the market. However, a fall in this required yield moves the market price of the bond to a premium above its face value, even though two interest payments have already been made.

Fig 1.1 ● The valuation of bonds

Basic equity valuation models

Shareholders can achieve a financial return on their investments in the form of either dividends received in cash, or as a capital gain through increases in the price of their shares; normally the total return takes the form of a mixture of the two. This is mathematically represented in Equation (1) below where K_E is the total return expected by the investor, D_1 is the dividend expected this year, P_0 is the current share price and P_1 is the share price at time t, either expected or actual:

$$K_E = \frac{D_1 + (P_1 - P_0)}{P_0} \qquad (1)$$

Equation (1) requires the estimation of this year's dividend and the share price at the end of this year with only the current share price (P_0) being actually known. It would obviously be easier if the formula could be driven by only one unknown variable and therefore it is logical to try to derive a relationship between the future share price and the future dividend payments.

By rearranging Equation (1) it becomes possible to derive the current share price (P_0) as Equation (2):

$$P_0 = \frac{D_1 + P_1}{(1 + K_E)} \qquad (2)$$

This can be applied to future share prices, giving us Equation (3):

$$P_1 = \frac{D_2 + P_2}{(1 + K_E)} \qquad (3)$$

and so on.

Therefore if investors are assumed to have a five-year investment horizon, they will receive dividends for the next five years plus a capital sum at the end of the five years when they sell their shares. This can be arrived at using the above relationship. This generates the present value of the cash flows received by the investors; the key being that the discount rate being used is the shareholders' total expected return on their investment (K_E).

TAKING RISK INTO ACCOUNT: THE CAPITAL ASSET PRICING MODEL

The positive correlation between risk and return is central to an understanding of financial economics. The theoretical framework for assessing the relevant level of risk needs to be briefly addressed here. This is one area of finance which has been the subject of massive empirical research because, in the major capital markets at least, there are detailed records of the actual returns achieved by a wide range of alternative financial investments for over more than 100 years. Some of these major research studies have compared the levels of average total return (including both dividend, or interest, income and capital gains) for different investment portfolios over almost this entire period. These analyses confirm the intuitive logic that investors *receive* a higher return on investments which have a higher risk. The problem of analyzing actual historic data and using the results to predict the future, which assumes that investors actually received in the past what they expected or wanted to receive when they made their investment decision, was discussed earlier.

This higher risk can be caused both by risk of default or non-recovery of the initial investment and changes in the level of financial return or the price of the underlying security. Both of these may be caused by high susceptibility to external environmental changes such as inflation or interest rate movements, etc.

Risk is therefore associated with volatility in the level of return received on a financial investment given that the guaranteed return on a short-term government-backed security makes such an investment much lower risk than an investment in the stock market. It is mathematically possible to describe this volatility by referring to only two measures for any investment; thus the expected return from the investment can be taken as the arithmetic mean of all the possible returns and the volatility can be described by calculating the standard deviation of these possible outcomes from the arithmetic mean. This ability to use only two measures, described in detail in Chapter 4, to describe a future or historic set of outcomes is only valid for normal distributions, the well-known bell-shaped curves beloved of statisticians. Thus returns on shares are assumed to be normally distributed. The higher the standard deviation, the greater the degree of volatility in return and hence the greater the risk that is associated with that particular investment.

However, this again raises a problem of measurement because, as stated above, what is required are calculations on the range of possible returns from each investment. Clearly these are unknown and therefore, once again, reliance must be placed on actual historic data from which estimated future standard deviations can be calculated. For these estimates, it would not be sensible to use data for individual companies for the last 100 years because the risk profiles and hence the associated standard deviations are likely to have changed significantly over this length of time. Shorter periods. normally the last five years, are used with more frequent observations being taken; e.g. daily, monthly or quarterly returns are measured with these then being annualized to get the data to calculate standard deviations for each company. Clearly the shorter the timescale used and the fewer observations taken, the less reliable are the statistical results obtained for predictive purposes.

An important element in financial economics relating to risk is that the total risk associated with an investment in shares can be split into two components. There is the unique risk associated with the particular company; this risk is also known as company risk, specific risk or unsystematic risk. By investing in a diversified portfolio of shares the impact of any single company's unique risk can be reduced. This works very simply because the returns from individual companies do not move entirely together; i.e. they are not perfectly correlated. Consequently external influences, which dramatically affect the price of one share in the portfolio, may have almost no influence, or even an opposite impact, on the price of another share in the same portfolio. Thus provided investors spread their total investment across a sufficient number of shares the risk of their overall portfolio should be reduced below the risk of the individual shares comprising the portfolio.

However, no level of diversification can reduce or get rid of the second component of risk. This is known as market or systematic risk and refers to the intrinsic risk of investing in the stock market given that companies are subject to greater volatility than many other financial investments such as government-backed bonds. There are external business environmental factors, such as worldwide recessions and economic booms, which affect all businesses, but they do not affect all businesses to the same extent. It is therefore important to rank businesses relatively by reference to the degree of impact which these external factors have on shares in general. (The impact of diversification is important to note because the standard deviation of most individual shares is greater than the standard deviation of any overall representation of the stock market such as is achieved by using some weighted total portfolio of all, or most, shares listed on the particular stock market.)

This relative sensitivity of a particular company's return to changes in the return of the total stock market is called *the beta* of the company. If a company's share price is twice as sensitive to the total stock market, it is said to have a beta of 2; i.e. when overall stock market returns increase by 5 per cent, the returns on this share rise by 10 per cent. Similarly a less sensitive company may have a beta of 0.75 which means that if returns on the stock market fall by 10 per cent, this company's return will only fall by 7.5 per cent. Clearly the stock market as a whole has a beta of 1 because the stock market is a weighted average of all shares.

Now comes the important part of the theory. As rational investors can diversify away the unique risk associated with any particular company, they do not need, and should not receive, any additional return to compensate for taking on this unnecessary risk. Therefore shareholders should only be compensated for taking the systematic risk, which is an inevitable consequence of investing in shares. Thus the increased return which should be expected by investors will be related to the beta of the company concerned. However, as investors should only invest in the stock market through a diversified portfolio, the return on a well diversified portfolio will be driven by the risk of the portfolio; this portfolio risk will, in turn, depend on the weighted market risk of the shares in the portfolio. Hence a large part of successful investing in the stock market comes down to designing efficient portfolios, and is discussed further in Chapters 8 and 9.

If the rate of return for risk-free securities can be established and the premium required for investing in the stock market can be measured, all that remains is to define the relationship between the relative market risk of a share and the specific risk premium required by investors. These factors have been defined in a strikingly simple way in the capital asset pricing model (CAPM) developed in the 1960s by Treynor (1965), Sharpe (1964) and Lintner (1965), working almost independently of each other. If the only relevant measure of risk is the degree of correlation between movements in the total stock market and movements in the value of a particular security, the beta of a short-term government security can be taken as almost nil.

The risk premium expected by investors for investing in any particular share is in direct proportion to its market risk or beta factor, according to the CAPM; i.e. the relationship is linear as is shown in Figure 1.2. This enables expected costs of equity capital to be calculated for any business.

Clearly the relevant risk-free return is the current level of interest available on zero risk securities, and the current market risk or beta or the particular company or portfolio must be assessed. However, up until recently, most applications of the theory used the historic level of market premium to drive the current expected premium over the risk-free rate.

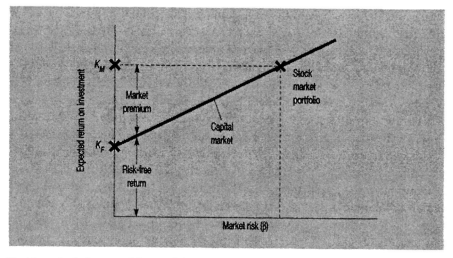

Fig 1.2 ● Capital asset pricing model

HOW DO YOU DESIGN AN EFFICIENT INVESTMENT PORTFOLIO?

If investors are expected to diversify so as to avoid the unique company risk of any particular investment, an important part of any investment strategy is to design the most suitable diversified portfolio. Some investment decisions are easy. All things being equal, investors will prefer a higher return for any level of risk and a lower risk for any given level of return. Therefore if two investments have the same standard deviation, investors will prefer the one with the higher expected return; while if the expected returns are the same, investors will choose the one with the lower risk, usually measured by the standard deviation. Normally, however, the company with the higher expected return also has the higher risk profile.

By using portfolio theory, as originally developed by Markowitz (1952), it is possible to reduce the risk associated with a combination of any potential investment by more than the return is reduced. Achieving this should increase investor value. The expected return from any portfolio is simply the weighted average of the individual expected returns of the shares comprising the portfolio. However, the risk of the portfolio is not the weighted average of the individual risks because the individual shares are not perfectly correlated with each other. In fact the lower the covariances, defined below, between the individual portfolio components, the greater is the reduction in the overall risk of the portfolio. Covariance is a measure of how tightly any two variables move together, it is driven by the correlation coefficient of the variables and their individual standard deviations. It is possible for correlation coefficients, and hence covariances, to be negative, which indicates that the variables normally move in opposite directions. Incorporating such negatively correlated investments in a portfolio can dramatically reduce the overall associated risks. (These statistical concepts are discussed in detail in Chapter 4.)

Obviously as the range of possible investments expands so do the potential ways of combining them into investment portfolios. However, only a limited number can be classified, in Markowitz's terms, as efficient portfolios, in that they represent the best return for any given level of risk, or the lowest risk for any given level of return. This is diagrammatically illustrated in Figure 1.3. As there are many efficient portfolios for any given range of investments the final choice appears to depend on the investor's risk appetite.

Clearly, the use of this portfolio management technique requires not only the estimation of expected returns and standard deviations for each prospective investment, but also the estimation of the covariance (via estimating the correlation coefficient) between each pair of shares. Interestingly, as the number of individual investments included in any portfolio increases, the relative total importance of the covariances between each pair of investments also increases. Not surprisingly, if the portfolio incorporated the appropriately weighted representatives of the entire stock market, its overall risk would be the market risk. After all, market risk is really the average covariance of all the shares making up the market. Thus diversification can eventually eliminate the unique risks of any shares, but cannot get rid of the covariances among shares.

The theory using efficient portfolios goes one stage further by introducing the ability for the investor to lend or borrow funds at the risk-free rate. The spread between lending and borrowing and the availability of finance are discussed further in Chapter 8. This additional principle enables the investor now to achieve any optimal desired position by simply investing in *one* efficient share portfolio and either lending or borrowing the necessary funds. This is illustrated

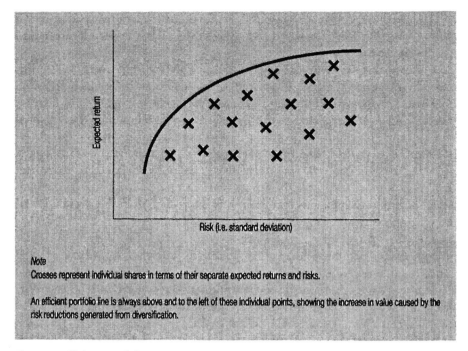

Note
Crosses represent individual shares in terms of their separate expected returns and risks.

An efficient portfolio line is always above and to the left of these individual points, showing the increase in value caused by the risk reductions generated from diversification.

Fig 1.3 ● Efficient portfolios

in Figure 1.4, which shows that this optimal line is drawn through the risk-free intercept and is tangential to the efficient portfolio curve. Thus, whatever the risk appetite of the investor, a better position can be achieved by using the potential to lend and borrow than by simply investing in any other efficient portfolio.

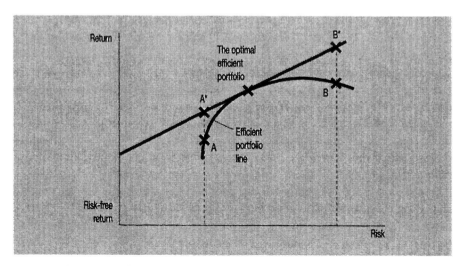

Fig 1.4 ● The optimal efficient portfolio

For risk-averse investors, who might otherwise have selected portfolio A, there is now a more attractive proposition. They can invest some of their funds in the optimal efficient portfolio and invest the rest in risk-free government bonds, so that they end up at position A*. This gives them their desired risk profile with a higher return. Conversely, high risk takers might have selected portfolio B but now they can borrow funds at the risk-free rate and invest all the money in the optimum portfolio which will move them to position B*. Once again, this shows a higher return for the same level of risk.

The beauty of this principle is that it means that investors can achieve their best financial position by holding either a mixture of their optimal investment portfolio and risk-free assets or a higher proportion of the same investment portfolio with borrowings to finance this extra investment in shares. In other words it is not necessary for a risk-averse investor to focus exclusively on low-risk shares nor for a high-risk taker to concentrate only on high volatility shares. Indeed, for most investors the most effective investment strategy using this logic is to use an appropriate mix, which reflects their appetite for risk, of risk-free lending or borrowing and an equity portfolio which mirrors the stock market, since this diversifies risk as completely as possible.

If this argument is applied to Figure 1.2 it becomes clear that the straight line drawn through K_F and the optimal efficient portfolio is actually the capital market line from Figure 1.4. In other words the stock market portfolio is an efficient investment portfolio, and this will certainly be the case in a perfectly competitive market.

The arbitrage pricing theory (APT) was propounded by Ross (1976) as a means of relating changes in returns on investments to unanticipated changes in a range of key value drivers for these investments. Thus, under APT, all investments have an 'expected return', and are affected by this range of basic economic forces (the exact nature of this range is not specified in the initial theory). Changes from the expected investment return are caused by the unanticipated movements in the factors and by the residual, unique risk associated with the company. Although all companies are affected by the same range of factors, the impact of each factor is not the same for each company; hence individual weightings for each factor are required. The key issue is obviously to define what the relevant factors are and to identify appropriate weightings for each company. As before, the theory assumes that investors avoid this unique risk by diversifying into an efficient portfolio.

This theory has been empirically tested but again the results are inconclusive, not least because of the potential range of economic factors which can be included. However, Roll and Ross (1980) believe that four major forces explain the majority of movements. These are the *unanticipated* changes in inflation, risk premiums, the term structure of interest rates and industrial production.

EFFICIENT MARKETS: HYPOTHESIS OR REALITY?

This subject has generated innumerable books, journal articles and other academic treatises and is discussed further in Chapters 10 and 12.

It is important at this stage to be precise about what is meant by the word 'efficient'. The term is not intended to mean that asset prices are always 'right' in the sense that expectations are always exactly, but only exactly, fulfilled. It simply means that today's prices incorporate all the information which is currently available to potential buyers and sellers. If this is true then price movements are caused by new information and as the nature of this new information is, by definition, unknown, the impact on prices cannot be predicted. Logically this would suggest no correlation between the direction and size of tomorrow's price movement and today's.

The theory of efficient markets was quite neatly broken down into three stages by Roberts (1959). The weak form of the efficient markets hypothesis (EMH) is that all historical price information is incorporated into current share prices. This means that price movements are random and are not controlled by past trends. Commonly referred to as the 'random walk' theory, this implies that technical analysis of past price movements (such as is done by 'chartists') cannot give investors a competitive advantage.

The semi-strong form argues that all published financial information is already included in the current share price. Consequently detailed analysis of a company's published financial statements should not give a consistently superior return.

The strong form of EMH says that current prices reflect all the available information which could be known. In other words, even insider and privileged information would not enable investors regularly to make a better than normal return.

The implications of an efficient market are substantial. If future price movements are random, it is fair to say that share prices have no memory. Thus talk of the market reaching record levels is irrelevant as share prices merely move to reflect the new information which has become available. Also if markets are efficient so that current prices are always 'as right as they can be', the most logical investment portfolio is an index of the whole stock market. With efficient markets no consistent gain can be achieved by active trading, i.e. moving from one share to another, and increased costs will be incurred.

THE THEORY OF OPTIONS

Options are one of the most exciting areas of financial economics. Unfortunately, they are also one of the most complicated. An option is a contractual right to buy or sell something at a particular time in the future, or during a given future period, at a fixed or specified price. Options can be divided into two basic types.

1   A call option gives its owner the future right to buy.

2   A put option gives its owner the future right to sell.

The key to the value of options is that ownership conveys the 'right' to do something, i.e. the choice of whether to exercise the option is left to the owner. This choice distinguishes options from future or forward contracts, where the obligation is binding on both parties. In an option contract, the obligation is only binding on the seller (normally known as the 'writer' of the option). The seller of a call option must deliver the asset in exchange for the agreed payment (known as the exercise or strike price) if required to do so by the buyer of the call option. The seller of a put option must pay the agreed price to the buyer of the put option if the asset is offered (put) to the seller.

All options contracts are made for a specified time period but there are two ways in which the contract may be determined. Under what is known as an American option, the owner can exercise the option at any time during the period of the contract, whereas, under a European option, exercise is only allowed at the maturity of the contract. The differences do not have a major impact on the prices of option contracts but theoretically European options are much easier to value.

Indeed, it is relatively straightforward to highlight the major factors which affect option values, *although* turning these factors into a mathematical relationship is considerably more complicated. This was originally done by Black and Scholes (1973), probably the most cited paper in financial economics. It is easier to consider the value of a call option first, say a call option to buy shares in a particular company at a specified time in the future (a European option).

The first factor is the relationship between the exercise price of the option and the current share price. If the share price is not above the exercise price at the maturity of the option contract, it will not be exercised and will be allowed to lapse. The buyer of the option has lost the investment made (the option purchase price) but cannot be forced to buy a share at a certain capital loss. However, the exercise price has to be paid only when the option is being taken up: hence the comparison should be between the present value of the exercise price and the current share price. In this case the risk-free discount rate should be used because the present value required is that sum of money which, if set aside today, will *guarantee* that sufficient funds are available at the maturity of the contract to exercise the call option if it is economically sensible to do so. This 'guarantee' means that the investment would have to be in a risk-free security. Thus the first factor in valuing options is the comparison of the present value of the exercise price to the current asset price. This is often described as the intrinsic value of the option and is why options are known as 'in the money' (the exercise price is below the current asset value) or 'out of the money' (the exercise price is above the current asset value).

The likelihood that the asset value will rise above the exercise price of the option is also a function of the time period involved and the volatility of the asset value in a single period of time. There is no value in owning an option to buy something if the price never changes! This volatility factor is usually measured by the variance or standard deviation of the asset value. The *greater* the variance and the larger the time period to maturity, the greater the value of any specific option.

If this theory is to be made useful in a practical way, it is clearly necessary to have some mathematical relationship among the key variables which determine option values. These key variables are the current asset price, the risk-free investment rate, the instantaneous volatility of the asset price and the time to maturity of the option, all of which are positive factors on the option value, together with the option exercise price (which is a negative factor on the value of the option).

The breakthrough in this area was achieved by Black and Scholes (1973) using some sophisticated mathematics. They produced a continuous time (i.e. using integration calculus rather than discrete binomial models) option pricing valuation model which, as seen in Equation (4), showed:

$$\text{Call option value} = P_0 N(d_1) - E e^{-K_f t} N(d_2) \tag{4}$$

where

P_0 = asset price now
E = option exercise price
K_f = risk-free
σ = standard deviation of the return on the asset
t = time to maturity of option

and

$$d_1 = \frac{\ln(P_0/E) + K_f t}{\sigma\sqrt{t}} + \tfrac{1}{2}\sigma\sqrt{t}, \text{ and } d_2 = d_1 - \sigma\sqrt{t}$$

and $N(d_1)$ and $N(d_2)$ are cumulative probabilities for a unit normal distribution, which is defined as having a mean of zero and a standard deviation of 1.

The problem with Equation (4) is not that it is complicated but that it is based on a series of restrictive assumptions. It represents the value of a simple call option on an asset which produces income stream during the life of the option (such as a non-dividend paying share). However, many real-life options are actually more complex. Options are discussed in more detail in Chapter 15.

TERM STRUCTURE OF INTEREST RATES

Another area of financial economics which needs to be examined is the structure of interest rates. Interest rates clearly have to compensate savers (lenders) for giving up their ability for immediate consumption; the higher the interest rate, the more *most* people would save. However as interest rates rise, the cost of funds increases to borrowers; thus they will demand less. Companies will find less economically attractive investment opportunities as their costs of funding increase. Equilibrium is achieved at the rate of interest where the supply of funds from savers equals the demand for borrowed funds. Thus equilibrium can be achieved at significantly different levels in different economies around the world at the same time. If individuals in one country have a high desire to save (normally expressed as a percentage of disposable income), they may only need to be offered a low rate of interest to stimulate sufficient savings to meet total investment needs: hence corporate funding costs are lower and funds are readily accessible. Alternatively if savings ratios are lower but the government is a very heavy borrower (it is running a large fiscal deficit), interest rates may be forced up to stimulate the level of saving needed to finance government needs as well as commercial investments. This would make company funding costs higher.

The above analysis ignores the ability of individuals to invest abroad if rates are higher, and for borrowers to raise funds from the cheapest source. By going abroad both parties potentially incur a foreign exchange risk which can be hedged by using a forward exchange contract or taking out an option contract. The costs of hedging this foreign currency risk clearly reduce the benefit obtained from the differences in interest rate.

Also interest rates have to compensate for more than just the loss of immediate use of the money. In periods of inflation the funds received back in the future will have lower purchasing power as general price levels will have increased. Thus interest rates must compensate for both the 'real' cost and the inflationary cost of lending money: hence nominal interest rates are the *product* of the required real rate of interest and the expected inflation rate. A key question is whether the real rate of interest is a function of the expected inflation rate or is constant over time; i.e. do investors in times of high expected future inflation, demand a greater real return as well? This is actually very difficult to test because measures of *expected* inflation, rather than actual inflation, are, as usual, difficult to obtain.

The nominal rate of interest is added to the risk premium required by the lender or investor in equities. This provides the cost of funding used to discount future expected cash flows to generate present values. Any casual examination of interest rates in any free financial market will indicate that interest rates do differ depending on the time period involved. The theoretical reasons for this are discussed in Chapter 5.

OLD FINANCE, MODERN FINANCE AND THE NEW FINANCE

In a controversial series of monographs, Robert Haugen, in analyzing the evolution of academic finance, characterizes its evolution into three groupings, namely what he calls the Old Finance, Modern Finance and the New Finance

(1999). The characteristics of these three groupings are summarized in Figure 1.5 which provides a useful taxonomy to plot the evolution of Financial Economics as a subset of Finance.

The Old Finance

    Theme: Analysis of Financial Statements and the Nature of Financial Claims
    Paradigms: *Analysis of Finance Statements*   *Uses and Rights of*
                  (Graham & Dodd)   *Financial Claims (Dewing)*
    Foundation: Accounting and Law

Modern Finance

    Theme: Valuation Based on Rational Economic Behaviour
    Paradigms: *Optimization*   *Irrelevance*   *CAPM*   *EMH*
                  (Markowitz)   *(Modigliani & Miller)*   *(Sharpe, Lintner & Mossen)*   *(Fama)*
    Foundation: Financial Economics

The New Finance

    Theme: Inefficient Markets
    Paradigms: Inductive ad hoc Factor Models
                  Expected Return   Risk   Behavioural Models
                  (Haugen)   (Chen, Roll & Ross)   (Kahneman & Tversky)
    Foundation: Statistics, Econometrics and Psychology

Fig 1.5 ● The evolution of academic finance

Source: The Inefficient Stock Market (Robert A. Haugen, Prentice Hall 1999)

The Old Finance

Accounting and Law, Haugen proposes, are the basic foundations of the Old Finance. The Old Finance drew heavily on two standard textbooks, *Security Analysis* by Benjamin Graham and David Dodd (1951) and *The Financial Policy of Corporations* by Arthur Stone Dewing (1953).

The focus of *Security Analysis* was to highlight how accounting statements could be adjusted so that the earnings and the balance sheets of different companies could be directly compared. The Dewing text took a more legalistic approach and stressed the laws relating to mergers and acquisitions as well as those governing bankruptcy and reorganization. These two texts established the rules of the game if finance, as an academic discipline, was to evolve.

Modern Finance

Modern Finance has four strands to it and we discuss these in more detail throughout the text. These four strands are:

1 *portfolio optimization as demonstrated by Harry Markowitz;*

2 *the irrelevance theorems as highlighted by Franco Modigliani and Merton Miller;*

3 *the capital asset pricing model as developed by Bill Sharpe, John Lintner and Jan Mossin;*

4 *the efficient market hypothesis, developed by Eugene Fama.*

1. Portfolio optimization

Markowitz's work was based, as Haugen demonstrates, on how one could build portfolios of stocks with the highest possible expected return given their risk or, alternatively, building a portfolio with the lowest possible risk given their rate of return. His work culminated in the development in what is known as the 'efficient set'. These efficient sets are the portfolios with the lowest risk, given return and those portfolios which give the highest return, given the risk. The efficient set was illustrated in Figure 1.3. Any portfolio which is below the efficient set, or efficient frontier as it became known, should be discarded, as there is another portfolio with a higher risk/return profile.

2. The irrelevance theorem

Why did Modligliani and Miller (M & M) (1958) come up with a theory which is so oddly named? What, in other words, is irrelevant about the theory of finance as it was then understood? What M & M claimed was that the structure of the liabilities of a company was irrelevant. What, however, was relevant was the nature and composition of the assets and investments of the company. So the capital structure of the company was irrelevant. It was the asset side of the balance sheet that determined the value of the company, as represented by the share price.

Prior to the work of M & M the view held on the effect of the capital structure on the price of shares was that there was an optimal debt-equity mix which maximized the value of the company's shares. This was based on the belief that the cost of equity does not rise sufficiently to offset the use of cheaper forms of financing, principally debt. Therefore, the overall cost of capital will fall and the value of the firm will be maximized at some optimum capital structure. This optimum is not 100 per cent debt financing as equity is regarded as a safety cushion which will absorb any losses which might be incurred during the ordinary course of trading and/or liquidation. Hence, the smaller the amount of equity the more likely it is that debt holders may have to bear some part of any losses. The traditional view argued that this factor only makes itself felt after a substantial proportion of total financing is in the form of debt.

The traditional view was challenged by Modigliani and Miller (1958). They argued that the level of gearing used by the firm should not affect the cost of capital or alter the value of the firm as the risk borne by shareholders and debenture holders was dependent on how the firm used the capital, not on how the firm raised the capital. In other words, what matters is the way in which funds are invested. Therefore, as the firm takes on more of the cheaper form of financing – debt – the cost of equity should rise so as to offset this advantage and maintain a constant cost of capital regardless of the debt-equity ratio. That this should happen is no accident, according to Modigliani and Miller. The means by which the cost of equity rises to offset exactly the use of cheaper debt is an arbitrage process and arises out of rational investors taking advantage of profitable opportunities if the market values companies according to factors other than their returns and the riskiness of the returns.

3. The capital asset pricing model (CAPM)

The CAPM assumes that there is universal and unrestricted use, by investors, of Markowitz's optimization process. If, as the theory assumes, all investors build their stock portfolios using this principle, how would this affect pricing in the securities market? Under these conditions a single factor it is argued would make one stock different from another in its expected return.

This factor is based on the principle that in the world of CAPM, investors hold widely diversified portfolios. In the simple form of the model all investors invest in the market index. Risk is then measured as variability in return to that index. The risk of an individual stock is measured by its contribution to that variability.

This contribution, known as Beta, is defined as the sensitivity of a security's return to changes in the periodic return to the market index. We return to Beta in later chapters.

4. The efficient market hypothesis (EMH)

An efficient capital market is one in which stock prices fully reflect available information. The efficient market hypothesis predicts that the stock price of a company at any one moment in time reflects all the information known about the company at that moment in time.

The efficient market hypothesis (EMH) has implications for investors and for firms.

1 Because information is reflected in stock prices immediately, investors should only expect to obtain an equilibrium rate of return.

2 Firms should expect to receive the fair value for securities that they sell. *Fair* means that the price they receive for the securities they issue is the present value.

Given the ease with which information on stocks is available and the desire for investors to make profits by selling overvalued stocks and buying undervalued stocks, the market becomes efficient. When a market is efficient with respect to information, prices fully incorporate the information. The effect of this is that an investor in an efficient market can only expect to earn an equilibrium, or normal, required return from an investment. Again, we return to the EMH in Chapters 10, 12 and 13.

Fama showed that stock prices appeared to change randomly from one period to the next (1970). If stocks were always responding instantly and accurately to the appearance of new and unanticipated information (which must come in randomly if it truly can't be anticipated) then the EMH indicates that that is how prices would move.

The New Finance

The New Finance, as Haugen describes it, starts with the principle that the EMH, following rigorous empirical tests, has been faced with so many anomalies, situations in which it does not hold, that its value must be open to question (2000). The stage then, Haugen suggests, is set for the age of 'The New Finance'.

What this stage of the evolution of Finance involves, Haugen suggests, is initially to discard those theories that have no predictive power. In doing this one must discard the requirement that all explanation of the behaviour of financial markets must be based on rational economic behaviour. Look carefully at the data and measure accurately without preconception, Haugen advocates. Discard the tradition that you must model first without looking and then verify. Carefully measure behaviour first, and then find reasonable and plausible explanation for what you see later. The test, for Haugen with his New Theory of Finance, is that a model is judged by whether it predicts accurately. The key to the New Finance, Haugen demonstrates, is the ad hoc, expected return, factor model.

The ad hoc, expected return, factor models

While we can't see the entire distribution for stock returns, we do have tools to give us estimates of two of its characteristics. Haugen advocates that one can use *expected return factor models* to estimate the expected return (as indicated by the vertical arrow in Figure 1.6) and *risk factor models* to estimate the possible variability or variance in return (as indicated by the horizontal arrow in Figure 1.6).

With a risk factor model you are seeking to identify factors that are able to account for the correlations between stock return, inflation, industrial output, etc.

In an expected return model, you use factors that help explain and predict which stocks have tended to, or will, drift up or down in value relative to others. These factors tend to be individual stock characteristics which differ in

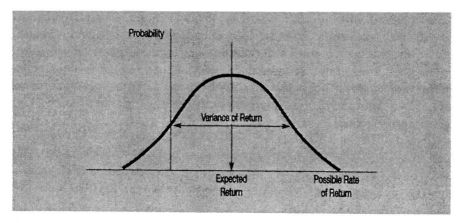

Fig 1.6 ● Probability distribution for returns to a portfolio

level from one stock to another. This would include say, the ratio of the accounting book value of a firm's equity capital to the total market value of the firm's common stock – the book-to-price ratio.

The relative expected return is the difference between a particular stock rate of return and the expected return to an average stock. The first step in building an expected return factor model is finding a list of factors that adequately describes the profile of a stock and its company. For each of the factors affecting the return you then multiply the stock's factor exposure by the projected pay-off to the factor and you arrive at the component of total expected return coming from the particular factor.

Factor Exposure × Projected Factor Pay-off =

Factor Component of Exposure Return

After doing this for each factor, you add up all the components to get the total relative expected return for the stock.

Drawing on empirical evidence, particularly Fama and French (1996), and applying the ad hoc expected return factor model, Haugen comes up with some controversial findings. Cheap stocks he finds tend to produce high returns while expensive stocks tend to produce low returns. At the same time cheap stocks tend to be not so risky and expensive stocks tend to be very risky. These findings appear to turn the normal risk/return profile upside down as low risk stocks have high expected returns.

Haugen's rationale for these surprising findings is that the stock market systematically fails to process information, the opposite of what EMH proponents assume. The stock market fails to appreciate the strength of competitive forces in a market economy by overestimating the length of the short run. The normal assumption in economics is that abnormal profits can only be earned in the short run. In the long run, competitive pressures will force down these profits so that only normal returns are earned in the long run.

Haugen asks, Just how long is the short run? He provides evidence that the short run lasts for only a few years at best. Investors, however, mistakenly project a continuation of abnormal profit levels for long periods into the future. Because of this mistaken projection, successful firms become overvalued. Unsuccessful firms becomes undervalued. As the process of competitive entry and exit drives performance to the mean faster than expected, investors in the formerly expensive stocks become disappointed with reported earnings, and investors in the formerly cheap stocks are pleasantly surprised.

By overestimating the length of the short run, Haugen argues, the stock market overreacts to records of success and failure for individual companies, driving the prices of successful companies too high and their unsuccessful counterparts too low.

Haugen's findings have provoked a fierce debate among financial economists, one which had reached no firm conclusions at the time of writing.

CHAPTER **2**

The foundations of financial economics

- Introduction
- Louis Bachelier (1870–1946)
- John Virgil Lintner (1916–1983)
- Benoit Mandelbrot
- Harry Markowitz
- Richard Roll
- Stephen Ross
- Merton Miller (1923–2000)
- Myron Scholes (1941–),
  Robert Merton (1944–),
  Fischer Black (1940–1995)
- Paul A. Samuelson
- William Sharpe
- James Tobin
- Appendix 2.1 The Nobel Prize in
  Economics

INTRODUCTION

One of the more noteworthy developments in economics over the past 30 years or so is the emergence of models of financial markets. Included within these models are the markets for financial securities, currencies, equities, bonds and derivatives. The chief building block and spur in this evolution has been the economics of uncertainty, which is itself of rather recent origin. The results of this new focus and the activities and synergies that it has generated is often broadly referred to as 'financial economics'. It is within this new sub-field that various models of financial markets occupy centre stage. This chapter provides the flavour of where the principal ideas in financial economics came from and provides the background to the rest of the book.

Any list of who has made the greatest contribution to any subject must by its nature be subjective. In this chapter the work of some of the more noteworthy contributors has been included. My choice of contributors has been guided by three principles. First, it includes those financial economists who have been awarded the Nobel Prize for Economics, more correctly called The Bank of Sweden Prize in Economic Sciences. Appendix 2.1 provides a description of the procedure for choosing Nobel Prize winners and lists the winners with the reasons for their awards. My second criterion was to include those economists whose death excluded them from winning the prize but whom, by common consent of the winners, would have shared the prize. The best example here is Fischer Black, most widely known for the Black and Scholes Option Pricing model. Third, included here are those financial economists whose articles are most frequently cited in the academic journals.

The contributors are listed alphabetically unless they shared the Nobel Prize. I make no claim to this list being in any sense definitive, a conclusion I came to following lengthy correspondence and numerous discussions with professors of financial economics around the world!

LOUIS BACHELIER (1870–1946)

The tragic hero of financial economics was the unfortunate Louis Bachelier. In his 1900 dissertation written in Paris, 'Theorie de la Spéculation', and in his subsequent work, he anticipated much of what was to become standard fare to financial economists: the random walk of financial market prices, what is known as 'Brownian motion'. Brownian motion, alternatively known as a martingale, is the relationship whereby the return on a security tomorrow is equal to the return on a security today plus an amount that depends on the new information generated between today and tomorrow, which is unpredictable given today's information set.

Bachelier was born in Le Havre, France, on 11 March 1870 and died in Saint-Servan-sur-Mer, Ille-et-Villaine, on 28 April 1946. He taught at Besançon, Dijon and Rennes and was a professor at Besançon from 1927 to 1937.

Bachelier invented efficient markets in 1900, 60 years before the idea came into vogue. He described the random walk model of prices, ordinary diffusion of probability and martingales, which, as already indicated, are the mathematical expression of efficient markets. He even attempted an empirical verification. But he remained a shadowy presence until 1960 or so, when his major work was revived in English translation.

His major work was his doctoral dissertation in the mathematical sciences, defended in Paris on 19 March 1900. Things went badly from the start: the committee failed to give it the 'mention très honorable', key to a University career. It was very late, after repeated failures, that Bachelier was appointed to the tiny University of Besançon. After he had retired, the University Archives were accidentally set on fire and none of his records survive, not even a single photograph.

Although, from today's perspective, the economics and mathematics of Bachelier's work are flawed, the connection of his research with the subsequent path of attempts to describe an equilibrium theory of option pricing is unmistakable.

JOHN VIRGIL LINTNER (1916–1983)

The contributions by John Lintner that are most frequently cited in the economic literature involve asset pricing, dividend policy, mergers, and capital formation under inflation. Along with others Lintner was one of the independent creators of the modern theory of asset pricing. This model is usually referred to as the Capital Asset Pricing Model (CAPM) which holds that the equilibrium rates of return on all risky assets are a function of their covariance with the returns on the market portfolio.

In addition to his major contribution to the creation of the modern theory of financial markets, Lintner wrote the seminal articles on dividend policy which provided the foundations for further research and remain the basic references on the subject.

In 1990 the Nobel Prize for economics was awarded to Harry Markowitz, Merton Miller and William Sharpe. Many financial economists said, at the time, that Lintner would have shared the prize, had he lived, for having devised, with William Sharpe, the Capital Asset Pricing Model.

BENOIT MANDELBROT

Mandelbrot is best known as author of *The Fractal Geometry of Nature* (1982). This work attempts to seek a measure of order in physical, mathematical or social phenomena that are characterized by extreme variability or roughness. Paul Samuelson, Nobel Economist, describes him thus: 'On the scroll of great non-economists who have advanced economics by quantum leaps, next to John von Neumann, we read the name of Benoit Mandelbrot' (1976).

Much of Mandelbrot's work involves analyzing efficient markets. If markets are efficient, the (technical) analysis of past price patterns to predict the future will be useless because any information from such an analysis will already have been discounted into current market prices. Suppose market participants were confident that a commodity price would double next week. The price will not gradually approach its new equilibrium value. Indeed, unless the price adjusted immediately, a profitable arbitrage opportunity would exist and could be expected to be exploited immediately in an efficient market. Similarly, if a reliable and profitable seasonal pattern for equity prices exists (e.g. a substantial Christmas rally) speculators will bid up prices sufficiently prior to Christmas so as to eliminate any unexploited arbitrage possibility. Samuelson (1965a) and Mandelbrot (1963, 1966) proved rigorously that if the flow of information is unimpeded and if there are no transactions costs, then tomorrow's price change in speculative markets will reflect only tomorrow's 'news'. But tomorrow's (news) is by definition unpredictable and thus the resulting price changes must also be unpredictable and random.

The term 'random walk' is usually used loosely in the financial economics literature to characterize a price series where all subsequent price changes represent random departures from previous prices. Thus, changes in price will be unrelated to past price changes. (More formally, the random walk model states that investment returns are serially independent, and that their probability distributions are constant through time.) It is believed that the term was first used in an exchange of correspondence appearing in *Nature* in 1905. The problem considered in the correspondence was the optimal search procedure for finding a drunk who had been left in the middle of a field. The answer was to start exactly where the drunk had been placed. That point is an unbiased estimate of the drunk's future position since he will presumably stagger along in an unpredictable and random fashion.

The earliest empirical work on the random walk hypothesis was performed by Bachelier (1900), as mentioned earlier. He concluded that commodities prices followed a random walk, although he did not use that term.

Mandelbrot's book, *The Fractal Geometry of Nature* (1982), builds on that and subsequent work and is a major contribution to the understanding of how speculative prices vary in time. The book presents and tests three successive rules of variation, tackling fast change and long distribution tails, then long dependence in time, and finally both features simultaneously.

Careful modelling is needed because prices do not perform a Random Walk to mimic the toss of a coin. They are not tossed around like Brownian Motion tosses a small piece of matter. As Mandelbrot showed, price change is often subjected to substantial sharp discontinuities, and periods of price activity are far from being uniformly spread over time (1997).

HARRY MARKOWITZ

Harry Markowitz, together with Merton Miller and William Sharpe, was awarded the Nobel Prize for economics in 1990. Markowitz built on the earlier work by James Tobin, ennobled in 1981, concerning the diversification of risk through building balanced portfolios.

James Tobin (1958), whose ideas we discuss later, utilized the foundations of portfolio theory to draw implications with regard to the demand for cash balances. He also demonstrated that given the possibility of an investment in a risk-free asset as well as in a risky asset (or portfolio), an investor can construct a combined portfolio of the two assets to achieve any desired combination of risk and return. Subsequently, William Sharpe, using one of the efficient methods for constructing portfolios discussed in the appendices to the Markowitz book (1959), developed what he called the 'diagonal model' in his dissertation, which was under the direction of Markowitz. The results of this were later summarized in an article, Sharpe (1963). This represented another step towards general equilibrium models of asset prices developed almost simultaneously by Treynor (1965), Sharpe (1964, 1970), Lintner (1965) and Mossin (1966, 1969). Important contributions were also made by Fama (1971, 1976) and Fama and Miller (1972).

These works resulted in the development of the relationship between return and risk summarized in what has since been called the Security Market Line of the Capital Asset Pricing Model (CAPM) and is described in Equation (1).

$$E(R_j) = R_F + \left[\frac{E(R_M) - R_F}{\sigma_M^2} \right] COV(R_j, R_M) \tag{1}$$

This equation says that the return required (*ex ante*) by investors on any asset is equal to the return, R_F, on a risk-free asset plus an adjustment for risk. Alternatively, the risk adjustment can be defined as the market risk premium weighted by the risk of the individual asset normalized by the variance of market returns. This latter measure has been referred to as the beta measure (β) of the risk of an individual asset or security. See Equation (2).

$$\beta = COV(R_j, R_M)/\sigma_M^2 \tag{2}$$

In the early 1950s Harry Markowitz developed a theory of portfolio selection, building on the work of Tobin, which has resulted in a revolution in the theory of finance leading to the development of modern capital market theory (1952, 1959). He formulated a theory of investor investment selection as a problem of utility maximization under conditions of uncertainty. Markowitz discusses mainly the special case in which investors' preferences are assumed to be defined over the mean and variance of the probability distribution of single-period portfolio returns.

Prior to Markowitz's work, portfolio theory focussed on picking 'winners'. All sorts of ad hoc ideas about security pricing, many found in the still popular book *Security Analysis* by Benjamin Graham and David Dodd (1934), supported the central investment goal of attempting to pick undervalued stocks to beat the market. Harry Markowitz, a mathematician by training and an expert on statistical theory, began thinking about the statistical properties of security returns around 50 years ago. He published an article called 'Portfolio Selection' in the *Journal of Finance* in 1952 and a book by the same title later the same year.

Markowitz defined the risk to owning securities as variance, a familiar statistical concept, and rigorously developed the principles governing how portfolio variance, or risk, is affected by adding and subtracting the individual securities from a portfolio which is simply a combination of securities. The major lesson implied by the mathematics is that portfolios offer far superior returns for given risk (variance) than do individual securities. This insight flew in the face of the conventional practice of emphasizing individual securities in an effort to pick winners. Markowitz showed that eschewing diversification was enormously risky and could only be justified economically as a general approach if financial markets were unbelievably inefficient.

The simple fact that securities carry differing degrees of expected risk leads most investors to the notion of holding more than one security at a time, in an attempt to spread risks by not putting all their eggs into one basket. However, there is disagreement over the 'right' kind of diversification and the 'right' reason. It was in providing answers to these questions that Markowitz made his major contribution to financial economics and which ultimately resulted in him being jointly awarded the Nobel prize.

Markowitz's approach to coming up with efficient portfolio possibilities has its roots in risk-return relationships. This is not at odds with traditional approaches in concept. The key differences lie in Markowitz's assumption that investor attitudes toward portfolios depend exclusively upon

● expected return and risk; and

● quantification of risk.

Risk is, by proxy, the statistical notion of variance, or standard deviation of return.

What Markowitz questioned was that, although holding two securities is probably less risky than holding either security alone, whether it *is possible to reduce the risk of a portfolio by incorporating into it a security whose risk is greater than that of any of the investments held initially?* For example, given two stocks, X and Y, with Y considerably more risky than X, a portfolio composed of some of X and some of Y may be less risky than a portfolio composed exclusively of the less risky asset, X.

The key to Markowitz's work was not that by investing in two stocks rather than one provided twice as much diversification as one, but that by investing in securities with negative or low covariances among themselves it was possible to reduce the overall risk of the portfolio. Markowitz's efficient diversification involves combining securities with less than positive correlation in order to reduce risk in the portfolio without sacrificing any of the portfolio's return. In general he showed that the lower the correlation of securities in the portfolio, the less risky the portfolio would be. This is true regardless of how risky the stocks of the portfolio are when analyzed in isolation. It is not enough to invest in *many* securities; it is necessary to have the *right* securities.

Markowitz devised an ingenious computational model designed to trace out what is known as an efficiency locus and to identify the portfolios that make it up. In other words, he produced a scheme whereby large numbers of feasible portfolios could be ignored completely where they were dominated by more efficient portfolios. See Figure 2.1.

In the calculations, Markowitz used the techniques of quadratic programming. He assumed that one could deal with N securities or fewer. Using the expected return and risk for each security under consideration, and covariance estimates for each pair of securities, he was able to calculate risk and return for

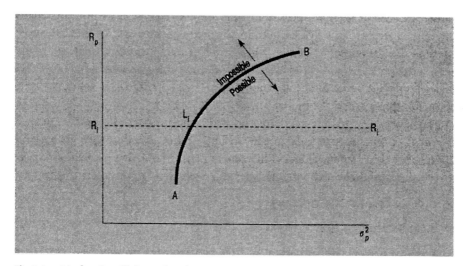

Fig 2.1 ● Markowitz efficiency frontier

any portfolio made up of some or all of these securities. In particular, for any specific value of expected return, using the programming calculation, he determined the least-risk portfolios. With another value of expected return, a similar procedure again yields the minimum-risk combination.

So the Markowitz model uses a matrix of covariances to compute the variance of a portfolio of securities. Each element of the matrix represents the covariance between the rates of return for two of the securities. To compute the variance of a portfolio of the securities, you multiply the covariance number by the fraction of the money that you are investing in each element in the matrix and add them up to obtain the variance of the portfolio.

This procedure is perfectly accurate, given the accuracy of the covariance estimates. Suppose, for example, that the covariance numbers are sample estimates, taken from the returns on the stocks over the last 12 months. This being the case, the portfolio variance that we get is the actual variance of the portfolio for the 12 months of the preceding year. While it may not be an accurate prediction of what the variance is going to be in the coming year – that depends on the stability of the covariance numbers over time – it is a perfectly accurate estimate of the variance in the year in which the sample estimates of the covariance are taken.

However, there is a problem in computing portfolio variance in this way. The problem becomes apparent when the number of securities in the population becomes large. When this happens, the number of elements in the covariance matrix becomes extremely large. Suppose, for example, we tried to determine the efficient set for 1600 stocks on the New York Stock Exchange. The matrix would be 1600 by 1600, and it would contain more than 2.5 million covariance numbers. Granted, for each covariance on one side of the diagonal, there is a matching number on the other side of the diagonal, but we still would have to estimate nearly 1.3 million variances and covariances.

Even if we went to the trouble of making that many estimates, our problems are just beginning. Think of the process a computer goes through in finding the efficient set. Every time it needs to compute the variance of a portfolio, it must add more than 2.5 million products. Even if we use the fastest computers and the most efficient computer programs, the problem becomes intractable.

Markowitz's procedure was relatively simple to perform for a portfolio consisting of a very small number of securities. However, as suggested earlier, the movement from three- to N-security portfolios not only highlights the enormity of the calculation problem and the assistance provided by the Markowitz algorithm, it also points up the expansion of the data bits required for fundamental analysis. The inputs to the portfolio analysis of a set of N securities are:

1 N expected returns

2 N variances of return

3 $(N^2 - N)/2$ covariances.

Thus the Markowitz calculation requires a total of [N(N + 3)/2] separate pieces of information before efficient portfolios can be calculated and identified. Table 2.1 illustrates the data requirements needed to use the Markowitz technique with large portfolios.

Table 2.1 ● Data requirements in applying the Markowitz algorithm

Number of Securities	Bits of Information*
10	65
50	1,325
100	5,150
1,000	501,500

*[100(100 +3)/2]

This is the problem with the Markowitz model. It employs an equation for portfolio variance that is perfectly accurate, but also *intractable*, when we are dealing with a large number of securities. What we need is an alternative formula for portfolio variance that is capable of dealing with large populations of stocks. We get such a capability with index models, particularly as developed by William Sharpe. These are discussed later in this chapter.

RICHARD ROLL

Roll's name is associated with the development of the capital asset pricing model (CAPM). The central feature of the CAPM, discussed in more detail in Chapters 9 and 17, is the role of mean-variance efficiency of the market portfolio and the emergence of the beta coefficient on the market portfolio as the determinant of the risk premium of an asset. Those features of an asset that contribute to its variance but do not affect its covariance with the market will not influence its pricing. Critically it is beta that matters for pricing; the idiosyncratic or unsystematic risk.

This finding produces some results that were at first viewed as counterintuitive. Prior to the acceptance of the CAPM the view was that the risk premium depended on the asset's variance. After the acceptance of the CAPM ideas, this was thought to be no longer appropriate, since if one asset had a higher covariance with the market than another, it would have a higher risk premium even if the total variance of its returns were lower. Even more surprising was the implication that a risky asset that was uncorrelated with the market would have no risk premium and would be expected to have the same rate of return as the riskless asset, and that assets that were inversely correlated with the market would actually have expected returns of less than the riskless rate in equilibrium.

These results for the CAPM were supposedly explainable by the twin intu-itions of diversification and systematic risk. There could be no premium for bearing unsystematic risk since a large and well-diversified portfolio (i.e. one whose asset proportions are not concentrated in a small subset) would elimi-nate it – presumably by the law of large numbers. This would leave only systematic risk in any optimal portfolio and since this risk cannot be eliminated by diversification, it has to have a risk premium to entice risk-averse investors to hold risky assets. From this perspective it becomes clear why an asset that is uncorrelated with the market bears no risk premium. One that is inversely cor-related with the market actually offers some insurance against the all-pervasive systematic risk and, therefore, there must be a payment for the insurance in the form of a negative risk premium.

The CAPM was the genesis for countless empirical tests. The general struc-ture of these tests was the combination of the efficient markets hypothesis with time series and cross-section econometrics. Typically some index of the market, such as the value weighted combination of all stocks would be chosen and a sample of firms would be tested to see if their excess returns, were 'explained' in cross-section analysis by their betas on the index, that is, whether the Security Market Line (SML) was rejected. The SML is discussed further in Chapter 8.

Roll (1977, 1978) put a stop to this indiscriminate testing by calling into question precisely what was being tested. Roll's critique (1977), as it is now known, has had a major impact on the way the CAPM has evolved ever since. Roll's major conclusions are as follows.

1 The only legitimate test of the CAPM is whether the market portfolio (which includes *all* assets) is mean-variance efficient.

2 If performance is measured relative to an index which is *ex post* efficient, then from the mathematics of the efficient set, no security will have abnormal performance when measured as a departure from the Security Market Line.

3 If performance is measured relative to an *ex post* inefficient index, then any ranking of portfolio performance is possible depending on which inefficient index has been chosen.

The Roll critique does not imply that the CAPM is invalid, but that tests of the CAPM are joint tests with market efficiency and that its uses must be imple-mented with due care.

STEPHEN ROSS

The empirical tests of CAPM are conducted in what is known in the literature as 'excess return form'. For the equation in this form to be valid it should have an intercept term not significantly different from zero, with a slope equal to the excess market portfolio return. The empirical tests have found an intercept term significantly above zero with a slope less than predicted. This implies that the empirical securities market line is tilted clockwise, implying that low beta securities earn more than the CAPM would predict and high beta securities earn less. But the main predictions of the CAPM of a positive market price for risk and a model linear in beta are broadly supported.

The intuition of the CAPM, as already discussed, is that idiosyncratic risk can be diversified away leaving only the systematic risk to be priced. Idiosyncratic risk is defined with reference to the market portfolio as the residual from a regression of returns on the market portfolio's returns. Since no further assumptions are made about the residuals, contrary to intuition, a largely diversified portfolio that differs from the market portfolio will not in general have insignificant residual risk.

The recognition that the market return alone might not explain all of the variation in the return on an asset or a portfolio gave rise to a multiple factor analysis of capital asset pricing. This more general approach formulated by Ross (1976) was called the Arbitrage Pricing Theory (APT). Requiring only that individuals be risk averse, the APT has multiple factors affecting stock returns and in equilibrium all assets must fall on the arbitrage pricing line. Thus the CAPM is viewed as a special case of the APT in which the return on the market portfolio is the single applicable factor.

The theory is controversial. For one thing, critics argue that, unlike the capital asset pricing model – which, for better or worse, tells investors what systematic risk is and how and to what extent expected returns of the stocks they buy are related to that risk – the arbitrage pricing theory is not that specific. It tells you only that certain factors in the economy move stock prices, but it doesn't tell you what those factors are or how much return you can expect by exposing yourself to them. And while Roll and Ross (1980) seem sure they have identified the most important factors, other modellers of the arbitrage pricing theory might look to, for example, oil prices or other economic indicators.

William Sharpe, a Nobel prize winner himself and the father of the capital asset pricing model, says APT 'is a valuable theory and tool, but if people thought they had problems with the instability of beta measurement, wait until they try models where they all choose different factors' (1990).

Nevertheless, given the problems with beta – that it has been a poor predictor of returns for some stocks, that it varies with the market benchmark one chooses, that it doesn't explain why small-capitalization stocks outperform the market – APT is gaining wider and wider acceptance among academics.

MERTON MILLER (1923–2000)

Merton Miller won his share of the Nobel prize for his contributions to the field of corporate finance, mainly the study of corporations' debt and dividend payout policies. Miller's seminal contribution came in an article co-authored with Franco Modigliani, entitled 'The Cost of Capital, Corporate Finance, and the Theory of Investment', which appeared in the *American Economic Review* in June 1958.

Corporate finance before Merton Miller was in a very sad shape. The study of corporate debt and dividend policies amounted to a series of rules of thumb that simply described widespread practice and justified them logically in consistent, normative assertions. Financial economists in academia were treated as second-class citizens at universities, and their weak, unpromising body of knowledge probably deserved this treatment. Miller's article applied the physics principle of conservation of matter to the study of the value and riskiness of the corporate entity. In his theory the corporation was a stream of expected future cash flows, or profits from operations. These were independent of the financial policies and dividend payout policies of the firm.

This approach allowed Miller and his followers to apply rigorous mathematical analysis in understanding how increasing long-term debt levels or changing dividend payout rates affected the overall value of the firm. Two revolutionary principles, called irrelevance propositions, emerged from this early work. The first proposition was that the value of the firm is independent of the degree of financial leverage employed by the firm, i.e. debt levels are irrelevant to firm value. The second proposition was that the value of the firm is independent of the level of dividends chosen by the firm, i.e. dividends, too, are irrelevant. These two propositions, derived mathematically, were completely counterintuitive and caused an enormous academic debate.

Miller's work paved the way to understanding how financial markets for securities and derivative instruments operate in arbitrage equilibriums and certainly raised the profile of financial economics.

MYRON SCHOLES (1941–), ROBERT MERTON (1944–), FISCHER BLACK (1940–1995)

Robert Merton, together with Myron Scholes, was awarded the Nobel Prize in economics in 1997. Their citation stated that the award was 'for a new method to determine the value of derivatives'. Undoubtedly Fischer Black would have shared the prize had he not suffered an untimely death, in his early fifties, in 1995. Markets for options and futures, derivatives for short, based on their work, have made important contributions to risk management.

Futures markets allow agents to hedge against upcoming risks; such contracts promise future delivery of a certain item at a certain price. To take an example, a firm might decide to engage in copper mining after determining that the metal to be extracted can be sold in advance at the copper futures market. This risk of future movements in the copper price is thereby transferred from the owner of the mine to the buyer of the copper futures contract.

Due to their design, options allow agents to hedge against one-sided risks; options give the right, but not the obligation, to buy or sell something at a pre-specified price in the future. An importing British firm that anticipates making a large payment in US dollars can hedge against the one-sided risk of large losses due to a future depreciation of sterling by buying call options for dollars on the market for foreign currency options. Effective risk management requires that such instruments be correctly priced.

The option pricing formula applied is now widely referred to as the Black and Scholes formula, given that they were the first to derive it.

Black and Scholes originally based their result on the capital asset pricing model (CAPM), for which Sharpe was awarded the 1990 Nobel Prize. While working on their 1973 paper, they were strongly influenced by Merton. Black described this in an article in 1989.

> 'As we worked on the paper we had long discussions with Robert Merton, who also was working on option valuation. Merton made a number of suggestions that improved our paper. In particular, he pointed out that if you assume continuous trading in the option or the stock, you can maintain a relation between them that is literally riskless. In the final version of the paper we derived the formula that way because it seemed to be the most general derivation.'

It was thus Merton who contributed the important generalization that market equilibrium is not necessary for option valuation; it is sufficient that there are no arbitrage opportunities. The method described in the journal article cited above is based precisely on the absence of arbitrage (and on stochastic calculus). It generalizes to valuations of other types of derivatives. Merton's 1973 article also included the Black-Scholes formula and some generalizations; for instance, he allowed the interest rate to be stochastic. Stochastic refers to a statistically random sequential process in which the probabilities at each step depend on the outcomes of previous steps, in other words they are broadly random. Four years later, he also developed, Merton (1976), a more general method of deriving the formula which uses the fact that options can be created synthetically by trading in the underlying share and a risk-free bond.

To fully understand the contribution made by Black, Scholes and Merton it is essential to look back at the early attempts to value options.

The history of option valuation

Attempts to value options and other derivatives have a long history. One of the earliest endeavours to determine the value of stock options was made by Louis Bachelier in his Ph.D. thesis at the Sorbonne in 1900, as was discussed earlier. The formula that Bachelier derived, however, was based on unrealistic assumptions, a zero interest rate, and a process that allowed for a negative share price.

The attempts at valuation before 1973 basically determined the expected value of a stock option at expiration and then discounted its value back to the time of evaluation. Such an approach requires taking a stance on which risk premium to use in the discounting. This is because the value of an option depends on the risky path of the stock price, from the valuation date to maturity. But assigning a risk premium is not straightforward. The risk premium should reflect not only the risk for changes in the stock price, but also the investors' attitude towards risk. And while the latter can be strictly defined in theory, it is hard or impossible to observe in reality.

The Black-Scholes formula

The insight by Black and Scholes that resolved these problems came about by recognizing that it is not necessary to use any risk premium when valuing an option. This does not mean that the risk premium disappears, but that it is already incorporated in the stock price. In 1973 Fischer Black and Myron S. Scholes published the famous option pricing formula that now bears their name, Black and Scholes (1973). They worked, as already mentioned, in close co-operation with Robert C. Merton, who, that same year, published an article which also included the formula and various extensions, Merton (1973).

The idea behind the new method developed by Black, Merton and Scholes can be explained in the following simplified way. Consider a so-called European call option that gives the right to buy a certain share at a strike price of $100 in three months. (A European option gives the right to buy or sell only at a certain date, whereas a so-called American option gives the same right at any point in time up to a certain date.) Clearly, the value of this call option depends on the current share price; the higher the share price today the greater the probability that it will exceed $100 in three months, in which case it will pay to exercise the option. A formula for option valuation should thus determine exactly how the value of the option depends on the current share price. How much the value of the option is altered by a change in the current share price is called the 'delta' of the option.

Assume that the value of the option increases by $1 when the current share price goes up $2 and decreases by $1 when the stock goes down $2 (i.e. delta is equal to one half). Assume also that an investor holds a portfolio of the underlying stock and wants to hedge against the risk of changes in the share price. He can then, in fact, construct a risk-free portfolio by selling (writing) twice as many options as the number of shares he owns. For reasonably small increases in the share price, the profit the investor makes on the shares will be the same as the loss he incurs on the options, and vice versa for decreases in the share price. As the portfolio thus constructed is risk free, it must yield exactly the same return as a risk free three-month Treasury bill. If it did not, arbitrage trading would begin to eliminate the possibility of making risk-free profits. These ideas are discussed in detail in Chapter 15.

As the share price is altered over time and as the time to maturity draws nearer, the delta of the option changes. In order to maintain a risk-free stock-option portfolio, the investor has to change its composition. Black, Merton and Scholes assumed that such trading can take place continuously without any transaction costs (transaction costs were later introduced by others). The condition that the return on a risk-free stock-option portfolio yields the risk-free rate, at each point in time, implied a partial differential equation, the solution of which is the Black-Scholes formula for a call option. See Equation (3):

$$C = SN(d) - Le^{-rt} N(d - \sigma \sqrt{t}) \tag{3}$$

where the variable d is defined by Equation (4):

$$d = \frac{\ln \frac{S}{L} + \left(r + \frac{\sigma^2}{2}\right)t}{\sigma\sqrt{t}} \tag{4}$$

According to this formula, the value of the call option C, is given by the difference between the expected share price – the first term on the right-hand side of Equation (4) – and the expected cost – the second term – if the option is exercised. The option value is higher, the higher the current share price S, the higher the volatility of the share price (as measured by its standard deviation) sigma (σ), the higher the risk-free interest rate r, the longer the time to maturity t, the lower the strike price L, and the higher the probability that the option will be exercised. (This probability is, under risk neutrality, evaluated by the standardized normal distribution function N.) All the parameters in the equation can be observed except sigma, which has to be estimated from market data. Alternatively, if the price of the call option is known, the formula can be used to solve for the market's estimate of sigma.

PAUL A. SAMUELSON

Samuelson was awarded the Nobel Laureate in Economics in 1970 'for the scientific work through which he has developed static and dynamic economic theory and actively contributed to raising the level of analysis in economic science'. He was the first American to win the prize.

Samuelson has made fundamental contributions to nearly all branches of economic theory. Despite his long-time personal interest in capital markets, Samuelson's contribution to finance theory started only as he turned 50. His two most important papers are 'Proof that properly anticipated prices fluctuate randomly' (1965a) and 'Rational theory of warrant pricing', (1965b) 'Proof ...' provides a first precise formulation of the consequences for speculative prices of market efficiency. The theorem describes the behaviour of the current price of a commodity for delivery at a given future date, e.g. June 1990 wheat. Assuming that speculators do not have to put up any money to enter the contract, the result is that the market price should be the expectation at each date of the June 1990 wheat price. Given rational expectations, there is no serial correlation in the changes in price. Hence 'properly anticipated prices fluctuate randomly'.

Samuelson says of this theorem 'This theorem is so general that I must confess to having oscillated over the years between regarding it as trivially obvious (and almost trivially vacuous) and regarding it as remarkably sweeping' (1965a).

Note what the theorem does not say, using the exchange rate as the example. The theorem is not that the exchange rate fluctuates randomly; predictable inflation or predictable business cycle fluctuations can cause predictable movements in the exchange rate. Rather it is the current price of foreign exchange at a *given* future date that fluctuates randomly. The notion that efficiency produces random motion is itself fascinating. But far more important is the restriction of empirical behaviour implied by efficiency that Samuelson derives in a well-defined context. Testing for efficiency of speculative markets has become a major industry.

Samuelson's 'Rational theory of warrant pricing' missed its target, but it is as Merton (1990) remarks, a near miss. Samuelson pursued option pricing for well over a decade. He was familiar with Bachelier's 1900 continuous time stochastic calculus calculation of rational option prices. Samuelson derived a partial differential equation for the option price that depends, among other variables, on the expected return on the stock and the required return on the option. The remarkable feature of the Black-Scholes solution to the problem, as discussed earlier, is that the rational price of the warrant does not depend on the expected return on the stock, but rather on the risk-free rate. Nonetheless, the Samuelson differential equation can be specialized to the correct Black-Scholes equation.

WILLIAM SHARPE

William Sharpe was the most notable of several financial economists, including names like Treynor, Lintner, Mossin and Black, who extended Markowitz's powerful insights and created the revolutionary theories of asset pricing based on Markowitz's mathematical treatment of security returns and variances. Specifically,

Sharpe, in his 1964 *Journal of Finance* article, 'Capital Asset Prices: A Theory of Market Equilibrium under Conditions of Risk', assumed that all investors looked at security risk and return in the same way as did Markowitz. Under these assumptions Sharpe developed a model of market equilibrium that showed how the risk of individual securities would be priced in a 'Markowitz world'.

The main insight here was that only the so-called systematic risk of individual securities (the famous beta risk) would be priced in such a market. The holding of unsystematic risk, which is the variance in returns to individual securities that could be eliminated through diversification, would earn no additional return. So, in such a market, diversification was imperative to sensible and successful investing. Refusing to diversify exposed one to additional risk with no market-based prospect for reward.

Sharpe's contributions were the genesis of a revolution in financial economics, leading to an explosion of theoretical and empirical advances that has yet to run its course. The emphasis on diversification and portfolio management is at the heart of practical investment management today.

One of Sharpe's most powerful insights was to develop a simplified variant of the Markowitz model that reduced substantially its data and computational requirements. The reasoning whereby this data simplification occurs is discussed below. In so called 'simplified models' it is assumed that fluctuations in the value of a stock relative to that of another do not depend primarily upon the characteristics of those two securities alone. The two securities are more likely to reflect a broader influence that might be described as general business activity. Relationships between securities occur only through their individual relationships with some index or indexes of business activity. This reduction in the number of covariance estimates needed eases considerably the job of security-analysis and portfolio-analysis computation. Thus the covariance data requirement reduces from $(N^2 - N)/2$ under the Markowitz technique to only N measures of each security as it relates to the index. See Table 2.2.

Table 2.2 ● Data requirements for Markovitz covariances versus the Sharpe index

Number of Securities	Markowitz Covariances	Sharpe Index Coefficients
10	65	10
50	1,325	50
100	5,150	100
1000	501,500	1000
2000	1,999,000	2000

However, some additional inputs are required using Sharpe's technique. Estimates are required of the expected return and variance of one or more indexes of economic activity. The indexes to which the returns of each security are correlated are likely to be some securities-market proxy, such as the Dow Jones Industrial Average or the Standard & Poor's 500 Stock Index. Overall then, the Sharpe technique requires $3N + 2$ separate bits of information, as opposed to the Markowitz requirement of $[N(N = 3)]/2$.

Risk-return and the Sharpe model

As mentioned above it is now necessary to explain how this reduction in the data demands could occur. Sharpe suggested that a satisfactory simplification would be to abandon the covariances of each security with each other security and to substitute information on the relationship of each security to the market. In his terms, it is possible to consider the return for each security to be represented by Equation (5):

$$R_i = \alpha_i + \beta_i I + e_i \tag{5}$$

where

R_i = expected return on security i
α_i = intercept of a straight line or alpha coefficient
β_i = slope of straight line or beta coefficient
I = expected return on index (market)
e_i = error term with a mean of zero and a standard deviation which is a constant

In other words, the return on any stock depends upon some constant (α), plus some coefficient (β), times the value of a stock index (I), plus a random component (e). Let us look at a hypothetical stock and examine the historical relationship between the stock's return and the returns of the market (index).

Assume we examine the historical relationship between the return on a hypothetical security and the return on the Dow Jones Industrial Average (DJIA). If we mathematically 'fit' a line to the small number of observations, we get an equation for the line of the form $y = \alpha + \beta x$. Say the equation turns out to be $y = 8.5 - 0.05x$.

The equation $y = \alpha + \beta x$ has two terms or coefficients that have become commonplace in the modern jargon of investment management. The 'α' or intercept term is called by its Greek name 'alpha'. The 'β' or slope term is referred to as the 'beta' coefficient. The alpha value is really the value of y in the equation when the value of x is zero. Thus, for our hypothetical stock, when the return on the DJIA is zero the stock has an expected return of 8.5 per cent $[y = 8.5 - 0.05(0)]$. The beta coefficient is the slope of the regression line and as such it is a measure of the sensitivity of the stock's return to movements in the market's return. A beta of +1.0 suggests that, ignoring the alpha coefficient, a 1 per cent return on the DIJA is matched by a 1 per cent return on the stock. A beta of 2.5 would suggest great responsiveness on the part of the stock to changes in the DJIA. A 5 per cent return on the index, ignoring the alpha coefficient, leads to an expected return on the stock of 12.5 per cent (2.5 times 5 per cent). While the alpha term is not to be ignored, we shall see a bit later the important role played by the beta term or beta coefficient.

The Sharpe index method permits us to *estimate* a security's return then by utilizing the values of α and β for the security and an estimate of the value of the index. Assume the return on the index (I) for the year ahead is expected to be 25 per cent. Using our calculated values of $\alpha = 8.5$ and $\beta = -0.05$ and the estimate of the index of $I = 25$, the return for the stock is estimated as:

$$R_i = 8.5 - 0.05(25)$$
$$R_i = 8.5 - 1.25$$
$$R_i = 7.25$$

The expected return on the security in question will be 7.25 per cent if the return on the index is 25 per cent, and if α and β are stable coefficients.

To calculate portfolio returns rather than individual stock returns we need merely to take the weighted average of the estimated returns for each security in the portfolio. The weights will be the proportions of the portfolio devoted to each security. For each security, we will require α and β estimates. One estimate of the index (I) is needed. This gives Equation (6):

$$R_P = \sum_{i=1}^{N} X_i(\alpha_i + \beta_i I) \tag{6}$$

where all terms are as explained earlier, except that R_p is the expected portfolio return, X_i is the proportion of the portfolio devoted to stock i, and N is the total number of stocks.

The notion of security and portfolio *risk* in the Sharpe model is a bit less clear on the surface than are return calculations. The plotted returns and some key statistical relationships are shown in Table 2.3.

Table 2.3 ● Risk in the Sharpe model

Year	Security Return (%)	Index Return (%)
1	6	20
2	5	40
3	10	30
Average	= 7	30
Variance from average	= 4.7	30
Correlation coefficient (r)	= − 0.189	66.7
Coefficient of determination (r^2)	= 0.0357	

Notice that when the index return goes up (down), the security's return generally goes down (up). Note changes in return from years 1 to 2 and 2 to 3. This reverse behaviour accounts for our negative correlation coefficient (r).

The *coefficient of determination* (r^2) tells us the percentage of the variance of the security's return that is explained by the variation of return on the index (or market). Only about 3.5 per cent of the variance of the security's return is explained by the index; some 96.5 per cent therefore is not. In other words, of the total variance in the return on the security (4.7), the following is true:

Explained by index   = 4.7 × 0.0357 = 0.17 = systematic risk
Not explained by index = 4.7 × 0.9643 = 4.53 = unsystematic risk

Sharpe noted that the variance explained by the index could be referred to as the *systematic risk*. The unexplained variance is called the residual variance, or *unsystematic risk*.

Sharpe suggested that systematic risk for an individual security can be seen as:

$$
\begin{aligned}
\text{Systematic risk} \quad &= \quad \beta^2 \times (\text{Variance of index}) \\
&= \quad \beta^2 \, \sigma_1^2 \\
&= \quad (-0.05)^2 \, (66.7) \\
&= \quad (0.0025)(66.7) \\
&= \quad 0.17
\end{aligned}
$$

Unsystematic risk = (Total variance of security return) − (Systematic risk)

$$
\begin{aligned}
&= \quad e^2 \\
&= \quad 4.7 - 0.17 \\
&= \quad 4.53
\end{aligned}
$$

Then:

$$
\begin{aligned}
\text{Total risk} \quad &= \quad \beta^2 \, \sigma_1^2 + e^2 \\
&= \quad 0.17 + 4.53 \\
&= \quad 4.7
\end{aligned}
$$

And portfolio variance is given by Equation (7):

$$
\sigma_P^2 = \left[\left(\sum_{i=1}^{N} X_i \beta_i \right)^2 \sigma_I^2 \right] + \left[\sum_{i=1}^{N} X_i^2 e_i^2 \right] \tag{7}
$$

where all symbols are as above, plus:

σ_P^2 = variance of portfolio return
σ_I^2 = expected variance of index
e_i^2 = variation in security's return not caused by its relationship to the index.

Given the importance of Sharpes' breakthrough it is worth reiterating his ideas with a simplified example.

EXAMPLE

Under the Markowitz system of portfolio analysis, we need three bits of information for each stock:

1 expected return for the holding period;

2 expected risk for the holding period; and

3 expected covariance for each pair of stocks.

The Sharpe simplification would require information on 1 and 2, and for 3, covariance estimates for each stock relative to the market (index). In addition, for the Sharpe model we need to estimate the return and variance on the index for the holding period.

Let us assume that we use the S & P index and that the return one year ahead was estimated at 11 per cent and the risk (variance) was 26 per cent. These two estimates, return and risk on the S & P serve as the focal point for estimating return and risk for each stock and, therefore, portfolios of stocks. Recall that, using the Sharpe method, return and risk estimates for portfolios are built by using the α, β and e^2 estimates for portfolios for individual stocks applied to the projected return-risk variables for the index.

Let us assume that we calculate for stock ABC the Alpha (%) at 1.47, the Beta at 1.73, and we apply equations (6) and (7) to calculate the one stock portfolio return and risk, we find the results as below:

PORTFOLIO RETURN FOR ABC

$$
\begin{aligned}
R_p &= \sum_{i=1}^{N} X_i\,(\alpha_i + \beta_i I) \\
&= 1.00\,[1.47 + (1.73)(11)] \\
R_p &= 20.5
\end{aligned}
$$

PORTFOLIO RISK FOR ABC

$$
\begin{aligned}
\sigma_p^2 &= \left(\sum_{i=1}^{N} X_i\beta_i\right)^2 \sigma_I^2 + \sum_{i=1}^{N} (X_i^2 e_i^2) \\
&= \beta_i^2\sigma_I^2 + e_i^2 \text{ (since } X_i = 1.00) \\
&= (2.99)(26.37) + (196.28) \\
&= 78.84 + 196.28 \\
&= 275.12 \\
\sigma_p &= 16.6
\end{aligned}
$$

The ideas of Sharpe greatly simplified the process of selecting the 'efficient' portfolio. In conclusion essentially the Sharpe Single Index Model assumes that security returns are correlated.

The Single Index Model

The Single Index Model assumes that security returns are correlated for only one reason. Each security is assumed to respond, in some cases more and in other cases less, to the pull of the market portfolio. As the market portfolio makes a significant movement upward, nearly all stocks go up with it. Some stocks rise in price more than others, but as we observe the movement of stock prices over time, it is assumed that variability in the market portfolio accounts for all of the co-movement that we see among the stocks. This is, in fact, the assumption of the Single Index Model. The model assumes that all the numbers in the covariance matrix can be accounted for by the fact that all of the stocks are responding to the pull of this single, common force, thereby simplifying the calculations.

JAMES TOBIN

James Tobin was awarded the Nobel Laureate in Economics in 1981 'for his analysis of financial markets and their relations to expenditure decisions, employment, production and prices'.

Tobin illustrated that investors can choose between portfolios of stocks on the basis of expected return and variance if either of two conditions hold.

The first condition is that the probability distributions for portfolio returns are all *normally distributed*. This means they all look something like the *bell-shaped* distribution of Figure 2.2. A normal distribution, as discussed further in Chapter 4, has only two relevant parameters, the expected value and the variance. If you know the expected value and the variance and that the distribution is normal, you know everything you need to know to accurately describe the distribution. A normal distribution is fully specified by its expected value and its variance. All normal distributions are identical in every respect, other than their expected value and variance. They are all, for example, perfectly symmetric, having no skewedness in either direction.

The assumption of normality isn't unreasonable in some cases. While the possible range for the return is truncated at the lower end (the lowest possible return is −100 per cent, but there is no bound on the highest possible return), this is of no *practical* consequence if the time horizon is relatively short, say, a month. Stocks rarely more than double in price or fall by more than 50 per

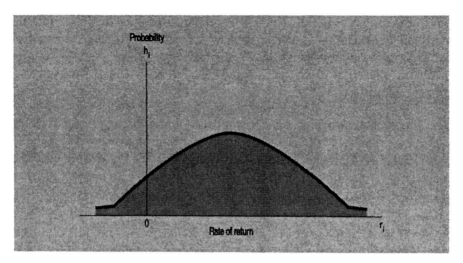

Fig 2.2 ● Normal probability distribution

cent in such a short period of time. As a consequence, if you were to observe the monthly returns on a typical stock over a period of time where there was no change in the underlying variance of the series, the frequency distribution for the returns would not depart significantly from that of normal distribution.

The second condition emphasized by Tobin, which allows investors to choose between portfolios solely on the basis of expected return and variance, is that the relationship between your utility u and the value of your portfolio V is *quadratic* in form. If so, then the utility associated with any ith value for your portfolio is given by Equation (8):

$$u_i = a_0 + a_1 V_i + a_2 V_i^2 \qquad (8)$$

In Equation (8), if the coefficient a_i were positive and a_2 were negative, the relationship between your utility and the value of your portfolio would look like the parabola of Figure 2.3. Utility increases as portfolio value increases, but it increases at a decreasing rate, finally reaching a maximum at V^1.

In choosing between portfolios, it is assumed investors want to maximize their expected well-being or utility. The formula for expected utility is given by Equation (9):

$$E(u) = \sum_{i=1}^{n} h_i u_i \qquad (9)$$

In the formula, h_i represents the probability of attaining the ith possible level of utility, which is associated with the ith possible portfolio value. Substituting Equation (8) into Equation (9), we get Equation (10):

$$E(u) = \sum_{i=1}^{n} b_i \left(a_0 + a_1 V_i + a_2 V_i^2 \right) \tag{10}$$

By bringing the summation into the parentheses and factoring out constants from the sums, we get Equation (11):

$$E(u) = a_0 \sum_{i=1}^{n} b_i + a_1 \sum_{i=1}^{n} b_i V_i + a_2 \sum_{i=1}^{n} b_i V_i^2 \tag{11}$$

Recognizing the formulas for expected values and the fact that the probabilities sum to 1.00, we obtain Equation (12):

$$E(u) = a_0 + a_1 E(V) + a_2 E(V^2) \tag{12}$$

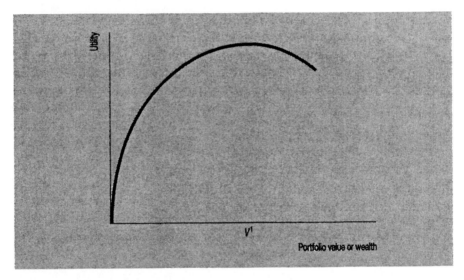

Fig 2.3 ● Quadratic utility function

Tobin then goes on to employ the following mathematical identity in Equation (13):

$$E(V^2) \equiv E(V)^2 + \sigma^2(V) \tag{13}$$

Substituting Equation (13) into Equation (12), we arrive at Equation (14)

$$E(u) = a_0 + a_1 E(V) + a_2 E(V)^2 + a_2 \sigma^2(V) \tag{14}$$

Thus, if you have a quadratic utility function, the utility you would expect to get from investing in a portfolio is related only to the expected value and variance of the portfolio. Even if the probability distribution of ending portfolio values (and, therefore, of portfolio returns as well) is skewed left or right, it makes no difference to you. Given two portfolios with the same variance, you prefer the one with the higher expected rate of return. Since a_2 is assumed to be a negative number, given two portfolios with the same expected return, you prefer the one with the lower variance.

Without these insights the distinguishing features of the Capital Asset Pricing Model (CAPM) could not have been established.

The major part of Tobin's analysis deals with the choice between a single risky asset and cash, but he demonstrated that nothing essential is changed if there are many risky assets, for they will always be held in the same proportions and can be treated as a single composite asset. This is known as the first separation theorem in portfolio theory, and is illustrated in Figure 2.4 which plots mean returns, μ, against the standard deviation, σ. In Figure 2.4 the curved locus AMOVB corresponds to the set of portfolios offering the lowest standard deviation for each level of mean return: the positively sloped segment is referred to as the efficient frontier, for points along it offer the highest μ for a given σ. In the absence of any riskless investment opportunities, risk averse mean-variance investors will select portfolios corresponding to the points at which their indifference curves in (μ,σ) space are tangent to the efficient frontier (Tobin shows that the indifference curves of risk averters will have the requisite curvature). Point C represents cash, which has zero risk and return. By combining cash with the portfolio of risky assets corresponding to the tangency portfolio O, investors are able to attain the (μ,σ) combinations along the line segment CO, and all investors who find it optimal to hold cash will find it optimal to combine their cash with the same risky portfolio O. Their portfolio decisions can be *separated* into the choice of the optimal combination of risky asset (O) and the choice of the cash/risky asset ratio, hence the term separation theorem.

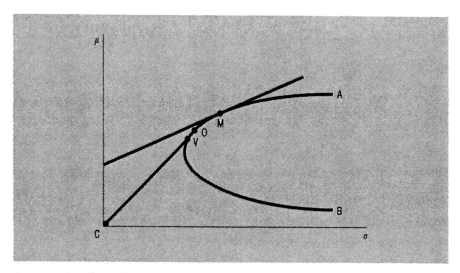

Fig 2.4 ● The efficient frontier and the CAPM

Six years elapsed before the equilibrium implications of the Tobin Separation Theorem were exploited by Sharpe (1964) and Lintner (1965). The reason for delay was undoubtedly the boldness of the assumption required for progress, namely that all investors hold the same beliefs about the joint distribution of security returns. Nevertheless, this assumption of homogeneous beliefs, combined with the further assumption that all investors can borrow as well as lend at the riskless rate, r, leads to the powerful conclusion that all investors hold the same portfolio of risk assets, denoted by M in Figure 2.4. Then the only risky assets that will be held by investors in equilibrium are those contained in portfolio M, and M must be the market portfolio of all risky assets in the economy. This identification of the tangency portfolio M with the aggregate market portfolio is the essence of the Sharpe-Lintner CAPM.

Tobin also introduced the idea of 'Tobin's q' as a measure to predict whether capital investment would increase or decrease. 'Tobin's q' is simply the ratio between the market value of an asset and its replacement cost. He believed this ratio could be used to predict future capital investment, and thus would be a good predictor of general economic conditions. Tobin's q ratio is discussed further in Chapter 7.

The Nobel Prize in Economics

The annual award of the Nobel Prize in Economics takes place every year in October. The winner, or winners, receive the prize for contributing the most outstanding ideas to the field of economics. But just what exactly is the Nobel Prize in Economics? From where did it come?

Few realize, especially outside of the economics profession, that the prize in economics is not an 'official' Nobel. The five original Nobels – physics, chemistry, peace, literature and medicine or physiology – were established in Alfred Nobel's will, in 1895, to honour the most important discoveries in these respective areas. The first awards were made in 1901.

The award for economics came almost 70 years later – bootstrapped to the Nobel in 1968 as a bit of a marketing ploy to celebrate the Bank of Sweden's 300th anniversary. The Bank established a foundation to award the annual prize money, and the new award became known officially as 'The Sveriges Riksbank (Bank of Sweden) Prize in Economic Sciences in Memory of Alfred Nobel'.

Awarded by the Royal Swedish Academy of Science (which also awards the prizes for chemistry and physics), the selection process for economics laureates is similar to that of the original Nobels, and the financial award is also $1 million.

THE NOBEL PRIZE SELECTION PROCESS

One of the enamouring idiosyncrasies of the Economics Prize is the degree of secrecy that surrounds the prize's selection and announcement.

If the award is anything, it is thorough in its selection process. Much of the legwork is handled by the Economics Prize Selection Committee, which consists of five eminent scholars. Every year in October, the committee sends invitations to economists throughout the world and to all living economics laureates, asking for nominations for the coming year.

The nominations received by the committee – usually around 250, covering roughly 100 individuals – are investigated with the help of specially appointed experts, who research and analyze the contributions of the top 20 or 30 candidates. These reports are then debated by the Prize Committee, and by Spring they send a recommendation to the Social Sciences Class, which endorses the recommendation by late Summer or early Autumn and sends it to the full Academy. The winner is selected by a simple majority vote and is announced immediately after the vote in mid-October each year.

Table 2.4 ● Winners of the Nobel Prize in Economic Sciences (1969–2000)

Year	Winner	Description
2000	James J. Heckman and Daniel L. McFadden	For extending the field of micro-econometrics in the analysis of individual and household behaviour within economics and other social sciences
1999	Robert A. Mundell	For his analysis of monetary and fiscal policy under different exchange rate regimes and his analysis of optimum currency areas
1998	Amartya Sen	For his contributions to welfare economics
1997	Robert C. Merton and Myron S. Scholes	For a new method to determine the value of derivatives
1996	James A. Mirrlees and William Vickrey	For their fundamental contributions to the economic theory of incentives under asymmetric information
1995	Robert Lucas	For having developed and applied the hypothesis of rational expectations, and thereby having transformed macroeconomic analysis and deepened our understanding of economic policy
1994	John C. Harsanyi, John F. Nash and Reinhard Selten (prize awarded jointly)	For their pioneering analysis of equilibria in the theory of non-co-operative games
1993	Robert W. Fogel and Douglass C. North (prize awarded jointly)	For having renewed research in economic history by applying economic theory and quantitative methods in order to explain economic and institutional change
1992	Gary S. Becker	For having extended the domain of microeconomic analysis to a wide range of human behaviour and interaction, including non-market behaviour
1991	Ronald H. Coase	For his discovery and clarification of the significance of transaction costs and property rights for the institutional structure and functioning of the economy
1990	Harry M. Markowitz, Merton M. Miller and William F. Sharpe (Prize awarded with one third each)	For their pioneering work in the theory of financial economics
1989	Trygve Haavelmo	For his clarification of the probability theory foundations of econometrics and his analyses of simultaneous economic structures
1988	Maurice Allais	For his pioneering contributions to the theory of markets and efficient utilization of resources

Table 2.4 ● Continued

1987	**Robert M. Solow**	For his contributions to the theory of economic growth
1986	**James M. Buchanan, Jr**	For his development of the contractual and constitutional bases for the theory of economic and political decision-making
1985	**Franco Modigliani**	For his pioneering analyses of saving and of financial markets
1984	**Sir Richard Stone**	For having made fundamental contributions to the development of systems of national accounts and hence greatly improved the basis for empirical economic analysis
1983	**Gerard Debreu**	For having incorporated new analytical methods into economic theory and for his rigorous reformulation of the theory of general equilibrium
1982	**George J. Stigler**	For his seminal studies of industrial structures, functioning of markets and causes and effects of public regulation
1981	**James Tobin**	For his analysis of financial markets and their relations to expenditure decisions, employment, production and prices
1980	**Lawrence R. Klein**	For the creation of econometric models and the application to the analysis of economic fluctuations and economic policies
1979	**Theodore W. Schultz and Sir Arthur Lewis** (prize divided equally)	For their pioneering research into economic development research with particular consideration of the problems of developing countries
1978	**Herbert A. Simon**	For his pioneering research into the decision-making process within economic organizations
1977	**Bertil Ohlin and James E. Meade** (prize divided equally)	For their pathbreaking contribution to the theory of international trade and international capital movements
1976	**Milton Friedman**	For his achievements in the fields of consumption analysis, monetary history and theory and for his demonstration of the complexity of stabilization policy
1975	**Leonid Vitaliyevich Kantorovich and Tjalling C. Koopmans** (prize awarded jointly)	For their contributions to the theory of optimum allocation of resources

Table 2.4 ● Continued

1974	**Gunnar Myrdal and Friedrich August Von Hayek** (prize divided equally)	For their pioneering work in the theory of money and economic fluctuations and for their penetrating analysis of the interdependence of economic, social and institutional phenomena
1973	**Wassily Leontief**	For the development of the input-output method and for its application to important economic problems
1972	**Sir John R. Hicks and Kenneth J. Arrow** (prize awarded jointly)	For their pioneering contributions to general economic equilibrium theory and welfare theory
1971	**Simon Kuznets**	For his empirically founded interpretation of economic growth which has led to new and deepened insight into the economic and social structure and process of development
1970	**Paul A. Samuelson**	For the scientific work through which he has developed static and dynamic economic theory and actively contributed to raising the level of analysis in economic science
1969	**Ragnar Frisch and Jan Tinbergen** (prize awarded jointly)	For having developed and applied dynamic models for the analysis of economic processes

Source: Nobel Prize Committee

CHAPTER 3

The time value of money: its role in the valuation of financial assets

- Introduction
- Future values – compounding
- Present value – discounting
- Bond and stock valuation
- Simple interest and compound interest
- Nominal and effective rates of interest

INTRODUCTION

Time value of money is a critical consideration in understanding the key areas in financial economics. *Compound interest* calculations are needed to determine future sums of money resulting from an investment. Discounting, or the calculation of *present value*, which is inversely related to compounding, is used to evaluate the cash flow associated with the valuation of financial assets.

FUTURE VALUES – COMPOUNDING

A dollar in hand today is worth more than a dollar to be received tomorrow because of the interest it could earn from putting it in a savings account. Compounding interest means that interest earns interest. In order to appreciate the concepts of compounding and time value we need some definitions. Let us define:

F_n = future value = the amount of money at the end of year n
P = principal
i = annual interest rate
n = number of years

Then,

F_1 = the amount of money at the end of year 1
= principal and interest = $P + iP = P(1 + i)$
F_2 = the amount of money at the end of year 2
= $F_1(1 + i) = P(1 + i)(1 + i) = P(1 + i)^2$

The future value of an investment compounded annually at rate i for n years is given by Equation (1)

$$F_n = P(1 + i)^n = P \cdot \text{FVIF}_{i,n} \tag{1}$$

where $\text{FVIF}_{i,n}$ is the future value interest factor for \$1. This can be found in Table 3.1.

EXAMPLE 1

Nadia placed $1000 in a savings account earning 8 per cent interest compounded annually. How much money will she have in the account at the end of four years?

$F_n = P(1 + i)^n$

$F_4 = \$1000(1 + 0.08)^4 = \$1000 \cdot \text{FVIF}_{8,4}$

From Table 3.1 the FVIF for four years at 8 per cent is 1.360. Therefore,

$F_4 = \$1000(1.360) = £1360.$

Table 3.1 • Compounded future value of $1

Years Hence	1%	2%	3%	4%	5%	6%	7%	8%	9%
1	1.010	1.020	1.030	1.040	1.050	1.060	1.070	1.080	1.090
2	1.020	1.040	1.061	1.082	1.102	1.124	1.145	1.166	1.188
3	1.030	1.061	1.093	1.125	1.158	1.191	1.225	1.260	1.295
4	1.041	1.082	1.126	1.170	1.216	1.262	1.311	1.360	1.412
5	1.051	1.104	1.159	1.217	1.276	1.338	1.403	1.469	1.539
6	1.062	1.126	1.194	1.265	1.340	1.419	1.501	1.587	1.677
7	1.072	1.149	1.230	1.316	1.407	1.504	1.605	1.714	1.828
8	1.083	1.172	1.267	1.369	1.477	1.594	1.718	1.851	1.993
9	1.094	1.195	1.305	1.423	1.551	1.689	1.838	1.999	2.172
10	1.105	1.219	1.344	1.480	1.629	1.791	1.967	2.159	2.367

PRESENT VALUES – DISCOUNTING

Present value is the present worth of future sums of money. The process of calculating present values, or *discounting*, is actually the opposite of finding the compounded future value. In connection with present value calculations, the interest rate i is called the *discount rate*.

Recall that $\qquad F_n = P(1 + i)^n$

Therefore $\qquad P = \dfrac{F_n}{(1 + i)^n} = F\left(\dfrac{1}{(1 + i)^n}\right) = F_n \cdot \text{PVIF}_{i,n}$ (2)

Where $\text{PVIF}_{i,n}$ represents the present value interest factor for $1. This can be found in Table 3.2.

EXAMPLE 2

Nadia has been given an opportunity to receive $20,000 six years from now. If she can earn 10 per cent on investments, what is the most she should pay for this opportunity? To answer this question, one must compute the present value of $20,000 to be received six years from now at a 10 per cent rate of discount. F_6 is $20,000, i is 10 per cent, which equals 0.1, and n is six years. $\text{PVIF}_{10,6}$ from Table 3.2 is 0.564.

$$P = \$20,000 \left(\frac{1}{(1 + 0.1)^6}\right) = \$20,000(\text{PVIF}_{10,6}) = \$20,000(0.564) = \$11,280$$

This means that Nadia, who can earn 10 per cent on her investment, should be indifferent to the choice between receiving $11,280 now or $20,000 six years from now since the amounts are time equivalent. In other words she could invest $11,280 today at 10 per cent and have $20,000 in six years.

Table 3.2 ● Present value of $1 (PVIF)

Years Hence	1%	2%	4%	5%	6%	8%	10%	12%	15%
1	.990	.980	.962	.952	.943	.926	.909	.893	.870
2	.980	.961	.925	.907	.890	.857	.826	.797	.756
3	.971	.942	.889	.864	.840	.794	.751	.712	.658
4	.961	.924	.855	.823	.792	.735	.683	.636	.572
5	.951	.906	.822	.784	.747	.681	.621	.567	.497
6	.942	.888	.790	.746	.705	.630	.564	.501	.432
7	.933	.871	.760	.711	.665	.583	.513	.452	.376
8	.923	.853	.731	.677	.627	.540	.467	.404	.327
9	.914	.837	.703	.645	.592	.500	.424	.361	.284
10	.905	.820	.676	.614	.558	.463	.386	.322	.247

BOND AND STOCK VALUATION

The process of determining security valuation, discussed in more detail in Chapters 6 and 7, involves finding the present value of an asset's expected future cash flows using the investor's required rate of return. Thus the basic security valuation model can be defined mathematically as Equation (3):

$$V = \sum_{t=1}^{n} \frac{C_t}{(1+r)^t} \tag{3}$$

where V = intrinsic value or present value of an asset
         C_i = expected future cash flows in period $t = 1,....,n$
         r = investor's required rate of return.

Bond valuation

The valuation process for a bond requires a knowledge of three basic elements:

1   the amount of the cash flows to be received by the investor, which is equal to the periodic interest to be received and the par value to be paid at maturity;

2   the maturity date of the loan; and

3   the investor's required rate of return.

The periodic interest can be received annually or semi-annually. The value of a bond is simply the present value of these cash flows.

If the interest payments are made annually then we derive Equation (4):

$$V = \sum_{t=1}^{n} \frac{I}{(1+r)^t} + \frac{M}{(1+r)^n} = I(\text{PVIFA}_{r,n}) + M(\text{PVIF}_{r,n}) \qquad (4)$$

where

   I = interest payment each year = coupon interest rate $\times$ par value
   M = par value, or maturity value, typically $1,000
   r = investor's required rate of return
   n = number of years to maturity
   PVIFA = present value interest factor of an annuity of $1 (which can be found in Table 3.3)
   PVIF   = present value interest factor of $1 (which can be found in Table 3.2).

EXAMPLE 3

Consider a bond, maturing in ten years and having a coupon rate of 8 per cent. The par value is $1000. Investors consider 10 per cent to be an appropriate required rate of return in view of the risk level associated with this bond. The annual interest payment is $80 (8% $\times$ $1000). The present value of this bond is given by Equation (5):

$$V = \sum_{t=1}^{n} \frac{I}{(1+r)^t} + \frac{M}{(1+r)^n} = I(\text{PVIFA}_{r,n}) + M(\text{PVIF}_{r,n}) \qquad (5)$$

$$= \sum_{t=1}^{10} \frac{80}{(1+0.1)^t} + \frac{1000}{(1+0.1)^{10}} = \$80(\text{PVIFA}_{10\%,10}) + \$1,000(\text{PVIF}_{10\%,10})$$

$$= \$80(6.145) + \$1000(0.386) = \$491.60 + \$386.00 = \$877.60$$

Table 3.3 • Present value of an annuity of $1 (PVIFA)

Years	1%	2%	4%	5%	6%	8%	10%
1	0.990	0.980	0.962	0.952	0.943	0.926	0.909
2	1.970	1.942	1.886	1.859	1.833	1.783	1.736
3	2.941	2.884	2.775	2.723	2.673	2.577	2.487
4	3.902	3.808	3.630	3.546	3.465	3.312	3.170
5	4.853	4.713	4.452	4.329	4.212	3.993	3.791
6	5.795	5.601	5.242	5.076	4.917	4.623	4.355
7	6.728	6.472	6.002	5.786	5.582	5.206	4.868
8	7.652	7.325	6.733	6.463	6.210	5.747	5.335
9	8.566	8.162	7.435	7.108	6.802	6.247	5.759
10	9.471	8.983	8.111	7.722	7.360	6.710	6.145

Common stock valuation

Like bonds, the value of a common stock is the present value of all future cash inflows expected to be received by the investor. The cash inflows expected to be received are dividends and the future price at the time of the sale of the stock. For an investor holding a common stock for only one year, the value of the stock would be the present value of both the expected cash dividend to be received in one year (D_1) and the expected market price per share of the stock at year-end (P_1). If r represents an investor's required rate of return, the value of the common stock (P_0) would be given by Equation (6):

$$P_0 = \frac{D_1}{(1+r)^1} + \frac{P_1}{(1+r)^1} \tag{6}$$

EXAMPLE 4

Assume an investor is considering the purchase of stock A at the beginning of the year. The dividend at year-end is expected to be $1.50, and the market price by the end of the year is expected to be $40. If the investor's required rate of return is 15 per cent, referring to Table 3.2 the value of the stock would be:

$$P_0 = \frac{D_1}{(1+r)^1} + \frac{P_1}{(1+r)^1} = \frac{\$1.50}{(1+0.15)} + \frac{\$40}{(1+0.15)^1}$$

$$= \$1.50(0.870) + \$40(0.870) = \$1.31 + \$34.80 = \$36.11$$

Since common stock has no maturity date and is held for many years, a more general, multiperiod model is needed. The general common stock valuation model is defined as follows:

$$P_0 = \sum_{t=1}^{\infty} \frac{D_t}{(1 + r)^t}$$

There are three cases of growth in dividends. They are:

1 zero growth;

2 constant growth; and

3 supernormal growth.

In the case of *zero growth*, if:

$$D_0 = D_1 = \ldots = D_{\infty}$$

then the valuation model becomes Equation (7):

$$P_0 = \sum_{t=1}^{\infty} \frac{D_t}{(1 + r)^t} \tag{7}$$

This reduces to Equation (8)

$$P_0 = \frac{D_1}{r} \tag{8}$$

EXAMPLE 5

Assuming D equals $2.50 and r equals 10 per cent, then the value of the stock is:

$$P_0 = \frac{\$2.50}{0.1} = \$25$$

In the case of *constant growth*, if we assume that dividends grow at a constant rate of g every year {i.e. $D_t = D_0(1 + g)^t$}, then Equation (7) is simplified to Equation (9):

$$P_0 = \frac{D_1}{r - g} \tag{9}$$

This formula is known as the *Gordon growth model*.

EXAMPLE 6

Consider a common stock that paid a $3 dividend per share at the end of last year and is expected to pay a cash dividend every year at a growth rate of 10 per cent. Assume that the investor's required rate of return is 12 per cent. The value of the stock would be:

$$D_1 = D_0(1 + g) = \$3(1 + 0.10) = \$3.30$$

$$P_0 = \frac{D_1}{r - g} = \frac{\$3.30}{0.12 - 0.10} = \$165$$

Finally, consider the case of *supernormal* growth. Firms typically go through life cycles, during part of which their growth is faster than that of the economy and then falls sharply. The value of stock during such super-normal growth can be found by taking the following steps:

1   compute the dividends during the period of supernormal growth and find their present value;

2   find the price of the stock at the end of the supernormal growth period and compute its present value; and

3   add these two PV figures to find the value (P_0) of the common stock.

EXAMPLE 7

Consider a common stock whose dividends are expected to grow at a 25 per cent rate for two years, after which the growth rate is expected to fall to 5 per cent. The dividend paid last period was $2. The investor desires a 12 per cent return. To find the value of this stock, take the following steps:

1   Compute the dividends during the supernormal growth period and find their present value. Assuming D_0 is $2, g is 15 per cent and r is 12 per cent:

$$D_1 = D_0(1 + g) = \$2(1 + 0.25) = \$2.50$$

$$D_2 = D_0(1 + g)^2 = \$2(1.563) = \$3.125$$

or $D_2 = D_1(1 + g) = \$2.50(1.25) = \$3.125$

$$\text{PV of dividends} = \frac{D_1}{(1 + r)^1} + \frac{D_2}{(1 + r)^2} = \frac{\$2.50}{(1 + 0.12)} + \frac{\$3.125}{(1 + 0.12)^2}$$

$$= \$2.50(\text{PVIF}_{12\%,1}) + \$3.125(\text{PVIF}_{12\%,2})$$

$$= \$2.50(0.893) + \$3.125(0.797) = \$2.23 + \$2.49 = \$4.72$$

2   Find the price of stock at the end of the supernormal growth period. The dividend for the third year is:

$$D_2 \quad = D_2(1 + g'), \text{ where } g' = 5\%$$
$$= \$3.125(1 + 0.05) = \$3.28$$

The price of the stock is therefore:

$$P_2 = \frac{D_3}{r - g'} = \frac{\$3.28}{0.12 - 0.05} = \$46.86$$

PV of stock price $= \$46.86(\text{PVIF}_{12\%,2}) = \$46.86(0.797) = \$37.35$

3. Add the two PV figures obtained in steps 1 and 2 to find the value of the stock.

$$P_0 = \$4.72 + \$37.35 = \$42.07$$

SIMPLE INTEREST AND COMPOUND INTEREST

Present values and future values for financial assets are very sensitive to the frequency with which interest is paid. In particular it is necessary to distinguish between simple interest and compound interest.

Simple interest

When money of value P on a given date increases in value to S at some later date,

P is called the *principal*
S is called the *amount* or *accumulated value of P*,

and

$I = S - P$ is called the *interest*.

When only the principal earns interest for the entire life of the transaction, the interest due at the end of the time is called *simple interest*. The simple interest on a principal P for t years at the rate r is given by Equation (10):

$$I = Prt \tag{10}$$

and the simple amount is given by Equation (11):

$$S = P + I = P + Prt = P(1 + rt) \tag{11}$$

EXAMPLE 8

Find the simple interest on $750 at 4 per cent for 6 months. What is the amount?

Here $P = 750$, $r = 0.04$, and $t = \frac{1}{2}$. Then

$$I = Prt = 750(0.04)\tfrac{1}{2} = \$15$$

and

$$S = P + I = 750 + 15 = \$765$$

Compound interest

If the interest due is added to the principal at the end of each interest period and thereafter earns interest, the interest is said to be *compounded*. The sum of the original principal and total interest is called the *compound amount* or *accumulated value*. The difference between the accumulated value and the original principal is called the *compound interest*. The interest period, the time between two successive interest computations, is also called the *conversion period*.

Interest may be converted into principal annually, semi-annually, quarterly, monthly, weekly, daily or continuously. The number of times interest is converted in one year, or compounded per year, is called the *frequency of conversion*. The rate of interest is usually stated as an annual interest rate, referred to as the *nominal* rate of interest. The phrases 'interest at 12%' or 'money worth 12%' means 12 per cent compounded annually; otherwise, the frequency of conversion is indicated, e.g. 16 per cent compounded semi-annually, 10 per cent compounded daily.

The following notation will be used:

P ≡ original principal, or the present value of S, or the discounted value of S

S ≡ compound amount of P, or the accumulated value of P

n ≡ total number of interest (or conversion) periods involved

m ≡ number of interest periods per year, or the frequency of compounding

j_m ≡ nominal (yearly) interest rate which is compounded (payable, convertible) m times per year

i ≡ interest rate per interest period

The interest rate per period, i, equals j_m/m. For example $j_{12} = 12\%$ means that a nominal (yearly) rate of 12 per cent is converted (compounded, payable) 12 times per year, $i = 1\% = 0.01$ being the interest rate per month.

Let P represent the principal at the beginning of the first interest period and i the interest rate per conversion period. It is necessary to calculate the accumulated values at the ends of successive interest periods for n periods.

At the end of the first period:

    interest due Pi

    accumulated value $P + Pi = P(1 + i)$

At the end of the second period:

    interest due $[P(1 + i)]i$

    accumulated value $P(1 + i) + [P(1 + i)]i = P(1 + i)(1 + i) = P(1 + i)^2$

At the end of the third period:

interest due $\quad\quad [P(1 + i)^2]i$

accumulated value $\quad P(1+ i)^2 + [P(1 + i)^2]i = P(1 + i)^2(1 + i) = P(1 + i)^2$

Continuing in this manner, we see that the successive accumulated values,

$P(1+ i), P(1+ i)^2, P(1+ i)^3, ...$

form a geometric progression whose nth term is Equation (12):

$$S = P(1+ i)^n \tag{12}$$

giving us Equation (12) where S is the accumulated value of P at the end of the n interest periods.

The application of compound interest is most clearly seen by working through some real world applications.

EXAMPLE 9

Find (a) the simple interest on $1000 for two years at 12 per cent,

(b) the compound interest on $1000 for two years at 12 per cent compounded semi-annually (that is, $j_2 = 12\%$).

(a) $I = Prt - 1000(0.12)(2) = \$240$

(b) Since the conversion period is six months, interest is earned at the rate of 6 per cent per period, and there are four interest periods in two years the answer can be seen from Table 3.4.

Table 3.4 ● Calculating compound interest

At the End of Period	Interest		Accumulated Value
1	1000(0.06)	= $60	$1060.00
2	1060(0.06)	= $63.60	$1123.60
3	1123.60(0.06)	= $67.42	$1191.02
4	1191.02(0.05)	= $71.46	$1262.48

The compound interest is 1262.48 – 1000 = $262.48.

Alternate solution

From Equation (12) with $P = 1000$, $i = 0.06$, and $n = 4$,

$S = P(1 + i)^n = 1000(1.06)^4 = \$1262.48$

and the compound interest is $S - P = \$262.48$.

EXAMPLE 10

Find the compound interest on \$1000 at (a) j_{12} = 6% for five years, (b) j_{12} = 15% for 30 years.

(a) We have P = 1000, i = 0.06/12 = 0.005, and n = 5 × 12 = 60. From Equation (12),

$$S = P(1 + i)^n = 1000(1.005)^{60} = \$1348.85$$

The compound interest is $S - P = \$348.85$.

(b) We have P = 1000, i = 0.15/12 = 0.0125, and n = 30 × 12 = 360. From Equation (12),

$$S = 1000(1.0125)^{360} = \$87,541.00$$

The compound interest is $S - P = \$86,541.00$, which is more than 86 times the original investment of \$1000. If the investment had been at 15 per cent simple interest, the interest earned would have been only:

$$I = 1000(0.15)(30) = \$4500$$

This illustrates the power of compound interest at a high rate of interest for a long period of time.

EXAMPLE 11

Tabulate and graph the growth of \$100 at compound interest rates j_{12} = 6%, 8%, 10%, 12% and times 5, 10, 15, 20, 25, 30, 35, 40, 45, 50 years. See Table 3.5 and Figure 3.1.

Table 3.5 • Compound interest rates

Years	n	j_{12} = 6%, i = 0.005	j_{12} = 8%, i = 0.08/12	j_{12} = 10%, i = 0.10/12	j_{12} = 12%, i = 0.01
5	60	134.89	148.98	164.53	181.67
10	120	181.94	221.96	270.70	330.04
15	180	245.41	330.69	445.39	599.58
20	240	331.02	492.68	732.81	1,089.26
25	300	446.50	734.02	1,205.69	1,978.85
30	360	602.26	1093.57	1,983.74	3,594.96
35	420	812.36	1629.26	3,263.87	6,530.96
40	480	1095.75	2427.34	5,370.07	11,864.77
45	540	1478.00	3616.36	8,835.42	21,554.69
50	600	1993.60	5387.82	14,536.99	39,158.34

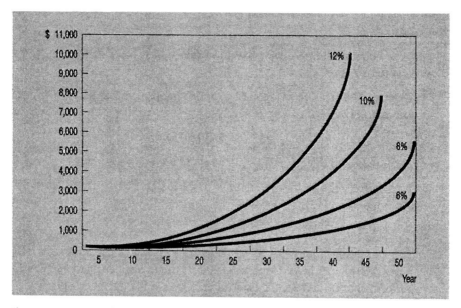

Fig 3.1 ● Compound interest rates

NOMINAL AND EFFECTIVE RATES OF INTEREST

The annual rates of interest with different conversion periods are called equivalent if they yield the same compound amount at the end of one year. Again, this is best understood using examples.

EXAMPLE 12

At the end of one year the compound amount of $100 at

(a) 4 per cent compounded quarterly is $100(1.01)^4 = \$104.06$

(b) 4.06 per cent compounded annually is $100(1.0406) = \$104.06$

Thus 4 per cent compounded quarterly and 4.06 per cent compounded annually are equivalent rates.

When interest is compounded more often than once per year, the given annual rate is called the *nominal annual rate* or *nominal rate*. The rate of interest actually earned in one year is called the *effective annual rate* of the *effective rate*. In Example 12 (a) 4 per cent is a nominal rate while in 12 (b) 4.06 per cent is an effective rate. As noted above, 4.06 per cent is the effective rate equivalent to a nominal rate of 4 per cent compounded quarterly.

EXAMPLE 13

Find the effective rate r equivalent to the nominal rate 5 per cent compounded monthly.

In one year 1 at r effective will amount to $1 + r$ and at 5 per cent compounded monthly will amount to $(1 + 0.05/12)^{12}$. Setting

$$1 + r = (1 + 0.05/12)^{12}$$

we find

$$r = (1 + 0.05/12)^{12} - 1$$

$$= 1.05116190 - 1 = 0.05116190 \text{ or } 5.116\%$$

EXAMPLE 14

Find the nominal rate j compounded quarterly which is equivalent to 5 per cent effective.

In one year 1 at j compounded quarterly will amount to $(1 + j/4)^4$ and at 5 per cent effective will amount to 1.05. Setting

$$(1 + j/4)^4 = 1.05$$

we find

$$1 + j/4 = (1.05)^{\frac{1}{4}}$$

Then

$$
\begin{aligned}
j \quad &= 4[(1.05)^{\frac{1}{4}} - 1] \\
&= 4(0.01227223) = 0.04908892 \text{ or } 4.909\%
\end{aligned}
$$

CHAPTER **4**

Measuring risk and return: a short guide to financial statistics

INTRODUCTION

Statisticians design procedures for collecting, describing, analyzing, evaluating and interpreting data. Despite the widespread application of computers, now arriving almost daily in all shapes and forms, it remains the case that it is essential to understand what lies behind the impressive looking printouts which have become increasingly familiar. Statistics are subject to differing degrees of reliance and the more these limitations are understood the more you will be qualified to understand the key issues in financial economics.

Statistics is all about uncertainty and this is best measured by probability theory. When the degree of uncertainty is established we can draw inferences and decide on actions.

RANDOM VARIABLES AND PROBABILITY DISTRIBUTIONS

Sample space refers to the set of outcomes that can happen in some context. Thus in the context of tossing a coin, the sample space is (heads, tails), in throwing a dice it is (1,2,3,4,5,6), in a football game it is (win, lose, draw).

Two more statistical concepts are important, a *random variable* and a *probability distribution*.

A *random variable is a function which assigns numbers to outcomes defined by elements in the sample space.*

Consider the dice-throwing context as an example. There are six possible outcomes, representing the possible numbers on which the dice could fall uppermost after the dice has been thrown. Hence S = (1,2,3,4,5,6) as we have noted already. We could define a random variable (X, say) as equal to 1 if the number thrown is odd, and equal to 2 if the number thrown is even.

A *probability distribution assigns numbers to values of the random variable.* In the dice-throwing example, we let the random variable take the value 1 if an odd number is thrown and the value 2 if an even number is thrown. Thus $f(1)$ is equivalent to P(X = 1) and $f(2)$ is equivalent to P(X = 2).

Means and variances

Let us now explore the concept of a mean and see how it relates to some of these ideas on probability.

The mean of a random variable may be calculated by multiplying each value the random variable can take by the probability of its taking that value, and adding together all the resulting products. Thus if the random variable X is defined as the number on the upper face of a thrown dice, we may compute its mean as:

$$(1 \times \tfrac{1}{6}) + (2 \times \tfrac{1}{6}) + \dots + (6 \times \tfrac{1}{6}) = 3.5$$

The mean of a random variable is sometimes called its *expected value*. *This is an instance of mathematicians taking an everyday word and using it to mean something much more precise than it does in everyday use.* In the case of the dice throwing, for example, the expected value is 3.5.

A term associated with the mean is the *variance*. The mean and the variance together provide a lot of information about a random variable. The variance can be calculated by finding the difference between each value the random variable can take and its mean, squaring it, multiplying that by the probability that the random variable takes that value, then adding together all the products. The square root of the variance is called the *standard deviation* of the random variable.

We may define mean and variance in a more convenient, shorter way, using Equations (1) and (2):

$$\text{Mean } (\mu) \quad = \sum x f(x) \tag{1}$$
$$\text{Variance } (\sigma^2) = \sum (x-\mu)^2 f(x) \tag{2}$$

The mean and variance are often useful as parameters of the distribution of a random variable. They give us an indication of its *central value* and its *degree of spread*, or variability.

The normal distribution

The best known distribution of all is the normal distribution. The normal distribution is a two-parameter distribution meaning that all we need to define it are the values of its mean and standard deviation. It does, however, differ in an important respect from other distributions so far in that it is *continuous* rather than *discrete*. What do these two words mean?

With respect to a continuous distribution, the question 'What is the probability that the random variable takes the value X?' cannot be answered unless you would be satisfied by the answer zero. The question that *can* be answered is 'What is the probability that the random variable takes a value *between* value A (say) and value B (say)?'. Thus, the probability that a 25-year-old Englishman is between 1.80 and 1.81 metres tall can be assessed, but the probability that a 25-year-old Englishman is exactly 1.80 metres tall is, if we have to answer the question, zero.

The standardized normal distribution

The normal distribution has several properties, but the property of most interest to financial economists is the useful fact that probability statements about any normal distribution may be made directly, knowing only its mean and standard deviation. All normal distributions are symmetrical, so the probability of a normal distributed random variable having a value greater than the mean is 0.5. The probability of a normally distributed random variable having a value more than two standard deviations away from the mean is 0.0456.

In financial markets, it has frequently been observed that the returns on securities typically have a normal distribution. This indicates that there is an equal probability that they will lie above the mean expected return as there is that they will lie below, and that as we move further from the mean the probability of the rate of return deviating from the expected rate of return decreases. A normal distribution is depicted in Figure 4.1, and its characteristics are described below.

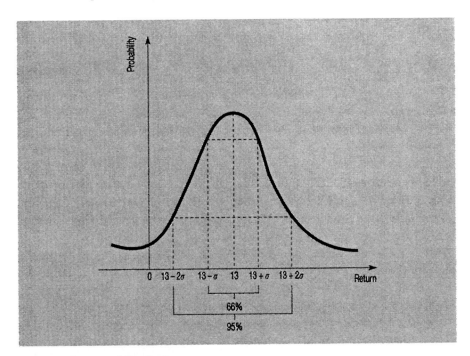

Fig 4.1 ● The normal distribution

If expected rates of return follow a normal distribution then the variance becomes a very useful measure of risk. The larger the variance then the greater the dispersion of values around the mean value and therefore the greater the degree of risk facing the investor.

The normal distribution has a number of useful properties.

1   The distribution is symmetric so that the total variability of returns is twice the size of the portfolio's variability below the mean expected return. Hence, if variability of return is used a proxy for risk in ranking alternative investment portfolios, the ranking will be identical to the case where variability of returns below the mean is used.

2   There is an approximately 95 per cent probability that the actual return on an investment portfolio will lie within two standard deviations of the expected return, and approximately 66 per cent probability that it will lie within one standard deviation. For example, if the mean expected return for the investment portfolio is 13 per cent and the standard deviation is 4, then there is a 95 per cent probability that the expected return will lie within the range 13% ± (2 × 4) = 5%–21% and a 66 per cent probability that it will lie in the region of 13 ± (1 × 4) = 9%–17%. This is a powerful finding for measuring the riskiness of stocks.

STATISTICS DESCRIBING THE PROPERTIES OF A SINGLE SECURITY

It is now time to more formally apply these business statistical ideas to financial markets. Suppose we are looking across some period of time in the future, say, over the next month, and are contemplating the potential for getting various rates of return on our investment. We might ask, 'What is the probability of getting a rate of return in the next month that is less than zero?' If we explore questions like this thoroughly, we might be able to see in our minds what is called a 'simple probability distribution' for the investment. The simple probability distribution shows the probabilities of getting various rates of return over the course of the month.

The distribution might look like the one in Figure 4.2. Horizontally, we are plotting the rates of return that might develop on the investment, which we will presume is a common stock. The symbol r is the rate of return that stock J might produce in some possible state of the world i.

The rate of return is the percentage increase in your wealth associated with holding the stock for the period. The dollar increase is equal to cash dividends received during the period plus any change in the value of the stock that occurs during the period. Your percentage rate of return is equal to the dollar increase divided by the market value of the stock at the beginning of the period, as shown below.

$$r = \frac{\text{Dividends} \times \text{Change in market value}}{\text{Beginning market value}}$$

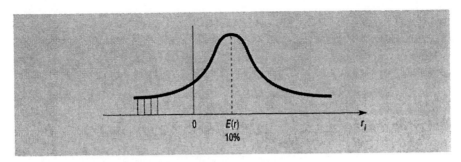

Fig 4.2 ● Marginal probability distribution for rates of return

On the vertical axis of Figure 4.2 we are measuring the probability of getting any particular rate of return. The graph is drawn as if the returns were continuous along the horizontal axis. Actually, assume that there are a series of discrete possible rates of return, each associated with one of the vertical bars drawn on the graph. The length of each bar represents the probability of getting the particular rate of return represented below the bar. If you summed the probabilities represented by all the bars, the sum would equal 1, or 100 per cent, because the returns plotted on the horizontal axis constitute everything that can happen to the stock in the next month.

The sample mean or average rate of return

Suppose you can't see the actual probability distributions that represent the likelihood of getting the various returns for individual securities. Is there any way to infer what the underlying distributions look like, given that you can't actually see them? This is an important question, because in the real world, you can't see the probability distributions for investments. We cannot actually see the probabilities as they exist in the example depicted in Figure 4.2. Consequently, you usually have to estimate the properties of the distribution by sampling.

In taking sample estimates, you assume that the underlying probability distribution for the returns remains constant as time goes by. If you are dealing with a probability distribution for monthly rates of return, you assume that the distribution doesn't change from month to month. You then observe the rates of return that are supposedly drawn from this distribution month after month.

In Figure 4.3 we have plotted a time series of such returns for a security. Rates of return are plotted vertically, and time is plotted horizontally, for six months. To illustrate, note that the security produces a positive return equal to 6 per cent in period 1. Given the returns produced in the six months, you can get an estimate of the underlying distribution by taking the sample mean of the returns:

$$\text{Sample mean} = r = \frac{\text{Sum of individual returns}}{\text{Number of sampled returns}}$$

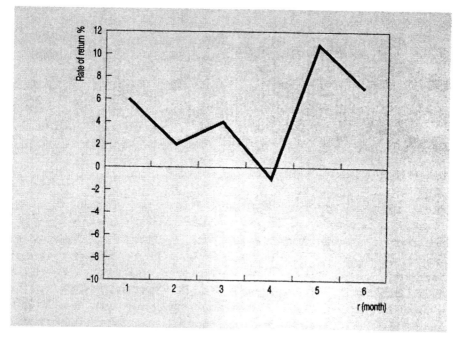

Fig 4.3 ● Time series of rates of return

In this example, the average of returns is equal to 6, and the sample mean is computed as the average of 6, 2, 4, –1, 12, and 7 per cent, giving a mean value of 5 per cent. The sample mean gives you an idea of what you can expect to get as a return from a stock in any given month.

The variance and standard deviation

What about the possibility of getting returns that deviate from the sample mean or average rate of return? The *variance* of return describes the propensity of the security to produce returns that are above or below the sample mean. To estimate the variance, you must once again resort to a sampling procedure. The sample variance is computed using the following formula in Equation (3):

$$\text{Variance} = \sigma^2 r = \frac{\text{Sum of squared deviations from sample mean}}{\text{Number of sampled returns less 1}} \tag{3}$$

where the squared deviation for a particular period, say a month, is the square of the difference between the return for the month and the sample mean return.

To compute the variance, again observe the stock's returns over a number of periods. In each period you subtract, from the return produced, the sample mean rate of return. You square the differences and sum them up. Then you divide the sum by the number of returns observed, less 1. You subtract 1 because you are using an *estimate* in the computation of the variance. The estimate is the sample mean. Subtracting 1 from the denominator gives an unbiased estimate for the variance when you are dealing with a relatively small sample. In our example, the variance is computed as follows:

$$(0.06 - 0.05)^2 = 0.0001$$
$$(0.02 - 0.05)^2 = 0.0009$$
$$(0.04 - 0.05)^2 = 0.0001$$
$$(-0.01 - 0.05)^2 = 0.0036$$
$$(0.12 - 0.05)^2 = 0.0049$$
$$(0.07 - 0.05)^2 = \underline{0.0004}$$
$$\text{Total} = 0.0100$$
$$0.0100/(6 - 1) = 0.0020 = \text{variance}$$

The propensity to deviate from the average rate of return can also be measured with another statistic called the 'standard deviation'. The standard deviation is computed merely by taking the square root of the variance.

Standard deviation = σ_r = square root of variance

In our example, the standard deviation is given by:

$$0.04 = (0.002)^{1/2}$$

Skewness and kurtosis

Skewness (S) is a measure of asymmetry of a probability distribution function (PDF), as can be seen in Figure 4.4. If the S value is positive the PDF is right or positively skewed and if it is negative, it is left, or negatively skewed.

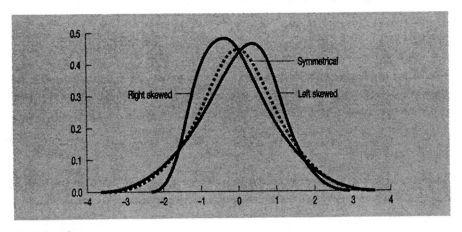

Fig 4.4 ● Skewness

Kurtosis is a measure of tallness or flatness of a PDF as can be seen from Figure 4.5. Fat or short-tailed PDFs are called platykurtic, slim or long-tailed PDFs are called leptokurtic and a normally distributed PDF would be called a mesokurtic distribution.

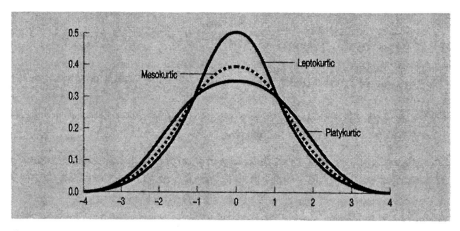

Fig 4.5 ● Kurtosis

STATISTICS DESCRIBING THE INTERRELATIONSHIPS AMONG SECURITIES

The average rate of return and the variance, or standard deviation, provide us with information about the probabilities for returns to a single security or for a portfolio of securities. However, these numbers tell us nothing about the way the returns on securities *interrelate*. Suppose in some given month one security produces a rate of return that is above its average return. If we know that this has happened, what does it do to our expectation for the rate of return produced on some other stock in the same period? When one stock produces a rate of return above its average value, do other stocks have a propensity to do so as well? A statistic that provides us with some information about this question is the covariance between the two stocks.

The covariance

To illustrate what the covariance is, suppose we have two securities, A and B. In a period of five months they produce the following rates of return, as shown in Table 4.1.

Table 4.1 ● The mean rate of return

Month	1	2	3	4	5	Mean
Stock A	0.04	−0.02	0.08	−0.04	0.04	0.02
Stock B	0.02	0.03	0.06	−0.04	0.08	0.03

To compute the simple covariance based on these five monthly rates of return, we compute the deviation that is occurring from the mean return for each of the stocks in each of the months. Then in each month we multiply together the deviations for each of the stocks to get a product. Then we use the formula in Equation (4):

$$\text{Covariance} = \text{Cov}(r_A, r_B) = \frac{\text{Sum of the products of the deviations}}{\text{Number of sampled returns less 1}} \quad (4)$$

Thus, we start with the first pair of monthly returns in Table 4.1. In this month stock A is producing 4 per cent, and stock B is producing 2 per cent. We first compute the deviation that these returns represent from the mean returns of each stock. Note that stock A is 2 per cent above its mean of 2 per cent, and stock B is 1 per cent below its mean of 3 per cent. After expressing the two deviations as decimals, we multiply them to get a product of −0.0002. We now do the same for each of the other four return pairs and sum them up as follows:

$$
\begin{array}{lll}
(0.04 - 0.02) & (0.02 - 0.03) = & -0.0002 \\
(-0.02 - 0.02) & (0.03 - 0.03) = & 0.0000 \\
(0.08 - 0.02) & (0.06 - 0.03) = & 0.0018 \\
(-0.04 - 0.02) & (-0.04 - 0.03) = & 0.0042 \\
(0.04 - 0.02) & (0.08 - 0.03) = & \underline{0.0010} \\
\text{Total} & = & 0.0068
\end{array}
$$

We then divide the total by the number of sampled returns less 1, to obtain the covariance.

$$0.0068/(5 - 1) = 0.0017$$

As a number, the covariance doesn't provide much detail about the relationship between the returns on the two stocks. In this case, because it is a positive number, the covariance tells you that when one security produces a return above its average return, the other security has a propensity to do the same thing.

The covariance number is important because it is a critical input in determining the variance of a portfolio of securities. However, as we said earlier, it doesn't describe very fully the nature of the relationship between the two investments. Nevertheless, we can standardize the covariance to obtain a better descriptor called the correlation coefficient.

The correlation coefficient

Theoretically, the possible range for the covariance extends all the way from minus infinity to plus infinity. We can bound it, however, by dividing it by the product of the standard deviation for the two investments as can be seen from Equation (5):

$$\text{Correlation coefficient} = \sigma_{A,B} = \frac{\text{Covariance}}{\text{Product of standard deviations}} \quad (5)$$

The resulting number is called the correlation coefficient, and it falls within the range of -1 to $+1$. In our example, the standard deviation of the five returns to security A is equal to 4.9 per cent and the standard deviation for B is equal to 4.6 per cent. The correlation coefficient is thus:

$$\text{Correlation coefficient} = \frac{0.0017}{0.049 \times 0.046} = 0.76$$

Given the above definition for the correlation coefficient, the covariance can be written as the correlation coefficient and the standard deviation of the two securities, as shown in Equation (6):

$$\text{Covariance} = \text{Correlation coefficient} \times \text{Product of standard deviations} \quad (6)$$

The coefficient of determination

If we square the correlation coefficient, we obtain the coefficient of determination. This is the percentage of the variability in the returns on one investment that can be associated with variability in the returns on some other. For example, if the correlation coefficient is $+0.90$, we can say that approximately 81 per cent of the variability in the returns on security A can be associated with, or explained by, returns on security B.

SOME APPLICATIONS OF STATISTICAL MEASURES OF RISK AND RETURN

The number of mutual funds in the USA (unit trusts in the UK) has grown dramatically over recent years. Their growth has raised major issues as to how to measure their performance. The two major issues that need to be addressed in any performance ranking are first, how to choose an appropriate benchmark for comparison and second, how to adjust a fund's return for risk. Some flavour of these issues will be discussed in this section and we will return to these ideas in later chapters.

Simple measures of return

The return on a mutual fund investment includes both income (in the form of dividends or interest payments) and capital gains or losses (the increase or decrease in the value of a security). The return is calculated by taking the change in a fund's net asset value, which is the market value of securities the fund holds divided by the number of the fund's shares during a given time period, assuming the reinvestment of all income and capital-gains distributions, and dividing it by the original net asset value. Thus a fund's monthly return can be expressed as shown in Equation (7):

$$R_t = \frac{NAV_t = DIST_t - NAV_{t-1}}{NAV_{t-1}} \tag{7}$$

where R_t is the return in month t, NAV_t is the closing net asset value of the fund on the last trading day of the month, NAV_{t-1} is the closing net asset value of the fund on the last day of the previous month, and $DIST_t$ is income and capital gains distributions taken during the month.

Investors are not interested in the returns of a unit trust in isolation but in comparison with some alternative investment. To allow for this a fund should meet some minimum hurdle, such as a return on a completely safe, liquid investment available at the time. Such a return is referred to as the 'risk-free rate' and is usually taken in the United States to be the rate on 90-day Treasury bills. A fund's monthly return minus the monthly risk-free rate is called the fund's monthly 'excess return'. Column 2 of Table 4.2 shows the risk-free rate as represented by 1996 monthly returns on a money market fund investing in Treasury bills. Column 3 of Table 4.2 shows monthly excess returns of XYZ Fund, derived by subtracting monthly returns on the money market fund from monthly returns on XYZ Fund. We see that XYZ Fund had an annual (geometric) mean return of 20.26 per cent in excess of the risk-free rate.

Comparing a fund's return to a risk-free investment is not the only relevant comparison. Domestic equity funds are often compared to a representative stock exchange index. The S&P 500 index is the most widely used benchmark for diversified US equity funds. However, other benchmarks may be more appropriate for some types of funds.

Measures of risk

Investors are interested not only in funds' returns but also in the risks taken to achieve those returns. We can think of risk as the uncertainty of the expected return, and uncertainty is generally equated with variability. Investors demand and receive higher returns with increased variability, suggesting that variability and risk are related.

Table 4.2 ● XYZ equity fund monthly returns and summary statistics

Month	XYZ Return (%) (1)	Risk-free Rate (%) (2)	XYZ Excess Return (%) (3)	Benchmark Excess Return (%) (4)
1	−1.66	0.46	−2.12	−0.30
2	3.37	0.41	2.96	3.02
3	3.26	0.43	2.83	1.44
4	4.61	0.41	4.20	5.18
5	4.40	0.43	3.97	3.51
6	−1.45	0.42	−1.87	−4.21
7	−6.23	0.44	−6.67	−8.89
8	4.82	0.44	4.38	5.50
9	3.86	0.43	3.43	3.33
10	1.56	0.44	1.12	−1.89
11	4.36	0.42	3.94	3.94
12	3.51	0.44	3.07	1.97
Geometric mean (%)				
Monthly	1.98		1.55	0.97
Annualized	26.53		20.26	12.22
Arithmetic mean (%)				
Monthly	2.03		1.60	1.05
Annualized	21.41		19.25	12.60
Standard deviation (%)				
Monthly	3.27		3.28	4.06
Annualized	11.34		11.36	14.08

Source: Simons K. *New England Economic Review*. September/October 1998

Standard deviation

The basic measure of variability is the standard deviation, also known as volatility. For a mutual fund, the standard deviation is used to measure the variability of monthly returns, as shown in Equation (8):

$$STD = \sqrt{1/T^* \sum (Rt - AR)^2} \tag{8}$$

where STD is the monthly standard deviation, *AR* is the average monthly return, and *T* is the number of months in the period for which the standard deviation is being calculated. The monthly standard deviation can be annualized by multiplying it by the square root of 12.

For mutual funds/unit trusts, we are most often interested in the standard deviation of excess returns over the risk-free rate. To continue with our example, XYZ Fund had a monthly standard deviation of excess returns equal to 3.27 per cent, or an annualized standard deviation of 11.34 per cent.

Risk adjusted performance: the Sharpe ratio

Investors can always obtain higher returns by accepting higher risks. In order to adjust returns for these higher risks, William Sharpe, a Nobel Prize winner in economics, as discussed in Chapter 2, designed just such a risk-adjusted measure. Not surprisingly this is known as the Sharpe ratio. The Sharpe ratio (Sharpe 1966) measures the fund's excess return per unit of its risk. The Sharpe ratio can be expressed as shown in Equation (9):

$$\text{Sharpe ratio} = \frac{\text{Fund's average excess return}}{\text{Standard deviation of fund's excess return}} \tag{9}$$

Column 3 of Table 4.2 shows that the (arithmetic) monthly mean excess return of XYZ Fund is 1.60 per cent, while the monthly standard deviation of its excess return is 3.28 per cent. Thus, the fund's monthly Sharpe ratio is 1.60%/3.28% = 0.49. The annualized Sharpe ratio is computed as the ratio of annualized mean excess return to its annualized standard deviation, or, equivalently, as the monthly Sharpe ratio times the square root of 12. Thus, XYZ's annualized Sharpe ratio is 19.25%/11.36% = 1.69.

The Sharpe ratio is based on the trade-off between risk and return. A high Sharpe ratio means that the fund delivers a lot of return for its level of volatility. The Sharpe ratio allows a direct comparison of the risk-adjusted performance of any two mutual funds, regardless of their volatilities and their correlations with a benchmark.

CAPITAL MARKET THEORY: HOW ARE RISK AND RETURN DEFINED?

Capital market theory deals with the relationship between risk and return. In particular capital market theory deals with how asset prices are determined in the marketplace. As we discuss in more detail in Chapter 9 prices of securities reflect the expected return and risk associated with an asset. In the jargon of financial economics capital market theories are *ex ante* theories, that is they deal with expected returns. In contrast *ex post* (historical) returns are what we know actually happened. *Ex ante* theories rely on probability theory to throw light on potential future outcomes whereas an *ex post* outcome is already known.

Tables 4.3 and 4.4 illustrate the different risk and return criteria depending on whether historical (*ex post*) or anticipated (*ex ante*) criteria are applied.

Table 4.3 ● Quantifying individual security returns

Historical (ex post) returns	Expected (ex ante) returns
Arithmetic mean return:	Expected return:

$$r_i = \frac{1}{n} \sum_{t=1}^{n} r_{itt}$$

$$E(r_i) = \sum_{s=1}^{n} r_{is}\pi_s$$

Variance	Variance:

$$\sigma_i^2 = \frac{1}{n-1} \sum_{t=1}^{n} (r_{it} - \bar{r_i})^2$$

$$\sigma_i^2 = \sum_{s=1}^{n} [r_{is} - E(r_i)]^2 \pi_s$$

Standard deviation	Standard deviation:

$$\sigma^2 = \sqrt{\frac{1}{n-1} \sum_{t=1}^{n} (r_{it} - \bar{r_i})^2}$$

$$\sigma^2 = \sqrt{\sum_{s=1}^{n} [r_{is} - E(r_i)]^2 \pi_s}$$

r_{it} = historical (*ex post*) return generated by the ith stock in time period t.

r_{is} = expected (*ex ante*) return for the ith stock assuming the s state of the world occurs.

π = probability that the s state of the world will occur.

Table 4.4 ● Quantifying portfolio returns

Historical (ex post) returns	Anticipated (ex ante) returns
Historical holding period return:	Historical holding period return:

$$r_{pt} = \sum_{t=1}^{n} r_{it}W_{it}$$

$$E(r_p) = \sum_{i=1}^{n} E(r_i) W_i$$

Variance:	Variance:

$$\sigma_p^2 = \sum_{t=1}^{n} \sum_{i=1}^{n} Cov_{ij}W_iW_j$$

$$\sigma_p^2 = \sum_{t=1}^{n} \sum_{i=1}^{n} Cov_{ij}W_iW_j$$

$$\sigma_p^2 = \sum_{i=1}^{n} \sigma_i^2 W_i^2 + 2 \sum Cov_{ij}W_iW_j$$

$$\sigma_p^2 = \sum_{i=1}^{n} \sigma_i^2 W_i^2 + 2 \sum Cov_{ij}W_iW_j$$

Covariance:	Covariance:

$$Cov_{ij} = \frac{1}{n-1} \sum_{t=1}^{n} (r_{it} - \bar{r_i})(r_{jt} - \bar{r_j})$$

$$Cov_{ij} = \sum_{s=1}^{n} [r_{is} - E(r_i)][r_{js} - E(r_j)]\pi_s$$

Correlation coefficient:	Correlation coefficient:

$$\rho_{ij} = \frac{Cov_{ij}}{\sigma_i\sigma_j}$$

$$\rho_{ij} = \frac{Cov_{ij}}{\sigma_i\sigma_j}$$

W_i = weight of the ith asset, defined as the market value of the ith asset divided by the market value of the portfolio

$\sum Cov_{ij}W_iW_j$ = sum of the unique covariances (multiplied by their weights); when there are n assets in a portfolio, there are $(n^2 - n)/2$ unique covariances.

THE EFFICIENT FRONTIER

A key idea in capital market theory is the concept of the efficient frontier. Figure 4.6 illustrates the principle. The vertical axis refers to expected return, the horizontal axis refers to risk as measured by the standard deviation of return, and the shaded area represents the set of all the possible portfolios that could be obtained from a given group of securities by varying the proportionate holdings of each security. A certain level of return and a certain risk will be associated with each possible portfolio. Thus each portfolio is represented by a single point in the shaded area of Figure 4.6.

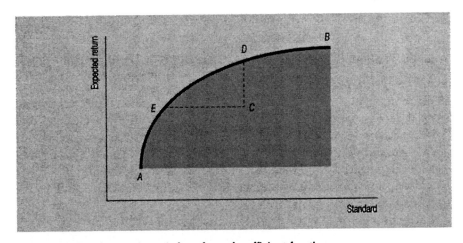

Fig 4.6 ● Risk and return in capital markets: the efficient frontier

What is the point of the portfolio possibility set, you may ask. It was this idea, first developed by Nobel Prize winner Harry Markowitz that launched the whole portfolio management industry. Building on Markowitz's ideas, and those of others, came the idea of the capital asset pricing model (CAPM) to which we return throughout this book.

If we make various assumptions regarding the behaviour of investors, as discussed further in Chapter 9, the concept of efficiency can be imposed on the choice of a portfolio. The efficiency set is represented by the upper left-hand boundary of the shaded area between points A and B. Portfolios along this efficient frontier dominate those below the line. Specifically, they offer higher return than those of an equivalent level of risk or, alternatively, entail less risk at an equivalent level of return. For example, note that portfolio C, which does not lie on the efficient boundary, is dominated by portfolios D and E, which do lie on the efficient boundary. Portfolio D offers greater return than portfolio C at the same level of risk, while portfolio E entails less risk than portfolio C at the same level of return.

Rational investors will thus prefer to hold efficient portfolios – that is, ones on the frontier and not those below it. The particular portfolio that an individual investor selects from the efficient frontier depends on the investor's degree of aversion to risk. An investor who is highly averse to risk will hold one on the lower left-hand segment of the frontier, while an investor who is not too risk-averse will hold one on the upper portion. In more technical terms, the selection depends on the investor's risk aversion, which might be characterized by the nature and shape of the investor's risk-return utility function.

Once the efficient set of portfolios is determined using the Markowitz model, investors must select from this set the portfolio most appropriate for them. The Markowitz model does not specify one optimum portfolio. It generates the efficient set of portfolios, all of which, by definition, are optimal portfolios (for a given level of expected return or risk).

What do we know about the ex *post* risk and returns on US stocks and bonds?

Jeremy Siegel, *Stocks for the Long Run* (1995), reported on the returns on stocks, bonds, gold and commodities from 1802 until 1992. Figure 4.7 tells the story. It depicts the total return indexes for the above mentioned assets. Total return means that all returns such as interest and dividends and capital gains are automatically reinvested in the asset and allowed to accumulate over time.

As Siegel illustrates, the total return for equities dominates all other assets. One dollar invested and reinvested in stocks in 1802 would have accumulated to $3,050,000 by the end of 1992.

Cochrane presented several measures of average return on stocks and bonds in the post-war period (1997). See Table 4.5. His data also provided measurement of risk. These findings are discussed in more detail in Chapters 16, 17 and 18.

Table 4.5 presents several measures of average real returns on stocks and bonds in the post-war period. The weighted value NYSE portfolio shows an impressive annual return of 9 per cent after inflation with a standard deviation of 16.7 per cent for the period 1947–1996. The S&P 500 is similar. Long-term government bonds earned only 1.8 per cent after inflation despite a standard deviation (11.1 per cent) more than half that of stocks at around (17 per cent). Corporate bonds earn a slight premium over government bonds, but at 2.1 per cent are still a poor investment compared to stocks. Treasury bills earn even less, 0.8 per cent on average after inflation.

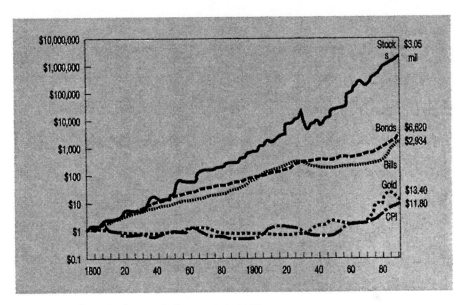

Fig 4.7 ● Total nominal return indexes (1802–1992)

Source: J. Siegel. *Stocks for the Long Run.* Reproduced with permission of McGraw Hill Companies

Table 4.5 ● Annual returns and risk in stocks and bonds 1947–1996

	New York Stock Exchange	Standard & Poors 500	Government Bonds	Corporate Bonds	Treasury Bills
Average Return E(R) %	9.1	9.5	1.8	2.1	0.8
Standard Deviation σ (R)%	16.7	16.8	11.1	10.7	2.6

Source: J. Cochrane, 1997

Table 4.5 highlights a crucially important fact. *The high returns are only earned as compensation for risk.* As Cochrane points out, the interesting question is why the market provides such a high compensation for bearing risk. The risk, as can be seen from Table 4.5, is substantial. A 16.7 per cent standard deviation for the NYSE means the market is quite likely to decline 9.1%–16.7% = –7.6% or rise 9.1%+16.7% = +25.8% in a year. (More precisely, there is about a 30 per cent probability that the decline will be bigger than –7.6 per cent or the rise bigger than 25.8 per cent.) We return to the question of why equities yield a disproportionate return when compared to their risk in our discussion of the 'equity premium' in Chapter 14.

CHAPTER **5**

The term structure of interest rates

- Introduction
- Functions of interest rates
- Determination of interest rates, demand and supply of funds
- International factors affecting interest rates
- Price and yield – a key relationship
- The term structure of interest rates
- Term structure theories
- Implied forward rates

INTRODUCTION

Decisions as to whether to spend or not to spend, whether to borrow (or lend) now or to postpone borrowing (or lending) for six or nine months, whether to buy securities today or hold cash for the present, whether borrowing or lending should be short term or long term are all decisions influenced by current and expected *interest rates*. Interest rates are at the centre of the key issues in financial economics. But what are the factors affecting interest rates and exactly what role do interest rates play within the financial system?

FUNCTIONS OF INTEREST RATES

Interest rates serve a number of significant functions. First, they provide investors with a guide for allocating funds among investment opportunities. As funds are directed into projects that have higher expected rates of return (risk and other factors being taken into account), the funds are optimally allocated from the viewpoint of both consumer and investor, since the highest returns normally prevail where effective consumer demand is strongest. Unless an investment opportunity promises a return high enough to pay the market rate of interest, it does not justify the required capital outlay. The money market, by channelling funds into projects that have an expected return in excess of the interest rate, provides a valuable service to investors, borrowers and society as a whole.

The interest rate also provides a measure of the relative advantage of current consumption compared to saving. By adjusting the available market rate for expected inflation and taxes, an individual can determine the real amount of additional future consumption that can be obtained by postponing current consumption.

Similarly, interest rates help business managers decide among alternative production methods. Suppose a product can be made either solely with labour or with a combination of labour and machinery. By calculating the capital cost of the machine (the interest rate times the amount invested in the machine), the expected labour-plus-capital cost can be compared with the labour-alone cost to determine the least expensive means of production.

DETERMINATION OF INTEREST RATES, DEMAND AND SUPPLY OF FUNDS

Interest rates are prices. Unlike other prices they are usually expressed as percentages of the amount borrowed or lent. But, like other prices, they are determined by supply and demand. Interest rates depend on the supply of and the demand for loanable funds. The sources of the supply of funds are savings, reductions in the demand for money and increases in the supply of money. The sources of the demand for funds are investment demands, consumption demands (for spending on consumer goods) and increases in the demand for money.

The supply of funds

Saving, which is the main source of supply of loanable funds, arises in all sectors of the economy and may take many forms. Personal saving, i.e. the excess of personal income over consumption spending, may consist, *inter alia*, of contributions to pension funds, the repayment of mortgage loans, deposits with building societies or banks, or the purchase of securities. Business saving comprises retained profits and, most important, depreciation charges. What is not reinvested in the business is usually held in a liquid form or used to reduce bank loans. The government, too, may contribute to saving in the economy by raising more in taxes than it needs for its own current expenditure; any surplus goes to offset part of the public sector's own investment.

It is important to distinguish between the potential and the actual supply of loanable funds. The reason for this is that households and businesses having savings may not be willing to make these funds available to borrowers. Money, remember, is a store of value. Households and businesses may not want to offer either their current savings or any of their accumulated savings to borrowers. On the contrary, they may choose to add a portion of their current savings to their accumulated balances.

Having made choices as to how to divide their incomes and receipts between spending and saving, households and businesses must then decide the specific form in which to hold their savings. The basic choice is between money in the form of either idle cash or bank accounts on the one hand, and securities of some sort on the other. Idle cash and bank accounts are highly liquid assets; securities acquired from borrowers are somewhat less liquid but generally yield a better rate of return. That part of savings (current or accumulated) which households and businesses want to hold as securities flows into the money market as the supply of loanable funds. That part which households and businesses want to hold as cash obviously does not. This division depends upon the liquidity preferences of households and businesses. More specifically, there are three main reasons why households and businesses prefer to hold cash rather than securities.

1 There is a transaction motive for holding money rather than securities. Households and businesses both need a stock of cash on hand to make ordinary day-to-day purchases. Households, for example, usually receive a sizeable chunk of income every week, or every month. Disbursements, on the other hand, occur more or less evenly over time. This means that households have an average money balance of some size bridging the gap between paydays. And it is simply more convenient to have one's assets in their most liquid form, that is, as idle cash balances or bank accounts, than in the form of securities. Furthermore, there are costs – brokerage fees – in transferring cash into securities and back again.

2 There is a precautionary motive for holding money. Households and businesses may hold cash balances to meet any rainy day contingencies which might arise. Particularly relevant are those risks which one cannot protect oneself against by purchasing insurance policies – prolonged illness, unemployment and so forth.

3 There is a speculative motive for holding money. At any point in time, there is a certain rate of interest which households and businesses as potential suppliers of loanable funds consider to be about 'normal'. If the rate of interest is currently low, that is, 'below normal', households and businesses may withhold a part of their savings which would otherwise flow into the money market as a part of the supply of loanable funds. They hold more money and fewer securities than they normally would. Why? Because they expect that the current below-normal interest rate will probably rise in the future. Conversely, if the current interest rate is unusually high, that is, 'above normal', households and businesses will choose to hold less money and more securities to take advantage of high current interest rates as opposed to the lower normal rate expected to prevail again in the future.

The supply of loanable funds is critically influenced by the level of interest rates, i.e. higher interest (real) rates will induce households and businesses (but obviously not necessarily governments) to be less liquid. At relatively high interest rates, households and firms will prefer to hold their assets in the form of interest-bearing securities rather than as non-interest bearing current accounts and idle cash balances.

The supply of loanable funds depends on the following.

1 *The rate of interest* A high rate of interest encourages savers to place their funds in financial institutions – the supply of loanable funds increases.

2 *The amount of savings* Some countries, such as Japan, are very thrifty. This increases the amount of funds available for borrowers.

3 *A Budget surplus* This occurs when the government spends less than its revenue. In these conditions the government has a surplus that it can lend to the private sector.

4 *International factors* When foreigners buy assets in another country they are lending to those domestic residents. Low interest rates overseas encourage funds to flow from the low interest rate country into the countries with higher interest rates, increasing the supply of funds available to borrowers in the high interest rate country (and vice versa).

The supply curve for loanable funds is upward sloping, i.e. higher interest rates increase the supply available, and vice versa.

The demand for funds

Now let us turn to the demand for funds. Again this can be by private individuals, companies or governments. Private individuals borrow in order to increase their current level of consumption either for housing, cars, holidays or whatever. Companies borrow to pay for factories, plant and equipment. Finally, governments borrow to pay for current and capital spending (e.g. on schools, roads, etc. which they cannot finance from taxation).

The demand for borrowed funds depends on the following.

1 *The rate of interest* When it becomes more expensive to borrow (i.e. when the interest rate rises) demand from the private sector falls (and vice versa).

2 *The level of income* The higher the level of income, the more individuals and businesses will want to borrow. For example, if investment is to increase, firms will, in general, require outside finance. Similarly, consumers borrow money to buy durable goods, washing machines, etc. More generally when incomes rise individuals increase borrowing for all purposes (houses, cars, etc.) and firms need more working capital.

3 *The government finances* In many countries governments are major borrowers of funds. This is known as the fiscal deficit or budget deficit (total government expenditure minus tax revenue).

4 *International factors* When foreigners buy domestic assets they are lending to domestic residents of the country concerned. Low overseas interest rates encourage domestic borrowers to borrow these overseas funds, increasing the supply of funds available to domestic borrowers (and vice versa).

The demand curve for loanable funds is clearly downward-sloping, i.e. lower interest rates raise the demand for funds. Businesses will find it profitable to purchase larger amounts of capital goods when the price of loanable funds declines. Similarly, lower interest rates may encourage some increases in consumer and government borrowing. (In practice it is 'real' interest rates which are relevant.)

Interest rate determination

In equilibrium the interaction between the demand for loanable funds and the supply of loanable funds will determine the interest rate.

Elementary economic analysis tells us that if the demand rises (I) or the supply falls (II) then the interest rate rises. Similarly if the demand falls (III) or if the supply rises (IV) then interest rates will fall. This is illustrated in Figure 5.1.

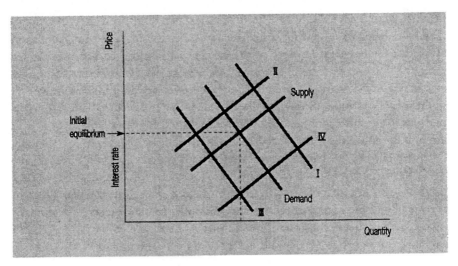

Fig 5.1 • The determination of interest rates

The effect on the interest rate of any shift in demand or supply will depend on the elasticities of both lines.

Following a change in demand, the less elastic (more elastic) the supply curve is, the greater (less) will be the change in interest rates. Following a change in supply, the less elastic (more elastic) the demand curve is, the greater (less) will be the effect on interest rates.

How can changes in the supply of funds and demand for funds change interest rates? If there is more saving (relative to demand) by businesses and consumers this will bring down interest rates. What happens if there is an increase in the supply of money? This adds to the savings in the capital market. To see how this can occur, suppose that instead of raising new funds through the stock market, companies borrow from their banks, and the banks increase the supply of money (remember bank loans create bank deposits which are in themselves the most important component of the money supply). Because companies are borrowing from the banks this will increase security prices (due to a lower demand) and the rate of interest on securities will fall correspondingly as companies can now raise funds more cheaply.

INTERNATIONAL FACTORS AFFECTING INTEREST RATES

Given the importance of international factors in affecting interest rates, it is worth explaining in some detail the mechanics whereby overseas interest rates affect domestic interest rates. The speed of the impact of international factors depends on official exchange rate policy.

If a country has a fixed exchange rate (i.e. the government is committed to official intervention in order to keep the rate fixed) and the currency is weak, i.e. it is being heavily sold on the foreign exchange market, the government may be induced to raise official interest rates. The objective is to make it more attractive for overseas holders of the currency to hold it and to make it less attractive for domestic holders to transfer it overseas. If a country has a fixed and strong exchange rate there may be pressure for the authorities to lower the interest rate. As funds flow into the currency the authorities, being forced to increase the domestic money supply to keep the exchange rate fixed, will, in an attempt to reduce the inflows, reduce domestic interest rates.

Under floating exchange rates the effects of capital flows on interest rates occur very quickly. With a weak currency investors will speedily reduce their holdings thereby driving up interest rates, e.g. by selling bonds. The link between bond prices and interest rates is outlined in the next section. Similarly investors will be keen to acquire liabilities in that currency since, if the exchange rate change occurs and is larger than the extra borrowing cost, the investor can repay (say, a bank loan) and make a profit. The combination of an increase in the supply of loanable funds and a decrease in the demand for loanable funds drives down interest rates.

The effect of international factors also depends on the size of the home economy and how developed the domestic financial system is. For a small economy a given foreign inflow of funds is likely to represent a relatively high proportion of the total capital market. The impact is likely to be bigger therefore in a country with limited facilities for foreign investors, e.g. because the capital market is undeveloped or exchange controls are in operation.

PRICE AND YIELD – A KEY RELATIONSHIP

The inverse relationship between price and yield is important in understanding how the financial system works. It is discussed further in Chapter 6. When interest rates rise, the market price of outstanding fixed-income securities, such as bonds and gilts, declines. When interest rates fall, the market price of fixed-income securities increases.

Holders of fixed-income securities then experience price depreciation on their portfolios during periods of rising interest rates. On the other hand, those who defer the purchase of fixed-interest securities during a period of falling interest rates will later pay higher prices. The following example illustrates this inverse relationship.

EXAMPLE

Assume that a €1,000 bond has a fixed coupon interest rate of 8 per cent and a maturity date, to make the arithmetic easy, of perpetuity. The bond pays €80 in interest per year, and the face value, or principal amount, is of €1000.

If, some time later, similar bonds of comparable maturity are paying €90 in interest a year, bond dealers will continue to buy and sell the 8 per cent issue, but they will lower its price until it also yields nine per cent. The principle behind this is that no one would buy a bond with an 8 per cent yield when one of the same quality with a 9 per cent yield could be bought.

At what price will the 8 per cent coupon bond yield a 9 per cent current return?

By using the formula for current yield:

$$\text{current yield} = \frac{\text{annual interest payment}}{\text{prevailing market price}}$$

and transposing it

$$\text{prevailing market price} = \frac{\text{annual interest payment}}{\text{current yield}}$$

the price can be determined $\frac{€80}{0.09} = €888.88$

At a price of €888.88, the 8 per cent coupon bond will yield 9 per cent. Since the bond is selling for less than €1000, i.e. less than par value, it is said to be priced at a discount.

What if market interest rates fall and new bonds are being sold with 7 per cent coupons? Again, the 8 per cent coupon bond must be brought into line with similar securities. In this case, the 8 per cent bond will be 'bid up' to yield 7 per cent.

$$\frac{€80}{0.07} = €1142.86$$

Since the bond is selling for more than par, i.e. €1142.86, it is said to be priced at a premium.

Instead of talking about the supply of and demand for credit or loanable funds determining the rate of interest, we could talk about the same thing in terms of the demand for securities and the supply of securities determining the price of securities, see Figure 5.2. To supply credit (lend) is equivalent to demanding financial assets (securities); financial institutions lend, for example, by purchasing financial assets. To demand credit (borrow) is the same as supplying securities; business firms borrow by selling their bonds or other IOUs. At a price of €833 (which corresponds, let us say, to 6 per cent yield, assuming a 5 per cent coupon on a €1000 bond), relative eagerness to buy securities – or lend – would drive the price of securities up, and it would drive the rate of interest down. And at a price of €1250, corresponding to a 4 per cent yield, relative eagerness to sell securities – to borrow – would drive the price of securities down, and would drive the rate of interest up.

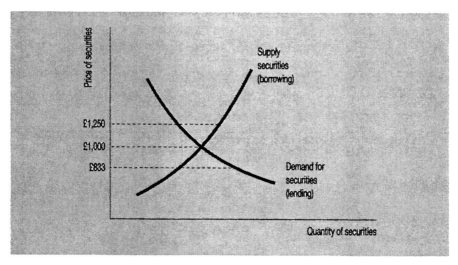

Fig 5.2 ● The determination of interest rates

Now let us drop the assumption about a single rate of interest and consider why it is the case that rates of interest or yields on different financial instruments vary. Why do some borrowers pay more than others? Why are the yields on long-dated securities different from those on short-dated ones? Why do interest rates on different currency denominated assets vary? It is to these questions that we now turn.

THE TERM STRUCTURE OF INTEREST RATES

The term structure of interest rates, or maturity structure as it is sometimes referred to, refers to the set of theories designed to explain why practically homogeneous bonds of different maturities have different interest rates. The starting point for understanding the term structure theories is the present value concept discussed in Chapter 3.

Because of the time value of money, $1 received at a future date has a present value of less than $1. If we denote the present (that is, time 0) value of $1 received n periods from now by D_n then the interest rate is the discount rate (denoted by R_n) that solves Equation (1):

$$D_n = \frac{1}{(1 + R_n)^n} \tag{1}$$

D_n represents both the *present value* of $1 received in period n and the *spot price* of a zero coupon bond with a par value of $1. The purchaser of this zero coupon bond pays the purchase price D_n at time zero and receives the par value of $1 at time n. The rate R_n is called the zero coupon discount rate or the *spot interest rate*. The spot market is the market for immediate delivery. Some observers call the spot market the 'cash' market.

The spot price D_n and the spot interest rate R_n are inversely related. When the spot interest rate goes up, the spot price goes down because the spot interest rate is in the denominator. As the spot interest rate increases, the denominator increases, and the ratio (that is, the price) decreases. Figure 5.3 and the present value tables at the back of the book illustrate this point. Look across any row of the present value table. As you move to the right, the interest rate increases and the present value decreases. In the present value table, the present value decreases as maturity increases for a given interest rate. To see this point, look down any column of the table. The lowest present values are in the lower right corner of the table for long maturities and high interest rates. (It is worth checking this point yourself.)

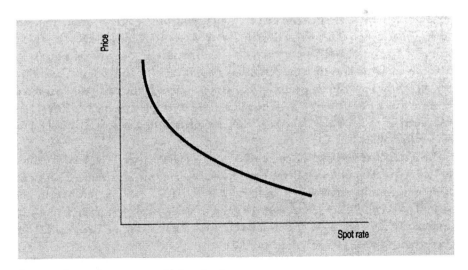

Fig 5.3 • Spot price versus spot interest rate

Consider the examples in Figure 5.4. The spot interest rate is 8 per cent for one-period, 10 per cent for two-periods, 12 per cent for three-periods. D_1 equals 0.93, meaning that the present value of $1 received one period from now is $0.93. D_2 is 0.83 meaning that the present value of $1 received two periods from now is $0.83. The present value of $1 received three periods from now, D_3, is $0.71.

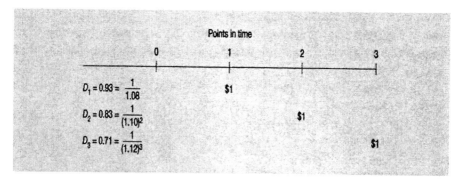

Fig 5.4 ● Present values

The pattern of spot interest rates for different maturities is called the *term structure of interest rates*.

Determination of forward interest rates

Assume the one-year spot interest rate for a risk-free security was determined to be 7 per cent. This means that the market has determined that the present value of $1 to be paid by the United States Treasury in one year is $1/1.07 or $0.9346. That means that the relevant discount rate for converting a cash flow one year from now to its present value is 7 per cent. If the two-year spot interest rate was 8 per cent, the present value of $1 to be paid by the US Treasury in two years is $1/1.08^2, or $0.8573. (You are advised to check this with the present value tables.)

An alternative view of $1 to be paid in two years is that it can be discounted in two steps. The first step determines its equivalent one-year value. That is, $1 to be received in two years is equivalent to $1/(1+f_{1,2})$ to be received in one year. The second step determines the present value of this equivalent one-year amount by discounting it at the one-year spot interest rate of 7 per cent. Thus its current value is given by Equation (2):

$$\frac{\$1/(1+f_{1,2})}{(1 + 0.07)} \tag{2}$$

However, this value must be equal to $0.8573, as it was mentioned earlier that, according to the two-year spot rate, $0.8573 is the present value of $1 to be paid in two years. That is,

$$\frac{\$1/(1+f_{1,2})}{(1 + 0.07)} = \$0.8573$$

which has a solution for $f_{1,2}$ of 9.01%.

This discount rate $f_{1,2}$ is known as the *forward rate* from year one to year two. That is, the discount rate for determining the equivalent value one year from now of $1 that is to be received two years from now. In the example, $1 to be received two years from now is equivalent in value to $1/1.0901 = $0.9174 to be received one year from now. (Note that the present value of $0.9174 is $0.9174/1.07 = $0.8573.)

The yield curve

Another important term to be familiar with is the yield curve. A yield curve is a graph that shows the yields-to-maturity (on the vertical axis) for identical securities of various terms to maturity (on the horizontal axis) as of a particular date. In order to eliminate the risk of default the calculations are normally done for risk-free, government-issued, securities.

The shape of the yield curve provides an estimate of the current term structure of interest rates and will change as yields to maturity change. Figure 5.5 illustrates the most commonly observed yield curves.

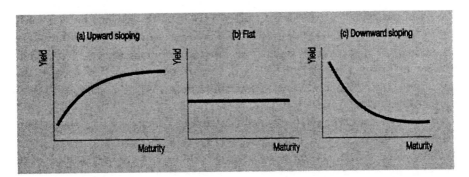

Fig 5.5 • Yield curves

TERM STRUCTURE THEORIES

Four primary theories are used to explain the term structure of interest rates. In discussing them, the focus will be on the term structure of spot interest rates, because these rates are critically important in determining the price of any risk-free security. Sharpe, Alexander and Bailey (1999) provide an excellent term structure survey and this has been drawn upon here.

1. Unbiased expectations theory

The *unbiased expectations theory* (or pure expectations theory, as it is sometimes called) holds that the forward rate represents the average opinion of what the expected future spot rate for the period in question will be. So, a set of spot interest rates that is rising can be explained by arguing that the marketplace (that is, the general opinion of investors) believes that spot interest rates will be rising in the future. Conversely, a set of decreasing spot interest rates is explained by arguing that the marketplace expects spot interest rates to fall in the future.

Upward sloping yield curves

In order to understand this theory more fully, consider an example in which the one-year spot rate was 7 per cent and the two-year spot rate was 8 per cent. The basic question is this: Why are these two spot interest rates different? Equivalently, why is the yield curve upward sloping?

Consider an investor with $1 to invest for two years. This investor could follow a 'maturity strategy', investing the money now for the full two years at the two-year spot interest rate of 8 per cent. With this strategy, at the end of two years the dollar will have grown in value to $1.1664 (= $1 × 1.08 × 1.08). Alternatively, the investor could invest the dollar now for one year at the one-year spot interest rate of 7 per cent, so that the investor knows that one year from now the investor will have $1.07 (=$1 × 1.07) to reinvest for one more year. Although the investor does not know what the one-year spot rate will be one year from now, the investor has an *expectation* about what it will be. The expected future spot interest rate will hereafter be denoted as $es_{1,2}$. If the investor thinks that it will be 10 per cent, then his $1 investment has an expected value two years from now of $1.177 (= $1 × 1.07 × 1.10). In this case, the investor could choose a 'rollover strategy', meaning that the investor would choose to invest in a one-year security at 7 per cent rather than in the two-year security, because he would expect to have more money at the end of two years by doing so given that $1.177 > $1.1664.

However, an expected future spot interest rate of 10 per cent cannot represent the general view in the marketplace. If it did, people would not be willing to invest money at the two-year spot interest rate, as a higher return would be expected from investing money at the one-year rate and using the rollover strategy. So the two-year spot interest rate would quickly rise as the supply of funds for two-year loans at 8 per cent would be less than the demand. Conversely, the supply of funds for one year at 7 per cent would be more than the demand, causing the one-year spot rate to fall quickly. Thus, a one-year spot interest rate of 7 per cent, a two-year spot interest rate of 8 per cent, and an expected future spot interest rate of 10 per cent cannot represent an equilibrium situation.

But now what if the expected future spot interest rate one year ahead is 6 per cent instead of 10 per cent? In this case, according to the rollover strategy the investor would expect $1 to be worth $1.1342 (= $1 × 1.07 × 1.06) at the end of two years. This is less than the value the $1 will have if the two-year investment strategy is followed given that $1.1342 < $1.664, so the investor would choose the two-year investment period strategy. Again, however, an expected future spot interest rate of 6 per cent cannot represent the general view in the marketplace because if it did, investors would not be willing to invest money at the one-year spot interest rate.

Earlier (page 105), it was shown that the forward rate in this example was 9.01 per cent. What if the expected future spot interest rate was of this magnitude? At the end of two years the value of $1 with the rollover strategy would be $1.1664 (= $1 × 1.07 × 1.0901), the same as the value of $1 with the two-year investment period strategy. In this case, equilibrium would exist in the marketplace because the general view would be that the two strategies have the same expected return. Accordingly, investors with a two-year holding period would not have an incentive to choose one strategy over the other.

The unbiased expectations theory asserts that the expected future spot rate is equal in magnitude to the forward rate. In this example, the current one-year spot rate is 7 per cent, and, according to this theory, the general opinion is that it will rise to a rate of 9.01 per cent in one year. This expected rise in the one-year spot rate is the reason behind the upward-sloping term structure where the two-year spot rate (8 per cent) is greater than the one-year spot rate (7 per cent).

Equilibrium

In equation form, the unbiased expectations theory states that in equilibrium the expected future spot interest rate is equal to the forward rate as shown in Equation (3):

$$es_{1,2} = f_{1,2} \tag{3}$$

The previous example dealt with an upward-sloping term structure; the longer the term, the higher the spot interest rate. Whereas the explanation for an upward-sloping term structure was that investors expect spot rates to rise in the future, the reason for the downward-sloping curve is that investors expect spot interest rates to fall in the future.

2. Liquidity preference theory

The *liquidity preference theory* starts with the notion that investors are primarily interested in purchasing short-term securities. That is, even though some investors may have longer holding periods, there is a tendency for them to prefer short-term securities. These investors realize that they may need their funds earlier than anticipated and recognize that they face less 'interest rate risk' if they invest in shorter term securities.

Interest rate risk

Investors with a two-year holding period would tend to prefer the rollover investment strategy because they would be certain of having a given amount of cash at the end of year one when it may be needed. An investor who followed a two-year investment strategy would have to sell the two-year security after one year if cash were needed. However, it is not known now what price that investor would get for the two-year security in one year. Thus there is an extra element of risk associated with the two-year investment strategy that is absent from the rollover strategy.

The upshot is that investors with a two-year holding period will not choose the two-year investment strategy if it has the same expected return as the rollover strategy because it is riskier. The only way investors will follow the two-year investment strategy and buy the two-year securities is if the expected return is higher. That is, borrowers will have to pay the investors a risk premium in the form of a greater expected return in order to get them to purchase two-year securities.

Will borrowers be inclined to pay such a premium when issuing two-year securities? Yes, they will, according to the liquidity preference theory. First, frequent refinancing may be costly in terms of registration, advertising and paperwork. These costs can be lessened by issuing relatively long-term securities. Second, some borrowers will realize that relatively long-term bonds are a less risky source of funds than relatively short-term funds because borrowers who use them will not have to be as concerned about the possibility of refinancing in the future at higher interest rates. Thus borrowers may be willing to pay more (via higher expected interest costs) for relatively long-term funds.

In the earlier example, the one-year spot interest rate was 7 per cent and the two-year spot interest rate was 8 per cent. According to the liquidity preference theory, the only way investors will agree to follow a two-year investment strategy is if the expected return from doing so is higher than the expected return from following the rollover strategy. So the expected future spot rate must be something *less* than the forward rate of 9.01 per cent. Perhaps it is 8.6 per cent. At 8.6 per cent the value of a $1 investment in two years is expected to be $1.1620 (= $1 × 1.07 × 1.086), if the rollover investment strategy is followed. Because the value of a $1 investment with the two- year invest-ment strategy is $1.1664 (= $1 × 1.08 × 1.08), it can be seen that the two-year investment strategy has a higher expected rate of return for the two-year period than can be attributed to its greater degree of risk.

Liquidity premium theory

The difference between the forward rate and the expected future spot interest rate is known as the *liquidity premium*. It is the 'extra' return given investors in order to entice them to purchase the riskier two-year security. In the example given earlier, it is equal to 0.41% (= 9.01% – 8.6%). More generally it is given by Equation (4):

$$f_{1,2} = es_{1,2} + L_{1,2} \tag{4}$$

where $L_{1,2}$ is the liquidity premium for the period starting one year from now and ending two years from now.

So, how does the liquidity preference theory explain the slope of the term structure? In order to answer this question, note that with the rollover invest-ment strategy the expected value of a dollar at the end of two years is $1 × (1 + s_1) × (1 × es_{1,2})$. Alternatively with the two-year investment strategy, the expected value of a dollar at the end of two years is $1 × (1 + s_2)^2$. According to the liquidity preference theory, there is more risk with the two-year invest-ment strategy, which in turn means that it must have a higher expected return. That is, the following inequality, shown in Equations (5) and (6) must hold:

$$\$1(1 + s_1) × (1 + es_{1,2}) < \$1(1 + s_2)^2 \tag{5}$$

or:

$$(1 + s_1) × (1 + es_{1,2}) < (1 + s_2)^2 \tag{6}$$

This inequality is the key to understanding how the liquidity preference theory explains the term structure.

Downward-sloping yield curves

Consider the downward-sloping case first, where $s_1 > s_2$. The above inequality will hold in this situation only if the expected future spot interest rate $(es_{1,2})$ is substantially lower than the current one-year spot interest rate (s_1). Thus a downward-sloping yield curve will be observed only when the marketplace believes that interest rates are going to decline substantially.

As an example, assume that the one-year spot interest rate (s_1) is 7 per cent and the two-year spot interest rate (s_2) is 6 per cent. Because 7 per cent is greater than 6 per cent, this is a situation in which the term structure is downward sloping. Now according to the liquidity preference theory, Equation (6) indicates that:

$$(1 + 0.07)(1 + es_{1,2}) < (1.06)^2$$

which can be true only if the expected future spot rate ($es_{1,2}$) is substantially less than 7 per cent. Given the one-year and two-year spot interest rates, the forward rate ($f_{1,2}$) is equal to 5.01 per cent. Assuming the liquidity premium ($L_{1,2}$) is 0.41 per cent, then, according to Equation (4) $es_{1,2}$ must be 4.6 per cent (= 5.01% – 0.41%). Thus, the term structure is downward-sloping because the one-year spot interest rate of 7 per cent is expected to decline to 4.6 per cent in the future.

The unbiased expectations theory would also explain the term structure by saying it was downward-sloping because the one-year spot rate was expected to decline in the future. However, the unbiased expectations theory would expect the spot rate to decline only to 5.01 per cent, not to 4.6 per cent.

Flat yield curve

Consider next the case of a flat yield curve, where $s_1 = s_2$. Equation (6) will be true in this situation only if $es_{1,2}$ is less than s_1. Thus a flat term structure will occur only when the marketplace expects spot interest rates to decline. Indeed, if $s_1 = s_2 = 7$ per cent and $L_{1,2} = 0.41$ per cent, then $f_{1,2} = 7$ per cent, and, according to Equation (4), the expected future spot rate is 6.59 per cent (= 7% – 0.41%), a decline from the current one-year spot rate of 7 per cent. This outcome is in contrast to the unbiased expectations theory, which would interpret a flat rate structure to mean that the marketplace expected interest rates to remain at the same level.

Upward-sloping yield curves

The last case is an upward-sloping yield curve where $s_1 < s_2$. A slightly upward-sloping curve can be consistent with an expectation that interest rates are going to decline in the future. For example, if $s_1 = 7$ per cent and $s_2 = 7.2$ per cent, then the forward rate is 7.2 per cent. In turn, if the liquidity premium is 0.41 per cent, then the expected future spot rate is 6.79 per cent (= 7.2% – 0.41%), a decline from the current one-year spot rate of 7 per cent. Thus the reason for the slight upward slope in the term structure is that the marketplace expects a small decline in the spot rate. In contrast, the unbiased expectations theory would argue that the reason for the slight upward slope was the expectation of a small increase in the spot rate.

If the term structure is more steeply sloped, then it is more likely that the marketplace expects interest rates to rise in the future. For example, if $s_1 = 7$ per cent and $s_2 = 7.3$ per cent, then the forward rate is 7.6 per cent. Continuing to assume a liquidity premium of 0.41 per cent, Equation (4) indicates that the marketplace expects the one-year spot interest rate to rise from 7 per cent to 7.19 per cent (= 7.6% – 0.41%). The unbiased expectations theory also would explain this steep slope by saying that the spot rate was expected to rise in the future, but by a larger amount. In particular, the unbiased expectations theory would state that the spot interest rate was expected to rise to 7.6 per cent, not to 7.19 per cent.

In summary, with the liquidity preference theory, downward-sloping term structures are indicative of an expected decline in the spot interest rate, whereas upward-sloping term structures may indicate either an expected rise or decline, depending on how steep the slope is. In general, the steeper the slope, the more likely it is that the marketplace expects spot interest rates to rise. If, roughly half the time, investors expect that spot rates will rise, and half the time investors expect that spot interest rates will decline, then the liquidity preference theory suggests that there will be more occurrences of upward-sloping term structures than downward-sloping ones.

3. The market segmentation theory

A third explanation for the determination of the term structure rests on the assumption that there is market segmentation. Various investors and borrowers are thought to be restricted by law, preference, or custom to certain maturities. Some investors may prefer short-term securities, others intermediate-term securities, whilst others prefer long-term securities. According to the *market segmentation theory*, spot interest rates are determined by supply and demand conditions in each market. Furthermore, investors and borrowers will not leave their market and enter a different one even when the current rates suggest to them that there is a substantially higher expected return available by making such a move.

With this theory, an upward-sloping term structure exists when the intersection of the supply and demand curves for shorter-term funds is at a lower interest rate than the intersection for longer-term funds. This situation could be due to either a relatively greater demand for longer-term funds by borrowers or a relatively greater supply of shorter-term funds by investors, or some combination of the two. Conversely, a downward-sloping term structure would exist when the intersection for shorter-term funds was at a higher interest rate than the intersection for longer-term funds.

4. The preferred habitat theory

According to this theory, investors and borrowers have segments of the market in which they prefer to operate, similar to the market segmentation theory. However, they are willing to leave their desired maturity segments if there are significant differences in yields between the various segments. These yield differences are determined by the supply and demand for funds within the segments.

As a result, as under the liquidity preference theory, the term structure under the preferred habitat theory reflects both expectations of future spot interest rates and a risk premium. Unlike the risk premium according to the liquidity preference theory, though, under the preferred habitat theory the risk premium does not necessarily rise directly with maturity. Instead, it is a function of the extra yield required to induce borrowers and investors to shift out of their preferred habitats. The risk premium may, therefore, be positive or negative in the various segments.

IMPLIED FORWARD RATES

Implied forward rates provide valuable information as to the market forecasts of future short-term interest rates, enabling futures markets and other derivatives contracts, discussed further in Chapter 15, to be priced. Consequently it is worth reiterating where they come from.

As already discussed, the yield curve depicts spot interest rates, which are current interest rates for immediate delivery securities of varying maturities. Forward rates are the yields on securities with deferred delivery. Therefore, there are two relevant time periods: the time to maturity and the time to delivery. Here we introduce notation that clearly specifies these two time periods. Yields will be expressed as $_nR_t$ where n is the time to delivery, t is the number of periods between delivery and maturity, and R is the choice of the yield format (i, i^*, y, y^*). Periods for n and t can be stated in terms of days, months or years. Thus, $n = 0$ for all spot interest rates since delivery takes place immediately. For example, the 90-day zero coupon security in Table 5.1 offers a simple interest yield denoted, using this notation, as $_0i_{90} = 4.097\%$ p.a. If delivery of this security were deferred for 180 days, then the forward rate (in simple interest format) would be denoted as $_{180}i_{90}$, with a compound interest rate of $_{180}i^*_{90}$. The maturity date of this forward transaction is 270 days from today: 180 days until delivery plus 90 days until maturity.

Table 5.1 ● The term structure of interest rates, 22 January 2000

Time to Maturity, t	Rate of Discount, d	Simple Interest Yield, i
85 days	5.00%	5.13%
176	5.46%	5.69%
274	5.67%	6.01%
358	5.85%	6.30%

The decomposition of the yield curve

Consider the term structure as of 22 January 2000. The simple interest yield is 5.69 per cent for a 176-day maturity Treasury security and 5.13 per cent for an 85-day maturity. If the expectations hypothesis holds, over the 176-day hold-ing period, the 5.69 per cent yield must be equalized with the yield on two consecutive transactions: the purchase of the 85-day Treasury today followed by, on the date of the maturity of the 85-day Treasury security, the purchase of a 91-day Treasury security for a total holding period of 85 plus 91 equals 176 days. We know the yield on the first leg of this transaction: the spot interest rate on the 85-day Treasury security, or 5.13 per cent (in simple interest format). If all 176-day holding period yields are equal, then we can solve for the 91-day *implied forward rate* – that is, the rate on the 91-day Treasury secu-rity that will be delivered in 85 days, denoted $_{85}i_{91}$.

Figure 5.6 shows the decomposition of the yield curve for the 176-day and 85-day spot yields. In the top transaction, the investor buys the 176-day secu-rity, with a face value set at $1, for simplicity, as shown in Equation (7) for a price of:

$$P = \frac{F}{1 + {}_0i_{176}(176)/365} = \frac{1}{1 + 0.569(176)/365} = \$0.973295959 \quad (7)$$

If the unbiased expectations hypothesis holds, then this investment must be the equivalent to the bottom transaction in Figure 5.6: the purchase of a spot 85-day security followed by the purchase of a 91-day security in 85 days. Setting the price of the 85-day security equal to $0.973295959, we find that the face value, upon maturity, is $F = P\left(1 + \frac{it}{365}\right) = 0.973295959\left(1 + \frac{0.0513(85)}{365}\right) = \$0.984923512$, thereby yielding the 85-day spot yield of 5.13 per cent.

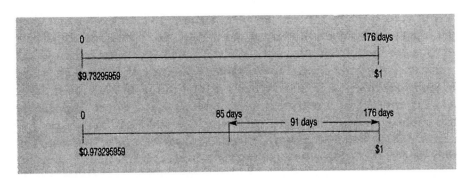

Fig 5.6 ● Decomposing the yield curve

This is immediately reinvested in a 91-day forward security to mature 176 days from today at a face value of $1. The yield on that security is given in Equation (8):

$$\frac{F-P}{P}\left(\frac{365}{t}\right) = \frac{1 - 0.984923512}{0.984923512}\left(\frac{365}{91}\right) = 6.14\% \tag{8}$$

This yield is the implied forward rate on the 91-day bill to be delivered in 85 days, denoted $_{85}i_{91}$.

Restating this in a simplified formula, we obtain:

Price of 176-day spot = Price of 85-day spot × Price of 91-day implied forward

$$\frac{1}{1 + \dfrac{_0 i_{176}(176)}{365}} = \left(\frac{1}{1 + \dfrac{_0 i_{85}(85)}{365}}\right) \times \left(\frac{1}{1 + \dfrac{_{85}i_{91}(91)}{365}}\right)$$

$$\frac{1}{1 + \dfrac{0.0569(176)}{365}} = \left(\frac{1}{1 + \dfrac{0.0513(85)}{365}}\right) \times \left(\frac{1}{1 + \dfrac{_{85}i_{91}(91)}{365}}\right)$$

where $_{85}i_{91}$ denotes the implied forward rate.

The implied forward rate of 6.14 per cent can be interpreted as the market's consensus that the expected spot interest rate on 91-day securities will be 6.14 per cent in 85 days from today. Thus, the upward slope of the yield curve suggests that the market expects interest rates to rise in the future. The implied forward rate can be used as an estimate of how high interest rates are expected to rise.

This process can be repeated for other maturity pairs of spot interest rates. For instance, we can use the 85-day and the 274-day spot rates of 22 January to solve for the implied forward rate, $_{85}i_{189} = 6.33$ per cent, on a 189-day maturity security to be delivered in 85 days. Similarly, using the 85-day and 358-day securities, we can show that the implied forward rate, $_{85}i_{273}$, on a 273-day maturity security to be delivered in 85 days is 6.59 per cent. Plotting the implied forward rates (see 6.14%, 6.33% and 6.59% in Figure 5.7) expected to prevail in 85 days, we obtain a *forward yield curve*, which graphically depicts the implied forward rates for different maturities on a specific date in the future. This can be used as a consensus estimate of expected future spot interest rates.

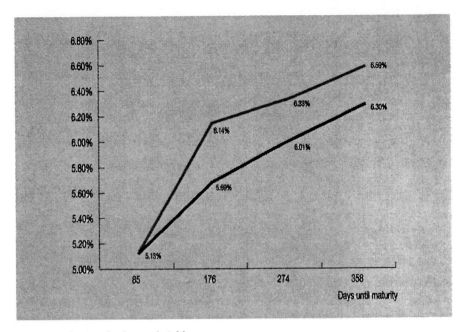

Fig 5.7 ● Plotting the forward yield curve

The implied forward rate is a forecast of expected future spot rates. If the expectations hypothesis holds, then the implied forward rate tells us the rate that investors expect to prevail on deferred delivery securities. This implied forward rate should be equal to the spot interest rate expected to prevail on the deferred delivery date.

CHAPTER 6

The valuation of financial assets: bonds

- Introduction
- The valuation principle
- Valuing bonds
- Bond concepts
- Bond yields and prices
- The basic components of interest rates
- Measuring bond yields
- Bond valuation principles
- Bond price changes over time
- Factors affecting the volatility of bond prices
- Measuring bond price volatility: duration and convexity

INTRODUCTION

Chapter 3 discussed the mathematics of compounding, discounting and present value. We now use the mathematics of compounding and discounting to determine the present values of financial instruments, beginning with a discussion of how bonds are valued. Since the future cash flows of bonds are known, the application of net present value techniques is fairly straightforward. The uncertainty of future cash flows with stocks makes the pricing of stocks applying, net present values, more difficult to apply. We turn to the valuation of stocks in Chapter 7.

THE VALUATION PRINCIPLE

What determines the price of a security? The answer is intrinsic or *estimated* value! A security's estimated value determines the price that investors place on it in the open market.

A security's intrinsic value, or estimated value, is the present value of the expected cash flows from that asset. Any security purchased is expected to provide one or more cash flows at some time in the future. These cash flows could be periodic, such as interest or dividends, or simply a terminal price or redemption value, or a combination of these. Since these cash flows occur in the future, they must be discounted at an appropriate rate to determine their present value. The sum of these discounted cash flows is the estimated intrinsic value of the asset. Calculating intrinsic value, therefore, requires the use of present value techniques. Equation (1) illustrates the concept:

$$\text{Value}_{t=0} \quad \sum_{t=1}^{n} \frac{\text{Cash flows}}{(1+k)^t} \tag{1}$$

where

$\text{Value}_{t=0}$ = the value of the asset now (time period 0)

Cash flows = the future cash flows resulting from ownership of the asset

k = the appropriate discount rate of rate of return required by an investor for an investment of this type

n = number of periods over which the cash flows are expected

To solve Equation (1) and derive the intrinsic value of a security, it is necessary to determine the following.

1 The expected *cash flows* from the security. This includes the size and type of cash flows, such as dividends, interest, face value *expected* to be received at maturity, or the *expected* price of the security at some point in the future.

2 *The timing* of the expected cash flows. Since the returns to be generated from a security occur at various times in the future, they must be properly documented for discounting back to time period 0 (today). Money has a time value and the timing of future cash flows significantly affects the value of the asset today.

3 *The discount rate*, or required rate of return demanded by investors. The discount rate used will reflect the time value of the money and the risk of the security. The discount rate is an *opportunity cost*, representing the rate foregone by an investor in the next best alternative with comparable risk.

VALUING BONDS

A *bond* is a certificate showing that a borrower owes a specified sum. In order to repay the money, the borrower has agreed to make interest and principal payments on designated dates. For example, imagine that Solovieva Associates has just issued 100,000 bonds for €1000 each, where the bonds have a coupon rate of 5 per cent and a maturity of two years. Interest on the bonds is to be paid yearly. This has the following implications.

1 The firm has borrowed €100 million (100,000 × €1000).

2 The firm must pay interest of €5 million (5% × €100 million) at the end of one year.

3 The firm must pay both €5 million of interest and €100 million of principal at the end of two years.

We now consider how to value pure discount bonds, coupon bonds and perpetuities.

Pure discount bonds

The pure discount bond is perhaps the simplest kind of bond. It promises a single payment, say €1000, at a fixed future date. If the payment is one year from now, it is called a *one-year discount bond*, if it is two years from now, it is called a *two-year discount bond*, and so on. The date when the issuer of the bond makes the last payment is called the *maturity date* of the bond, or just its *maturity* for short. The bond is said to mature or *expire* on the date of its final payment. The payment at maturity (€1000 in this example) is termed the bond's face value.

Table 6.1 • Bond payments

Years	Year 1		Year 2		Year 3		Year 4		Year 5		Year 6	
Months	6	12	18	24	30	36	42	48	54	60	66	72
Pure discount bonds								F				
Coupon bonds	C	C	C	C	C	C	C	F+C				
Consols	C	C	C	C	C	C	C	C	C	C	C	C

Pure discount bonds are often called *zero-coupon bonds* or zeros to emphasize the fact that the holder receives no cash payments until maturity. We will use the terms *zero*, *bullet* and *discount* interchangeably to refer to bonds that pay no coupons.

The first row of Table 6.1 shows the pattern of cash flows from a one-year pure discount bond. Note that the face value, F, is paid when the bond expires in the 48th month. There are no payments of either interest or principal prior to this date.

In Chapter 3 we indicated that one discounts a future cash flow to determine its present value. The present value of a pure discount bond can easily be determined using the techniques of Chapter 3.

Consider a pure discount bond that pays a face value of F in T years, where the interest rate is R in each of the T years. (We also refer to this rate as the market interest rate.) Because the face value is the only cash flow that the bond pays, the present value of this face amount is calculated by applying Equation (2) below.

Present value of a pure discount bond:

$$PV = \frac{F}{(1 + R)T} \tag{2}$$

The present-value formula can produce some surprising results. Suppose that the interest rate is 10 per cent. Consider a bond with a face value of €1 million that matures in 20 years. Applying the formula to this bond, its PV is given by

$$PV = \frac{€1 \text{ million}}{(1.1)^{20}} = €148,644$$

or only about 15 per cent of the face value.

Coupon bonds

Many bonds, however, are not of the simple, pure discount variety. Typical bonds issued by either governments or corporations offer cash payments not just at maturity, but also at regular times in between. For example, payments on US government issues and American corporate bonds are made every six months until the bond matures. These payments are called the coupons of the bond. The middle row of Table 6.1 illustrates the case of a four-year, *coupon bond*. The coupon, C, is paid every six months and is the same throughout the life of the bond.

Note that the face value of the bond, F, is paid at maturity (end of year 4). F is sometimes called the *principal*. Bonds issued in the USA typically have face values of $1000, though this can vary with the type of bond.

As mentioned above, the value of a bond is simply the present value of its cash flows. Therefore, the value of a coupon bond is merely the present value of its stream of coupon payments plus the present value of its repayment of principal. Because a coupon bond is just an annuity of C each period, together with a payment at maturity of $1000, the value of a coupon bond is given below:

Present value of a coupon bond:

$$PV = \frac{C}{1+r} + \frac{C}{(1+r)^2} + \dots + \frac{C}{(1+r)^T} + \frac{\$1000}{(1+r)^T}$$

where C is the coupon and the face value, F, is $1000. The value of the bond can be rewritten as Equation (3).

Present value of a coupon bond:

$$PV = C \times A_r^T + \frac{\$1000}{(1+r)^T} \tag{3}$$

A_r^T is the present value of an annuity of $1 per period for T periods at an interest rate per period of r.

EXAMPLE 1

Suppose it is November 1998 and we are considering investing in a US government bond. We see in the *Wall Street Journal* some 13s of November 2002. This jargon means the annual coupon rate is 13 per cent. The face value is $1000, implying that the yearly coupon is $130 (13% × $1,000). Interest is paid each May and November, implying that the coupon every six months is $65 ($130/2). The face value will be paid out in November 2002, four years from now. From this we mean that the purchaser obtains claims to the following cash flows:

5/99	11/99	5/00	11/00	5/01	11/01	5/02	11/02
$65	$65	$65	$65	$65	$65	$65	$65 + $1000

If the stated annual interest rate in the market is 10 per cent per year, what is the present value of the bond?

Note that the coupon rate is specific to the bond. The coupon rate indicates what cash flow should appear in the numerator of Equation (1). The coupon rate does *not* appear in the denominator of Equation (1).

The discussion on compounding in Chapter 3 showed that the interest rate over any six-month interval is one-half of the stated annual interest rate. In the current example, this semi-annual rate is 5 per cent (10%/2). Since the coupon payment in each six-month period is $65, and there are eight of these six-month periods from November 1998 to November 2002, the present value of the bond is:

$$PV = \frac{\$65}{(1.05)} + \frac{\$65}{(1.05)^2} + \ldots + \frac{\$65}{(1.05)^8} + \frac{\$1000}{(1.05)^8}$$
$$= \$65 \times A^8_{0.05} + \$1000/(1.05)^8$$
$$= (\$65 \times 6.463) + (\$1000 \times 0.677)$$
$$= \$420.095 + \$677$$
$$= \$1097.095$$

The discount factors can be found in the Appendix at the end of the book. The figure of 6.463 can be found in Table A-4 and the figure of 0.677 in Table A-2 in the Appendix.

Traders will generally quote the bond as 109.7095 indicating that it is selling at 109.7095 per cent of the face value of $1000.

At this point, it is worthwhile to relate the above example of bond pricing to the effect of compounding. We must distinguish between the stated annual interest rate and the effective annual interest rate, in line with our discussion in Chapter 3. The effective annual interest rate is given in Equation (4):

$$(1 + r/m) - 1 \tag{4}$$

where r is the stated annual interest rate and m is the number of compounding intervals. Since $r = 10\%$ and $m = 2$ (because the bond makes semi-annual payments), the effective annual interest rate is:

$$(1 + 0.10/2)2 - 1 = (1.05)2 - 1 = 10.25\%$$

In other words, because the bond is paying interest twice a year, the bond-holder earns a 10.25 per cent return when compounding is considered.

One final note concerning coupon bonds: Although the above example concerns government bonds, corporate bonds are identical in form. For example, DuPont Corporation has an $8\frac{1}{2}$ per cent bond maturing in 2006. This means that DuPont will make semi-annual payments of $42.50 ($8\frac{1}{2}\%/2 \times \$1000$) between now and 2006 for each face value of $1000.

Perpetuities/consols

Not all bonds have a final maturity date. Consols are bonds that never stop paying a coupon, have no final maturity date, and therefore never mature. Thus, a consol is a perpetuity. In the eighteenth century the Bank of England issued such bonds, called 'English consols'. These were bonds that the Bank of England guaranteed would pay the holder a cash flow forever! Through wars and depressions, the Bank of England continued to honour this commitment, and you can still buy such bonds in London today. Table 6.1 on page 121 illustrates the cash flows associated with consols.

BOND CONCEPTS

In Chapter 5 we introduced two important interest rate concepts. These must now be considered further. First, we examine the relationship between interest rates and bond prices. Second, we define the concept of yield to maturity.

Interest rates and bond prices

EXAMPLE 2

Assume the interest rate is 10 per cent. A two-year bond with a 10 per cent coupon pays interest of €100 = (€1000 × 10%). For simplicity we assume that the interest is paid annually. The bond is priced at its face value of €1000, i.e.

$$€1,000 = \frac{€100}{1.10} + \frac{€100 + €1000}{(1.10)^2}$$

If the interest rate unexpectedly rises to 12 per cent, the bond sells at:

$$€966.20 = \frac{€100}{1.12} + \frac{€100 + €1000}{(1.12)^2}$$

Because €996.20 is below €1000 the bond is said to sell at a discount. This makes sense. Now that the interest rate is 12 per cent, a newly issued bond with a 12 per cent coupon rate will sell at €1000. This newly issued bond will have coupon payments of €120 (0.12 × €1000). Because our bond has interest payments of only €100, investors will pay less than €1000 for it.

If interest rates fell to 8 per cent, the bond would sell at:

$$€1035.67 = \frac{€100}{1.08} + \frac{€100 + €1000}{(1.12)^2}$$

Because €1035.67 is above €1000, the bond is said to sell at a *premium*.

Thus we find that bond prices fall with a rise in interest rates and rise with a fall in interest rates. The general principle is that a coupon bond sells in the following ways.

1 At the face value of €1000 if the coupon rate is equal to the market interest rate.

2 At a discount if the coupon rate is below the market interest rate.

3 At a premium if the coupon rate is above the market interest rate.

Yield to maturity

Let's now consider the previous example *in reverse*. If our bond is selling at €1035.67, what return is a bondholder receiving? This can be answered by considering Equation (5):

$$€1035.67 = \frac{€100}{1 + y} + \frac{€100 + €1000}{(1 + y)^2} \tag{5}$$

The unknown, y, is the rate of return that the holder is earning on the bond. The example above implies that $y = 8\%$. Thus, traders state that the bond is yielding an 8 per cent return. Bond traders would also state that the bond has a yield to maturity of 8 per cent.

BOND YIELDS AND PRICES

In addition to the total return concept considered earlier, which is applicable to any security, bond investors must also understand specific measures of bond yields. It is traditional in the bond markets to use various yield measures and to quote potential returns to investors on the basis of these measures. However, these measures can mislead unwary investors who fail to understand the basis on which they are constructed. Investors must understand that bond yields shown daily in sources such as *The Wall Street Journal* do not indicate the 'true' yield that investors are promised when they buy bonds in the marketplace and hold them to maturity.

How is the price of a bond determined? This question introduces the subject of asset price valuation. The basic valuation principles set out here are very important and will be used when considering other investing alternatives, particularly common stocks in Chapter 7. In addition to calculating the price of a bond, it is essential to understand why bond prices change and why some bonds are more sensitive to a change in market interest rates than others. As part of this analysis we will consider the important concepts of duration and convexity.

Bond yields and interest rates are the same concept seen from a different viewpoint. Therefore, we need to go over some of the discussion of bond yields with a briefer consideration of interest rates, discussed in Chapter 5.

Interest rates measure the price paid by a borrower to a lender for the use of resources over some time period, i.e. interest rates are the price for loanable funds. The price differs from case to case, based on the demand and supply for these funds, resulting in a wide variety of interest rates. The spread between the lowest and highest rates at any point in time could be as much as 10 to 15 percentage points. In bond parlance, this would be equivalent to 1000 to 1500 points since one percentage point consists of 100 basis points.

It is convenient to focus on the one interest rate that provides the foundation for other rates. This rate is referred to as the short-term riskless rate, usually designated RF, and is typically proxied by the rate on short-term default free government securities, usually Treasury bills. All other rates differ from RF because of two factors:

1 maturity differentials, and

2 risk premiums.

THE BASIC COMPONENTS OF INTEREST RATES

We can analyze the basic determinants of nominal (current) interest rates with an eye toward recognizing the factors that affect such rates and cause them to fluctuate.

The basic foundation of market interest rates is the opportunity cost of foregoing consumption, representing the rate that must be offered to individuals to persuade them to save rather than consume. This rate is sometimes called the real risk-free rate of interest, because it is not affected by price changes or risk factors. We will refer to it simply as the *real rate* and designate it here as RR.

Nominal interest rates on Treasury bills consist of the RR plus an adjustment for inflation. A lender who lends $100 for a year at 10 per cent will be repaid $110. But if inflation is 12 per cent a year, the $110 that the lender receives upon repayment of the loan is worth only (1/(1.12)($1.10), or $98.21. Lenders therefore expect to be compensated for the *expected* rate of price change in order to leave the real purchasing power of wealth unchanged. As an approximation, this inflation adjustment can be added to the real risk-free rate of interest. Unlike RR, which is often assumed by market participants to be reasonably stable over time, adjustments for expected inflation vary widely over time.

Thus, for short-term risk-free securities, such as three-month Treasury bills, the nominal interest rate is a function of the real rate of interest and the *expected inflationary premium*. This is expressed as an approximation by Equation (6):

$$RF = RR + EI \qquad (6)$$

where

RF = short-term Treasury bill rate
RR = the real risk-free rate of interest
EI = the expected rate of inflation over the term of the instrument

Equation (6) is known as the *Fisher hypothesis*, named after Irving Fisher (1930). It implies that the nominal rate on short-term risk-free securities rises point-for-point with anticipated inflation, with the real rate of interest remaining unaffected. Turning Equation (6) around, estimates of the real risk-free rate of interest can be *approximated* by subtracting the *expected* inflation rate from the observed nominal interest rate.

All market interest rates are affected by a time factor which leads to maturity differentials. That is, although long-term government Treasury bonds are free from default risk in the same manner as Treasury bills, Treasury bonds typically yield more than Treasury bills. This typical relationship between bond maturity and yield applies to all types of bonds, whether Treasuries, corporates or municipals. The *term structure of interest rates*, discussed in Chapter 5, explains the relationship between time to maturity and yield to maturity.

Market interest rates other than those for riskless Treasury securities are also affected by a third factor, a *risk premium*, which lenders require as compensation for the risk involved. This risk premium is associated with the issuer's own particular situation or with a particular market factor. The risk premium is often referred to as the *yield spread* or yield differential.

MEASURING BOND YIELDS

Several measures of the yield on a bond are used by investors. It is very important for bond investors to understand which yield measure is being discussed, and what the underlying assumptions of any particular measure are.

Current yield

Current yield is defined as the ratio of the coupon interest to the current market price. The current yield is clearly superior to simply citing the coupon rate on a bond because it uses the current market price as opposed to the face amount of a bond (almost always, $1000). However, current yield is not a true measure of the return to a bond purchaser because it does not account for the difference between the bond's purchase price and its eventual redemption at par value.

Yield to maturity

The rate of return on bonds most often quoted for investors is the yield to maturity (YTM), which is defined as the *promised* compounded rate of return an investor will receive from a bond purchased at the current market price and held to maturity. It captures the coupon income to be received on the bond as well as any capital gains and losses realized by purchasing the bond for a price different from face value and holding to maturity. Similar to the Internal Rate of Return (IRR) applied in financial management, *the yield to maturity is the periodic interest rate that equates the present value of the expected future cash flows (both coupons and maturity value) to be received on the bond to the initial investment in the bond, which is its current price.*

To calculate the yield to maturity (YTM), we use Equation (7) where the market price, the coupon, the number of years to maturity, and the face value of the bond are known, and the discount rate or YTM is the variable to be determined.

$$P = \sum_{t=1}^{2n} \frac{C_t / 2}{(1 + YTM / 2)^t} + \frac{MV}{(1 + YTM / 2)^{2n}} \tag{7}$$

where

$$
\begin{aligned}
P &= \text{the market price of the bond, which is known} \\
n &= \text{the number of years to maturity} \\
YTM &= \text{the yield to maturity} \\
C &= \text{the coupon in dollars} \\
MV &= \text{the maturity value (or face value or par value)}
\end{aligned}
$$

Since both the left-hand side of Equation (7) and the numerator values (cash flows) on the right side are known, the equation can be solved for YTM. Because of the semi-annual nature of interest payments, the coupon is divided in half and the number of periods is doubled. What remains is a trial-and-error process to find a discount rate (YTM) that equates the inflows from the bond (coupons plus maturity value) with its current price (cost). Different rates are tried until the left-hand and right-hand sides are equal. It is now easy to find financial calculators or personal computers that are already set up to solve YTM problems.

We illustrate the trial-and-error (iteration) process involved in a yield-to-maturity calculation by referring to the present value tables at the end of the text. The purpose is simply to demonstrate conceptually how to calculate the YTM. As already mentioned, investors will normally use a calculator or computer to do computations such as these.

EXAMPLE 3

A 10 per cent coupon bond has ten years remaining to maturity. Assume that the bond is selling at a discount with a current market price of $885.30. *A bond is selling at a discount if the coupon rate is less than the current yield.* Because of the inverse relation between bond prices and market yields, it is clear that yields have risen since the bond was originally issued, because the price is less than $1000. Using Equation (7) to solve for yield to maturity:

$$\$885.50 \; = \; \sum_{t=1}^{20} \frac{\$50}{(1 + YTM / 2)^2} \; + \; \frac{\$1000}{(1 + YTM / 2)^{20}}$$

$885.50 = $50 (present value of an annuity, 6 per cent for 20 periods)
+ $1000 (present value factor, 6 per cent for 20 periods)

$885.50 = $50(11.4700) + $1000(0.312)

$885.50 = $885.30

The present value of an annuity factor for 6 per cent for 20 periods, 11.4700, is taken from Table A-4 in the Appendix at the end of the book; 0.312, the present value of $1 for 6 per cent for 20 periods, is taken from Table A-2 in the Appendix.

An approximation formula exists for calculating YTM. It relates the net annual effective cash flow to the average amount of money invested in the bond during the ownership period. Effectively, the investor is assumed to have an average investment of this amount in the bond as the price gradually converges to $1000, as it must by the maturity date. An approximation to this result is given in Equation (8):

Approximate yield to maturity = (Current market price + Par value)/2 (8)

EXAMPLE 4

Consider the bond in Example 3 with a 10 per cent coupon and a term to maturity of ten years. If an investor purchases it at a current market price of $885.50, the approximate yield to maturity is [$100 + ($114.70/10)]/ [($885.50 + 1000)/21 = 11.83%.

The YTM calculation for a zero-coupon bond is based on the same process expressed in Equation (7) equating the current price to the future cash flows. Because there are no coupons, the process reduces to Equation (9), with all terms as previously defined:

$$YTM = [MV/P]^{1/2n} - 1 \tag{9}$$

EXAMPLE 5

A zero-coupon bond has 12 years to maturity and is sold for $300. Given the 24 semi-annual periods, the power to be used in raising the ratio of $1000/$300, or 3.333, is 0.04167 (calculated as 1/(2 × 12)). Using a calculator with a power function produces a value of 1.0514. Subtracting the 1.0 and multiplying by 100 leaves a semi-annual yield of 5.145 per cent.

Because YTM numbers are stated on an annual basis, the yield as calculated from Equation (9) must be doubled, which produces in this case an annual yield of 10.29 per cent.

It is important to understand that YTM is a promised yield, because investors earn the indicated yield only if the bond is held to maturity and the coupons are reinvested at the calculated YTM. Obviously, no trading can be done for a particular bond if the YTM is to be earned. The investor simply buys and holds. What is not so obvious to many investors, however, is the reinvestment implications of the YTM measure. Because of the importance of the reinvestment rate, we consider it in more detail by analyzing what is known as reinvestment risk.

Reinvestment risk

The YTM calculation assumes that the investor reinvests all coupons received from a bond at a rate equal to the computed YTM on that bond, thereby earning *interest on interest* over the life of the bond *at the computed YTM rate.* In effect, this calculation assumes that the reinvestment rate is the yield to maturity.

If the investor spends the coupons, or reinvests them at a rate different from the assumed reinvestment rate of 10 per cent, the realized yield that will actually be earned at the termination of the investment in the bond will differ from the promised YTM. And, in fact, coupons almost always will be reinvested at rates higher or lower than the computed YTM, resulting in a realized yield that differs from the promised yield. This gives rise to *reinvestment rate risk.*

This interest-on-interest concept significantly affects the potential total dollar return. The exact impact is a function of coupon and time to maturity, with reinvestment becoming more important as either coupon or time to maturity, or both, rises. In principle, we know the following.

1 Holding everything else constant, the longer the maturity of a bond, the greater the reinvestment risk.

2 Holding everything else constant, the higher the coupon rate, the greater the dependence of the total dollar return from the bond on the reinvestment of the coupon payments.

Horizon return

Bond investors today often make specific assumptions about future reinvestment rates in order to cope with the reinvestment rate problem illustrated above. This is sometimes referred to as *horizon analysis.* Given their explicit assumption about the reinvestment rate, investors can calculate the horizon return to be earned if that assumption turns out to be accurate.

The investor makes an assumption about the reinvestment rate expected to prevail over the planned investment horizon. The investor may also make an assumption about the yield to maturity expected to prevail at the end of the planned investment horizon, which in turn is used to estimate the price of the bond at that time. Based on these assumptions, the total future dollars expected to be available at the end of the planned investment horizon can be determined. The horizon return is then calculated as the interest rate that equates the total future dollars to the purchase price of the bond.

BOND VALUATION PRINCIPLES

The intrinsic value of a bond should equal the present value of its expected cash flows. The coupons and the principal repayment are known, and the fundamental value is determined by discounting these future payments from the issuer at an appropriate required yield, r, for the issue. Equation (10) is used to solve for the value of a coupon bond. We will state the left-hand side as P, or price.

$$P = \sum_{t=1}^{2n} \frac{C_t / 2}{(1 + r/2)^t} + \frac{MV}{(1 + r/2)^{2n}} \tag{10}$$

where

$\quad P \;=\;$ the present value of the bond today (time period 0)
$\quad C \;=\;$ the annual coupons or interest payments
$\quad MV \;=\;$ the maturity value (or par value) of the bond
$\quad n \;=\;$ the number of years to maturity of the bond
$\quad r \;=\;$ the appropriate discount rate or market yield

In order to conform with the existing payment practice on bonds of paying interest semi-annually rather than annually, the discount rate being used (r) and the coupon (C) on the bond must be divided by 2, and the number of periods must be doubled. Equation (10) is the equation that underlies published bond quotes and standard bond investment practices.

For *expositional purposes*, we will illustrate the calculation of bond prices by referring to the present value tables at the end of the text; in actuality, a calculator or a computer is used. The present value process for a typical coupon-bearing bond involves three steps, given the dollar coupon on the bond, the face value, and the current market yield applicable to a particular bond.

1 Using the *present value of an annuity* table (Table A-4 in the Appendix at the end of the book), determine the present value of the coupons (interest payments).

2 Using the *present value* table (Table A-2 in the Appendix at the end of the book), determine the present value of the maturity (par) value of the bond; for our purposes, the maturity value will always be $1000.

3 Add the present values determined in steps 1 and 2 together.

Consider newly issued bond A with a three-year maturity, sold at par with a 10 per cent coupon rate. Assuming semi-annual interest payments of $50 per year for each of the next three years, the price of bond A, based on Equation (10), is:

$$P(A) = \sum_{t=1}^{6} \frac{\$50}{(1 + 0.05)^t} + \frac{\$1000}{(1 + 0.05)^6} = \$50(5.076) + \$1000(0.746)$$

$$= \$999.99, \text{ or } \$1000$$

which, of course, confirms that the bond's price should be $1000 since it has just been sold at par.

Now consider bond B, with characteristics identical to A's, issued five years ago when the interest rate demanded for such a bond was 7 per cent. Assume that the current discount rate or required yield on bonds of this type is 10 per cent and that the bond has three years left to maturity. Investors certainly will not pay $1000 for bond B and receive the dollar coupon of $70 per year, or $35 semi-annually, when they can purchase bond A and receive $100 per year. However, they should be willing to pay a price determined by the use of Equation (10):

$$P(B) = \sum_{t=1}^{6} \frac{\$35}{(1 + 0.05)^t} + \frac{\$1000}{(1 + 0.05)^6} = \$35(5.076) + \$1000(0.746)$$

$$= \$923.66$$

Thus, bond B is valued, as is any other asset, on the basis of its future stream of benefits (cash flows), using an appropriate market yield. Since the numerator is always specified for coupon-bearing bonds at time of issuance, the only problem in valuing a typical bond is to determine the denominator or discount rate. The appropriate discount rate is the bond's required yield.

The required yield, r, in Equation (10) is specific for each particular bond. It is the current market rate being earned by investors on comparable bonds with the same maturity and the same credit quality. (In other words, it is an opportunity cost.) Thus, market interest rates are incorporated directly into the discount rate used to solve for the fundamental value of a bond.

Since market interest rates fluctuate constantly, required yields do also. When solving for a bond price it is customary to use the yield to maturity. If the YTM is used, we can, for convenience, restate Equation (10) in terms of price and YTM, as in Equation (11):

$$P = \sum_{t=1}^{2n} \frac{C_t / 2}{(1 + YTM / 2)^t} + \frac{MV}{(1 + YTM / 2)^{2n}} \tag{11}$$

BOND PRICE CHANGES OVER TIME

We now know how to calculate the price of a bond, using the cash flows to be received and the YTM as the discount rate. Assume that we calculate the price of a 20-year bond issued five years ago and determine that it is $910. The bond has 15 years to maturity. What can we say about its price over the next 15 years?

When everything else is held constant, including market interest rates, any bond price that differs from the bond's face value (assumed to be $1000) must change over time. Why? On a bond's specified maturity date, it must be worth its face value or maturity value. Therefore, over time, holding all other factors constant, a bond's price must converge to $1000 on the maturity date.

After bonds are issued, they sell at discounts (prices less than $1000) and premiums (prices greater than $1000) during their lifetimes. Therefore, a bond selling at a discount will experience a rise in price over time, holding all other factors constant, and a bond selling at a premium will experience a decline in price over time, holding all other factors constant, as the bond's remaining life approaches the maturity date.

Figure 6.2 illustrates bond price movements over time, assuming constant yields. Bond 2 in Figure 6.2 illustrates a 10 per cent coupon, 30-year bond assuming that yields remain constant at 10 per cent. The price of this bond does not change, beginning at $1000 and ending at $1000. Bond 1, on the other hand, illustrates an 8 per cent coupon, 30-year bond assuming that required yields start, and remain constant, at 10 per cent. The price starts

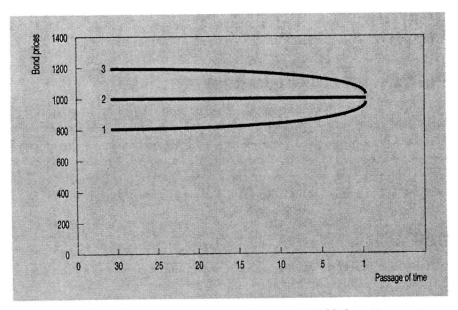

Fig 6.1 ● Bond price movements over time assuming constant yields for a 10 per cent coupon, 30-year bond

below $1000 because bond 1 is selling at a discount as a result of its coupon of 8 per cent being less than the required yield of 10 per cent. Bond 3 illustrates a 12 per cent coupon, 30-year bond assuming that required yields start, and remain constant, at 10 per cent. The price of bond 3 begins above $1000 because it is selling at a premium (its coupon of 12 per cent is greater than the required yield of 10 per cent).

If all other factors are held constant, the price of all three bonds must converge to $1000 on the maturity date. In actuality, however, other factors do not remain constant, in particular interest rates or yields to maturity. As interest rates change, and they do constantly, bond prices change. Furthermore, the sensitivity of the price change is a function of certain variables, especially coupon and maturity. We now examine these variables.

FACTORS AFFECTING THE VOLATILITY OF BOND PRICES

Bond prices change because interest rates and required yields change. Understanding how bond prices change given a change in interest rates is critical to applying modern portfolio theory. The basics of bond price movements as a result of interest rate changes have been known for many years. For example, nearly 40 years ago Burton Malkiel derived five theorems about the relationship between bond prices and yields (1962). These have stood the test of time. Using the bond valuation model, Malkiel showed the changes that occur in the price of a bond (i.e. its volatility), given a change in yields, as a result of bond variables such as time to maturity and coupon. We will use Malkiel's bond theorems to illustrate how bond prices change as a result of changes in interest rates.

Bond prices move inversely to interest rates

Investors must always keep in mind a fundamental fact about the relationship between bond prices and bond yields: *bond prices move inversely to market yields*. When the level of required yields demanded by investors on new bond issues changes, the required yields on all bonds already outstanding will also change. For these yields to change, the prices of these bonds must also change. This inverse relationship is the basis for understanding, valuing and managing bonds.

EXAMPLE 6

Table 6.2 shows prices for a 10 per cent coupon bond for market yields from 6 to 14 per cent and for maturity dates from 1 to 30 years. For any given maturity, the price of the bond declines as the required yield increases and increases as the required yield declines from the 10 per cent level. Figure 6.3 shows this relationship using data from Table 6.2.

An interesting corollary of the inverse relationship between bond prices and interest rates is as follows: *holding maturity constant, a decrease in interest rates will raise bond prices on a percentage basis more than a corresponding increase in interest rates will lower bond prices.*

EXAMPLE 7

Table 6.2 shows that for the 15-year 10 per cent coupon bond, the price would be $1172.90 if market rates were to decline from 10 per cent to 8 per cent, resulting in a price appreciation of 17.29 per cent. On the other hand, a rise of two percentage points in market rates from 10 per cent to 12 per cent results in a change in price to $862.35, a price decline of only 13.77 per cent, for the same 15-year bond.

Obviously, bond price volatility can work for, as well as against, investors.

Table 6.2 • Bond price and market yields for a 10 per cent coupon bond

Time to Maturity (Years)	Bond Prices at Different Market Yields and Maturities				
	6%	8%	10%	12%	14%
1	$1038.27	$1018.86	$1000	$981.67	$963.84
5	$1170.60	$1081.11	$1000	$926.40	$859.53
10	$1297.55	$1135.90	$1000	$885.30	$788.12
15	$1392.01	$1172.92	$1000	$862.35	$751.82
20	$1462.30	$1197.93	$1000	$849.54	$733.37
25	$1514.60	$1214.82	$1000	$842.38	$723.99
30	$1553.51	$1226.23	$1000	$838.39	$719.22

Although the inverse relationship between bond prices and interest rates is the basis of all bond analysis, a complete understanding of bond price changes as a result of interest rate changes requires additional information. An increase in interest rates will cause bond prices to decline, but the exact amount of decline will depend on important variables unique to each bond, such as time to maturity and coupon. We will examine each of these in turn.

The effects of maturity

The effect of a change in yields on bond prices depends on the maturity of the bond. An important principle is that *for a given change in market yields, changes in bond prices are directly related to time to maturity.* Therefore, as interest rates change, the prices of longer-term bonds will change more than the prices of shorter-term bonds, everything else being equal.

EXAMPLE 8

Given two 10 per cent coupon bonds and a drop in market yields from 10 per cent to 8 per cent, we can see from Table 6.2 that the price of the 15-year bond will be $1172.90, while the price of the 30-year bond will be $1226.23.

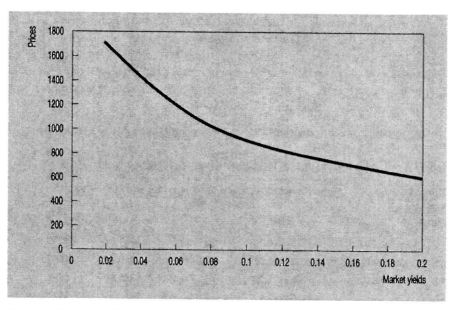

Fig 6.2 ● The relationship between bond prices and market yields

The principle illustrated here is simple but important. Other things being equal, bond price volatility is a function of maturity. Long-term bond prices fluctuate more than short-term bond prices.

A related principle regarding maturity is as follows. *The percentage price change that occurs as a result of the direct relationship between a bond's maturity and its price volatility increases at a diminishing rate as the time to maturity increases.*

EXAMPLE 9

As we saw above, a two percentage point drop in market yields from 10 per cent to 8 per cent increased the price of the 15-year bond to $1172.90, a 17.29 per cent change, while the price of the 30-year bond changed to $1226.23, a 26.23 per cent change.

This example shows that the percentage of price change resulting from an increase in time to maturity increases, but at a decreasing rate. Put simply, a doubling of the time to maturity will not result in a doubling of the percentage price change resulting from a change in market yields.

The effects of coupon

In addition to the maturity effect, the change in the price of a bond as a result of a change in interest rates depends on the coupon rate of the bond. We can state this principle as (other things being equal): *Bond price fluctuations (volatility) and bond coupon rates are inversely related.* Note that we are talking about percentage price fluctuations. This relationship does not necessarily hold if we measure volatility in terms of dollar price changes rather than percentage price changes.

What are the implications of Malkiel's theorems for investors?

Malkiel's theorems for bond investors lead to the practical conclusion that the two bond variables of major importance in assessing the change in the price of a bond, given a change in interest rates, are its coupon and its maturity. This conclusion can be summarized as follows:

A decline (rise) in interest rates will cause a rise (decline) in bond prices, with the most volatility in bond prices occurring in longer maturity bonds and bonds with low coupons.

This leads to the following propositions.

1 A bond buyer, in order to receive the maximum price impact of an expected change in interest rates, should purchase low-coupon, long-maturity bonds.

2 If an increase in interest rates is expected (or feared), an investor contemplating their purchase should consider those bonds with large coupons or short maturities, or both.

These relationships provide useful information for bond investors by demonstrating how the price of a bond changes as interest rates change. Although investors have no control over the change and direction in market rates, they can exercise control over the coupon and maturity, both of which have significant effects on bond price changes. Nevertheless, it is still cumbersome to calculate various possible price changes on the basis of these theorems.

Furthermore, maturity is an inadequate measure of the sensitivity of a bond's price change to changes in yields because it ignores the coupon payments and the principal repayment.

Investors managing bond portfolios ideally need a measure of time designed to more accurately portray a bond's 'average' life, taking into account all of the bond's cash flows, including both coupons and the return of principal at maturity. Such a measure is called duration.

MEASURING BOND PRICE VOLATILITY: DURATION

In managing a bond portfolio, perhaps the most important consideration is the effect of yield changes on the prices and rates of return for different bonds. The problem is that a given change in interest rates can result in very different percentage price changes for the various bonds that investors hold. We saw earlier that both maturity and coupon affect bond price changes for a given change in yields.

Although maturity is the traditional measure of a bond's lifetime, it is inadequate because it focuses only on the return of principal at the maturity date. Two 20-year bonds, one with an 8 per cent coupon and the other with a 15 per cent coupon, do not have identical *economic* lifetimes. An investor will recover the original purchase price much sooner with the 15 per cent coupon bond. Therefore, a measure is needed that accounts for the entire pattern (both size and timing) of the cash flows over the life of the bond – the *effective maturity of the bond*. Such a concept, called duration, was conceived over 60 years ago by Frederick Macaulay (1938). Duration is very useful for bond management purposes because it combines the properties of maturity and coupon.

Duration defined

Duration measures the weighted average maturity of a bond's cash flows on a present value basis; that is, the present values of the cash flows are used as the weights in calculating the weighted average maturity. Thus,

Duration = number of years needed to fully recover the purchase price of a bond, given the present values of its cash flows

= weighted average time to recovery of *all* interest payments plus principal

Figure 6.3 illustrates the concepts of both time to maturity and duration for a bond with five years to maturity, a 10 per cent coupon, and selling for $1000. As Figure 6.3 indicates, the stream of cash flows generated by this bond over the term to maturity consists of $50 every six months, or $100 per year, plus the return of principal of $1000 at the end of the five years. The last cash flow combines the interest payment of $50 with the principal repayment of $1000 which occurs at the maturity date.

Although the term to maturity for the bond illustrated in Figure 6.3 is five years, its duration is only 4.17 years as indicated by the arrow. This means that the weighted average maturity of the bond's cash flows is 4.17 years from the beginning date. It is important that we understand how this duration value is calculated.

How do we calculate duration?

To calculate duration, it is necessary to calculate a weighted time period. The time periods at which the cash flows are received are expressed in terms of years and denoted by t in this discussion. When all of these t's have been weighted and summed, the result is the duration, stated in years.

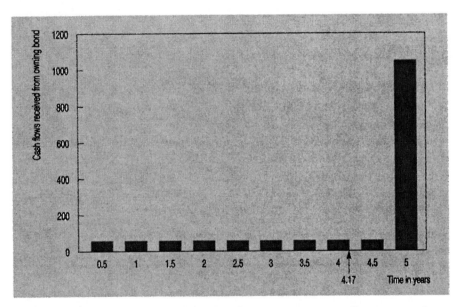

Fig 6.3 ● Illustration of the cash flow pattern of a 10 per cent coupon, five-year maturity bond paying interest semi-annually and returning the principal of $1000 at maturity

The present values of the cash flows serve as the weighting factors to apply to the time periods. Each weighting factor shows the relative importance of each cash flow to the bond's total present value, which is simply its current market price. The sum of the weighting factors will be 1.0, indicating that all cash flows have been accounted for.

Putting this all together gives us the equation for duration as shown in Equation (12):

$$\text{Macaulay Duration} = D = \sum_{t=1}^{n} \frac{PV(CF_t)}{\text{Market price}} \; X_t \qquad (12)$$

where

t = the time period at which the cash flow is expected to be received

n = the number of periods to maturity

$PV(CF_t)$ = present value of the cash flow in period t discounted at the yield-to-maturity

Market price = the bond's current price or present value of all the cash flows

As Equation (12) shows, duration is obtained by multiplying each year's weighted cash receipt (weighted by the price of the bond) by the number of years when each is to be received, and summing. *Note that duration is measured in years.*

EXAMPLE 10

Table 6.3 provides an example of calculating the duration for a bond, using the same bond as shown in Figure 6.3 except now *for ease of exposition, the calculation is done on an annual basis*. Assume that this is a 10 per cent coupon bond with five years remaining to maturity. The bond is priced at $1000 and the YTM is 10 per cent.

Table 6.3 • An example of calculating the duration of a bond using a 10 per cent coupon, five-year maturity bond priced at $1000 and paying annual interest

(1)	(2)	(3)	(4)$	(5)	(6)
Years	Cash Flow	PV Factor	(2)/(3)	(4)/Price	(1) × (5)
1	$100	0.909	90.90	0.0909	0.0909
2	100	0.826	82.60	0.0826	0.1652
3	100	0.751	75.10	0.0751	0.2253
4	100	0.683	68.30	0.0683	0.2732
5	1100	0.621	683.10	0.6831	3.4155
				Duration =	4.1701

The cash flows consist of five $100 coupons plus the return of principal at the end of the fifth year. Notice that the fifth-year cash flow of $1100 ($100 coupon plus $1000 return of principal) accounts for 68 per cent of the value of the bond and contributes 3.42 years to the duration of 4.17 years. In this example, the other cash flows *combined* contributed less than one year to the duration. The duration of 4.17 years is almost one year less than the term to maturity of five years. As we will see, duration will always be less than time to maturity for bonds that pay coupons.

Understanding duration

How is duration related to the key bond variables previously analyzed? An examination of Equation (12) shows that the calculation of duration depends on three factors:

1 Final maturity of the bond;

2 Coupon payments;

3 Yield to maturity.

This gives us the following characteristics of bond duration.

1 Holding the size of coupon payments and the yield to maturity constant, *duration expands with time to maturity but at a decreasing rate*, particularly beyond 15 years' time to maturity. Even between five and ten years' time to maturity, duration is expanding at a significantly lower rate than in the case of a time to maturity of up to five years, where it expands rapidly.

   Note that for all coupon-paying bonds, duration is always less than maturity. For a zero-coupon bond, duration is equal to time to maturity.

2 Holding maturity and yield to maturity constant, *coupon is inversely related to duration*. This is logical because higher coupons lead to quicker recovery of the bond's value, resulting in a shorter duration, relative to lower coupons.

3 Holding coupon payments and maturity constant, *yield to maturity is inversely related to duration*.

Why is duration important in bond analysis and management? First, it tells us the difference between the effective lives of alternative bonds. Bonds A and B, with the same duration but different years to maturity, have more in common than bonds C and D with the same maturity but different durations. For any particular bond, as maturity increases the duration increases at a decreasing rate. Example 11 below illustrates this relationship.

Second, the duration concept is used in certain bond management strategies, particularly immunization.

Third, duration is a measure of bond price sensitivity to interest rate movements, which is a very important part of any bond analysis. Malkiel's bond price theorems are thereby inadequate to examine all aspects of bond price sensitivity.

EXAMPLE 11

Given the 10 per cent coupon bond discussed above with a yield to maturity of 10 per cent and a five-year life, we saw that the duration was 4.17 years. If the maturity of this bond was ten years, it would have an effective life (duration) of 6.76 years, and with a 20-year maturity it would have an effective life of 9.36 years – quite a different perspective. Furthermore, under these conditions, a 50-year maturity for this bond would change the effective life to only 10.91 years. The reason for the sharp differences between the term to maturity and the duration is that cash receipts received in the distant future have very small present values and therefore add little to a bond's value.

Estimating price changes using duration

The real value of the duration measure to bond investors is that it combines coupon and maturity, the two key variables that investors must consider in response to expected changes in interest rates. As noted earlier, duration is positively related to maturity and negatively related to coupon. However, bond price changes are directly related to duration; that is, the percentage change in a bond's price, given a change in interest rates, is proportional to its duration. Therefore, duration can be used to measure interest rate exposure.

The term modified duration refers to Macaulay's duration in Equation (12) divided by $(1 + r)$. This gives us Equation (13) or:

Modified duration $= D^* = D / (1 + r)$ (13)

where

     D^* = modified duration
     r = the bond's yield to maturity

EXAMPLE 12

Using the duration of 4.17 years calculated earlier and the YTM of 10 per cent, the modified duration based on annual interest would be:

$D^* = 4.17 / (1 + 0.10) = 3.79$ years

The modified duration can be used to calculate the percentage price change in a bond for a given change in the r. This is shown by Equation (14), *which is an approximation.*

Percentage change

in bond price $\approx \dfrac{-D}{(1 + r)} \times$ Percentage point change in the r (14)

or

$\Delta P / P \approx -D^* \, \Delta r$ (15)

where

ΔP = change in price
P = the price of the bond
$-D^*$ = modified duration with a negative sign
Δr = the instantaneous change in yield

EXAMPLE 13

Using our same bond with a modified duration of 3.79 years, assume an instantaneous yield change of 20 basis points (+0.0020) in the YTM, from 10 per cent to 10.20 per cent. The approximate change in price, based on Equation (15) would be:

$$\Delta P/P = -3.79 \times (+0.0020) \times 100 = -0.758\%$$

Given the original price of the bond of $1000, this percentage price change would result in an estimated bond price of $992.42. For very small changes in yield, Equations (14) or (15) produce a good approximation.

Convexity

Although Equation (15) is only an approximation, for very small changes in the required yield the approximation is quite close. However, as the changes become larger the approximation becomes poorer. The problem is that modified duration produces symmetric percentage price change estimates using Equation (13). If r had decreased 0.20 per cent, the price change would have been +0.758 per cent when, in actuality, the price-yield relationship is not linear. This relationship is, in fact, convex, and calculations of price changes should properly account for this convexity. *Convexity* is the term used to refer to the degree to which duration changes as the yield to maturity changes.

To understand the convexity issue, Figure 6.4 repeats the analysis from Figure 6.3 which shows a 10 per cent coupon bond at different market yields and prices. We can think of modified duration graphically as the slope of a line that is tangent to the convex price-yield curve of Figure 6.4 at the current price and yield of the bond, which is assumed to be $1000 and 10 per cent.

In effect, we are using a tangent line to measure the slope of the curve that depicts the inverse relationship between bond price and yield. For a very small change in yield, such as a few basis points, the slope of the line – the modified duration – provides a good approximation for the rate of change in price given a change in yield. As the change in yield increases, the error that results from using a straight line to estimate a bond's price behaviour as given by a curve,

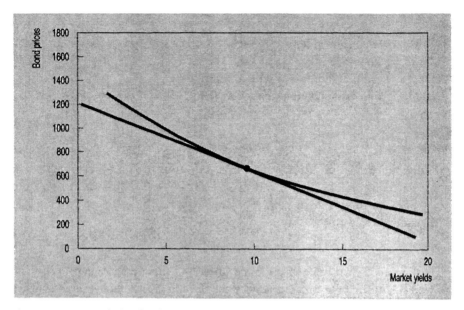

Fig 6.4 ● Convex relationship between yields and prices and tangent line representing modified duration for a 10 per cent, ten-year bond

increases. As we move away from the point of tangency in Figure 6.4 in either direction, we underestimate the price of the bond using modified duration. That is, the price change is always more favourable than suggested by the modified duration. Figure 6.4 captures the convexity areas both above and below the starting point of 10 per cent and $1000. If yields decrease, prices increase, and the duration tangent line fails to indicate the true higher price. Conversely, when yields increase, prices decrease, but the duration tangent line overstates the amount of the price decrease relative to the true convex relationship. This helps illustrate what is meant by the term *positive convexity*.

Convexity is largest for low coupon bonds, long-maturity bonds, and low yields to maturity. If convexity is large, large changes in duration are implied, with corresponding inaccuracies in forecasts of bond price changes.

Some conclusions on duration

What does this analysis of price volatility mean to bond investors? The message is simple. To obtain the maximum (minimum) price volatility from a bond, investors should choose bonds with the longest (shortest) duration. If an investor already owns a portfolio of bonds, he or she can act to increase the duration of the portfolio if a decline in interest rates is expected and the investor is attempting to achieve the largest price appreciation possible.

Fortunately, duration is additive, which means that a bond portfolio's duration is a weighted average of each individual bond's duration.

Although duration is an important measure of bond risk, it is not necessarily always the most appropriate one. Duration measures volatility, which is important but is only one aspect of the risk in bonds. If an investor considers volatility an acceptable proxy for risk, duration is the measure of risk to use along with the correction for convexity. Duration may not be a complete measure of bond risk, but it does reflect some of the impact of changes in interest rates.

CHAPTER **7**

The valuation of financial assets: stocks/equities

- What is value?
- The valuation principle
- Common stock valuation – present value approach: capitalization of income
- The dividend discount model
- Common stock valuation – fundamental analysis for valuing stocks
- Fundamental valuation methods for stocks
- What evidence is there that stock prices are not too high?
- Appendix 7.1 Is the stock market overvalued?

WHAT IS VALUE?

When analyzing stock markets the starting point is not to confuse price with value. Price is what you pay: value is what you get. Investors do not (or should not) buy financial assets for emotional reasons – they should buy them for profit. Value is directly related to the level and expected growth of those cash flows. Ben Graham, in writing *The Intelligent Investor* (1949), the founding father of investment analysis, neatly summed up the valuation dilemma: 'In the short term, the stock market is a voting machine: in the long term it's a weighing machine.'

While day-to-day market prices are largely driven by investors' emotions, long term they are based on the fundamental values of profits, earnings and cash flows, as discussed below.

Most analysts rely on the fundamental building blocks of stock value – the dividends and earnings of firms – to make stock valuation decisions. Stocks have value because of the potential cash flows, called dividends, which a stockholder expects to receive from ownership of the firm. Stocks also have value if, in the future, other stockholders may decide that the valuation of these future dividends is not fully reflected in the then current share price. It is by forecasting and valuing potential future dividends and earnings and deciding whether someone will, in the future, value these differently that enables one to judge the investment value of stocks.

Since the future cash flows of bonds are known, application of net present value techniques in valuing bonds, as was illustrated in Chapter 6, is fairly straightforward. The uncertainty of future cash flows makes the pricing of stocks according to net present values more difficult. In this chapter we examine the valuation principles applicable to stocks.

THE VALUATION PRINCIPLE

As we discussed in Chapter 6, a security's intrinsic value, or estimated value, is the present value of the expected cash flows from that asset. Any security purchased is expected to provide one or more cash flows some time in the future. These cash flows could be periodic, such as interest or dividends, or simply a terminal price or redemption value, or a combination of these. Since these cash flows occur in the future, they must be discounted at an appropriate rate to determine their present value. The sum of these discounted cash flows is the estimated intrinsic value of the asset. Calculating intrinsic value, therefore, requires the use of present value techniques. Equation (1) expresses the concept:

$$\text{Value}_{t=0} = \sum_{t=1}^{n} \frac{\text{Cash flows}}{(1+k)^t} \tag{1}$$

where

$\text{Value}_{t=0}$ = the value of the asset now (time period 0)
Cash flows = the future cash flows resulting from ownership of the asset
k = the appropriate discount rate of rate of return required by an investor for an investment of this type
n = number of periods over which the cash flows are expected

To solve Equation (1) and derive the intrinsic value of a security, it is necessary to determine the following:

1 the expected *cash flows* from the security;

2 the *timing* of the expected cash flows;

3 the *discount rate*, or required rate of return demanded by investors. The discount rate used will reflect the time value of the money and the risk of the security. It is an *opportunity cost*, representing the rate foregone by an investor in the next best alternative with comparable risk.

What determines the value of common stocks? Two basic approaches to the valuation of common stocks using *security analysis* are:

1 the present value approach (capitalization of income method);

2 the price earnings (PE) ratio (multiple of earnings) approach (fundamental analysis).

COMMON STOCK VALUATION – PRESENT VALUE APPROACH: CAPITALIZATION OF INCOME

The classic method of calculating intrinsic value applies present value analysis. This technique is often referred to as the *income method*. The present value process involves the capitalization (discounting) of future cash flows. That is, the *intrinsic value* of a security is equal to the discounted (present) value of the future stream of cash flows an investor expects to receive from the asset. This is illustrated with Equation (2):

$$\text{Estimated value of security} = \sum_{t=1}^{n} \frac{\text{Cash flows}}{(1+k)^t} \tag{2}$$

where

k = the appropriate discount rate or required rate of return.

To use such a model, an investor must:

1   estimate an appropriate required rate of return;

2   estimate the amount and timing of the future stream of cash flows;

3   use these two components in a present value model to estimate the value of the security. This is then compared to the current market price of a security.

Figure 7.1 summarizes the present value process used. This emphasizes the factors that go into valuing common stocks. The exact present value process used by investors in the marketplace depends on assumptions made about the growth rate in the expected stream of cash flows, as explained later in this chapter.

The required rate of return

An investor who is considering the purchase of a common stock must assess its risk and, given its risk, the *minimum expected rate of return* that will be

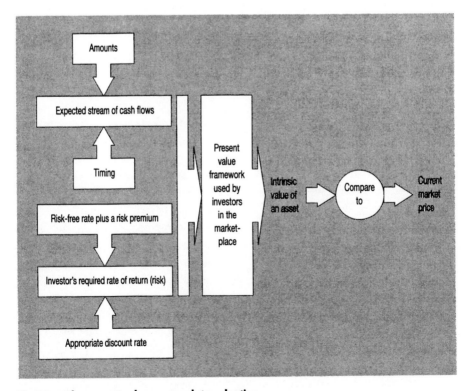

Fig 7.1 • The present value approach to valuation

required to induce the investor to make the purchase. This minimum expected return, or *required rate of return*, is an opportunity cost. It is the same concept as the required yield used to value bonds.

The *required rate of return, capitalization rates*, and *discount rate* are interchangeable terms in valuation analysis. While in theory we know what this variable is, in practice it is not easy to determine the precise number to use. Because of this complexity, we will generally assume that we know the capitalization rate and concentrate on the other issues involved in valuation.

The expected cash flows

The other component that goes into the present value framework is the expected stream of cash flows. Just as the value of a bond is the present value of any interest payments plus the present value of the bond's face value that will be received at maturity, the value of a common stock is the present value of all the cash flows to be received from the issuer. The questions that arise are as follows.

1 What are the cash flows to use in valuing a stock?

2 What are the expected amounts of the cash flows?

3 When will the expected cash flows be received?

Stockholders may plan to sell their shares some time in the future, resulting in a cash flow from the sales price. As shown later, however, even if investors think of the total cash flows from common stocks as a combination of dividends and a future price at which the stock can be sold, this is equivalent to using the stream of all dividends to be received on the stock as the key valuation principle.

What about earnings? Are they important? Can they be used in valuing a stock? The answer to both questions is yes. Dividends are paid out of earnings, so earnings are clearly important. The second stock valuation approach, fundamental analysis, to be considered later, uses earnings and a P/E ratio to determine intrinsic value. Therefore, earnings are an important part of fundamental analysis; in fact, earnings receive more attention from investors than any other single variable.

If all earnings are paid out as dividends, they will be accounted for as dividends. If earnings are retained by the corporation, they presumably will be reinvested, thereby enhancing future earnings and, ultimately, dividends. The present value analysis should not count the earnings reinvested currently and also count them again paid later as dividends. If properly defined and separated, these two variables produce the same results. This means that more than one present value model is possible. However, it is always correct to use dividends in the present value analysis, and this is what is almost always done when investors use the present value approach to valuation.

Because dividends are the only cash flow stream to be received directly by investors under normal conditions, it is appropriate to have a valuation model based on dividends. We now consider such a model, the dividend discount model, which is the basis for understanding the fundamental valuation of common stocks.

THE DIVIDEND DISCOUNT MODEL

Since dividends are the only cash payment a stockholder receives directly from a firm, *they provide the foundation of valuation for common stocks*. Applying Equation (2) specifically to value common stocks, the cash flows are the dividends *expected* to be paid in each future period. An investor or analyst using this approach carefully studies the future prospects for a company and estimates the likely dividends to be paid. In addition, the analyst estimates an appropriate required rate of return or discount rate based on the risk foreseen in the dividends, taking account of the alternatives available. Finally, the investor would discount to the present the entire stream of estimated future dividends, properly identified as to amount and timing.

The present value approach to calculating the value of a common stock is conceptually no different from the approach used earlier to value bonds. Specifically, Equation (2) adapted for common stocks, where dividends are the cash flows, results in Equation (3). This equation, known as the *dividend discount model* (DDM), states that the value of a stock today is the discounted value of all future dividends:

$$\hat{P}_{cs} = \frac{D_1}{(1+k_{cs})} + \frac{D_2}{(1+k_{cs})^2} + \frac{D_3}{(1+k_{cs})^3} + \dots \frac{D_\alpha}{(1+k_{cs})^\infty}$$

$$= \sum_{t=1}^{n} \frac{D_t}{(1+k_{cs})^t} \tag{3}$$

= Dividend discount model

where

$\hat{P}_{cs}$ = intrinsic value or estimated value of a common stock today based on the model user's estimates of the future dividends and the required rate of return

$D_1, D_2,...$ = the dividends expected to be received in each future period

k_{cs} = the required rate of return for this stock, which is the discount rate applicable for an investment with this degree of riskiness

There are two immediate problems with Equation (3).

1   The last term in Equation (3) indicates that investors are dealing with infinity. They must value a stream of dividends that may be paid forever, since common stock has no maturity date.

2   The dividend stream is uncertain:

(a) there are no specified number of dividends, if, in fact, any are paid at all. Dividends must be declared periodically by the firm's board of directors;

(b) the dividends for most firms are expected to grow over time; therefore, investors usually cannot simplify Equation (3) to a *perpetuity*. Only if dividends are not expected to grow can such a simplification be made.

How are these problems resolved? The first problem, that Equation (3) involves an infinite number of periods and dividends, will be resolved when we deal with the second problem, specifying the expected stream of dividends. However, from a practical standpoint this problem is not as troublesome as it appears. At reasonably high discount rates, such as 12 per cent, 14 per cent, or 16 per cent, dividends received 40 or 50 years in the future are worth very little today, so that investors need not worry about them. For example, the present value of \$1 to be received 50 years from now, if the discount rate is 15 per cent, is a mere 0.0009 cents.

The conventional solution to the second problem, that the dollar amount of the dividend is expected to grow over time, is to make some assumptions about the *expected growth rate* of dividends. That is, the investor or analyst estimates or models the expected *percentage* rate of growth in the future stream of dividends. To do this, they classify each stock to be valued into one of three categories, discussed below, based on the *expected growth rate in dividends*. In summary: *the dividend discount model is operationalized by estimating the expected growth rate(s) in the dividend stream.*

All stocks that pay a dividend, or that are expected to pay dividends some time in the future, can be modelled using this approach. It is critical to remember in using the dividend discount model (DDM) that an investor must account for all dividends from now to infinity by modelling the growth rate(s). As shown below, the mechanics of this process are such that we don't actually see all of these dividends because the formulas reduce to a simplified form, but nevertheless we are accounting for all future dividends when we use the DDM.

It is necessary in using the DDM to remember that the dividend currently being paid on a stock (or the most recent dividend paid) is designated as D_0 and is, of course, known. Specifically, D_0, designates the current dividend being paid, or the most recent dividend paid. Investors must estimate the future dividends to be paid, starting with D_1, the dividend expected to be paid in the next period.

The three-growth *rate* models for dividends are as follows.

1. The zero growth model

A dividend stream with a zero growth rate resulting from a fixed dollar dividend equal to the current dividend being paid, D_0, being paid every year from now to infinity. This is typically referred to as the no-growth rate or zero-growth rate model:

$$\frac{D_0 D_0 D_0 D_0 + \ldots + D_0}{0 \quad 1 \quad 2 \quad 3 + \ldots + \infty} \quad \begin{array}{l} \text{Dividend stream} \\ \text{Time period} \end{array}$$

2. Constant growth model

A dividend stream that is growing at a constant rate g, starting with D_0. This is typically referred to as the constant or normal growth version of the dividend discount model:

$$\frac{D_0 D_0(1+g)^1 D_0(1+g)^2 D_0(1+g)^3 + \ldots + D_0(1+g)^\infty}{0 \quad 1 \quad 2 \quad 3 \quad + \ldots + \quad \infty} \quad \begin{array}{l} \text{Dividend stream} \\ \text{Time period} \end{array}$$

3. The multiple growth model

A dividend stream that is growing at variable rates, for example, g_1, for the first four years and g_2 thereafter. This is referred to as the multiple-growth version of the dividend discount model:

$$\frac{D_0 D_1 = D_0(1+g_1) D_2 = D_1(1+g_1) D_3 = D_2(1+g_1) D_4 = D_3(1+g_1)}{0 \qquad 1 \qquad\qquad 2 \qquad\qquad 3 \qquad\qquad 4}$$

$$\frac{D_5 = D_4(1+g_2) + \ldots + D_\infty = D_{\infty-1}(1+g_2)}{5 \quad + \ldots + \qquad\qquad \infty} \quad \begin{array}{l} \text{Dividend stream} \\ \text{Time period} \end{array}$$

The zero-growth model

The fixed dollar dividend model reduces to a perpetuity. Assuming a constant dollar dividend, Equation (3) simplifies to the *no-growth model* shown as Equation (4).

$$\hat{P}_0 = \frac{D_0}{k_{cs}} = \quad \begin{array}{l} \text{Zero – growth version} \\ \text{of the dividend discount model} \end{array} \tag{4}$$

where D_0 is the constant dollar dividend expected for all future time periods and k_{cs} is the opportunity cost or required rate of return for this particular common stock.

A zero growth rate common stock is a perpetuity and is easily valued once k_{cs} is determined.

It is extremely important in understanding the valuation of common stocks using the DDM to recognize that in all cases an investor is discounting the future stream of dividends from now to infinity. This fact tends to be over-looked when using the perpetuity formula involved with the zero growth rate case because the discounting process is not visible. Nevertheless, we are accounting for all dividends from now to infinity in this case, as in all other cases. It is simply a mathematical fact that dividing a constant dollar amount by the discount rate, k_{cs} produces a result equivalent to discounting each dividend from now to infinity separately and summing all of the present values.

The constant growth model

The other two versions of the DDM, the constant growth model and the multi-ple growth case indicate that to establish the cash flow stream of expected dividends, which is to be subsequently discounted, it is first necessary to com-pound some beginning dividend into the future. Obviously, the higher the growth rate used, the greater the future amount. Furthermore, the longer the time period, the greater the future amount.

A well-known scenario in valuation is the case in which dividends are expected to grow at a constant rate over time. This *constant-* or *normal-growth model* is shown as Equation (5):

$$\hat{P}_0 = \frac{D_0(1+g)}{(1+k_{cs})} + \frac{D_0(1+g)^2}{(1+k_{cs})^2} + \frac{D_0(1+g)^3}{(1+k_{cs})^3} + \ldots + \frac{D_0(1+g)^\infty}{(1+k_{cs})^\infty} \qquad (5)$$

where D_0 is the current dividend being paid and growing at the constant rate g, and k_{cs} is the appropriate discount rate.

Equation (5) can be simplified to the following equation:

$$\hat{P}_0 = \frac{D_1}{k-g} = \begin{array}{l} \text{Constant – growth version of} \\ \text{the dividend discount model} \end{array} \qquad (6)$$

where D_1 is the dividend expected to be received at the end of year one.

Equation (6) is used whenever the *growth rate* of future dividends is esti-mated to be a constant. In actual practice, it is used quite often because of its simplicity and because it is the best description of the actual behaviour of a large number of companies and, in many instances, the market as a whole. Example 1 illustrates how the constant growth model can be applied to value stocks.

EXAMPLE 1

Assume Nadia Corporation is currently paying $1 per share in dividends and investors expect dividends to grow at the rate of 7 per cent a year for the foreseeable future. For investments at this risk level, investors require a return of 15 per cent a year. The estimated price of Nadia Corporation is:

$$\hat{P}_0 = \frac{D_1}{k - g}$$

$$= \frac{\$1.00\ (1.07)}{0.15 - 0.07} = \$14.38$$

Note that a current dividend (D_0) must be compounded one period because the *constant growth version of the DDM specifies the numerator as the dividend expected to be received one period from now, which is* (D_1). In valuation terminology, D_0 represents the dividend currently being paid, and D_1 represents the dividend expected to be paid in the next period. If D_0 is known, D_1 can always be determined:

$$D_0 = \text{Current dividend } D_1 = D_0(1 + g)$$

where g is the expected growth rate of dividends.

To completely understand the constant-growth model, which is widely used in valuation analysis, it is instructive to think about the process that occurs under constant growth. Table 7.1 illustrates the case of Nadia's growth stock with a current dividend of $1 per share (D_0), an expected constant growth rate of 7 per cent, and a required rate of return, k, of 15 per cent. Table 7.1 is taken from Table A-2 in the Appendix at the back of the book.

Table 7.1 • Present value of 60 years of dividends (current dividend = $1, g = 7 per cent, k = 15 per cent)

Period	Dollar Dividend	PV Factor	PV of Dollar Dividend
1	1.07	0.8696	0.93
2	1.14	0.7561	0.87
3	1.23	0.6576	0.81
4	1.31	0.5718	0.75
5	1.40	0.4972	0.70
6	1.50	0.4323	0.65
7	1.61	0.3759	0.60
8	1.72	0.3269	0.56
9	1.84	0.2843	0.52
10	1.97	0.2472	0.49
11	2.10	0.2149	0.45
12	2.25	0.1869	0.42
13	2.41	0.1625	0.39
14	2.58	0.1413	0.36
15	2.76	0.1229	0.34
16	2.95	0.1069	0.32
17	3.16	0.9385	0.29
18	3.38	0.0808	0.27

Table 7.1 ● Continued

Period	Dollar Dividend	PV Factor	PV of Dollar Dividend
19	3.62	0.0703	0.25
20	3.87	0.0611	0.24
21	4.14	0.0531	0.22
22	4.43	0.0462	0.20
23	4.74	0.0402	0.19
24	5.07	0.0349	0.18
25	5.43	0.0304	0.16
26	5.81	0.0264	0.15
27	6.21	0.0230	0.14
28	6.65	0.0200	0.13
29	7.11	0.0174	0.12
30	7.61	0.0151	0.11
31	8.15	0.0131	0.11
32	8.72	0.0114	0.10
33	9.33	0.0099	0.09
34	9.98	0.0086	0.09
35	10.68	0.0075	0.08
36	11.42	0.0065	0.07
37	12.22	0.0057	0.07
38	13.08	0.0049	0.06
39	13.99	0.0043	0.06
40	14.97	0.0037	0.06
41	16.02	0.0032	0.05
42	17.14	0.0028	0.05
43	18.34	0.0025	0.05
44	19.63	0.0021	0.04
45	21.00	0.0019	0.04
46	22.47	0.0016	0.04
47	24.05	0.0014	0.03
48	24.73	0.0012	0.03
49	27.53	0.0011	0.03
50	29.46	0.0009	0.03
51	31.52	0.0008	0.03
52	33.73	0.0007	0.02
53	36.09	0.0006	0.02
54	38.61	0.0005	0.02
55	41.32	0.0005	0.02
56	44.21	0.0004	0.02
57	47.30	0.0003	0.02
58	50.61	0.0003	0.02
59	54.16	0.0003	0.01
60	57.95	0.0002	0.01
Sum of dividends	$870.47		$13.20

Sum of first 60 years of discounted dividends is $13.20.

As Table 7.1 shows, the expected dollar dividend for each period in the future grows by 7 per cent. Therefore, D_1 = $1.07, D_2 = $1.14, D_3 = $1.23, and so forth. Only the first 60 years of growth are shown, at the end of which time the dollar dividend is $57.95. The last column of Table 7.1 shows the discounted value of each of the first 60 years of dividends. Thus, the present value of the dividend for period one, discounted at 15 per cent, is $0.93, while the present value of the actual dollar dividend received in year 60, $57.95, has a present value of only $0.01.

The message from Table 7.1 is that dividends received far in the future, assuming normal discount rates, are worth very little today. It is useful to check Table 7.1 in detail. It provides a simple technique for understanding the principles of stock valuation.

The estimated price of Nadia Corporation as illustrated in Table 7.1 is the sum of the present values of each of the future dividends. Adding each of these present values together from now to infinity would produce the correct estimated value of the stock. Note from Table 7.1 that adding the present values of only the first 60 years of dividends together produces an estimated present value of $13.20. The correct answer, as obtained from adding all years from now to infinity, or using Equation (7), is:

$$\hat{P}_0 = \text{Estimated price} = \frac{\$1.07}{0.15 - 0.07} = \$13.38 \qquad (7)$$

Thus, years beyond 40 to 50 typically add very little to the estimated value of a stock. Adding all of the discounted dividends together for the first 60 years produces a present value, or estimated value for the stock, of $13.20, which is only $0.18 different from using Equation (7). Therefore, years 61 to infinity add a total value of only $0.18 to the stock price.

Example 1 illustrates the very important point about these valuation models that was explained earlier. The constant-growth version model takes account of all future cash flows from now to infinity, although this is not apparent from simply looking at the equation itself. Although Equation (7) has no summation or infinity sign, the results produced by this equation are equivalent to those that would be obtained if the dividend for each future period is determined and then discounted back to the present. Again, the mathematics of the process masks the fact that all dividends from now to infinity are being accounted for.

To fully understand the constant growth rate version the DDM, it is also important to realize that the model implies that the stock price for any one period is estimated to grow at the same rate as the dividends, which is g. This means that the growth rate in price plus the growth rate in dividends will equal k, the required rate of return.

For Nadia Corporation the estimated price today is $13.38 and for the end of period one, using D_2 in the numerator of Equation (7) gives us:

$$\hat{P}_0 = \frac{(\$1.07)\,(1.07)}{0.15 - 0.07}$$

$$= \$14.31$$

This estimated price at the end of period one is 7 per cent higher than the estimated price today of $13.38.

$$\text{Price change} = \frac{\text{Ending price} - \text{Beginning price}}{\text{Beginning price}}$$

$$= (\$14.31 - \$13.38) / \$13.38 = 7\%$$

An examination of Equation (7) quickly demonstrates the factors affecting the price of a common stock, assuming the constant-growth version of the dividend discount model to be the applicable valuation approach:

1 if the market lowers the required rate of return for a stock, the stock price will *rise* (other things being equal);

2 if investors decide that the expected growth in dividends will be higher as the result of some favourable development for the firm, the stock price will also rise (other things being equal). Of course, the converse for these two situations also holds; a rise in the discount rate or a reduction in the expected growth rate of dividends will lower price.

The present value or intrinsic value calculated from Equation (7) is quite sensitive to the estimates used by the investor in the equation. Relatively small variations in the inputs can change the estimated price by large percentage amounts. This is illustrated in Examples 2, 3 and 4.

EXAMPLE 2

For Nadia Corporation assume the discount rate used, k, is 16 per cent instead of 15 per cent, with other variables held constant:

$$\hat{P}_0 = \frac{\$1\,(1.07)}{0.15 - 0.07}$$

$$= \$13.38$$

$$\frac{\$1(1.07)}{0.16 - 0.07}$$

$$P = \$11.89$$

In this example, a one percentage point rise in k results in an 11.14 per cent decrease in price, from today's price of $13.38 to $11.89.

EXAMPLE 3

Assume that for Nadia the growth rate, g, is 6 per cent instead of 5 per cent, with other variables held constant:

$$\frac{\$1(1.06)}{0.15 - 0.06} = \$11.77$$

In this example, a one percentage point decline in g results in a 12 per cent decrease in price, from $13.38 to $11.77.

EXAMPLE 4

Assume that for Nadia the discount rate rises to 16 per cent, and the growth rate declines to 4 per cent:

$$\frac{\$1(1.04)}{0.16 - 0.04} = \$8.67$$

In this example, the price declines from today's price of $13.38 to $8.67, a 35 per cent change.

These wide differences suggest why stock prices constantly fluctuate as investors make their buy and sell decisions. Even if all investors use the constant-growth version of the dividend discount model to value a particular common stock, many different estimates of value will be obtained because of the following.

1 Each investor has his or her own required rate of return, resulting in a relatively wide range of values of k.

2 Each investor has his or her own estimate of the expected growth rate in dividends. Although this range may be reasonably narrow in most valuation situations, small differences in g can produce significant differences in price, everything else remaining constant.

Thus, at any point in time for a particular stock, some investors are willing to buy, whereas others wish to sell, depending on their evaluation of the stock's prospects. This helps to make markets active and liquid.

The multiple-growth model

Many firms grow at a rapid rate (or rates) for a number of years and then slow down to an 'average' growth rate. Other companies pay no dividends for a period of years, often during their early growth period. The constant-growth model, discussed earlier, is unable to deal with these situations; therefore, a different model is needed. Such a variation of the DDM is the *multiple growth model*.

Multiple growth is defined as a situation in which the expected future growth in dividends must be described using two or more growth rates. Although any number of growth rates is possible, most stocks can be described using two or possibly three. It is important to remember that at least two different growth rates are involved; this is the distinguishing characteristic of multiple-growth situations.

A number of companies have experienced rapid growth that could not be sustained forever. During part of their lives their growth exceeded that of the average company in the economy, but later the growth rate slowed. Examples from the past would include McDonald's, Disney, IBM, Microsoft and Amazon.

To capture the expected growth in dividends under this scenario it is necessary to model the dividend stream during each period of differential growth. It is reasonable to assume that at some point the company's growth will slow down to that of the economy as a whole. At this time the company's growth can be described by the constant-growth model. What remains, therefore, is to model the exact dividend stream up to the point at which dividends slow to a normal growth rate and then to find the present value of all the components.

A well-known multiple-growth model is the two-stage growth rate model. This model assumes near-term growth at a rapid rate for some period (typically, two to ten years) followed by a steady long-term growth rate that is sustainable (i.e. a constant-growth rate as discussed earlier). Equation (8) describes the multiple growth model:

$$\hat{P}_0 = \sum_{t=1}^{n} \frac{D_0(1+g_1)^t}{(1+k)^t} + \frac{D_n(1+g_c)}{k-g_c} \frac{1}{(1+k)^n} \tag{8}$$

where

$\hat{P}_0$ = the intrinsic or estimated value of the stock today
D_0 = the current dividend
g_1 = the supernormal (or subnormal) growth rate for dividends
g_c = the constant growth rate for dividends
k = required rate of return
n = the number of periods of supernormal growth
D_n = the dividend at the end of the abnormal growth period

Notice in Equation (8) that the first term on the right side defines a dividend stream covering n periods, growing at a high (or low) growth rate of g, and discounted at the required rate of return, k. This term covers the period of supernormal growth, at which time the dividend is expected to grow at a constant rate forever. The second term on the right-hand side is the constant growth version discussed earlier, which takes the dividend expected for the next period $n + 1$, and divides by the difference between k and g. Notice, however, that the value obtained from this calculation is the value of the stock at the beginning of period $n + 1$ (or the end of period n), and it must be discounted back to time period zero by multiplying by the appropriate discount (present value) factor. Conceptually, the valuation process being illustrated here is:

$\hat{P}_0$ = discounted value of all dividends through the unusual growth period n plus the discounted value of the constant-growth model which covers the period $n + 1$.

It is useful to think about the second term in Equation (8) as representing a $\hat{P}_0$ or the expected price of the stock derived from the constant-growth model as of the end of period n. The constant-growth version of the dividend discount model is used to solve for expected price at the end of period n, which is the beginning of period $n + 1$. Therefore,

$$P_n = \frac{D_{n+1}}{k - g_c}$$

Because P is the expected price of the stock at the end of period n, it must be discounted back to the present. When added to the value of the discounted dividends from the first term, the estimated value of the stock today (P_0) is produced. Example 5 illustrates the multiple growth model.

EXAMPLE 5

Figure 7.2 illustrates the concept of valuing a multiple-growth rate company. In this example, the current dividend is $1 and it is expected to grow at the higher rate (g_1) of 12 per cent a year for five years, at the end of which time the new growth rate (g_c) is expected to be a constant 6 per cent a year. Assume the required rate of return is 10 per cent.

The first step in the valuation process, illustrated in Figure 7.2, is to determine the dollar dividends in each year of supernormal growth. This is done by compounding the beginning dividend, $1, at 12 per cent for each of five years, producing the following expected dividend stream:

$D_0 = \$1.00$

$$
\begin{aligned}
D_0 &= \$1.00(1.12) &&= \$1.12 \\
D_1 &= \$1.00(1.12)^2 &&= \$1.25 \\
D_2 &= \$1.00(1.12)^3 &&= \$1.40 \\
D_3 &= \$1.00(1.12)^4 &&= \$1.57 \\
D_4 &= \$1.00(1.12)^5 &&= \$1.76
\end{aligned}
$$

Once the stream of dividends over the supergrowth period has been determined, they must be discounted to the present using the required rate of return of 10 per cent. Thus:

$1.12(0.909) = \$1.02$
$1.25(0.826) = \$1.03$
$1.40(0.751) = \$1.05$
$1.57(0.683) = \$1.07$
$1.76(0.621) = \$1.09$
$\overline{\$5.26}$

Summing the five discounted dividends produces the value of the stock for its first five years only, which is $5.26. To evaluate years six and later, when constant growth is expected, the constant growth model is used.

$$P_n = \frac{D_{n+1}}{k - g_c}$$

$$= \frac{D_6}{k - g_c}$$

$$= \frac{D_5(1.06)}{k - g_c}$$

$$= \frac{1.76(1.06)}{0.10 - 0.06}$$

$$= \$46.64$$

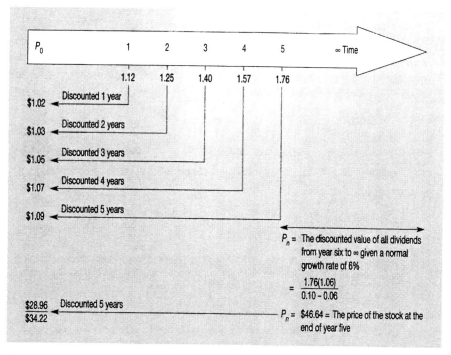

P_n = The discounted value of all dividends from year six to ∞ given a normal growth rate of 6%

$= \dfrac{1.76(1.06)}{0.10 - 0.06}$

P_n = \$46.64 = The price of the stock at the end of year five

Fig 7.2 ● Valuing a multiple-growth rate company

Thus, $46.64 is the expected price of the stock at the beginning of year six (end of year five). It must be discounted back to the present, using the present value factor for five years and 10 per cent, which is 0.621, and can be found from the Statistical Tables in the Appendix at the end of the book. Therefore,

$$P_n \text{ discounted to today} = P_n \text{ (PV factor for five years, 10\%)}$$
$$= \$46.64(0.621)$$
$$= \$28.96$$

The last step is to add the two present values together:

$5.26 = present value of the first five years of dividends
$28.96 = present value of the price at the end of year five, representing
_____ the discounted value of dividends from year six to ∞
= $34.22 = $\hat{P}_0$, the present value of this multiple growth rate stock

COMMON STOCK VALUATION – FUNDAMENTAL ANALYSIS FOR VALUING STOCKS

The approach to stock valuation discussed above is often referred to as the capitalization of income method. In the remainder of this chapter we describe other valuation techniques, often referred to collectively as fundamental analysis.

Appendix 7.1 describes some of the benchmarks used in this chapter and applies them to the controversial issue as to how one could decide whether the US stock market was or was not overvalued.

As already discussed, the value of any asset is determined by the *discounted value of all future expected cash flows. Discounted* means that future cash flows are not valued as highly as current flows. For stocks, cash flows come primarily in the form of dividends, but occasionally from other distributions resulting from the sale of assets or other transactions. For most assets – and especially for all stocks – the future cash flows are uncertain and depend on the financial circumstances of the firm.

The future cash flows from assets are discounted because cash received in the future is not worth as much as cash received in the present. There are many reasons for this: the innate *preferences* of most individuals to enjoy their consumption now rather than wait for tomorrow; *productivity*, which allows funds invested today to yield a higher return tomorrow; *inflation*, which reduces the future purchasing power of cash received in the future; and the *uncertainty* associated with any event which takes place in the future.

Since dividends generally increase over time, the value of most stocks depends on what may happen many decades hence.

Estimates of *all* future cash flows are important for the valuation of equities – not only the ones received during the time the investor holds the asset. However, for a short-term investor, the return on an investment will depend not only on the *investor's* assessment of the cash flows but also on the *market's* assessment of the cash flows at the time of the sale. This is because a large part of the return for a short-term stockholder comes from the proceeds of the sale of the asset and not from the dividends received. Unless one intends to hold the asset forever, one must take into account how much other investors in the market will value the asset at the time of its sale in order to estimate one's return.

As a consequence, for most investors, the return on an asset is composed of two parts: the cash flows received while holding the asset and the change in valuation of the asset by the market from the time of purchase to the time of sale. An investor might be enthusiastic about the dividend prospects of a certain stock, but if the intention is to sell the stock next year, the investor is at the mercy of what *other* investors will think of the firm's prospects at that time.

Most investors attempt to profit in the market by buying a stock with what they consider attractive future returns, hoping that other investors will come to agree with their judgement. If this comes to pass, the price of the stock will rise. In fact, the fastest way to make money in the market is to successfully forecast how *other* investors might change the basis on which *they* make judgements about stocks' values in the near future. For example, if you think that other investors will turn optimistic about technology stocks, then you may make money buying such stocks whether or not you believe they are good value.

Accordingly, success for short-term investors comes primarily from discerning how the public will view stocks in the future, and quite secondarily from the cash flows realized by the investment itself. The tension between investing in the long run and the short run was best described by John Maynard Keynes in 1936 when he wrote:

> 'most of these (professional investors and speculators) are, in fact, largely concerned, not with making superior long-term forecasts of the probable yield of an investment over its whole life, but with foreseeing changes in the conventional basis of valuation a short time ahead of the public. They are concerned, not with what an investment is really worth to a man who buys it "for keeps", but with what the market will value it at, under the influence of mass psychology, three months or a year hence.'

The game of forecasting future investor sentiment is difficult. But you need not forecast market sentiment in order to profit in stocks. Although investment advice geared to the short run hinges on predicting the judgement of other investors, in the long run one can ride out the waves of investor sentiment and profit from your own predictions. Investing for the long run does, however, necessitate first a knowledge of stock market history and second the ability to apply some suitable stock valuation models.

So we need to know some stock market history and then we must ask whether there are any other stock valuation models available which would enable us to compare our results with those of the capitalization of income method already discussed. So, does history tell us anything about the performance of stock markets, in this case examining US stock market history?

What do we know about US stock market history?

When predicting future returns on the market, the price-to-earnings ratio and the dividend yield compared to historical standards, are the most frequently cited criteria for judging the valuation of the market.

Table 7.2 displays the dividends and earnings yield on stocks represented by the US S&P 500 Index for the period 1871–1994. It can be seen that the average historical earnings yield during this period is 8.1 per cent giving an average price-earnings ratio of 13.6. This means that investors priced stocks on average at about 12 to 15 times their annual earnings. Despite the stability of the average, the P/E ratio for the period has shown considerable annual variation, ranging from a high of 27 in 1894 to a low of 6 in 1950. It should be noted that, as can be seen from Appendix 7.1, that more recent P/E ratios have been around 30.

Another yardstick used to judge the future of the market is the dividend yield. The dividend yield has averaged 4.9 per cent from 1871, with a high of 8.71 per cent in 1959 and a low of 2.85 per cent in 1973. The dividend yield shows far less variability than the earnings yield, as managers pursue policies to stabilize the cash payments to stockholders.

Table 7.2 ● Historical averages of dividend yield and earnings yield 1871–1994

Period	Dividend Yield (%)	Price/ Earnings	Earnings Yield (%)	Period	Dividend/ Earnings (%)	Growth of Real Dividends (%)	Growth of Real Earnings (%)	Growth of Real S&P (%)
1871 – 1994	4.9	13.6	8.1	1871 – 1994	64.0	1.2	1.5	1.8
1871 – 1958	5.3	13.4	8.2	1871 – 1958	71.5	0.7	1.0	0.8
1959 – 1994	3.8	14.1	7.8	1959 – 1994	51.8	2.0	2.1	3.4

Source: J. Siegel (1995) *Stocks for the Long Run: A Guide to Selecting Markets for Long-Term Growth.* Reproduced with permission of the McGraw-Hill Companies

In contrast to the long-term stability of the earning yield, the US dividend yield has fallen significantly in recent years. Between 1959 and 1994, the average dividend yield was 3.8 per cent, and has fallen since to below 2 per cent. Again, this is illustrated in Appendix 7.1. From 1871 to 1958 the dividend yield averaged 5.3 per cent. The primary cause of the reduction in the dividend yield is not the higher valuation of shares, but the reduction in the dividend pay out ratio – the fraction of earnings firms pay as dividends. The increase in US personal and corporate taxes made it advantageous for firms to retain earnings, rather than pay them to stockholders in the form of taxable dividends.

FUNDAMENTAL VALUATION METHODS FOR STOCKS

Numerous stock valuation methods are available for investors to choose between. It must be said that stock picking, as it is known, is an art rather than a science. However, there are scientific elements to the exercise and this section summarizes the techniques available. It must be stressed that each technique has limitations and these should be kept in mind.

The fundamental techniques listed below cover:

- the price/earnings ratio

- the price/earnings growth factor (PEG ratio)

- the dividend yield

- the yield ratio: bond yield to the dividend yield

- Tobins q ratio

- price to book value

- price to sales ratio

The price/earnings ratio

The cash flows which are received by shareholders come primarily from dividends, and these dividends in turn come from earnings. Obviously, then, two of the most important financial statistics about stocks are earnings and dividends. The earnings per share divided by the current stock price is referred to as the *earnings yield* on the stock. Many investors prefer to think in terms of the inverse of the earnings yield – called the *price/earnings*, or *P/E ratio*. The P/E ratio, also called the *earnings multiple*, measures how many times current (or prospective) earnings the market is paying for a stock. The P/E ratio is the most popular fundamental variable for valuing both stocks and the market.

There are many measures of profit, but a particular definition is earnings – the profit after taxes and any other changes that are attributable to ordinary shareholders. Earnings are reported by companies on a per share basis, and that can be translated by analysts into earnings yield, to parallel the dividend yields discussed below. As mentioned above, the ratio is presented the other way round from the price earnings ratio. Thus a 5 per cent earnings yield represents a P/E ratio of 20.

The price earnings ratio indicates how many years' purchase of a company's earnings are reflected in its share price. The higher the ratio, the more optimistic investors must be about growth in order to pay the market price. Thus growth stocks, most recently represented by technology stocks, are on high P/Es. Stocks on low P/Es may represent bargains, but more likely they are stocks facing troubled times.

Determinants of the P/E ratio

What determines the P/E ratio? The P/E ratio can be derived from the dividend discount model discussed earlier.

Start with Equation (6), the estimated price of a stock using the constant growth version of the model. We use P_0 to represent estimated price from the model.

$$P_0 = \frac{D_1}{k - g}$$

Dividing both sides of Equation (6) by expected earnings, E_1, gives us Equation (9):

$$P_0/E_1 = \frac{D_1/E_1}{k - g} \tag{9}$$

Equation (9) indicates those factors that affect the estimated P/E ratio are:

1 The dividend pay out ratio, D/E;

2 The required rate of return, k;

3 The expected growth rate of dividends, g.

The following relationships should hold, other things being equal.

(i) The higher the payout ratio, the higher the P/E ratio.

(ii) The higher the expected growth rate, g, the higher the P/E ratio.

(iii) The higher the required rate of return, k, the lower the P/E ratio.

It is important to remember the phrase 'other things being equal' because usually other things are not equal and the preceding relationships do not hold by themselves. It is quite obvious, upon reflection, that if a firm could increase its estimated P/E ratio, and therefore its market price by simply raising its payout ratio, it would be very tempted to do so. However, such an action would in all likelihood reduce future growth prospects, lowering g, and thereby offsetting the increase in the payout ratio. Similarly, trying to increase g by taking on particularly risky investment projects would cause investors to demand a higher required rate of return, thereby raising k. Again this would work to offset the positive effects of the increase in g.

Factors 2 and 3 above are typically the most important factors in the determination of the P/E ratio because a small change in either can have a large effect on the P/E ratio. This is illustrated in Example 6.

EXAMPLE 6

Assume that the payout ratio is 60 per cent. By varying k and g, and therefore changing the difference between the two (the denominator in Equation (9)), investors can assess the effect on the P/E ratio as follows:

Assume $k = 0.15$ and $g = 0.07$
$$P/E = \frac{D_1/E_1}{k-g}$$

$$P/E = \frac{0.60}{0.15 - 0.07}$$

$$P/E = \frac{0.60}{0.08} = 7.5$$

Now assume $k = 0.16$ and $g = 0.06$ $\quad P/E = \dfrac{0.60}{0.16 - 0.06} = 6$

or that $k = 0.14$ and $g = 0.08$ $\quad P/E = \dfrac{0.60}{0.14 - 0.08} = 10$

What are the limitations of P/E ratios?

There are several limitations to P/E ratios. They do not tell you:

1 at what rate a company's earnings are expected to grow;

2 whether a company's earnings growth is expected to accelerate or decelerate;

3 how its earnings generating capability compares with other investments offering the same risk-reward relationship;

4 exactly how earnings between companies differ. Earnings suffer from fundamental measurement problems because they depend on subjective judgements made by companies and their auditors. In bull markets, stan-

dards often deteriorate as companies bend the rules to meet the over ambitious expectations of investors;

5 how to adjust the ratio when accounting for massive structural change within an economy. As discussed in Chapter 11, the rising importance of intangible assets has meant that new methods of accounting for valuing companies need to be introduced. This forms a key component of the debate on the New Economy.

Prospective price/earnings ratio

Some analysts calculate the prospective price/earnings ratio based on what they predict companies will earn in the future. Since expectations of future earnings differ between analysts it is not easy to apply this method for the overall stock index, but it may be useful for individual stocks and sectors.

Price/earnings growth factor (PEG)

A concept that has become popular in the past few years is the price/earnings growth factor, or PEG. This is the P/E ratio divided by the annualized growth rate of earnings.

Dividing the P/E ratio by the estimated growth of earnings is a gauge of how quickly the company is growing. This is known as the prospective PEG. For instance, two companies may have a P/E ratio of 20, but show different rates of earnings growth. Company A has earnings growth of 20 per cent, while Company B has earnings growth of 5 per cent. Company A's PEG ratio would be 1 (20 divided by 20), whereas Company B would have a PEG of 4 (20 divided by 5). The lower the PEG ratio, the better the potential value of the company. In this example, company A is growing very quickly and could represent better potential.

A PEG of significantly less than 1 is regarded as attractive, so a share with a moderate P/E ratio of 15 would need a growth rate of close to 20 per cent a year to be a strong buy.

PEG can only be used for growth stocks. It would be inapplicable for cyclical stocks or turnaround situations. When calculating the estimated sustainable growth ratio in earnings it is expected that these can be sustained for over five years. So a company with a P/E of 10, for example, growing at 20 per cent would have a PEG of 0.5, or half the estimated growth rate. A PEG of less than 1 as discussed above, usually means that the share is good value.

The essential drawback in valuation with all multiples is that they do not take account of changes in inflation and interest rates. Increases in interest rates will usually cause share values to fall, as the real net present value of companies' future earnings streams is eroded. Falling interest rates have the opposite effect.

Dividend yield

Table 7.3 illustrates that US stocks earned significantly higher average returns between 1927 and 1995 than other financial assets such as corporate bonds or US Treasury Bills. While the stock returns shown in the Panel A of Table 7.3 are impressive, investors are more concerned with inflation adjusted returns. Panel B of Table 7.3 presents average real returns after adjusting for inflation.

One approach to deciding whether the stock market is overvalued is to examine the dividend yield, defined as the rate of dividends to stock prices. When the dividend yield is low, stock prices are considered relatively high and vice versa.

The cash income from shares is the most basic foundation for stock valuation. The dividends and cash flows from the stock are rarely identical to the earnings. Some earnings are usually retained by management to generate funds for future operations or expansion, or sometimes used to repurchase shares. The current cash return to the stockholder is called the *dividend yield* and is represented by the dividend per share divide by the current share price.

Earnings that are not paid out as dividends are called retained earnings. Management has two uses to which such retained earnings can be put. One is the purchase of either real or financial assets. As long as these assets are productive, their acquisition will increase future earnings and hence the future price of the shares. The second use of retained earnings is the purchase of the firm's own shares in the open market. Reducing the number of shares will also increase future per-share earnings and dividends and hence the future prices of

Table 7.3 ● Nominal and real returns on US financial assets 1927–1995

A. Nominal returns

	1927–95	1946–95
	(% per year)	
Stocks	9.54	11.23
Corporate bonds	5.39	5.46
Government bonds	4.85	5.04
Treasury bills	3.64	4.72

B. Real returns

	1927–95	1946–95
	(% per year)	
Stocks	6.43	7.03
Corporate bonds	2.28	1.25
Government bonds	1.74	0.84
Treasury bills	0.52	0.52

Source: Cochrane (1997)

the shares. Therefore if the firm buys productive assets or buys its own shares, per share earnings and dividends will increase.

Table 7.4 shows that the average dividend yield from 1927 to 1995 was about 4.4 per cent.

Table 7.4 ● US dividend yields, returns and dividend growth, 1927–95

	1927–95	1927–45	1946–95	1927–71	1972–95
			% per year		
Dividend yield	4.37	4.95	4.14	4.52	4.14
Real returns	6.43	4.86	7.03	6.73	6.40
Real dividend growth	1.12	–1.62	2.15	0.71	2.34

Source: Cochrane (1997)

Apart from the historic low of the dividend yield, two other questions need to be asked in using this as a form of calculating investment returns.

First: how safe is it? If the next payment is cut, the apparently attractive yield of, say 7 per cent return for 1946–1975 may be largely an illusion. Usually the market's expectation of the next or *prospective* annual total dividend is more important for the share price than the amount actually paid in the past year. Stability of profits, and the dividend *cover* – the ratio of available earnings to dividends – are also important factors here. Second: how rapidly is the dividend likely to grow? A fast growing dividend stream is clearly worth more than a static one, as we discussed earlier, with the effect that growth stocks are worth buying on much lower dividends than mature companies.

Professional analysts use the dividend discount models discussed earlier to compute the impact of different growth assumptions. Due to the power of compound arithmetic, valuations can be very sensitive to the forecast of the growth rate and this explains why company shares can fall so sharply when they produce disappointing results or issue profit warnings.

To illustrate, suppose that the current low dividend yield adjusts back to its mean. In this case, either stock prices will fall or dividends will increase. On 14 March 1998, Warren Buffet, a famous value investor, told stockholders that he believed the historically high stock prices are justified as long as interest rates remain low and corporations continue to produce 'remarkable' returns on equity. Buffet apparently believed that future dividends will rise to justify the low dividend to price ratio. Unfortunately history tells a different story. It is adjustments in stock prices, not dividends, that historically have driven the dividend yield back toward its mean value. If dividend yields do revert to their long-run mean over the next few years, the long-term prospects for the stock market over this period are not favourable. This is discussed in more detail in Appendix 7.1.

Unfortunately the analysis of dividends has become more complex than it used to be. Tax considerations cloud the calculations. Companies are therefore

much more interested than they used to be in finding alternative, more tax efficient, ways of returning cash to shareholders. Share buybacks are increasingly
popular. Analysts now agree that it is necessary to take buybacks into account
in valuing dividend flows.

Bond/equity yield ratio

Investors always have a choice between equities and bonds. In the long run, the
two asset classes ought to achieve similar returns, or at any rate similar returns
after adjusting for differences in risk and liquidity. In the UK it is usual historically for government bonds to pay a little more than twice as much as dividend
yields. In the USA the historical average is nearer three.

Analysts use the bond/equity yield ratio as a benchmark as to whether bond or
equity prices will revert back to the historical average. Table 7.5 illustrates how
this would work.

Table 7.5 ● Why bond yields drive dividend yields (and vice versa)

Historical Average Bond Yield/Equity Yield	Assumed Current Ratio	Expectation			
		Share Price	Dividend Yield	Bond Price	Bond Yield
3	< 3	↑	↓	↓	↑
3	> 3	↓	↑	↑	↓

However, the dividend yield has to be sensitively interpreted. If the dividend
yield is low due to the effect on earnings of a forthcoming recession, then the
ratio has to be treated cautiously.

Tobins q ratio

In addition to comparing a company's dividends or earnings to the price of the
stock it can also be useful to compare the value of the company's securities to
the value of its assets. The ratio of the market capitalization to the replacement
cost of the underlying corporate assets is known as Tobins q. It is named after
its creator, James Tobin, Yale University's Nobel Laureate, whose other contributions to financial economics we discussed in Chapter 2.

Tobins q is a simple enough idea. The ratio of (a) the value of companies according to their market capitalization to (b) the replacement of the cost of their assets
should be a number equal to 1. The numerator and the denominator of the ratio
are, after all, just two ways of measuring the same thing, the value of companies.

The value of the company on the financial markets exceeds the value of its
assets when its expected earnings are high or rising rapidly. Conversely the

company can be worth less than its assets when its prospects are especially poor or uncertain.

If q was for some reason greater than 1 this would imply that the stock market put a higher value on assets owned by companies than those same assets cost to acquire. So there would be a kind of arbitrage opportunity. If q were greater than 1, companies could be expected to increase their investment, presumably until the market reckoned the company was now worth what its assets cost. At that point q would again be equal to 1.

Estimates of Tobins q for non-financial corporations by the US Federal Reserve for 1998–2000, show the highest valuations since 1925. Using the Feds calculations it has fluctuated between a minimum of 0.4 and a maximum of 1.8, its level at the time of writing. The average level is 0.7.

A value higher than unity, the case since 1991, for the first time in 25 years, indicates that it is more advantageous for firms to issue shares in order to finance the accumulation of productive capital (land, plant) than to buy such assets 'secondhand' through purchasing the corresponding securities on the stock market.

In the early 1970s and early 1980s the value was usually less than 1, suggesting that companies were quite cheap. If this ratio was to revert to the long-term average, the US stock market would decline by 50 per cent.

Smithers and Wright (2000), have recently analyzed the US stock market and come up with a figure of a q ratio of well over 2. They find that when the ratio (suitably adjusted to take account of accounting discrepancies) moves far above unity, equilibrium is indeed eventually restored – not, however, by a surge in the replacement value of companies' assets – but by a dramatic fall in their share price. As Smithers and Wright point out, that is what happened in 1968–74 after earlier peaks in q. The current value of q, they note, is higher now than in either 1929 or 1986.

A ratio of this type has to be handled with great care, because of the problems posed by the valuation of assets both tangible and intangible. Intangible assets – intellectual property, trademarks, patents, know-how – for example, tend to be undervalued in the denominator of q, causing the ratio to be overstated. This argument is often advanced to explain the present high level of q, on the grounds that intangible assets are now of much greater importance than they were. We return to these ideas in Chapter 11.

Price to book value (P/BV)

Company balance sheets display a figure for the book value of shareholders funds, which can be expressed as net worth per share. US stocks in year 2000 are selling at a record 4.9 times book value. Book value refers to the value of the assets on a company's balance sheet. A the time of writing it is about 2.5 times the average multiple over the past 20 years.

But there is an old investment saying that 'assets are only worth what they can earn'. Asset analysis is most useful when companies possess unexploited assets that could be sold or put to other uses – office blocks, say, or stakes in other companies. Inflexible assets such as machinery or oil wells may need to be analyzed more cautiously.

The decline of manufacturing industry has highlighted, as mentioned above, the importance of intangible assets in today's companies – brand names, software, royalty rights and the skills of the workforce. Because it is so hard to value these satisfactorily in the balance sheet, the use of asset value analysis and with it price to book value, has declined in importance.

Price to sales ratio (PSR)

This is simply the ratio of the value of the company's equity (that is its market capitalization) to its sales. This might seem a confusing indicator, because profit margins can vary so much between different kinds of industry. But in an influential book, *What Works On Wall Street* published in 1996, the American quantitative investor James O'Shaughnessy described the price to sales ratio as the 'king of value factors'.

O'Shaughnessy found that low capitalization-to-sales ratios stocks beat the market more than any other value ratio. He stressed that investors should be cautious of stocks where the market capitalization is more than twice the level of the company's sales.

Using data going back to 1951 O'Shaughnessy analyzed all of the basic investment strategies used to select common stock, such as book value, cash flow, P/E, ROE, yield, and so forth. O'Shaughnessy found that the 50 stocks with the lowest PSRs based on an annual rebalancing of the portfolio, performed at an annual rate of 15.42 per cent over the 40 years from 1954 to 1994, compared to 12.45 per cent annually for his universe of all stocks. Stocks with the highest PSRs earned only 4.15 per cent annually. Furthermore, combining low PSR stocks (generally, a PSR of 1.0 or lower) with stocks showing *momentum* (the best 12-month price performance) produced results of 18.14 per cent annually over the full 40-year period.

WHAT EVIDENCE IS THERE THAT STOCK PRICES ARE NOT TOO HIGH?

Greenspan's (1996) speech, famously commented on the 'irrational exuberance' of the level of the stock market, indicating that it was, to his mind, reaching unsustainable peaks. Appendix 7.1 illustrates different criteria that would indicate he was correct to send out warning signals. One standard measure of 'fundamentals' is US average earnings over the past ten years, a period considered long enough for business cycle fluctuations to average out. In a typical year, a typical stock is priced about 15 times its ten year average of earnings. Today the typical US stock sells for nearly 30 times its ten year average of earnings.

The argument that the stock market is overvalued – and that it will gradually deflate or crash – is simple. Stocks are tradable pieces of paper that are merely a claim on a corporation's future earnings. And the ratio of stock price to earnings is twice what it traditionally has been. In the past, whenever general stock prices have risen as high, relative to fundamentals, as they are at the time of writing, the next decade has been an extremely bad one in which to invest in the stock market.

However, many participants in the markets suggest other theories which envisage a rosier outlook. The optimists offer three main theories as to why current stock prices, despite recent volatility, are not too high.

1   Some claim that information technology is ushering in a generation-long economic boom. Past rule of thumb valuations based on earnings and dividends assume that economic and profit growth will continue in the future at roughly the pace it did in the past. But (the argument goes), because we are on the threshold of the post-industrial transformation, economic growth – and earnings growth, and dividend growth, and stock price growth – will be faster than in the past. The arrival of the ideas surrounding the 'New Economy' it is argued, have changed the old rules of economics.

2   Others claim that the rate of return that the average investor expects to receive on stocks has fallen. This would mean that any given level of profit can sustain a higher stock price. In the past, demand for stocks was limited by fear of the risk. Investors could look to the bond market and see the chance for a decent return with total safety. But (the argument goes) the 1970s inflation taught investors the brutal lesson that there is no safety in bonds: your investment can evaporate if interest rates rise, or inflation devalues the bonds purchasing power. Investors today also have less fear of the business cycle and other risks associated with stocks. So investors are willing to pay more for stocks than they used to. We return to the prospects for the equity premium in Chapter 14.

3   Over the past generation, corporations have learned better how to avoid paying taxes. Some companies have pushed up their debt-equity ratios – raising more money through bonds and less through stocks – and thus changed payments (to investors) that used to be called 'dividends' into 'interest'. Dividends are paid out of post-tax earnings, whereas debt interest is a tax-deductible business expense. Other companies have decided to buy back shares with money that would otherwise have been paid out in dividends. The money shareholders receive in this way is taxed as a capital gain, usually at a lower rate, whereas dividends are taxed as ordinary income. Furthermore, investors can choose whether to participate in the buyback or to hold onto their shares and defer taxes completely. All these various tax techniques make stocks more valuable, per dollar of corporate earnings, than previously.

Is the stock market overvalued?*

With apologies to T. S. Eliot, October is the cruellest month. In 1929 October saw the start of the Great Crash which led to the depression of the early 1930s; the 1987 Crash occurred, effectively, on only two days, 16 and 19 October; and both of the last two years have seen trouble in October. October 1997 had the biggest-ever one-day points fall in the US stock market (until then) on 27 October; and, at the low point of the American stock market on 8 October 1998, it was over 20 per cent down on three months earlier. (Other stock markets suffered even larger peak-to-trough declines in 1998, but a big rebound occurred everywhere after 8 October.)

October's rogue behaviour is puzzling. In theory efficient markets ought to demolish seasonal fluctuations in share prices. Despite the oddness of the apparent monthly pattern, we can still ask: 'Will 1999 be different?'. The analysis In the accompanying research paper argues that the American stock market is heading for a big fall, although the precise timing is inherently unknowable. The central tension is between valuations far in excess of long-run norms and unsustainable macroeconomic trends. The paper reviews various well-known value benchmarks. All of them show serious over-valuation, although its extent varies from a third for the most favourable benchmark to over 100 per cent on the least favourable. (If an over-valuation of 100 per cent sounds strange, it means that share prices have to halve to return to 'normal'.) This might be acceptable if the USA's macroeconomic prospects were excellent, but they are not. The domestic economy is over-heating, while the plunge into external deficit cannot continue. October 1999 may or may not break the mould, but – sooner or later – a collapse in the American stock market will be part of the return to a more balanced macroeconomic situation.

Historically, the link between American and UK share prices has been close, but the movements have not been identical. Although a similar analysis of UK share prices would also identify over-valuation, the extent of the over-valuation would be less marked. A standard comment in recent months has been 'a big fall in American (and British/European/Asian) share prices would cause a recession'. Is that really so? An alternative view is that some drop in share prices is needed as a corrective to the above-trend growth in domestic demand which has been seen in the UK as well as the USA in the last three years. The Bank of England's decision to raise interest rates by 1/4% on 8 September 1999 be seen as an attempt to pre-empt eventual inflationary trouble from the buoyancy of demand. But it cannot be justified by the immediate inflation outlook, which is fine. It might also look a little peculiar if financial markets are as turbulent in October 1999 as they have been in the last two years.

*This appendix is reprinted, with permission, from *Lombard Street Research Monthly Economic Review*, September 1999. The date of publication is relevant when reading the text.

TRYING TO MAKE SENSE OF THE AMERICAN STOCK MARKET

Valuations defy historical norms, while over-heating and the external payments deficits are unsustainable

October seems to be the favourite month for big fails in the American stock market and, by a knock-on effect, in other leading stock markets. The 1987 Crash occurred on Black Monday, 16 October, although it had in fact been preceded by a topsy-turvy few months since a peak in July. October 1997 was a difficult month, with 27 October recording the largest one-day points fall until then. Last year the stock market was weak from July until early October, reaching a trough on the S & P 500 index on 8 October which was over 20 per cent lower than three months earlier.

Could October 1999 repeat the pattern? There is no doubt that – by most conventional valuation yard sticks – American equities are extremely expensive. However, the verdict about the degree of over-valuation depends on the approach adopted. A standard method is to compare the *price/earnings multiple* and *the dividend yield* today with an average over the past. This has the advantages of simplicity and familiarity, but it suffers from at least two weaknesses. First, it is unclear which concept of 'the past' should be truly representative. Is a period as long as a decade sufficient and appropriate? Or should it be 20 or 50 years? Moreover, shouldn't some allowance be made for cycles? And, if so, doesn't that affect the choice of start and end dates?

Second, equities are only one asset class. The correct valuation of equities ought to depend partly on asset values in general. Of course, the idea of 'asset values in general' is rather elusive and some sort of proxy is needed. The usual proxy in these exercises is the level of bond yields. The implication is that measures of equity market valuation should be qualified by 'bond yields'. That opens up a Pandora's Box of competing benchmarks. Which 'bond yield' is the right one to adopt? Should the yield be short-dated or long-dated? And should it be of a bond free from default risk (i.e. a government bond) or a corporate bond? And isn't the correct notion a bond yield adjusted for inflation (i.e. a real yield) instead of a nominal yield? Without going into all the complications, three measures have been recognized as valuable:

1 The ratio of the nominal yield on a long-dated government bond to the dividend yield on equities (or 'the yield ratio' for short);

2 The ratio of the nominal yield on a long-dated government bond to the earnings yield on equities (where the earnings yield is the inverse of the P/E ratio, expressed as a percentage), and

3 The ratio of the inflation-adjusted yield on a long-dated government bond to the earnings yield on equities.

The yield ratio has the drawback that it is sensitive to changes in companies' dividend pay-out behaviour, which may have no connection with underlying value. This is largely overcome by the two other measures, with many commentators believing that the third measure has the cleanest economic meaning. (A real bond yield is compared with the long-run ability to pay dividends on a 'real asset', i.e. equities.)

However, in practice the crudely-calculated yield ratio has been more stable in the world's large and long-established stock markets (i.e. those in the USA and the UK) than either of the two other measures. The stability of the yield ratio in the UK since the late 1960s has indeed been remarkable.

At any rate, all five of the possible valuation benchmarks for US equities are now giving an unequivocal message. US equities are stratospherically expensive on three simple measures (i.e. the P/E ratio, the dividend yield and the yield ratio), as these imply falls of 50 per cent or more to achieve a return to 'normal'. (See pp. 181–3.) Meanwhile they are very expensive on the two more ambitious measures (i.e. the ratio of the bond yield – either nominal or inflation-adjusted – to the earnings yield on equities). (See pp. 184–5.) The key numbers are set out in the accompanying charts, which relate to August when the average value of the S & P 500 index was 1327.5. The conclusion needs to be qualified to some extent if 'US equities' are defined as the stocks in the Dow Jones Industrial Average, as the valuation of these companies departs less from historical experience. However, the so-called 'tech stocks' in the NASDAQ index are on even more extraordinary P/E ratios and yields than those in the S & P 500.

A bull market in bonds might rescue analysts who focus on the relatively mild over-valuations suggested by the ratios of the bond yield to the dividend yield and of the real bond yield to the dividend yield. If the American bond market were on a threshold of a bull phase which cut yields to, say, 4 per cent from the current 6 per cent, US equities would look quite reasonably valued relative to bonds. The difficulty here is that the macroeconomic background is unhelpful. The rate of pay inflation in the USA has been rising for over three years, with the important message that unemployment (at 4.2 per cent of the workforce) is well beneath the so-called 'natural rate'. (The concept of the natural rate of unemployment was proposed by Professor Milton Friedman in 1967; it Is that rate at which wage increases, and so inflation, are stable.) The standard instruction of macroeconomic theory is that inflation will increase until unemployment returns to the natural rate, implying that several quarters of rising inflation are to be expected.

Meanwhile the emergence of trade deficits of about $25 billion a month is disturbing, although widely foreseen. The stability of American asset prices, and to some extent American financial stability more broadly, have become dependent on continued large-scale buying of American assets by foreigners. Yet – if such buying persists – it is simple to show that the USA's external liabilities become unmanageable in the medium and long runs. The final phase of the Greenspan Boom promises to be very interesting. It is difficult to see how the over-extended equity market valuations can be reconciled with the unsustainable macroeconomic trends for much longer.

THE VALUATION OF US EQUITIES

1. The P/E ratio

The most straightforward and perhaps the most reliable measure of stock market valuation is the ratio of price to earnings (i.e. profits after interest and tax). The P/E ratio has the important merit that it is not affected by changes in dividend distribution

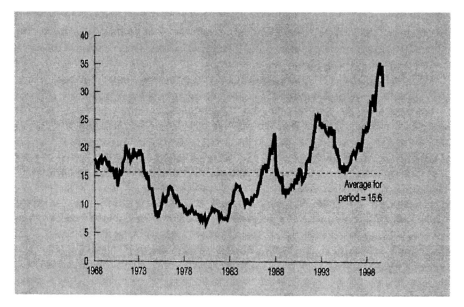

Fig 7.3 ● The fall required to restore 'normal' valuations: 50 per cent

Source: Datastream

policy, which may be motivated by extraneous factors such as inflation, the tax system and corporate fashion. (However, note that reductions in company taxation do affect post-tax profits and, hence, the value of companies.) The P/E ratio in the US stock market has been volatile from decade to decade, but in the long run it has tended to revert to an average value in the 15–20 range. The underlying logic for this value is discussed in an Appendix on p. 187. Against this background, the experience of the 1990s has been remarkable. The P/E ratio in the early 1990s was in the 20–25 area, similar to that in the late 1920s and the late 1960s but otherwise unparalleled. More recently it has exceeded 30, roughly twice the historical norm, even though company earnings are cyclically high because of the boom in the American economy.

2. The dividend yield

A standard valuation benchmark for equities used to be the dividend yield. Most academic studies until the 1990s found that the dividend yield had a much clearer pattern of reverting to its long-run mean value than the P/E ratio. But in the 1990s the dividend yield has collapsed and it has proved a very poor basis for asset allocation decisions. Part of the explanation is that American companies have reduced the ratio of dividend distributions to company earnings, which has boosted retentions and so the value of their capital assets. (The ratio of dividends to corporate post-tax profits was 47.6 per cent in 1998, compared with 56.3 per cent in 1989.) Logically, shareholders should take out their returns to a greater extent from capital gains and less from dividends. Another influence has been the increased role of share buy-backs. In the final quarter of 1998 US companies were

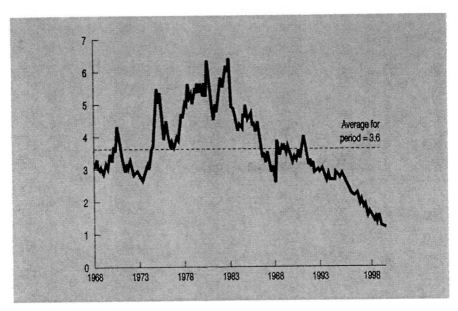

Fig 7.4 ● The fall required to restore 'normal' valuation: at least 60 per cent

Source: Economic Indicators

net buyers of corporate equities on a record scale, partly because they were involved in an unprecedented boom in acquisition activity, but partly also because of the increasing popularity of share buy-backs. It is important to recognize that – insofar as such buy-backs increase share prices – they protect the value of managements' share options.

3. The yield ratio

Investors can hold either equities or bonds. In the long run the two asset classes ought to achieve similar returns or, at any rate, similar returns after adjusting for differences in risk and liquidity. The conventional view is that bonds can have somewhat lower returns and still be acceptable assets, because they give greater certainty about their nominal value at future dates. In the USA the 1980s and early 1990s were years of mostly 5 per cent or sub-5 per cent inflation, with dividend growth of 7–8 per cent a year, and numbers like these were recorded fairly consistently. Equities with a dividend yield in the 3–4.5 per cent area therefore gave better or similar returns to bonds with yields typically between 7 per cent and 11 per cent. (With the yield stable, the total return on equities is the initial yield plus the dividend growth rate.) By extension, the ratio of the bond yield to the dividend yield ('the yield ratio') was remarkably stable in the 2.2–2.9 band between 1982 and 1996, with the significant exception of 1987. However, in the last three years the yield ratio has moved into uncharted territory. If bond yields were to stay at current levels and the yield ratio returned to 2½, the US stock market would halve.

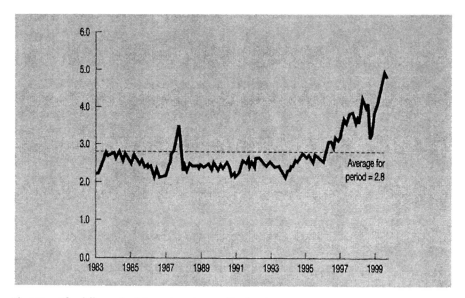

Fig 7.5 ● The fall required to restore 'normal' valuation: 50 per cent

Source: Datastream

4. The ratio of the bond yield to the earnings yield

The yield ratio, as conventionally understood, is the ratio of the yield on a representative bond to the dividend yield on equities. (See p. 183.) One drawback is that it

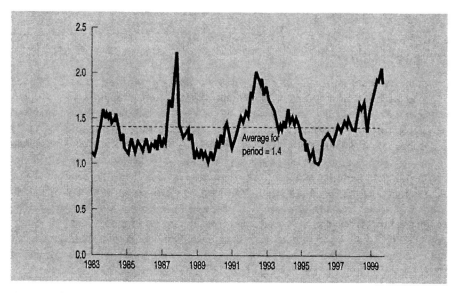

Fig 7.6 ● The fall required to restore 'normal' valuation: 30–35 per cent

Source: Economic Indicators

can be affected by changes in corporate attitudes towards dividend distribution, even though such changes may not alter the underlying economic value of business assets. (Shareholders have lower dividends, but higher retained equity.) A useful alternative value measure is therefore the ratio of the bond yield to the earnings yield on equities, where the earnings yield is the ratio of post-tax, post-interest profits to the equity market's market capitalization. (It is of course the inverse of the P/E ratio and is normally expressed as a percentage.) The bond yield/earnings yield ratio has averaged 1.4 in the period of sub-5 per cent inflation since 1982. It soared to almost 2.3 in 1987, giving an excellent 'sell' signal for equities. But a similar jump to about 2 in 1992 could also have been interpreted as 'sell', which would have been a duff message. At any rate, this valuation measure is once again testing its historical highs. An equity market fall of a third would take it back to 'normal'.

5. The ratio of real bond yield to earnings yield

A weakness of the bond yield/earnings yield ratio (see p. 184) is that it compares one asset (i.e. corporate equity) with a rising income stream and so some protection against inflation with another (i.e. bonds) where the income is fixed. The assets can be made more comparable if the bond yield is adjusted for the inflation rate. The resulting ratio of the real bond yield to the real earnings yield has been quite volatile since the early 1980s, with a typical value somewhat beneath one. Despite its theoretical attractions, it has not had a particularly reliable track record in terms of 'buy' and 'sell' signals in the last 15 years. (However, the 'buy') signal in the late 1990s was magnificent.) Its current value is virtually the highest ever recorded. If the real bond yield were to stay at about 3.5–4 per cent, an equity market fall of 40 per cent would be required

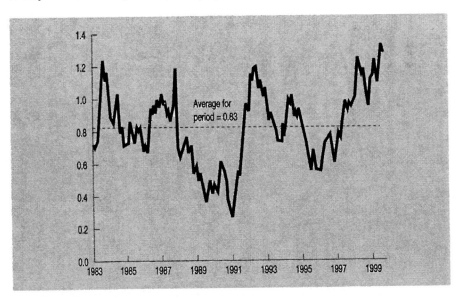

Fig 7.7 ● The fall required to restore 'normal' valuation: almost 40 per cent

Source: Economic Indicators and Bloomberg

to take the ratio back to the 0.83 average for the period. Some economists say that real bond yields are rather high at present, but they are in fact much lower than in the early 1980s. In 1982 the yield on a triple-A corporate bond averaged 13.79 per cent, while consumer prices rose by 3.8 per cent in the year to December.

THE MACROECONOMIC BACKGROUND TO BOND YIELDS

Figures 7.3 and 7.4 argue that in terms of its own specific yardsticks (i.e. the P/E ratio and the dividend yield) the US equity market is roughly double a 'normal' valuation. Implicitly, the valuation can make sense either if dividends and profits are in future to grow at rates well above the historical average or if help is in prospect from a bull market in bonds. Figures 7.5–7.7 suggest that equity valuations are already very stretched compared with bond yields. So – if a permanent acceleration in profits growth is deemed implausible – a huge fall in bond yields is needed to restore the equity market to a sensible valuation. Figure 7.8 argues that, on the contrary, bond yields have further to rise. Contrary to some newspaper comment, pay inflation has increased significantly in recent years. Using a quarterly series on 'hourly compensation in the business sector' the move upwards has been from 2 per cent in the mid-1990s to about 5 per cent today. (This series is probably more reliable than the 'hourly earnings' number published with the monthly payroll statistics.) By implication, unemployment is beneath the so-called 'natural rate' at which pay settlements are stable. Several quarters of rising inflation lie ahead.

Competing theories have been proposed to explain how the USA has been able in the late 1990s to reconcile a boom in spending with low inflation. One view is opti-

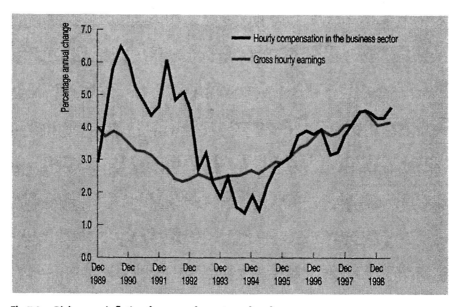

Fig 7.8 ● Rising pay inflation for several quarters ahead

Source: Bureau of Labour Statistics

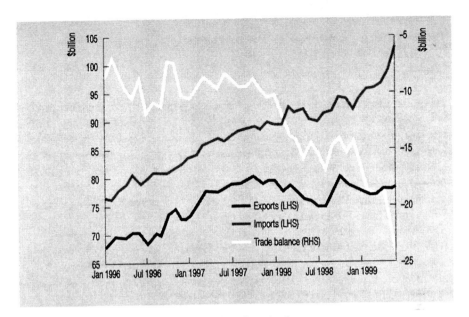

Fig 7.9 ● Plunging trade deficit belies supply-side 'miracle'

mistic, that the supply-side performance of the American economy has improved fundamentally. It is claimed, for example, that the trend annual growth rate of output has increased from under 2.5 per cent to over 3 per cent. An alternative hypothesis is more cautious, that exceptional international developments – notably the Asian crisis, the associated fall in commodity prices and the strong dollar – have enabled the USA to suppress inflation temporarily. If so, the USA has not defied the laws of macroeconomics, but merely postponed the inflationary consequences of excess demand. If the optimists were right, the stronger supply-side performance ought to have supported American international competitiveness and faster export growth; if the second argument were correct, the USA's external payments would have deteriorated, with the rest of the world acting as the vent for over-spending. In fact, the trade balance has plunged heavily into the red since mid-1997 and may average between $25 billion and $30 billion a month in the rest of 1999.

APPENDIX

The analytical rationale for a long-run P/E ratio in the 15–20 band

A standard textbook in finance theory has a straightforward and well-known formula for the determinants of the P/E ratio. Let D be dividends and E be earnings. Then the dividend pay-out ratio, d, is equal to D/E. The value of a stream of dividend payments over many time periods (i.e. of a sequence of dE's) has to be adjusted upwards for its growth rate (g), but reduced by a discount rate (r). On the assumption that corporate equity will outlive any individual and indeed any member of the current generation, there is no harm in regarding equities as having 'infinite lives'. The expression for the P/E ratio is then a geometric series whose value becomes:

$$\frac{d}{r-g}$$

The value of the discount rate partly reflects investors' time-preferences, but it is also influenced by the perceived riskiness of equities as an asset class and other attributes, such as the cost and ease of transactions. Ample historical evidence is available that a long-run real yield on a default-free long-dated government bond in politically-stable societies ought to be 3–3.5 per cent a year. Yields beneath that have never persisted for more than a few years. The discount rate on equities has to be higher. Suppose that the appropriate 'excess' is 2 per cent. That gives a value of 5.25 per cent for the discount rate in the above expression for the P/E ratio.

What about the growth rate of dividends? In the long run the growth rate of dividends has to be related to the growth rate of profits and, at the aggregate level, to the growth rate of national output. The analysis all runs in real terms. (It becomes complicated if inflation is introduced.) The long-run growth rate of real output in countries like the USA and the UK, which have been 'advanced industrial societies' for over a century, is 2–2.5 per cent a year, with productivity growth more like 1.5–2 per cent. Assume that the long-run real growth rate of dividends is 2.5 per cent a year. So the excess of the discount rate over the dividend growth (i.e. $r - g$) is 2.75 per cent or 0.0275.

The pay-out ratio in the UK stock market has been between 40 per cent and 45 per cent for most of the last 50 years or so, Of course, there is a trade-off between dividend distributions and growth. It appears that investors must accept that – in the aggregate – their companies have to retain more than half today's earnings in order to secure the 2.5 per cent real growth rate of dividend streams to which they are accustomed. Another complication is that distribution policy is sensitive to the structure of company taxation. Nevertheless, a value of 0.425 for the pay-out ratio looks reasonable. So the 'equilibrium' value of the P/E ratio is 0.425 divided by 0.0275, which is 15.5. This compares with an average P/E ratio on the FT non-financials index in the last 30 years of 13.5. The US data are different, although not that dissimilar, and – as already noted – the average P/E ratio on the S & P 500 since 1968 has been 15.1. The historical record therefore appears to be consistent with this analysis of the fundamental determinants of the P/E ratio.

CHAPTER **8**

Modern portfolio theory

- Building an efficient investment portfolio
- Stage 1: use the Markowitz portfolio selection model
- Apply the efficient frontier concept
- Stage 2: consider how borrowing and lending possibilities affect the efficient portfolio set
- The Separation Theorem
- Stage 3: how should investors select an optimal portfolio of risky assets?
- Portfolio return and risk: the role of diversification
- The Capital Market Line (CML)

BUILDING AN EFFICIENT INVESTMENT PORTFOLIO

In Chapter 4 we showed how the statistical concepts of risk and return can be applied to individual securities and to portfolios of securities. In this chapter we examine the principles involved in building an efficient investment portfolio.

What are the stages in building an efficient investment portfolio?

To build a portfolio of financial assets, investors follow certain stages. Specifically they follow this course of action.

1 They identify optimal risk return combinations available from the set of risky assets being considered by using the Markowitz efficient frontier analysis.

2 They consider the impact of a risk-free asset on the Markowitz efficient frontier. The introduction of borrowing and lending possibilities leads to an optimal portfolio of risky assets and has a significant impact on the way investors should think about the investment process.

3 They choose the final portfolio, consisting of the risk-free asset and the optimal portfolio of risky assets, based on their preferences for risk and return.

STAGE 1: USE THE MARKOWITZ PORTFOLIO SELECTION MODEL

Random diversification does not use the full information set available to investors and does not, in general, lead to optimal diversification.

To take the full information set into account, we use an alternative approach based on *portfolio theory* as developed by Markowitz (1952). Portfolio theory is normative, meaning that it tells investors how they should act to diversify optimally. It is based on a small set of assumptions, including:

1 a single investment period; for example, one year;

2 no transaction costs;

3 investor preferences based only on a portfolio's expected return and risk, as measured by variance or standard deviation.

What is an efficient portfolio?

Markowitz's approach to portfolio selection is that an investor should evaluate portfolios on the basis of their expected returns and risk as measured by the standard deviation. Markowitz was the first to derive the concept of an *efficient portfolio*, defined as one that has the smallest portfolio risk for a given level of expected return or the largest expected return for a given level of risk. Investors can identify efficient portfolios by specifying an expected portfolio return and minimizing the portfolio risk at this level of return. Alternatively, they can specify a portfolio risk level they are willing to assume and maximize the expected return on the portfolio for this level of risk. Rational investors will seek efficient portfolios because these portfolios are optimized on the two dimensions of most importance to investors, expected return and risk.

APPLY THE EFFICIENT FRONTIER CONCEPT

To begin the analysis, we must first determine the risk-return opportunities available to an investor from a given set of securities. Figure 8.1 illustrates the opportunities available from a given set of securities. A large number of possible portfolios exist when we realize that varying percentages of an investor's wealth can be invested in each of the assets under consideration. Is it necessary to evaluate all of the possible portfolios illustrated in Figure 8.1? Fortunately, the answer is no, because investors should be interested in only that subset of the available portfolios known as the *efficient set*.

The assets in Figure 8.1 generate the *attainable* set of portfolios, alternatively known as the *opportunity set*. The attainable set is the entire set of all portfolios that could be found from a group of *n* securities. However, risk-averse investors should be interested only in those portfolios with the lowest possible risk for any given level of return. All other portfolios in the attainable set are said to be *dominated*.

In order to select those assets that are on the efficient frontier it is necessary to apply mean-variance analysis, sometimes also referred to as the Dominance Principle. This states when choosing between two assets with different risks and return:

1 if expected *returns* are identical, choose the asset with the least risk;

2 if expected *risks* are the same, choose the asset with the highest return.

Point A in Figure 8.1 illustrates the best combination of assets which yield a 9 per cent return. This is the most efficient asset mix for that return because it is the portfolio with the least variability. Its standard deviation is 4 per cent, so two-thirds of the return from portfolio A are expected to fall between 5 per cent and 13 per cent (9+4=13%, 9–4=5%). Any other portfolio will carry greater variability of return and thus greater risk. Portfolio B is the most efficient choice of asset mix to achieve a 13 per cent return.

The efficient portfolio is provided by the locus XZ. Points inside the efficient frontier should not be considered by a rational investor as there is always a better combination of risk and return available.

Technically Markowitz showed that the actual efficient frontier provided the best combination of asset mix by applying the dominance principle. This is found by applying quadratic programming.

Why is the efficient frontier convex?

You may be wondering why the efficient frontier is not a straight line between risk and return. The explanation for the convex shape of the efficient frontier arises from the fact that there is a limited set of assets which produce higher returns. As the investor seeks higher and higher returns, there are fewer and fewer securities to choose from. This limits the extent to which risk can be moderated. Proportionately smaller returns are achieved for each additional unit of risk. Similarly, at the less risky end of the efficient frontier, the investor also has the choice of fewer and fewer less risky securities for inclusion in the efficient portfolio. Thus for every unit of return foregone, the investor achieves diminishing reductions in the risk level.

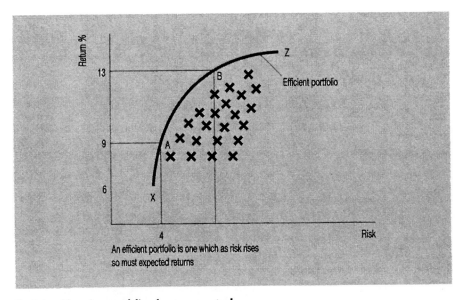

Fig 8.1 ● Choosing portfolios from many stocks

How do we apply the efficient frontier when it comes to choosing the mix of assets to invest in?

Let us assume that we make the assumption in Table 8.1 about how we see the predicted returns from different asset classes. Also assume that risk rises as we move from low-risk cash as an asset class to high-risk US Technology equities as an asset class.

Table 8.1 ● Predicted returns from different asset classes

	Predicted return per cent
Cash	9
Gilts	10
UK equities	15
US equities	10
European equities	14
Japanese equities	20
US Technology equities	25

We can then calculate the different combinations of asset returns and risk as seen in Table 8.2. The higher the proportion of cash held, as in portfolios A and B, the lower the risk. The higher the proportion of risky assets held, here equities, the higher the risk, as in portfolios C and D.

Table 8.2 ● Portfolio risk and return

Asset mix in portfolio	A	B	C	D
Cash	75	10	0	0
Gilts	10	30	10	0
UK equities	5	10	30	0
US equities	0	0	0	0
European equities	0	10	5	0
Japanese equities	10	30	40	10
US Technology equities	0	10	15	90
	100	100	100	100

This in turn gives us our efficient frontier as can be seen from Figure 8.2.

So the Markowitz analysis generates an entire set, or frontier, of efficient portfolios all of which are equally 'good'. What the analysis does not do is to

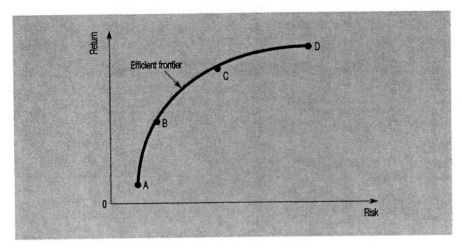

Fig 8.2 ● Using the efficient frontier in asset allocation decisions

deal with the question of whether, when we allow for risk-free borrowing and risk-free investing, the efficient portfolio principles are affected.

STAGE 2: CONSIDER HOW BORROWING AND LENDING POSSIBILITIES AFFECT THE EFFICIENT PORTFOLIO SET

As we saw above, investors can use the Markowitz analysis as a portfolio optimizer. This analysis determines the best combinations of expected return and risk for a given set of inputs for risky assets. However, investors always have the option of buying a risk-free asset such as Treasury bills. The portfolio selection question remains the same: What is the best portfolio of assets, given *any* set of assets under consideration, to hold?

Lending is best thought of as an investment in a riskless security. This security might be Treasury bills. Borrowing and lending options transform the efficient frontier into a straight line. See Figure 8.3 for the standard efficient frontier ABCD. Assume that an investor can lend at the rate of $R_F = 0.05$, which represents the interest rate on US Treasury bills. Hence the point R_F represents a risk-free investment ($R_F = 0.05$; $\sigma_p = 0$). The investor could place all or part of his funds in this riskless asset. If the investor placed part of his funds in the risk-free asset and part in one of the portfolios of risky securities along the efficient frontier, what would happen? The investor could generate portfolios along the straight-line segment $R_F B$ as seen in Figure 8.3.

Let us examine the properties of a given portfolio along the straight-line segment $R_F B$. Consider point B on the original efficient frontier ABCD in Figure 8.3 where, say, $R_p = 0.10$ and $\sigma_p = 0.06$. If we placed one-half of available

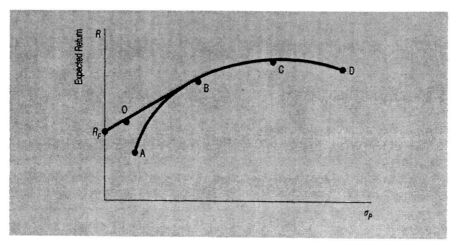

Fig 8.3 ● Efficient frontier with the introduction of lending

funds in the riskless asset and one-half in the risky portfolio, B, the resulting combined risk-return measures for the mixed portfolio, O, can be found from Equations (1) and (2):

$$R_p = XR_M + (1 - X) R_F \tag{1}$$

where

R_P = expected return on portfolio
X = percentage of funds invested in risky portfolio
$(1 - X)$ = percentage of funds invested in riskless asset
R_M = expected return on risky portfolio
R_F = expected return on riskless asset

and

$$\sigma_P = X\sigma_M \tag{2}$$

where

σ_P = expected standard deviation of the portfolio
X = percentage of funds invested in the risky portfolio
σ_M = expected standard deviation on the risky portfolio

From Equations (1) and (2) we calculate risk-return measures for portfolio M as being:

R_p = $(\frac{1}{2})(0.10) + (\frac{1}{2})(0.05) = 7.5\%$
σ_p = $(\frac{1}{2})(0.06) + (\frac{1}{2})(0.00) = 3.0\%$

The result indicates that our return and risk have been reduced (formerly it was 10 per cent and 6 per cent). All points between R_F and B can be similarly determined using Equations (1) and (2). As stated, the locus of these points will be a straight line.

Introduction of the possibility of borrowing funds will change the shape of our efficient frontier in Figure 8.3 to the right of point B. In borrowing, we consider the possibilities associated with the total funds invested being enlarged.

Consider three cases. If we assume that X is the percentage of investment wealth or equity placed in the risky portfolio. then where $X = 1$, investment wealth is totally committed to the risky portfolio. Where $X < 1$, only a fraction of X is placed in the risky portfolio, and the remainder is lent at the rate R_F. The third case, $X > 1$, signifies that the investor is borrowing rather than lending. It may be easier to visualize this by rewriting Equation (1) as follows:

$$R_P = XR_M - (X-1)R_B \tag{3}$$

where all terms are as in Equation (1) and the term R_B is the borrowing rate. For simplicity, the borrowing rate and lending rate are assumed to be equal, at 5 per cent. The first component of Equation (3) is the gross return made possible because the borrowed funds, as well as the original wealth or equity, are invested in the risky portfolio. The second term refers to the cost of borrowing on a percentage basis. For example, $X = 1.25$ would indicate that the investor borrows an amount equal to 25 per cent of his or her investment wealth. The investor's net return on the investment would become:

$$R_P = (1.25)(0.10) - (0.25)(0.05) = 11.25\%$$

The associated risk would become:

$$\sigma_P = X\sigma_p = (1.25)(0.06) = 7.5\%$$

THE SEPARATION THEOREM

This theorem, initially developed by Nobel prize winner James Tobin, and discussed in Chapter 2, states that all investors, conservative or aggressive, should hold the same mix of stocks from the efficient set. In contrast to popular thinking, this implies that both risk-averse and risk-loving investors should hold identically risky portfolios. They should use borrowing or lending to attain their preferred risk class. The separation theorem highlights two separate steps in the investment selection process.

Step 1

Choose the asset mix at the point on the efficient frontier which generates the highest risk/return mix. This is Point S in Figure 8.4.

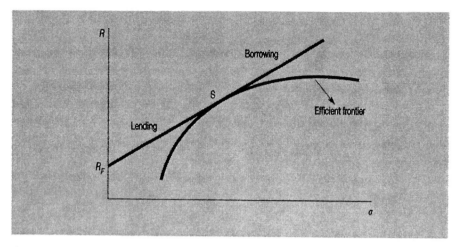

Fig 8.4 ● Borrowing and lending with the efficient frontier

Step 2

Second, we blend this asset mix of S by borrowing and lending depending on whether we want more or less risk. Taking the data from Table 8.3 enables us to generate Table 8.4.

Table 8.3 ● Risk and return data

	r	σ
1. Portfolio	15	16
2. Risk free rate (r_f)	5	0

Table 8.4 ● Risk and return from a portfolio consisting of 50 per cent in the efficient portfolio and 50 per cent in the risk-free asset

$$r = \left[\frac{1}{2} \times ER(S)\right] + \left[\frac{1}{2} \times r_f\right] = 7.5\% + 2.5\% = 10\%$$

$$\sigma = \left(\frac{1}{2} \times \sigma_s\right) + \left(\frac{1}{2} \times \sigma r_f\right) = 8\% + 0\% = 8\%$$

If we then examine the alternative of a risk lover borrowing the maximum amount possible and then investing all this into the efficient portfolio S, using S as collateral gives us Table 8.5.

Table 8.5 ● Portfolio of a risk lover

$r = [2 \times ER(S)] - [1 \times r_f)] = 30\% - 5\% = 25\%$

$\sigma = (2 \times \sigma_s) - (1 \times \sigma r_f) = 32\% - 0\% = 32\%$

Clearly Table 8.5 provides a more desirable risk/return profile than ignoring borrowing and lending altogether.

So the introduction of the risk-free asset significantly changes the Markowitz efficient set of portfolios. By introducing risk-free investing and borrowing into the analysis a set of expected return-risk possibilities is created *which did not exist previously*. As illustrated in Figure 8.4, the new risk return trade-off is a straight line tangent to the efficient frontier at point S and with a vertical intercept R_F.

We will return to this idea below in discussing the Capital Market Line.

STAGE 3: HOW SHOULD INVESTORS SELECT AN OPTIMAL PORTFOLIO OF RISKY ASSETS?

Once the efficient set of portfolios is determined using the Markowitz model, investors must select from this set the portfolio that is most appropriate for them. The Markowitz model does not specify one optimum portfolio. It generates the efficient set of portfolios, all of which, by definition, are optimal portfolios (for a given level of expected return or risk).

The central vehicle for choosing an optimal portfolio is the satisfaction an investor receives from investment opportunities. Satisfaction is best represented by utility functions or indifference curves. At this stage we must demonstrate what indifference curves are and describe the different shapes that indifference curves can take.

Where do indifference curves fit into the investment decision process?

To select the expected risk return combination that will satisfy an individual investor's personal preferences, indifference curves, which are assumed to be known for an investor, are used. These curves describe investors preferences for risk and return. Each indifference curve represents all combinations of portfolios that are equally desirable to a particular investor.

A few important points about indifference curves should be noted.

1 Indifference curves cannot intersect since they would then represent different levels of desirability.

2 Investors have an infinite number of indifference curves.

3 The curves for all risk-averse investors will be upward-sloping, but the shapes of the curves can vary depending on risk preferences.

4 Higher indifference curves are more desirable than lower indifference curves.

5 The greater the slope of the indifference curves, the greater the risk aversion of investors.

Figures 8.5, 8.6, 8.7 and 8.8 provide examples of the different shapes that indifference curves can take, depending on the investor's approach to risk and return.

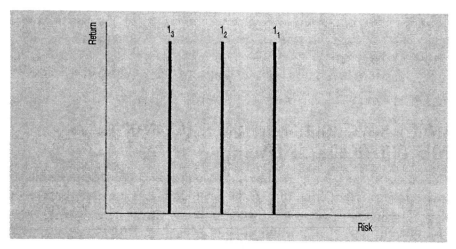

Fig 8.5 ● Risk-averse investors

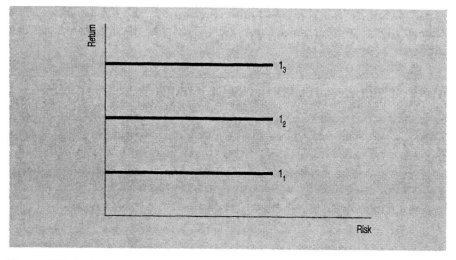

Fig 8.6 ● Risk-loving investors

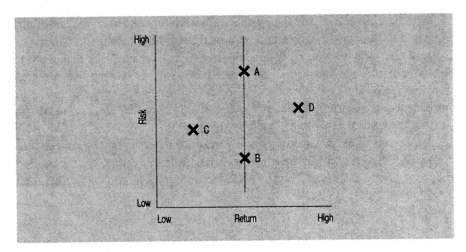

Fig 8.7 ● Risk-neutral investors

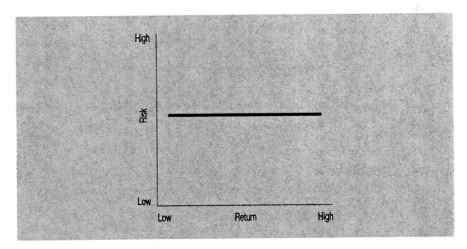

Fig 8.8 ● Return-neutral investors

The higher a curve, the more desirable the situation lying along it. Each curve carries equal satisfaction along its length. The problem for an investor is to find the feasible portfolio tangent to the best attainable (highest) indifference curve. If we combine the efficient frontier with the family of indifference curves, as we do in the next section, we can derive the optimal portfolio an investor should hold.

Although differences may occur in the slope of indifference curves, they are assumed to be positive sloping for most rational investors. A more important question is whether indifference curves are curves and not straight lines, as depicted so far.

Since most investors would be expected to seek more return for additional risk assumed, utility or indifference curves (lines) are not simply horizontal or vertical, they are positively sloped. Figures 8.9, 8.10 and 8.11 demonstrate indifference curves (lines) for a risk lover, depending on whether they are constant risk lovers, decreasing risk lovers or increasing risk lovers. The indifference curves are negative sloping and convex toward the origin. As risk rises so does utility.

The degree of slope associated with indifference curves will indicate the degree of risk aversion for the investor. A risk-averse investor's set of indifference curves are shown in Figures 8.12, 8.13 and 8.14. The very risk-averse

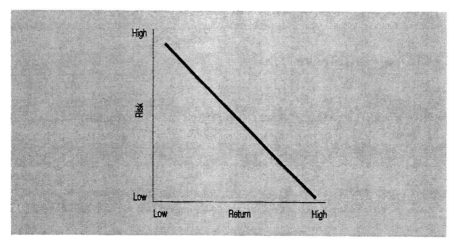

Fig 8.9 ● Constant risk lovers

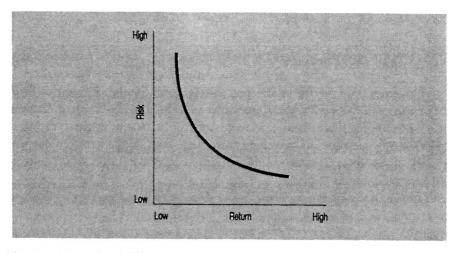

Fig 8.10 ● Decreasing risk lovers

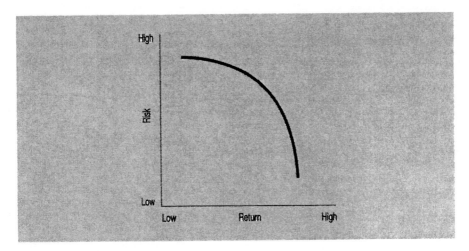

Fig 8.11 ● Increasing risk lovers

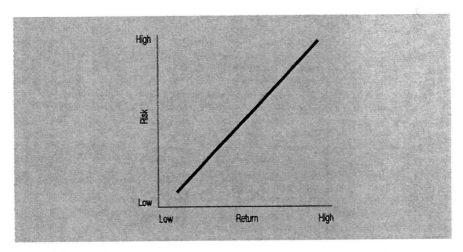

Fig 8.12 ● Constant risk aversion

investor requires large increases in return for large increases in risk, as in Figure 8.13.

With risk averters, the lower the risk of their portfolios, the happier they are; risk lovers are happier the higher the level of risk. A less risk-averse investor's set of indifference curves are shown in Figure 8.14. This investor will accept smaller increases in return for large increases in risk. Both investors dislike risk but they trade off risk and return in different degrees.

As already highlighted, different utility accrues to given increments of return. The utility received from $100,000 may or may not be worth twice that received from $50,000. In effect, in Figure 8.15 we can see three different

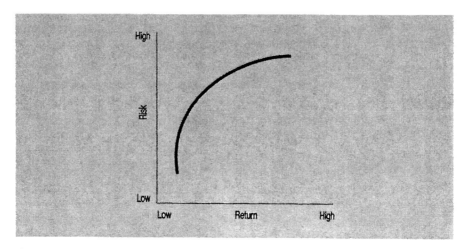

Fig 8.13 ● Increasing risk aversion

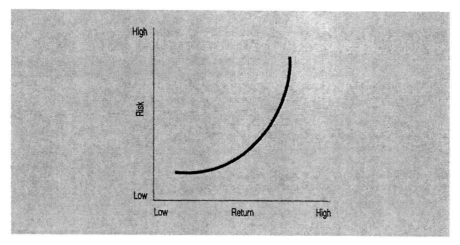

Fig 8.14 ● Decreasing risk aversion

slopes to an indifference or utility curve (line). Curve A depicts increasing marginal utility, curve B constant utility, and curve C diminishing marginal utility. While constant marginal utility (straight line) would suggest that, say, doubling return doubles utility (satisfaction), increasing marginal utility means that increasingly larger satisfaction is to be found from the same increase in return. Increasing marginal utility would suggest the case of the inveterate gambler who is, in fact, a risk lover. Curve C, diminishing marginal utility, is probably identified with the way most investors behave. In sum, constant marginal utility of return means that an investor is risk-neutral; decreasing marginal utility means that the investor is risk-averse; increasing marginal utility suggests that the investor likes risk.

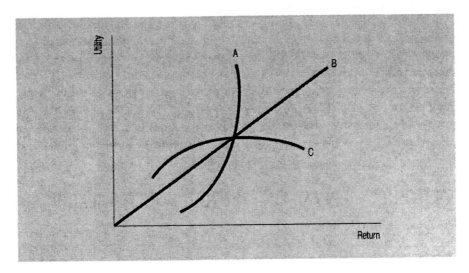

Fig 8.15 ● Marginal-utility curves

Given investors' preferences, what is the optimal portfolio?

The optimal portfolio for a risk-averse investor occurs at the point of tangency between the investor's highest indifference curve and the efficient set of portfolios. In Figure 8.16 this occurs at point O. This portfolio maximizes investor utility because the indifference curves reflect *investor preferences*, while the efficient set represents *portfolio possibilities*. Notice that curves U_2 and U_1 are

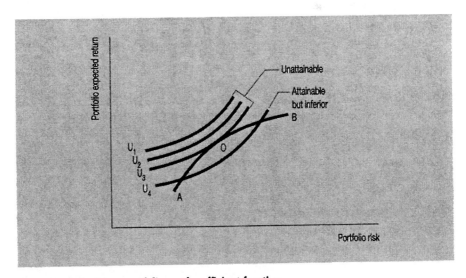

Fig 8.16 ● Selecting a portfolio on the efficient frontier

unattainable and that U_3 is the highest indifference curve for this investor that is tangent to the efficient frontier. On the other hand, U_4, though attainable, is inferior to U_3, which offers a higher expected return for the same risk (and therefore more utility).

A conservative investor would select portfolios on the left end of AB in Figure 8.16 because these portfolios have less risk and less expected return. Conversely, aggressive investors would choose portfolios towards the right of AB because these portfolios offer higher expected returns as well as higher risk.

PORTFOLIO RETURN AND RISK: THE ROLE OF DIVERSIFICATION

Individual securities, as we saw in Chapter 4, have risk-return characteristics of their own. Portfolios which are combinations of securities may, or may not, take on the aggregate characteristics of their individual parts. It is to whether they do or do not that we now turn.

Expected return from individual securities carries some degree of risk. *Risk* was defined as the standard deviation around the expected return. In effect, we equated a security's risk with the variability of its return. More dispersion or variability about a security's expected return meant the security was riskier than one with less dispersion.

The simple fact that securities carry differing degrees of expected risk leads most investors to the notion of holding more than one security at a time, in an attempt to spread risks by not putting all their eggs into one basket. Diversification of one's holdings is intended to reduce risk in an economy in which every asset's returns are subject to some degree of uncertainty.

Efforts to spread and minimize risk take the form of diversification.

Portfolio return

The return of a portfolio simply consists of the weighted average of the expected return E(R) of each asset in the portfolio. This is illustrated in Equation (4):

$$E(R) = \sum_{i=1}^{n} X_{i\mu_i} \qquad (4)$$

where

    E(R) = expected portfolio return
    X_i = proportion of security i in the portfolio
    μ_i = expected return of security i

For a two-asset portfolio this reduces to Equation (5):

$$E(R) = X_1\mu_1 + (1 - X_1)\mu_2 \tag{5}$$

The return of each investment, weighted for its size as a proportion of the whole, may be added to give a weighted average return as in Equation (6):

$$R_P = X_1R_1 + X_2R_2 + \dots + X_nR_n \tag{6}$$

where

R_P is the return on the portfolio

R_1, R_2, R_n are the returns of the individual investments in the portfolio

X_1, X_2, X_n are the proportions in which the assets are held.

An example of portfolio expected returns is given in Table 8.6.

Table 8.6 • Portfolio returns weighted average of expected returns

	μ	Weights (X_i) (25% of $100,000)
IBM	14	0.25
Microsoft	13	0.25
Amazon	20	0.25
Yahoo	18	0.25
Expected Return =		16.25%

The components of the risk of the portfolio are given in Figure 8.17.

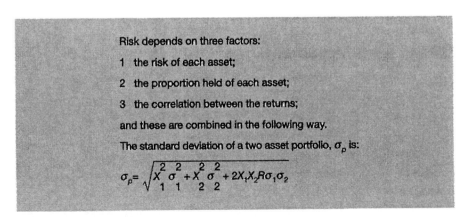

Risk depends on three factors:

1 the risk of each asset;

2 the proportion held of each asset;

3 the correlation between the returns;

and these are combined in the following way.

The standard deviation of a two asset portfolio, σ_p, is:

$$\sigma_p = \sqrt{X_1^2\sigma_1^2 + X_2^2\sigma_2^2 + 2X_1X_2R\sigma_1\sigma_2}$$

Fig 8.17 • Portfolio risk

In order to best understand the importance of the correlation coefficient between the returns on assets when calculating the risk of the whole portfolio, it is useful to break down the components of the variance of the portfolio of two or more stocks. See Table 8.7.

x_1 = proportion invested in stock 1

x_2 = proportion invested in stock 2

σ_1^2 = variance of return on stock 1

σ_2^2 = variance of return on stock 2

$\sigma_{1,2}$ = covariance of stocks 1 and 2 $(P_{1,2}\,\sigma_1\sigma_2)$

$P_{1,2}$ = correlation between returns on stocks 1 and 2.

Table 8.7 ● Components of the portfolio variance

	Stock 1	Stock 2
Stock 1	$x_1^2\sigma_1^2$	$x_1x_2\sigma_{1,2} = x_1x_2P_{1,2}\sigma_1\sigma_2$
Stock 2	$x_1x_2\sigma_{12} = x_1x_2P_{1,2}\sigma_1\sigma_2$	$x_2^2\sigma_2^2$

Tables 8.8, 8.9 and 8.10 illustrate that where a portfolio is split with 50 per cent being invested in stock W and 50 per cent being invested in stock Y that the expected return of the portfolio does not change when the correlation coefficient (r) varies. However, the risk of the portfolio varies from 22.6 per cent if r = +1.0, to 20.6 per cent if r = +0.65, to 0 if r = −1.0. The portfolio risk, as illustrated in Tables 8.8–8.10, is not a weighted average of the standard deviations, it depends on the correlation coefficient between the returns on the two stocks.

Table 8.8 ● Expected return and risk (r = +1.0)

Year	ER(W)%	ER(Y)%	Portfolio WY%
1995	(10)	(10)	(10)
1996	40	40	40
1997	(5)	(5)	(5)
1998	35	35	35
1999	15	15	15
Average Return	15	15	15
Standard Deviation	22.6	22.6	22.6

Diversification is a waste of time: portfolio risk is not reduced at all.

Table 8.9 ● Expected return and risk ($r = +0.65$)

Year	ER(W)%	ER(Y)%	Portfolio WY%
1995	40	28	34
1996	(10)	20	5
1997	35	41	38
1998	(5)	(17)	(11)
1999	15	3	9
Average Return	15	15	15
Standard Deviation	22.6	22.6	20.6

Diversification is better news: portfolio risk comes down slightly.

Table 8.10 ● Expected return and risk ($r = +1.0$)

Year	ER(W)%	ER(Y)%	Portfolio WY%
1995	40	(10)	$20 + -5 = 15$
1996	(10)	40	$-5 + 20 = 15$
1997	35	(5)	$17\frac{1}{2}\ 2\frac{1}{2} = 15$
1998	(5)	35	$-2\frac{1}{2} + 17\frac{1}{2} = 15$
1999	15	15	$7\frac{1}{2} + 7\frac{1}{2} = 15$
Average Return	15	15	15
Standard Deviation	22.6	22.6	0.0

Diversification is very good news: risk falls to zero.

THE CAPITAL MARKET LINE (CML)

Having illustrated the importance of the correlation coefficient to a diversified portfolio, it is now important to introduce the concept of Capital Market Line.

What does the Capital Market Line show?

The CML shows the equilibrium conditions that prevail in the market for efficient portfolios. All investors will hold portfolios along the capital market line. *The CML shows the efficient risk/return trade-off for all investors.*

How do we get to the Capital Market Line?

Looking at Figure 8.18, point C is the asset mix for a risk-averse investor and point A is the asset mix for a risk-loving investor. Applying the separation theorem, as discussed earlier, an investor at point C can improve the risk return profile by investing in asset mix M which raises the risk return profile.

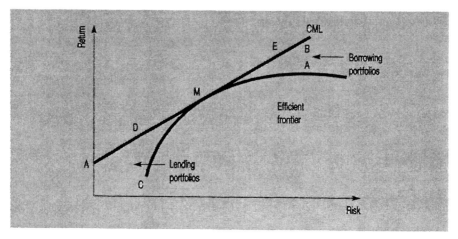

Fig 8.18 ● The Capital Market Line (CML)

The Capital Market Line and the components of its slope

The slope of the CML is the market price of risk for efficient portfolios. It indicates the additional return that the market demands for each percentage increase in a portfolios risk, that is, in its standard deviation of return. See Figure 8.19.

To take an example, assume that the expected return on portfolio M is 13 per cent, with a standard deviation of 25 per cent, and that RF is 7 per cent. The slope of the CML would be:

$$(0.13 - 0.07) / 0.25 = 0.24$$

In our example a risk premium of 0.24 indicates that the market demands this amount of return for each percentage increase in a portfolio's risk.

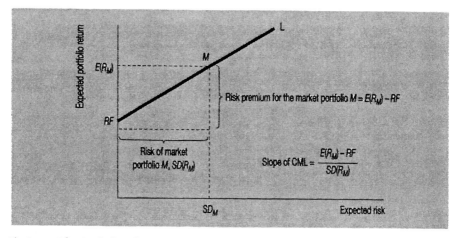

Fig 8.19 ● The Capital Market Line and the components of its slope

CHAPTER 9

Capital market theory

INTRODUCTION

Capital market theory is an extension of portfolio theory. Portfolio theory considers how investors should act in selecting an optimal portfolio of risky securities. Capital market theory extends portfolio theory by asking: what happens to security markets if all investors seek portfolios of risky securities under the Markowitz framework? How will this affect equilibrium security prices and returns? The model enabling us to analyze this is the capital asset pricing model (CAPM). CAPM allows us to measure the relevant risk of an individual security as well as to assess the relationship between risk and the returns from investing. Before we discuss the CAPM it is useful to reiterate some of the key findings from Chapter 8.

THE EFFICIENT FRONTIER REVISITED

A key idea in capital market theory is the concept of the efficient frontier. Figure 9.1 illustrates the principle. The vertical axis refers to expected return, the horizontal axis refers to risk as measured by the standard deviation of return, and the shaded area represents the set of all the possible portfolios that could be obtained from a given group of securities by varying the proportionate holdings of each security. A certain level of return and a certain risk will be

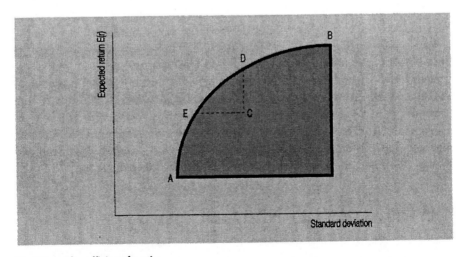

Fig 9.1 ● The efficient frontier

associated with each possible portfolio. Thus each portfolio is represented by a single point in the shaded area of Figure 9.1.

What is the point of the portfolio possibility set, you may ask? It was this idea, first developed by Nobel Prize winner Harry Markowitz, as discussed in Chapters 2 and 8, that launched the whole portfolio management industry. Building on Markowitz's ideas, and those of others, came the idea of the capital asset pricing model (CAPM) to which we return throughout this book.

The Markowitz model and the CAPM have three common assumptions.

1 Investors are risk-averse expected utility maximizers.

2 Investors choose portfolios based on their expected mean and variance of return.

3 A single holding period is assumed that is the same for all investors.

In addition, the following assumptions are also frequently made.

4 Unrestricted borrowing and lending at the risk-free rate is possible.

5 Investors have homogeneous expectations regarding the means, variances and covariances of security returns.

6 No taxes and no market imperfections such as transactions costs exist.

The importance of these assumptions is that the concept of efficiency can be imposed on the choice of a portfolio. The efficiency set is represented by the upper left-hand boundary of the shaded area between points A and B. Portfolios along this efficient frontier dominate those below the line. Specifically, these portfolios offer higher returns than those of an equivalent level of risk or, alternatively, entail less risk at an equivalent level of return. For example, note that portfolio C, which does not lie on the efficient boundary, is dominated by portfolios D and E, which do lie on the efficient boundary. Portfolio D offers greater return than portfolio C at the same level of risk, while portfolio E entails less risk than portfolio C at the same level of return.

Rational investors will thus prefer to hold efficient portfolios – that is, ones on the line and not those below it. The particular portfolio that an individual investor selects from the efficient frontier depends on the investor's degree of aversion to risk. An investor who is highly averse to risk will hold one on the lower left-hand segment of the frontier, while an investor who is less risk-averse will hold one on the upper portion. In more technical terms, the selection depends on the investor's risk aversion, which might be characterized by the nature and shape of the investor's risk-return utility function.

SELECTING AN OPTIMAL PORTFOLIO OF RISKY ASSETS

Once the efficient set of portfolios is determined using the Markowitz model, investors must select from this set the portfolio most appropriate for them.

The Markowitz model does not specify one optimum portfolio. It generates the efficient set of portfolios, all of which, by definition, are optimal portfolios (for a given level of expected return or risk).

In economics in general, and within financial economics in particular, we assume investors are risk averse. This means that investors, if given a choice, will not take a 'fair gamble', defined as one with an expected pay-off of zero and equal probabilities of a gain or a loss. In effect, with a fair gamble, the disutility from the potential loss is greater than the utility from the potential gain. The greater the risk aversion, the greater the disutility from the potential loss.

To select return-risk combination that will satisfy an individual investor's personal preferences, indifference curves, which are assumed to be known for an investor, are used. These curves, shown in Figure 8.16 on page 205 for a risk-averse investor, describe investor preferences for risk and return. Each indifference curve represents all combinations of portfolios that are equally desirable to a particular investor.

SYSTEMATIC AND NON-SYSTEMATIC RISK

In discussing the CAPM it is essential to stress the importance of distinguishing between two types of risk, systematic risk and non-systematic risk.

The risk applicable to common stocks can be divided into two types:

1 a general component representing that portion in the variability of a stock's total returns that is directly associated with overall movements in general economic (or stock market) activity; and

2 a specific (issuer) component, representing that portion in the variability of a stock's total return that is not related to the variability in general economic (market) activity.

These two components, referred to in investment analysis as systematic risk and non-systematic risk, or by the alternative names shown in Figure 9.3 below, are additive:

Total risk	=	Systematic risk + non-systematic risk
	=	Market risk + non-market risk
	=	Non-diversifiable risk + diversifiable risk

Variability in a security's total returns that is directly associated with overall movements in the general market or economy is called *systematic (market) risk*. Virtually all securities have some systematic risk, whether bonds or stocks, because systematic risk directly encompasses interest rate risk, market risk and inflation risk. Let us concentrate here on the systematic risk of common stocks.

After the non-systematic risk is eliminated, what is left is the non-diversifiable portion, or the market risk (systematic part). This part of the risk is inescapable because no matter how well investors diversify their portfolios, the risk of the overall market cannot be avoided. If the stock market declines sharply, most stocks will be adversely affected; most stocks will depreciate in value, and vice versa. These movements occur regardless of what any single investor does. See Figure 9.2.

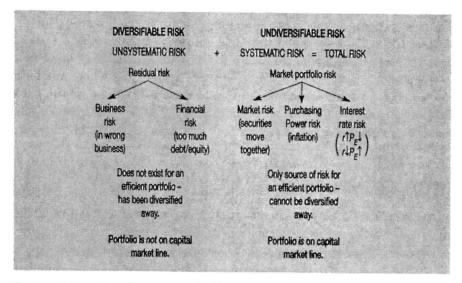

Fig 9.2 ● Systematic and non-systematic risk

Investors can construct a diversified portfolio and eliminate part of the total risk, i.e. the diversifiable or non-market part (non-systematic risk). Figure 9.3 illustrates the concept of declining non-systematic risk in a portfolio of securities. As more securities are added, the non-systematic risk becomes smaller and smaller, and the total risk for the portfolio approaches its systematic risk. Since diversification cannot reduce systematic risk, total portfolio risk can be reduced no lower than the total risk of the market portfolio. So diversification can substantially reduce the unique risk of a portfolio. However, Figure 9.3 indicates that no matter how much we diversify, we cannot eliminate systematic risk. The declining total risk curve in Figure 9.3 levels off.

How many securities does it take to eliminate most or all of the non-systematic risk? It has become commonplace to say that approximately 10–15 securities will provide a diversified portfolio. However, newer evidence suggests that at the very least 30 stocks, and perhaps more, are needed for a *well-diversified* portfolio.

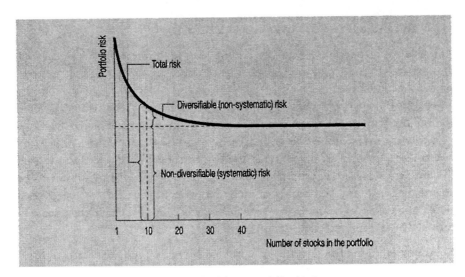

Fig 9.3 ● Systematic and non-systematic risk as portfolio size increases

The key contribution made by Markowitz is that all the risk of a fully diversified portfolio is systematic risk and the stock contribution to the risk of a fully
diversified portfolio depends on its sensitivity to this systematic risk (1952). As
is shown in Figure 9.4, this market sensitivity is known as beta.

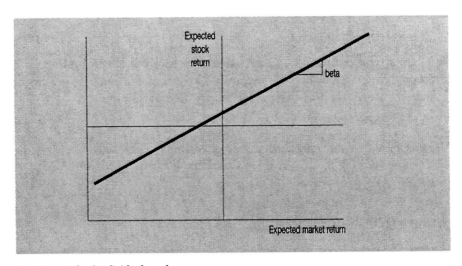

Fig 9.4 ● Risk of individual stocks

THE CAPITAL ASSET PRICING MODEL (CAPM)

The CAPM is concerned with the equilibrium relationship between the risk and expected return on risky assets. The CAPM rests at the heart of modern financial economics.

The CAPM involves a set of predictions concerning equilibrium expected returns on risky assets. Capital market theory builds on the previous work of Markowitz. Investors are assumed to diversify their portfolios, following Markowitz's principles, diversifying their portfolios towards that position on the efficient frontier that matches their market return profile. In order to be able to aggregate the behaviours of many individuals, the CAPM then makes a series of assumptions about investor behaviour some of which we discussed earlier. These assumptions are as follows.

1 All investors use the same information with regard to the expected returns, the variance of returns and the correlation matrix.

2 All investors have the same one-period time horizon.

3 All investors can borrow or lend money at the risk-free rate of return (designated RF).

4 There are no transaction costs.

5 There are no personal income taxes – investors are indifferent between capital gains and dividends.

6 There is no inflation.

7 There are many investors, and no single investor can affect the price of a stock through his or her buying and selling decisions. Investors are price-takers and act as if prices are unaffected by their own trades.

8 Capital markets are in equilibrium.

Most of these assumptions can be relaxed without significant effects on the capital asset pricing model or its implications; in other words, the CAPM is robust.

So where do these assumptions take us?

The implications of these assumptions can be summed up as follows.

1 All investors will choose to hold the aggregate market portfolio, which includes all assets in existence.

2 This market portfolio will be on the Markowitz efficient frontier and will be the optimal risky portfolio to hold.

3   All efficient portfolios will plot on the trade-off between the standard deviation and the expected return for efficient portfolios (the CML), and all securities and inefficient portfolios will plot on the trade-off between systematic risk and expected return (the Security Market Line (SML) discussed below).

We consider the implications of these findings below.

Figure 9.5 illustrates the market portfolio available to rational investors who would have open to them the choice of an efficient portfolio set plus the availability of a risk free asset. All investors would want to be on the optimal line RF-M-L. Point M is the optimal portfolio of risky assets.

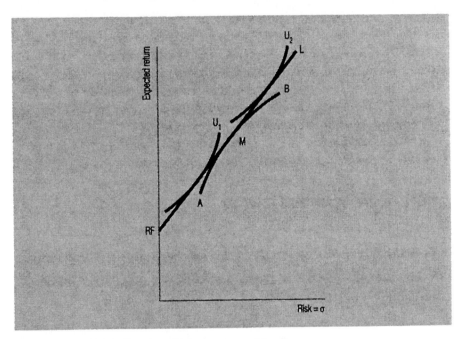

Fig 9.5 ● The efficient frontier with borrowing and lending

But why would all investors hold identical risky portfolios? As all investors use the same Markowitz analysis and assume the same properties about risk and return they will arrive at the same optimal risky portfolio, and it will be the market portfolio, designated M. The reasoning behind this revolves around the concept of diversifiable versus undiversifiable risk, discussed earlier. The distinction between systematic and unsystematic risk is, in fact, at the heart of the CAPM.

As discussed earlier modern portfolio theory divides the risk of each security (or each portfolio of securities such as a mutual fund) into two parts: systematic and unsystematic. Systematic risk (or market risk) is the risk associated with the correlation between the return on the security and the return on the market portfolio. Unsystematic risk is the 'leftover' risk, which is associated with the variability of returns of that security alone. The distinction between the two components of risk is important because they behave differently as one increases the number of securities in the portfolio. The unsystematic component of risk can be diversified away because it gets 'averaged out' as the number of securities gets larger, and so it can be ignored in a well-diversified portfolio. Systematic risk, on the other hand, cannot be diversified away and investors expect to be compensated for bearing it.

How does the CAPM connect the CML and the SML?

The CAPM is an equilibrium model that encompasses two important relationships: the Capital Market Line (CML) and the Security Market Line (SML). The CML, which was discussed in Chapter 8, specifies the equilibrium relationship between *expected return and total risk for efficiently diversified portfolios*. So the CML shows the equilibrium conditions that prevail in the market for efficient portfolios. All investors will hold portfolios along the capital market line. *The CML shows the efficient risk/return trade-off for all investors.*

The second relationship, the Security Market Line, specifies the equilibrium relationship between *expected return and systematic risk*.

Capital asset pricing model: a summary

It is complicated but it can be reduced to five simple ideas.

1 Investors can eliminate some risks by diversifying across sectors and regions.

2 Some risks, such as global recession, cannot be eliminated, so a fully diversified portfolio will still have risk.

3 Investors must be rewarded with higher returns if they invest in risky assets.

4 The return on a specific investment depends only on the extent to which it affects systematic risk.

5 Systematic risk can be measured by beta – the relationship between the investments risk and the markets.

THE SECURITY MARKET LINE

For well-diversified portfolios, non-systematic risk tends to go to zero, and the only relevant risk is systematic risk, measured by beta. Since we assume that investors are concerned only with expected return and risk, the only dimensions of a security that need be of concern are expected return and beta.

All investments and all portfolios of investments lie along a straight line in the return-to-beta space. To determine this line we need only connect the intercept (beta of zero, or riskless security) and the market portfolio (beta of one and return of R_M). These two points identify the straight line shown in Figure 9.6. The equation of a straight line is:

$$R_i = \alpha + b\beta_i$$

The first point on the straight line in Figure 9.6 is the riskless asset with a beta of zero, so:

$$R_F = \alpha + b(0)$$
$$R_F = \alpha$$

The second point on the line is the market portfolio with a beta of 1. Thus:

$$
\begin{aligned}
R_M &= \alpha + b(1) \\
R_M - \alpha &= b \\
(R_M - R_F) &= b
\end{aligned}
$$

Combining the two results gives us:

$$R_i = R_F + \beta_i(R_M - R_F)$$

This is a key relationship called the security market line and is illustrated in Figure 9.6. It describes the expected return for all assets and portfolios of assets, *efficient or not*. The difference between the expected return on any two assets can be related simply to their difference in beta. The higher beta is for any security, the higher must be its expected return, and vice versa.

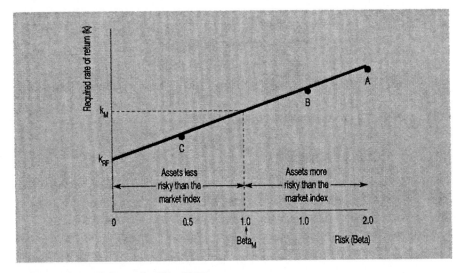

Fig 9.6 ● The security market line (SML)

If investors are to seek higher expected returns, they must assume a larger risk as measured by beta, the relative measure of systematic risk. The trade-off between expected return and risk must always be positive. In Figure 9.6 the vertical axis can be thought of as the expected return for an asset. In equilibrium, investors require a minimum expected return before they will invest in a particular security. That is, given its risk, a security must offer some minimum expected return before a given investor can be persuaded to purchase it. Thus, in discussing the SML concept, we are simultaneously talking about the required and expected rate of return.

So the SML depicts the trade-off between risk and return for ALL assets, individual securities and inefficient portfolios. The CML, it will be remembered, depicts the risk-return trade-off if the financial markets are in equilibrium. However, it is limited in its application in that it applies only to efficient portfolios and cannot be used to assess the equilibrium expected return on a single security.

Figure 9.7 illustrates how both aggressive investors and conservative investors can both take advantage of the SML concept.

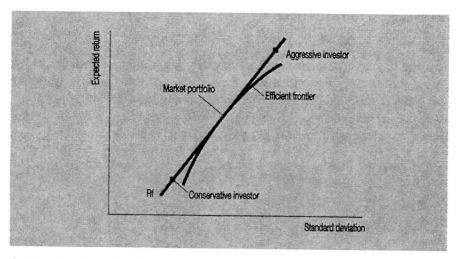

Fig 9.7 ● Security Market Line and the efficient frontier

How can investors use the SML?

The SML has important implications for security prices. In equilibrium, each security should lie on the SML because the expected return on the security should be that needed to compensate investors for the systematic risk.

What happens if investors determine that a security does not lie on the SML? In Figure 9.9 two securities are plotted around the SML. Security X has a high expected return derived from fundamental analysis and plots above the SML; security Y has a low expected return and plots below the SML. Which is undervalued?

Security X, plotting above the SML, is undervalued because it offers more expected return than investors require, given its level of systematic risk. Investors require a minimum expected return of $E(R_X)$, but security X, according to fundamental analysis, is offering $E(R_X^1)$. If investors recognize this, they will purchase security X, because it offers more return than required. This demand will drive up the price of X, as more of it is purchased. The return will be driven down, until it is at the level indicated by the SML.

Now consider security Y. This security, according to investors' fundamental analysis, does not offer enough expected return given its level of systematic risk. Investors require $E(R_Y)$ for security Y, based on the SML, but Y offers only $E(R_Y^1)$. As investors recognize this, they will sell security Y because it offers less than the required return. This increase in the supply of Y will drive down its price. The return will be driven up for new buyers because any dividends paid are now relative to a lower price, as is any expected price appreciation. The price will fall until the expected return rises enough to reach the SML and the security is once again in equilibrium.

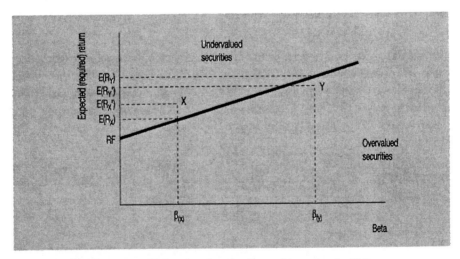

Fig 9.8 ● Identifying overvalued and undervalued securities using the SML

EXPECTED RETURN, BETA AND THE CAPM

The capital asset price model formally relates the expected rate of return for any security or portfolio with the relevant risk measure. The CAPM's *expected return–beta relationship* is the most-often cited form of the relationship. Beta is the relevant measure of risk that cannot be diversified away in a portfolio of securities and, as such, is the measure that investors should consider in their portfolio management decision process.

The CAPM in its expected return–beta relationship form is a simple but elegant statement. It says that the expected rate of return on an asset is a function of the two components of the required rate of return: the risk-free rate and the risk premium. Thus,

$$k_i = \text{Risk-free rate} + \text{Risk premium}$$
$$= RF + \beta_i[E(R_M) - RF]$$

where

$$k_i = \text{the required rate of return on asset } i$$
$$E(R_M) = \text{the expected rate of return on the market portfolio}$$
$$\beta_i = \text{the beta coefficient for asset } i$$

This relationship provides an explicit measure of the risk premium. It is the product for the beta for a particular security i and the market risk premium, $E(R_M) - RF$ thus,

Risk premium for security i
$$= \beta i \text{ (market risk premium)}$$
$$= \beta i \left[E(R_M) - RF\right]$$

The CAPM's expected return–beta relationship is a statement that formalizes the basis of investments, which is that the greater the risk assumed, the greater the expected (required) return should be. This relationship states that the investor requires (expects) a return on a risky asset equal to the return on a risk-free asset plus a risk premium, and the greater the risk assumed, the greater the risk premium.

Assume that the beta for IBM is 1.15. Also assume that RF is 0.05 and the expected return on the market is 0.12. The required return for IBM can be calculated as:

$$k_{IBM} = 0.05 + 1.15(0.12 - 0.05)$$
$$= 13.05\%$$

The required (or expected) return for IBM is, as it should be, larger than that of the market because IBM's beta is larger; once again, the greater the risk assumed the larger the required return. Figure 9.9 illustrates the relationship between the expected return from a security and its beta.

The role beta plays for investors

Beta is a measure of the systematic risk of a security that cannot be avoided through diversification. Beta is a *relative measure* of risk – the risk of an individual stock relative to the market portfolio of all stocks. If the security's returns move more (less) than the market's returns, then as the latter change, the security's returns have more (less) *volatility* (fluctuations in price) than

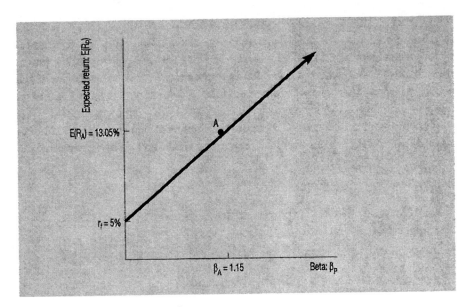

Fig 9.9 ● Expected return versus beta

those of the market. It is important to note that beta measures a security's volatility, or fluctuations in price relative to a benchmark, the market portfolio of all stocks.

Securities with different slopes have different sensitivities to the returns of the market index. If the slope of this relationship for a particular security is a 45 degree angle, as shown for security B in Figure 9.10, the beta is 1.0. This means that for every 1 per cent change in the market's return, *on average* this security's returns change 1 per cent. The market portfolio has a beta of 1.0.

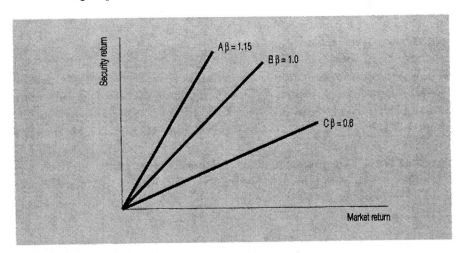

Fig 9.10 ● Illustrative betas of 1.5(A), 1.0(B), and 0.6(C)

In Figure 9.10 Security A's beta of 1.15 indicates that, on *average*, security returns are 1.15 times as volatile as market returns, both up and down. A security whose returns rise or fall on average 15 per cent when the market return rises or falls 10 per cent is said to be an aggressive, or volatile, security. If the line is less steep than the 45 degree line, beta is less than 1.0; this indicates that, *on average*, a stock's returns have less volatility than the market as a whole. For example, security C's beta of 0.6 indicates that if the market moves up or down by 10 per cent this stock moves up or down by only 6 per cent.

What is the scoreboard on the CAPM?

The CAPM states that the expected return on a given security or portfolio is determined by three factors:

1 the sensitivity of its return to that of the market portfolio (known as beta);

2 the return on the market portfolio itself; and

3 the risk-free rate.

Two problems arise in applying the CAPM to real-world investment. One problem concerns the definition of the 'market portfolio', and the second, the definition of the 'efficient portfolio'. Roll (1977) pointed out that the CAPM can never be definitely tested because, as a practical matter, it is impossible to define the 'market portfolio' with any degree of precision. Should foreign assets be included? How about commodities? Real estate? Antiques? Art? Some of these assets are traded so infrequently that it would be quite difficult to construct a reliable series of monthly returns. Finally, some assets, such as the present value of the investor's labour income, cannot be traded at all, yet they constitute an important part of the investor's overall 'portfolio'. Generally, as the definition of the 'market' becomes broader, the estimate of its monthly returns become less reliable.

The second problem is that no one truly 'efficient' portfolio exists that would be appropriate for all investors. Because research is costly, not all investors have access to the same information, nor do they have the same opinions and beliefs. As long as investors have differing expectations about the future risks and returns of various investments, they will not agree on the same 'efficient' portfolio but rather choose securities that have the best prospects according to their own judgement. In this case, instead of being efficient in some absolute sense, as Lintner (1965) showed, the market portfolio balances the divergent assessments of all investors.

CHAPTER 10

The efficient markets hypothesis

- Background
- Random walk theory
- The efficient markets hypothesis
- Implications of the efficient markets hypothesis for investors
- Testing for market efficiency
- Event studies
- The anomalies literature
- Efficient markets, the 1987 stock market crash and catastrophe theory

BACKGROUND

In the mid-1960s a group of professors, including the future Nobel laureate Paul Samuelson, discovered what became known as the efficient market hypothesis (1965a). It was a revolutionary proposition.

The gist of it is this: financial markets like Wall Street are made up of an army of investors actively seeking profits. If there is the slightest bit of breaking news that impinges on the value of stocks, these investors will pounce on it, swiftly driving shares up or down. In this way the market efficiently incorporates new information into stock prices. Obvious profit opportunities tend to vanish before they can be seized, and investors who chase them hoping to 'beat the market' will see their minimal gains more than offset by transaction costs.

There is more. If today's stock prices reflect all available information, then tomorrow's price movements must be unforeseeable, since any information that might be used to forecast them will have already been incorporated by traders into today's prices. Thus – paradoxically – the more efficient the stock market is, the more it will lurch unpredictably from day to day, like a drunkard meandering down the street. In other words, stock prices in an efficient market appear to take what economists call a 'random walk'.

Chapter 7 illustrated that the fundamental approach to security valuation focuses on the factors such as product demand, earnings dividends and management, in order to calculate an intrinsic value for the firm's securities. Investors reach their investment decisions by comparing this value with the current price of the security. These fundamentals are described in detail in Kettell (1998, 1999 and 2000).

In contrast, technical analysts, or chartists, as they are commonly called, believe that they can discern patterns in price or volume movements, and that by observing and studying the past behaviour patterns of given stocks, they can use this accumulated historical information to predict the future price movements in the security. Technical analysis comprises many different subjective approaches, but all have one thing in common – a belief that these past movements are very useful in predicting future movements.

In essence, the technician says that it is somewhat of an exercise in futility to evaluate accurately a myriad of detailed information, as the fundamentalist attempts to do. The technician chooses not to engage in this type of activity, but prefers to allow others to do it for him. Thus, after numerous analysts and investors evaluate the mountain of information on stocks, their undoubtedly diverse opinions will be manifested in the price and volume activity of the stocks in question. As this occurs, technicians act solely on the basis of that price and volume activity, without cluttering their minds with all the detail that they feel is superfluous to their analysis. They also believe that their price and volume analyses incorporate one factor that is not explicitly incorporated in the fundamentalist approach – namely, the psychology of the market.

RANDOM WALK THEORY

Can a series of historical stock prices or rates of return be an aid in predicting future stock prices or rates of return? This, in effect, is the question posed by the random-walk theory.

The empirical evidence in the random-walk literature existed before the theory was established. That is to say, empirical results were discovered first, and then an attempt was made to develop a theory that could possibly explain the results afterwards. After these initial occurrences, more results and more theory were uncovered. This has led then to a diversity of theories, which are generically called the theory of random walk.

THE EFFICIENT MARKET HYPOTHESIS

Imagine a world in which:

1 all investors have free access to currently available information about the future;

2 all investors are capable analysts; and

3 all investors pay close attention to market prices and adjust their holdings appropriately.

In such a market a security's price will be a good estimate of its intrinsic value, where intrinsic value is the present value of the security's future prospects, as estimated by well-informed and skillful analysts who use the information that is currently at hand. That is, an efficient market, defined as one in which every security's price equals its intrinsic value at all times, will exist.

It is advantageous to view the random-walk model or hypothesis as a special case of the more general efficient market model or hypothesis. In fact, one might more readily understand the distinctions and variations of the various forms of the more general efficient market hypothesis by viewing this hypothesis and its variations as lying on a continuum, with the so-called random-walk model at one end. It is necessary to briefly consider the three generally discussed forms of the efficient market hypothesis (EMH), namely the weak form, the semi-strong form and the strong form. These will be discussed in more detail later in this chapter.

Weak form

The weak form of the EMH says that the current prices of stocks already fully reflect all the information that is contained in the historical sequence of prices. Therefore, there is no benefit – as far as forecasting the future is concerned – in examining the historical sequence of prices. This weak form of the efficient market hypothesis is popularly known as the random-walk theory. Clearly, if this weak form of the efficient market hypothesis is true, it is a *direct* repudiation of technical analysis. If there is no value in studying past prices and past price changes, there is no value in technical analysis.

So a weak form efficient market is one where it is impossible to make abnormal profits (other than by chance) by using past prices to formulate buying and selling decisions.

Semi-strong form

The semi-strong form of the EMH says that current prices of stocks not only reflect all the informational content of historical prices, but also reflect all *publicly available knowledge* about the companies being studied. Furthermore, the semi-strong form says that efforts by analysts and investors to acquire and analyze public information will not yield consistently superior returns to the analyst. Examples of the type of public information that will not be of value on a consistent basis to the analyst are corporate reports, corporate announcements, information relating to corporate dividend policy, forthcoming stock splits and so forth.

In effect, the semi-strong form of the EMH maintains that as soon as information becomes publicly available, it is absorbed and reflected in stock prices. Even if this adjustment is not the correct one immediately, it will, in a very short time be properly analyzed by the market. Thus an analyst would have great difficulty trying to profit using fundamental analysis.

So the semi-strong form efficient market is one where it is impossible to make abnormal profits (other than by chance) by using publicly available information to formulate stock buying and selling decisions.

Strong form

The strong form of the EMH maintains that not only is publicly available information useless to the investor or analyst, but all information is useless. Specifically, no information that is available, be it public information or 'inside information' can be used to consistently earn superior investment returns. Figure 10.1 highlights that as the information set available to investors increases, so does the degree of market efficiency.

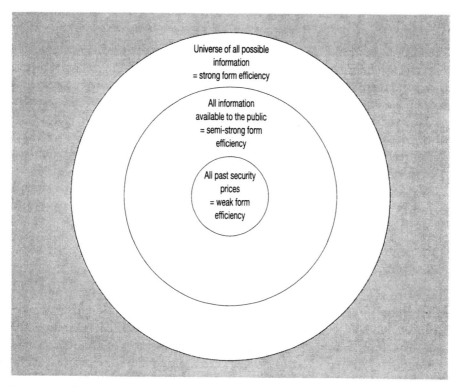

Fig 10.1 ● Subsets of market efficiency

The strong form of the efficient market hypothesis states that two conditions are met: first, that successive price changes or changes in return are independent; and second, that these successive price changes or return changes are identically distributed, i.e. these distributions will repeat themselves over time. In a practical sense, this seems to imply that in a random-walk world, stock prices will at any time fully reflect all publicly available information, and furthermore, that when new information becomes available, stock prices will instantaneously adjust to reflect it.

The more general efficient market model, when interpreted loosely, acknowledges that the markets may have some imperfections, such as transactions costs, information costs, and delays in getting pertinent information to all market participants; but it states that these potential sources of market inefficiency do not exist to such a degree that it is possible to develop trading systems whose expected profits or returns will be in excess of expected normal equilibrium returns or profits. Generally, we define *equilibrium profits* as those that can be earned by following a simple buy-and-hold strategy rather than a more complex, mechanical system. Thus, we see that the random-walk model represents a special, restrictive case of the efficient market model.

IMPLICATIONS OF THE EFFICIENT MARKET HYPOTHESIS FOR INVESTORS

The existence of securities markets that are at least semi-strong form efficient strongly indicates the following implications about investment management.

1 Stock prices cannot be predicted; prices will be affected by events in the future that at present are unknown.

2 Analysis of individual securities in an attempt to find undervalued ones will not increase portfolio returns. The costs of obtaining the information will probably offset any increased returns that are earned. It is extremely unlikely that the analysis of public information using standard techniques will identify securities that will out-perform the market.

3 Transaction costs should be minimized. Investors should adopt a buy-and-hold philosophy and trade as little as possible.

4 Economies of scale should be exploited in portfolio management. Searching for appropriate securities requires the same effort whether spending small amounts or large amounts. Thus it is much more efficient to manage large sums of money than smaller amounts.

5 The best portfolio management style is a passive one. Rather than attempting to pick winners and losers and trading stocks frequently, the investor should invest in a diversified portfolio that will be held through time. The portfolio should have a level of risk appropriate for the particular investor, and stocks should be selected based on their risk. Taxes and cash flow requirements of the investor should also be considered.

6 There will always be winners and losers in the market. Just because some investors or fund managers have outperformed the market over an extended period does not necessarily mean the market is not efficient. Either these individuals have unique abilities not possessed by others, or they are luckier than the rest. The problem is to identify who will outperform the market in the future.

Indeed, there is much anecdotal evidence about the success of certain investors which can be very misleading. It could be argued that their performance is merely due to chance. Think of a simple model in which half of the time the stock market has an annual return greater than Treasury bills (an 'up' market) and the other half of the time its return is less than Treasury bills (a 'down' market). With many investors attempting to forecast whether the stock market will be up or down each year and acting accordingly, in an efficient market about half the investors will be right in any given year and half will be wrong. The next year, half of those who were right the first year will be right the second year too. Thus, $\frac{1}{4}\left(=\frac{1}{2}\times\frac{1}{2}\right)$ of all the investors will have been right both years. About half of the surviving investors will be right in the third year, so in total $\frac{1}{8}\left(=\frac{1}{2}\times\frac{1}{2}\times\frac{1}{2}\right)$ of all the investors can show that they were right all three years. Thus, it can be seen that $\left(\frac{1}{2}\right)^T$ investors will be correct every year over a span of T years. Hence if $T = 6$, then 1/64 of the investors will have been correct all five years, but only, it can be argued, because they were lucky, not because they were skillful.

TESTING FOR MARKET EFFICIENCY

Over the years an impressive body of literature has been developed describing empirical tests of the random walk. It is useful to summarize the methodology of some of these tests used to determine if markets are perfectly efficient, reasonably efficient or not efficient at all. Three methodologies are discussed here, Serial-Correlation Tests, Runs Tests and Filter Tests, although other methodologies have been employed.

Serial-correlation tests

Since the random walk theory is interested in testing for independence between successive price changes, correlation tests are particularly appropriate. These tests determine whether price changes or proportionate price changes in some future period are related. For example, we are interested in seeing if price changes in a period $t + 1$ are correlated to price changes in the preceding period, period t. If, in fact, price changes are correlated, points plotted on a graph will tend to lie along a straight line. In Figure 10.2 we see such a relationship.

Figure 10.2 (a) implies that, on average, a price rise in period t is followed by a price rise in period $t + 1$, implying a correlation coefficient of close to 1.

Figure 10.2 (b) implies that, on average, a price decline in period $t + 1$ follows a price rise in period t; implying a correlation coefficient of close to -1.

Figure 10.2 (c), in which there does not appear any linear relationship in the scatter diagram, implies a correlation coefficient close to zero. In other words, the correlation coefficient can take on a value ranging from -1 to $+1$; a positive number indicating a direct correlation.

Runs tests

There is a potential problem, however, when one uses a correlation coefficient to evaluate the possibility of independence in a particular series. This problem arises because correlation coefficients can be dominated by extreme values. That is, an extremely large or extremely low value or two in the series can

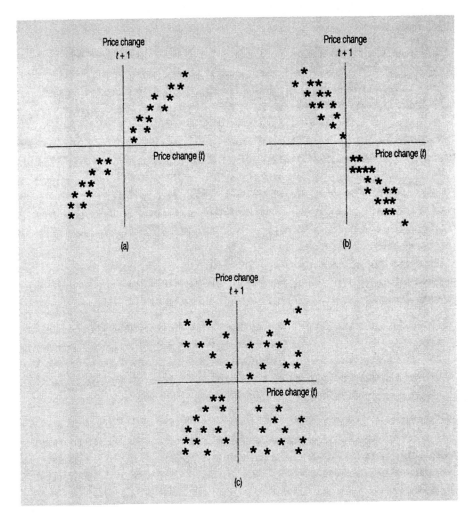

Fig 10.2 • Scatter diagrams to 'observe' correlation

unduly influence the results of the calculation used to determine the correlation coefficient. To overcome this possible shortcoming, some researchers have employed what is known as the runs test.

Runs tests ignore the absolute values of the numbers in the series and observe only their sign. The researchers then merely count the number of runs – consecutive sequences of signs – in the same direction. For example, the sequence – – – + + + – – – has three runs. The actual number of runs observed is then compared with the number that are to be expected from a series of randomly generated price changes.

Filter tests

The empirical tests of random walk examined thus far have been aimed at testing directly whether successive price or return changes are in fact independent, or, to put it in statistical terms, that their serial-correlation coefficients are not statistically significantly different from zero. If this is so, then an inference can be made that stock price changes appear to be random, and therefore it would be extremely difficult to develop successful mechanical trading systems. It is, however, necessary to discuss briefly another set of tests that examine the random-walk hypothesis from a different, but more direct, approach. Categorized as filter tests, they have been developed as direct tests of specific mechanical trading strategies. In other words, no inferences about such trading strategies need be made, for the approach is to examine directly the validity of specific systems.

One such test is based on the premise that once a movement in price has surpassed a given percentage movement, the security's price will continue to move in the same direction. This gives the following rule.

> If the daily closing price of a security moves up at least X per cent, buy the security until its price moves down at least X per cent from a subsequent high, at which time simultaneously sell and go short. The short position should be maintained until the price rises at least X per cent above a subsequent low, at which time cover and buy.

The selection of a high filter will cut down the number of transactions and will lead to fewer false starts or signals, but it will also decrease the potential profit because investors would have missed the initial portion of the move. Conversely, the selection of a smaller filter will ensure that investors share in the great bulk of the security's price movement, but they will have the disadvantage of performing many transactions with their accompanying high costs, as well as often operating on false signals.

What is the outcome of tests of market efficiency?

Empirical tests of market efficiency demonstrate that US security markets are highly efficient, discounting relevant information about investment values into security prices quickly and accurately. Investors cannot easily expect to earn abnormal profits trading on publicly available information, particularly once the costs of research and transactions are considered. Nevertheless, numerous pockets of unexplained abnormal returns have been identified which are known as the 'anomalies literature', and it is to these that we now turn.

EVENT STUDIES

Event study methodology is a commonly used empirical tool in research into security prices. The objective of an event study is to determine whether security holders earn abnormal returns in response to the arrival of information on a specific event. An event may be related to the release of company-specific information (e.g. an earnings announcement), a government action (e.g. a change in the tax law), or any other well-defined instance that may result in a re-evaluation of security prices. The focus of this analysis is upon an *event period*, which is a period of time during which information concerning an event reaches market participants. An abnormal return is the difference between an observed return and the expected return during the event period.

The analysis of abnormal returns is basically the analysis of forecast errors. The expected return is a forecasted return for the event period, where the forecast is often developed using data from a benchmark period. The benchmark period is selected to represent the typical return for the security in the absence of the event. This benchmark period may lie before the event, following the event, or both before and after the event. The key element is to make sure that the benchmark period is not contaminated by the arrival of information concerning the particular event.

There are many variations in event study methodologies. These variations occur primarily in the determination of the expected return. The expected return may be generated using:

1   a market model;

2   a mean-adjusted model; or

3   a market-adjusted model.

If the market model approach is used, parameters are estimated, using regression analysis, which represent the relation between the returns on the security and the returns on a market index. The expected return during the event period is calculated using the estimated parameters and the return on the market during the event period. If the mean-adjusted model approach is used, the mean return is calculated for the security (or for securities of similar risk) during the benchmark period. This mean return is then used as the expected return during the event period. If the market-adjusted model approach is used, then the return on the market during the event period is the expected return for the individual security during the event period.

Several problems arise in performing an event study. These problems include:

1   the choice of market index for models that require an index;

2   statistical problems, relating to the independence or observations when events are clustered (either by time or by risk);

3 the handling of missing returns; and

4 the potential for changing variances of returns.

Once the abnormal returns for individual cases are calculated, these returns are accumulated across securities to allow tests of hypotheses. Tests of the statistical significance of these abnormal returns are performed to determine whether the returns for the sample (or for a sub-sample of cases) are different from zero.

THE ANOMALIES LITERATURE

Until recently the proponents of the EMH were so strong that it was difficult to publish an article in an academic journal which questioned its robustness. From the beginning of the 1980s empirical evidence started to emerge that there were so called anomalies, empirical regularities that appeared to be inconsistent with the EMH. We concentrate here on various groups of these regularities, namely calendar effects, the small firm effect and the relationship between the return to securities and market-to-book ratios, earnings-price ratios and firm size. These have been well summarized by Blake (1999).

Calendar effects

These occur when excess returns from stocks can be achieved due to events associated with specific times of the day, days of the week or months of the year. The five most persistent of these calendar effects are: the *January effect*, the *turn-of-the-month effect*, the *Monday* (or *weekend*) *effect*, the *day-end effect* and the *holiday effect*.

Rozeff and Kinney (1976), using data on equities listed on the New York Stock Exchange, found that, between 1904 and 1974, the average return on shares in January exceeded the average return on shares for the other 11 months by 3.06 per cent. Ariel (1987) found that returns during the first half of any month (defined to include the last business day of the previous month) were much higher than the returns during the second half of the month. Lakonishok and Smidt (1988) found that the turn-of-the-month effect was actually concentrated in the first three trading days of the month. French (1980) and Gibbons and Hess (1981) found that the average return on shares was negative on Mondays, whereas it was positive for the other days of the week. The French study, for example, found that the average returns on US shares over the period 1953 to 1977 for each day of the week (beginning on Monday) were as follows:

- −0.17 per cent, Mondays

- 0.02 per cent, Tuesdays

- 0.10 per cent, Wednesdays

- 0.04 per cent, Thursdays

- 0.09 per cent, Fridays.

Harris (1986, 1989) found that the negative return for Mondays was actually concentrated in the first hour of trading on Monday morning and that thereafter Monday's share price movements behaved in the same way as on other days of the week. In particular Harris found that there was a significant upward movement in prices during the last half-hour of trading for every day of the week, including Mondays. Ariel (1990) found that returns on the two trading days prior to national holidays in the USA (especially Labor Day, Thanksgiving and Good Friday) were between 9 and 14 times higher than the average daily returns for the rest of the year. All these calendar effects seem to be inconsistent with the semi-strong form EMH, since they are examples of empirical regularities that could be exploited by a simple trading rule to generate excess returns.

The small firm effect

A number of studies have documented the fact that even when adjusted for risk, the returns to portfolios of small capitalization shares is substantially higher than the returns from large capitalization stocks. A notable feature is that this difference varies substantially between countries. Studies by Levis (1985) for the UK show the average out performance to be 6 per cent per year. Banz (1981) estimated the size premium at 0.84 per cent per month. The largest premium has been estimated for Australia at nearly 6 per cent per month (Brown, Kiem, Kleidon and Marsh, 1983).

Fama and French (1992) also found a strong negative relationship between returns and firm size: the shares of smaller firms tended to have higher average returns that the shares of larger firms (1.64 per cent per month compared with 0.90 per cent per month on average), again confirming the existence of the small firm effect. All these results are incompatible with semi-strong form market efficiency since it should not be possible to earn excess returns on the basis of characteristics of firms that are readily observable and thereby exploitable.

Differences between return and various accounting ratios

Fama and French (1992) examined the relationship between the return on securities and market-to-book ratios, earnings-price ratios and firm size. The market-to-book ratio is the ratio of the market value of a firm's share to its book value, using the firm's latest balance sheet. These accounting criteria are often used to divide company shares into two categories: growth shares (which have high market-to-book ratios) and value shares (which have low market-to-book ratios). Fama and French (1992) found a strong negative relationship between returns and market-to-book ratios. Firms with the lowest 1/12 market-to-book ratios (1.83 per cent per month compared with 0.30 per cent per month over the period 1963–1990). This result suggests that value shares tend to outperform growth shares.

Value investing as applied by the great value investor, Warren Buffet, involves seeking out companies with the following characteristic:

- a proven record, e.g. Coca-Cola, Gillette, McDonald's, Walt Disney

- strong management

- steady growth

- few competitors

- surplus cash

- good international exposure

- a 'margin of safety'.

Applying these principles has made Warren Buffet one of the richest men in America, thereby refuting, it is often argued, the EMH.

Fama and French also found a strong positive relationship between returns and earnings-price ratios. Firms with the largest 1/12 earnings-price ratios had higher average returns than firms with the lowest 1/12 earnings-price ratio (1.72 per cent per month compared with 1.04 per cent per month). Since value shares tend to have higher earnings-price ratios than growth shares, this result provides further evidence for the conclusion that value shares outperform growth shares. Haugen (1999), as discussed in Chapter 1, makes great play of this finding in his *New Finance*.

EFFICIENT MARKETS, THE 1987 STOCK MARKET CRASH AND CATASTROPHE THEORY

There is a famous joke about a physicist, an engineer and an economist ship-wrecked on a desert island with only a can of beans to eat. 'I can help open it', volunteers the physicist, 'I'll start a small fire, put the can on it, and compute how long it will take for the can to explode'. 'Great', says the engineer, 'I can calculate the trajectory that the beans will take and where we should stand to catch them'. 'Wait a minute!' the economist interrupts, 'You fellows are approaching the whole thing the wrong way ... first, assume we have a can opener ...'

Economists are notorious for making assumptions – assumptions that are at once crucial to their analysis and often completely unrealistic. Are the assumptions underlying the EMH, one must ask, such that they can explain wide swings in stock prices without the fundamentals fluctuating widely?

Economists have put forward many different arguments to explain the stock market crash of 19 October 1987. However, while there is no shortage of individual arguments, difficulties remain in bringing them together in a theoretical framework. This section examines one of the less well-known models which are able to explain large stock market movements: catastrophe theory. Chapter 12 examines another widely discussed theory, the theory of speculative bubbles.

The 1987 stock market crash: the basic facts

On 19 October 1987 the Dow Jones industrials index plunged 508 points from 2247 to 1739 in just a few hours. This was, at the time, the largest crash in stock exchange history, and amounted to an index drop of more than 22 per cent (compared with a 15 per cent decline in the 29 October 1929 crash). During and after 1987's 'Black Monday' there was a large increase in the volatility of equity prices, reflecting the rapidly changing expectations. Trading volume also went up dramatically. The crash was immediately transmitted to other financial centres via global telecommunications links.

Why it is necessary to concentrate on less well-known theories?

Economists typically attribute large swings in financial asset prices to the impact of important economic news. New information can cause investors to make drastic reassessments of the size of future cash flows or the future discount rates at which these cash flows are capitalized. But the adverse economic news that preceded the fall in US share prices on Monday, 19 October 1987, i.e. disappointing US trade deficit figures announced the previous Friday and reports of a possible tax law that would negatively affect mergers and acquisitions, does not appear dramatic enough to have caused the unusual drop of 22 per cent.

It is for this reason that it is useful to focus on one of the less well-known models which are able to explain large stock market movements.

Catastrophe theory

The model outlined here which could be used to explain the crash draws on the 'catastrophe theory' developed by René Thom, a French mathematician. He wrote in 1875 that:

'"Catastrophes" are characterised by abrupt changes in dynamic properties due to small shifts in parameter values. Catastrophes can only appear within non-linear dynamic systems.'

Zeeman (1974) set up a catastrophe model to investigate unstable stock exchange behaviour. Two classes of investors are defined; let's call them 'fundamentalists' and 'speculators'.

'Fundamentalists' are defined as being guided by estimates of economic variables which relate to general macroeconomic developments as well as to microeconomic analysis of specific industries and firms. 'Fundamentalists', thus, use all available information to form forecasts based on some kind of 'rational expectations'.

'Speculators', on the other hand, are defined as basing their investment policy on the behaviour of the market itself, using recent patterns to predict future trends. 'Speculators', as we define them here, thus typically relate to 'adaptive expectations'.

Of course, all investors who take risks in order to gain from differences in prices over time are speculators in the normal sense of the term. Thus, our 'fundamentalists' could also be involved in speculation. The point is that 'fundamentalists' usually follow a longer-range investment strategy, whereas 'speculators' have basically a short-term orientation.

The model

It is assumed that all investors can be divided into these two groups. The activities of these classes of investors can then be represented by the following two variables.

1   The proportion of the stock market held by 'speculators', which is denoted by S.

2   The excess demand for stock by 'fundamentalists', which is denoted by F.

The actual market of a stock exchange can be characterized by an equity price index, J, such as the Dow Jones or the S & P 500. The rate of change in the designated index, $J = dI/dt$, is the state-variable of the model. It is assumed that equity prices (and, therefore, J), respond very quickly to market imbalances so that price adjustments clear the markets instantaneously. $J = 0$ represents a static market, and $J > 0$ ($J < 0$) characterizes a bull (bear) market.

While J (= quick variable) responds very swiftly to changes in S and F, J has a much slower feedback effect on S (= slow variable).

Whereas 'fundamentalists' typically invest in a recuperating bear market (rising F), when equity prices are likely to be undervalued on average, 'speculators' wait for an uptrend to establish itself before buying, thereby intensifying the upward trend. Thus, during the bull period, the degree of 'speculation' (S) increases and leads to self-fulfilling price rises.

In this process, the wedge between share prices and their fundamental values becomes larger, inducing 'fundamentalists' to sell equities (reduction of F). If the market is about to decline, the 'speculators' tracking the market trend will start to sell their positions as well – this is the transition from a bull to a bear market.

These feedback effects of J on S and F are shown by the dotted flow lines in Figure 10.3.

If speculators are in the minority (S is small), then J is a continuous monotonic increasing function of F, which means that if 'fundamentalists' induce an excess demand (or excess supply) on the stock exchange, the equity price index will increase (decrease) continuously. There is a smooth change from bull to bear market.

On the other hand, instability is introduced into the stock exchange if the proportion of speculators is substantial (S is large). This means any changes in the equity price index will be amplified by the speculators. If the index begins to rise (fall), there will be a rapid move into a bull (bear) market.

Figure 10.3 shows the equilibrium surface of the Zeeman model, involving the variables, J, S and F.

If the proportion of 'speculators' in the market is small, i.e. if $S < S_0$, the transition from the bull to the bear market results in smooth movements of J. Catastrophe points appear only for a large degree of 'speculation', S, i.e. for $S > S_0$.

The larger the degree of speculation S, the more pronounced are the possible catastrophe events. During extended bull periods, intensified speculation leads to strong index increases, which indicate a market over-valuation of equities with respect to their fundamentals. 'Fundamentalists' usually start to pull

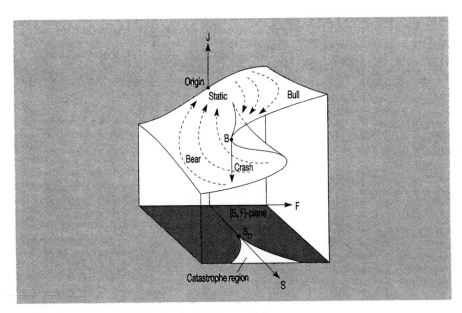

Fig 10.3 ● Stock price changes in the Zeeman model

Source: Zeeman, E. C. (1974) 'On the Unstable Behaviour of Stock Exchanges', *Journal of Mathematical Economics*, 1, 39–49

out from the market before it reaches its peak. Market declines are amplified as the 'speculators' – due to their adaptive expectations – reinforce the downward trend. At point B (Figure 10.3) – a point which will be reached if 'speculation' is in addition amplified by outside events – only a slight further reduction in the excess demand of equity from 'fundamentalist', F, leads to a 'crash' – i.e. an abrupt fall in J.

An explanation of the stock market crash?

Both the catastrophe theory and the speculative bubble theory can explain a crash if there is a large amount of 'speculation', i.e. investors who invest on the basis of adaptive expectations. During the extended bull period after 1982, these types of investors seemed to become more and more prominent (large S). This was particularly true for the 1987 stock markets, when the Dow Jones index gained 10 per cent in just three months. At the same time the fundamentals (the huge US budget and current account deficits) tended to be adverse, indicating a pronounced overvaluation of equity prices.

The situation became problematic in the months prior to the crash when the value of bond portfolios went down drastically, as long bond yields rose. These increasing bond yields, together with the growing awareness of the economic imbalances (as evidenced also by the very unstable exchange rate situation) eventually resulted in pessimistic expectations in the stock markets, with the result that the market crashed.

CHAPTER 11

The new economic paradigm: how does it affect the valuation of financial assets?

- What is the new economic paradigm?
- NAIRU and the new paradigm: why the sudden prominence?
- The new paradigm and the price earnings ratio

WHAT IS THE NEW ECONOMIC PARADIGM?

The new economic paradigm may be summarized as the view that globalization and information technology have led to a surge in the productivity of US workers. This, in turn, has produced a sharp increase in the rate of growth that the US economy can achieve without running up against inflationary capacity limits. At the heart of the new economic paradigm is the belief that the economy is in a phase of structural, rather than cyclical, improvement.

The essence of the new paradigm, and of its followers, the new paradigmatics, as the proponents of this idea are known, is the claim that the changes everyone can see in the US economy – the rise of digital technology, the growing volume of international trade and investment – have qualitatively altered the economic rules as represented by standard economic theories. Rapid technological change means that the economy can grow much faster than it used to. One implication being put forward by the new paradigmatics is that the US Federal Reserve should adopt higher economic growth targets in its monetary targeting.

There is no doubt that there has been a revolution in information technology. It is all around us – fax machines, cellular phones, personal computers, modems, the Internet, to name just some of the changes taking place. The changes taking place are, in fact, deeper than a cursory examination would indicate.

Information – words, pictures, data and so on – has now been digitized. This digital technology is creating new companies and new industries before our very eyes. In Silicon Valley alone, 11 new companies are created every week. Not all succeed, obviously, but in 1999.

Housing and cars used to drive the US economy. Now information technology accounts for a quarter to a third of economic growth. Information technology affects every other industry. It boosts productivity, reduces costs, cuts inventories and facilitates electronic commerce. It is, in short, a transcendent technology – like railways in the nineteenth century and cars in the twentieth.

The new paradigmatics argue that productivity growth has accelerated, which means that the old speed limit, meaning the acceptable rate of economic growth without inflationary pressures building up, has been repealed. They would argue that it is a fact that official productivity statistics do not show any dramatic acceleration. Here the statistics are clear. Measured productivity growth in the 1990s has been about 1 per cent per year, an unimpressive performance. But the new paradigmatics would argue that the official statistics understate true productivity. As Robert Solow (1998), Nobel Prize winner for Economics famously commented 'The computer is everywhere except in the productivity statistics'.

A second theme of the new paradigmatics is that global competition means that the economy does not need to fear overheating and the subsequent inflation. The implication being propounded here is that because of globalization, monetary expansion can now be pursued without the risk of inflation.

The globalization of business refers to the fact that capitalism is spreading around the world. This may not be full blown capitalism but at least we are seeing the widespread introduction of market forces, freer trade and widespread deregulation. It's happening in the former communist countries and in the developing world of Latin America and Asia.

These two trends of globalization and information technology are undermining the old order, forcing business to restructure. If you want to compete in global markets or take advantage of rapid technological change, so the argument goes, you have to move quickly – and that often means getting rid of layers of technology. The effect is a radical restructuring that makes business more efficient.

Critics, particularly Krugman (1997), contend that there are conceptual and empirical holes in the new paradigm which mean that we have not entered a new world of higher economic growth without the undesirable effects of inflation.

Krugman's reasoning goes along the following lines. Let us assume that the official statistics understate productivity growth by 1 per cent. This must also mean that official statistics, by implication, understate true output growth by exactly the same amount. So if true productivity growth is 2 per cent, not the 1 per cent measured rate, and if the labour force is growing at 1 per cent, then the economy's true speed limit is 3 per cent, and not 2 per cent. But when the economy is actually growing at 3 per cent, the statistics will say that it is growing at 2 per cent. Whichever number is agreed upon, that remains the rate at which it cannot grow any faster. One cannot cite the understatement of productivity figures, to prove one case, without simultaneously accepting the concomitant understatement of output growth.

Moving on to the next aspect of the new paradigm thinking the argument claims that the happy combination of low unemployment and low inflation proves the pay-off from higher productivity growth. There is no doubt that higher productivity growth would mean lower inflation for any given rate of wage increase. And if it is true that official productivity statistics understate the real rate of progress by 1 per cent, then official price statistics also overstate inflation by exactly the same amount. But what one could call covert productivity increases, Krugman claims, doesn't help explain why even measured inflation remains so subdued.

Turning now to the new importance of global competition. Unlike in the past, the story goes, US companies now have to face actual or potential competition from rivals in Europe and Asia; thus even in the face of strong demand they will not dare raise prices, for fear that these rivals will seize the market.

As in the case of the claim of understated productivity growth, it is possible to question this assertion on the facts. There are without question many American firms facing international competition to an unprecedented degree. However, such global competition mainly occurs in the goods-producing sector – very few services are traded on international markets – and even within manufacturing there are many industries that remain largely isolated from foreign competitors (as Krugman comments, 'Seen any Chinese refrigerators lately?'). Since the USA is mainly a service economy, this means that no more than 25 per cent, probably less than 15 per cent of employment and value-added are actually subjected to the kind of global market discipline that the new paradigm emphasizes.

But, Krugman continues, discussion of the true extent of globalization, like discussion of the true rate of productivity growth, is beside the point. Even if global competition played a bigger role in the US economy than it really does, such global competition would not raise the economy's speed limit, because no matter how big the world economy may be, once any economic slack has been taken up the maximum possible growth rate of any piece of that economy is still equal to the sum of productivity and labour force growth in that piece.

So is there a limit which the economy can achieve without running up against capacity limits?

Remember the new paradigmatics say that there is not. The conventional view that the economy has a 'speed limit' of around 2–2.5 per cent growth does not come out of thin air. It is based on the real-life observation that, when the output of the US economy, as measured by real gross domestic product, is growing rapidly, the unemployment rate falls. When the output is growing slowly or is shrinking, the unemployment rate rises. Over the last 20 years, the break-point – the growth rate at which unemployment neither rises nor falls – has been between 2 per cent and 2.5 per cent. And this break-point does not seem to have changed much in recent years.

What causes changes in the rates of inflation and unemployment? How are the price level and the level of employment related? These have been key questions facing economists for at least 50 years. Discussions about them usually centre on an approach to explaining the inflation/unemployment relationship that dates back to the 1960s and 1970s. According to this approach, inflation is caused by an excessively tight labour market that drives up wages and forces firms to respond by raising prices.

An important element of this approach is the concept of a non-accelerating rate of unemployment, or NAIRU, as it is most commonly referred to. As its name suggests, the NAIRU is supposed to be an unemployment rate (or range of unemployment rates) that produces a stable rate of inflation. If the actual unemployment rate is lower than the NAIRU then the inflation rate will tend to rise, and vice versa.

But the unemployment rate can only fall so far. Both logic and history tell us that when workers are very scarce and jobs very abundant, employers will start bidding against each other to attract workers, wages will begin rising rapidly, and real growth will give way to inflation. That means that while the economy can grow faster than two percentage points, or whatever per cent for a while if it starts from a high rate or unemployment, in the long run, that growth rate cannot remain higher than the rate that keeps unemployment constant. And that is where the infamous 'speed limit' comes from.

Behind that speed limit, in turn, lies another bit of arithmetic: The rate of growth of output, by definition, is the sum of the rate of growth of employment (which is limited by the size of the potential labour force) and that of productivity, normally referred to as output per worker.

NAIRU AND THE NEW PARADIGM: WHY THE SUDDEN PROMINENCE?

Many economists, e.g. Meyer (1997), subscribe to the view that there is some threshold level of the unemployment rate at which supply and demand are balanced in the labour market (and perhaps in the product market as well). This balance yields a constant inflation rate. If the unemployment rate falls below this threshold level – NAIRU – inflation tends to rise progressively over time. The unemployment rate at the time of writing is widely believed to be below this threshold; hence the puzzlement at the low inflation rate.

The concept of NAIRU has acquired significance since it seems to be embraced by both Laurence Meyer (1997), a Governor of the Fed and Alan Greenspan (1997), Chairman of the Fed. The application of NAIRU to predicting Fed actions would suggest that if the Fed foresees low unemployment, it will tighten monetary policy and slow the economy. If the current unemployment rate is below the non-accelerating rate, there will be wage and price pressures with inflation rising. Periods when the actual unemployment rate is below the national rate suggest a booming economy and pressure for the Fed to raise interest rates. Periods when the actual unemployment rate is above the natural rate are periods of recessionary pressures when the Fed could be expected to lower interest rates.

One of the problems with monetary policy is that there are time lags between when a policy action is taken and when it takes effect. In controlling inflation it is, therefore, dangerous to look only at current rates of inflation. By the time inflation actually begins to rise, inflationary pressures may have been brewing for a year or two and it may take a substantial tightening of policy (possibly leading to a recession) to slow them down.

According to standard thinking of the way the economy works, using the NAIRU concept, if there is an increase in overall spending in the economy it will be followed by inflation. So increases in demand raise real GDP relative to its potential level, which increases the demand for labour to produce the additional goods and services, and therefore lowers the unemployment rate relative to the NAIRU. Excess demand in goods and labour markets leads to higher inflation in goods, prices and wages with a lag. Because of this, the unemployment rate can help in generating the inflation forecasts that are crucial in formulating monetary policy.

A possible explanation of the recent failure of inflation to rise in the face of strong GDP growth and low unemployment is that the NAIRU has declined, i.e. the level of the unemployment rate at which the supply of and demand for labour are in balance may be lower than it used to be. The argument, expressed, for example, by Federal Reserve Board Chairman Alan Greenspan (1997), that technological change has added to workers' insecurity in recent years and made them less willing to push for higher wages, may be thought of as one version of this explanation. Greater insecurity might reduce the upward pressure on wage rates at any unemployment rate and so lower the threshold rate at which wages (and prices) would begin to move upward.

However, any improvement in the trade-off between real GDP growth and inflation coming from a decrease in the NAIRU, the argument goes, would be temporary. Once the NAIRU settled at a new (lower) level, further declines in unemployment coming from rapid GDP growth would again put upward pressure on inflation. Put differently, although workers may be temporarily inhibited from seeking wage hikes if they are insecure in their jobs, insecurity will not increase continually. At some point, strong GDP growth will cause unemployment to fall so low that workers will overcome their inhibitions, and wages (and prices) will begin to accelerate again. A permanent improvement in the trade-off between real growth and inflation can come only from an increase in the steady-state or potential growth rate of real GDP. Such an increase in potential growth makes it possible for output to grow correspondingly faster without pushing the unemployment rate below its threshold, wherever that happens to be.

In the long run, the growth in the nation's real GDP depends on the growth of the available supply of labour and the productiveness of that labour. Most recent estimates of this steady-state growth rate for the USA put it at about 2 per cent annually, comprised of one percentage point of growth in the labour supply and another one percentage point of productivity growth. A higher potential growth rate would mean that policymakers could aim for faster growth in nominal aggregate demand while continuing to keep inflation under control. The Federal

Reserve, with its stated goal of moving the economy toward price stability, has a strong interest in the determinants of potential growth.

So what are the facts about the trends in the US supply of labour. Over the last three decades the supply of labour to the US economy has been boosted by a substantial rise in labour force participation. This may be traced largely to the increased participation of women in the paid labour force. The proportion of adult women who spend any time in the labour force during any year (the female experience rate) has risen, as has the proportion of the year that these women with labour force experience actually participate.

The annual weeks of participation of women with labour force experience now is only slightly below that of men (48 weeks compared to 50 weeks). This means both that there is not much scope for boosting female participation by further increasing the time that women spend in the workforce and that the lower participation rate of women compared to men is due mostly to the smaller proportion of women who spend *any* time in the labour force. Krugman speculates that the lower experience rate of females is due primarily to the greater role of women in child-raising. Although this role may change, any such change seems unlikely to occur quickly.

Overall labour supply depends not only on the rate of participation but also on such other factors as the amount of time actually spent on the job (measured by the ratio of numbers at work to numbers employed) and average weekly hours. Both these indicators increased during the 1980s, largely offsetting the slowing in the labour force participation. The working/employed ratio may now be close to its practical maximum. In 1996, this ratio exceeded 95 per cent and was higher than at any time since 1960, implying that there is little scope left for increasing the supply of labour by reducing the amount of time away from the job due to such factors as vacation, sickness and labour disputes. Similarly, the rise in weekly hours of work during the 1980s seems to have petered out in the 1990s. The earlier increase in workhours seems to have been associated with an increase in the proportion of workers who hold more than one job. In recent years, the number of multiple jobholders appears to have stabilized at around 6 per cent of total employment. In particular, the increase in labour force participation that has occurred in the last year or so has not been associated with an increase in multiple jobholding. Finally, during the 1980s, the supply of workhours was boosted by demographic changes that increased the proportion of the population in the prime working years of their lifetimes, during which persons are more willing to work more hours per week and more weeks per year. Looking forward, Krugman suggests, it is plausible to expect that this demographic effect will go into reverse early in this century as the baby-boom generation ages.

These various considerations suggest that faster labour force growth is unlikely to make a significant contribution to raising overall GDP growth over the years ahead. If anything, a slowing of labour force growth is more likely. This does not, of course, mean that GDP growth cannot be increased, but only that any increase will have to come from faster growth in labour productivity rather than from faster growth in the supply of labour. Despite some controversies over the potential prospect for the continuation of the new paradigm, there is no doubt that it has fundamentally altered the traditional rules applied to valuing companies, discussed in Chapter 7, and it is to this that we now turn.

THE NEW PARADIGM AND THE PRICE EARNINGS RATIO

The changing structure of the US economy, it can be argued, has radically altered the business environment in a manner not yet fully recognized in company accounts by current accounting conventions. Newly developed products, widely used, have necessitated large-scale investment in what accountants call intangible assets, raising the value of copyrights and patents.

Microsoft's Windows 98, Paramount's movie 'Titanic', Pfizer's Viagra, and Gillette's Mach3 razor blades are four prominent examples of this. Developing each product required its corporate sponsor to invest hundreds of millions of dollars. For example, Gillette invested $700 million to develop the Mach3 razor blade in an effort begun in 1990. Paramount spent over $200 million to bring director James Cameron's vision of 'Titanic' to the screen.

These investment expenditures gave rise to economically valuable, legally recognized intangible assets, including copyrights ('Titanic' and Windows 98) and patents (Viagra and Mach3) that give the investing firms the exclusive right for a certain period to sell the newly developed products. Pfizer sold over $700 million worth of Viagra in 1998 after its introduction in April; 'Titanic' sold $1 billion in cinema tickets before it entered video sales; and Gillette's Mach3 razor blade was the top seller in the USA by the end of 1998, having secured more than 10 per cent of the razor blade replacement market in less than a full year.

Patents and copyrights on new consumer products are not the only types of intangible assets. New processes for making *existing* goods, such as the process for coating cookie wafers with chocolate, and new *producer* goods, like PC servers and fibre optic telephone cables, can also be patented or copyrighted or, perhaps, protected as trade secrets. Other intangible assets are brand names and trademarks, which can help a firm certify the quality of an existing product or introduce new products to potential purchasers. Not only can a reputation for quality persuade shoppers to try an item for the first time, but a clever use of advertisements can go a long way toward targeting precisely those who will gain the most from the product and thereafter become loyal, repeat customers.

Yet, because they are not investments in tangible assets, most expenditures on *intangible* assets are not fully recognized as investments, in either US companies' financial accounts or the US national income and product accounts. This practice may have been reasonable when investment in such assets was a negligible portion of US total investment, but that is no longer the case.

The effect of this lack of recognition is that corporate profits are understated because corporations are investing more of their cash flow in intangible assets. As a result price/earnings ratios are overstated, making comparison between differing time periods and different companies difficult to use as bases for deciding whether markets or individual companies are overvalued or undervalued.

As we discussed in Chapter 7, other things being equal, the price/earnings ratio should be high when the expected growth rate of profits (and thus of earnings per share) is high relative to the rate of return that stockholders require on the shares they own. That can happen when profits are temporarily low and expected to bounce back, as was the case during the 1990–91 recession in the USA. It can also happen when profits are high, as during the second half of the 1990s, if they are expected to grow rapidly in the future.

But over the long run, profits have tended to grow at the same rate as the economy as a whole. It is therefore legitimate to ask if there is any rational reason to believe that profits should grow strongly in the future and thereby justify the until recent high valuations placed on stocks. In fact, as Nakamura (1999) has shown, there is. As Nakamura shows, rising investment in intangible assets reduces measured current profits and raises expected future profits. Thus, rising new product development can help explain a high price/earnings ratio.

The accurate measurement of profits is fundamental to financial accounting. Profit tells us two things: how much revenue exceeded costs (a measure of the economic value of current operations of the firm) and how much the assets of the corporation have increased (before any cash distributions to shareholders). Formally accountants define profit as 'The excess of revenues over all expenses'. Expenses are 'the costs of goods, services, and facilities used in the production of current revenue' (Estes, 1981). To the extent that a firm buys things that are not used up in production, those additional costs are investments, not expenses, and are capitalized, i.e. considered as assets. A capital asset gives rise to an expense only to the extent that the capital asset's value falls while in use, a process called depreciation or capital consumption.

Research and Development costs are treated as part of the current expenses of the firm, and this treatment reduces reported profits. If R&D expenditure was treated as investment and capitalized and depreciated accordingly, the profitability of US non-financial corporations would have been much higher. Thus the high P/E ratios of the 1990s become easier to understand.

CHAPTER 12

Bubbleology and financial economics

INTRODUCTION

'How do we know when irrational exuberance has unduly escalated asset values?' Alan Greenspan (1996)

The above quote by Alan Greenspan, Chairman of the US Federal Reserve, provoked a large fall in the US stock market and opened up the debate as to whether stock markets are prone to speculative bubbles and, if so, as to how financial economists can identify them.

Movements in prices in any market which are thought to be self-fulfilling prophecies are often called 'bubbles' to denote their dependence on events that come from outside the market being studied. Proponents of the idea that bubbles in financial markets occur are usually referred to as 'Bubbleologists'. The idea that bubbles exist is often traced to John Maynard Keynes, writing in 1936:

'Professional investment may be likened to those newspaper competitions in which the competitors have to pick out the six prettiest faces from a hundred photographs, the prize being awarded to the competitor whose choice most nearly corresponds to the average preferences of the competitors as a whole; so that each competitor has to pick, not those faces which he himself finds prettiest, but those which he thinks likeliest to catch the fancy of other competitors, all of whom are looking at the problem from the same point of view. It is not a case of choosing those which, to the best of one's judgement are really the prettiest, nor even those which average opinion genuinely thinks the prettiest. We have reached the third degree where we devote our intelligences to anticipating what average opinion expects the average opinion to be. And there are some, I believe, who practise the fourth, fifth and higher degrees.'

The stock market, Keynes wrote, 'is a game of musical chairs, of Snap, where the winner is the one who makes his move fractionally ahead of everyone else' (1936). So the stock market, in Keynes' view, was an environment in which speculators anticipate 'what average opinion expects average opinion to be' rather than focusing on factors fundamental to the market itself, including expected future dividends, etc. The implication here is that if bubbles exist in asset markets, prices will differ from the fundamental values that were described in Chapter 7.

It is only recently that serious research has taken place on the existence of bubbles. Economic theory, until recently, placed essentially no restrictions on how agents formed expectations of future prices. Thus a folklore of bubbles grew up. These would include the tulip bubble in seventeenth-century Holland, the South Sea bubble in eighteenth-century England and the increase in equity prices during the 1920s in the USA. All these events, when followed by subsequent collapses in asset values have been labelled as bubbles. However, the widespread adoption of rational expectations, discussed below, provides a model amenable to the empirical study of bubbles.

But first of all we need to describe the terminology used by 'bubbleologists'.

BUBBLE TERMINOLOGY

Following the technical language of financial economics, a 'bubble' is any deviation from 'fundamental values', whether up or down. Fundamental values are a concept easier to define in theory than in practice. The fundamental term refers to the prices stocks ought to sell for, based on a business's real economic value, separating out speculation. The assumption is that stock prices will ultimately (whenever that is) return to their fundamental values, however much extraneous factors may be influencing them at any one moment.

A bubble is an upward price movement over an extended range that then implodes. An extended negative bubble is a crash. 'Noise' refers to small price variations about fundamental values. So a bubble is a situation in which the price of an asset differs from its fundamental market value. With a rational bubble, as discussed below, investors can have rational expectations that a bubble is occurring because the asset price is above its fundamental value, but continue to hold the asset anyway. They might do this because they believe that someone else will buy the asset for a higher price in the future. In a rational bubble, asset prices can therefore deviate from their fundamental value for a long time because the bursting of the bubble cannot be predicted and so there are no unexploited profit opportunities.

THE ROLE OF EXPECTATIONS IN ANALYZING BUBBLES

Beliefs about the future are an important determinant of behaviour today. Important disagreements between differing views of how expectations are formed lie at the centre of the discussion as to the existence or otherwise of 'bubbles'. Different views about expectations can be usefully broken down into three groups: exogenous expectations, extrapolative expectations and rational expectations. We will discuss these three groups in turn examining how standard economic analysis can explain economic phenomena.

Exogenous expectations

Some economists remain almost completely agnostic on the vital question of how expectations are formed. When analyzing the behaviour of the economy they simply treat expectations as exogenous or given. Expectations are one of the inputs to the analysis. The analysis can display the consequences of a change in expectations. For example, an increase in expected future profits might increase the share price of a firm. But this assumption of exogenous expectations means that the analysis does not investigate the *cause* of the change in expectations. In particular, it is unrelated to other parts of the analysis. With given expectations, there is no automatic feedback from rising output to expectations of higher profits in the future.

Thus, at best, economists using exogenous expectations in their analysis give an incomplete account of how the economy works. At worst, they completely neglect some inevitable feedback from the variables they are analyzing to the expectations that were an input to the analysis. On the other hand, since modelling expectations remains a contentious issue, proponents of this approach might argue that the various types of possible feedback on expectations can be explored in an *ad hoc* manner.

Extrapolative expectations

One simple way to make expectations endogenous, or determined by what is going on elsewhere in the analysis, when discussing the existence or otherwise of bubbles, is to assume that people forecast future profits by extrapolating the behaviour of profits in the recent past, or extrapolate past inflation in order to form expectations of inflation in the near future. Proponents of this approach suggest that it offers a simple rule of thumb and corresponds to what many people seem to do in the real world.

Rational expectations

Suppose the rate of money growth is steadily increasing and inflation is steadily accelerating. Extrapolating past inflation rates will *persistently* under-forecast future inflation. Many economists believe that it is implausible that people will continue to use a forecasting rule that makes the same mistake (under-forecasting of future inflation, say) period after period. The hypothesis of rational expectations makes the opposite assumption: on average, people guess the future correctly. They do not use forecasting systems that systematically give too low a forecast or too high a forecast. Any tendency for expectations to be systematically wrong will quickly be detected and put right.

This in no way says that everybody gets everything exactly right all the time. We live in a risky world where unforeseeable things are always happening. Expectations will be fulfilled only rarely. Rational expectations says that people make good use of the information that is available today and do not make forecasts that are already knowably incorrect. Only genuinely unforeseeable things cause present forecasts to go wrong. Sometimes people will under-predict and sometimes they will over-predict. But any systematic tendency to do one or other will be noticed and the basis of expectations formation will be amended until guesses are, on average, correct.

BUBBLES AND THE FORMATION OF EXPECTATIONS

The existence or otherwise of 'bubbles' depends on which one of these models of expectations one applies.

The adoption of the rational expectations assumption has clarified considerably the nature of price bubbles. With rational expectations a researcher can specify a model of bubbles which is then testable. If the expected rate of market price change influences the current market price, the researcher has a model to work with. This is not to say that this is straightforward. There is an indeterminacy in the model as a researcher is, in fact, faced with something to explain, the market equilibrium price, with two variables, the market price and the expected rate of market price change, both of which are interrelated within the economic system.

A bubble can arise when the actual market price depends positively on its own expected rate of change, as normally occurs in asset markets. Since agents forming rational expectations do not make systematic prediction errors, the positive relationship between price and its expected rate of change implies a similar relationship between price and its actual rate of change. In such conditions, the arbitrary, self-fulfilling expectation of price changes may drive actual price changes independently of *market fundamentals*. This situation is referred to as a *price bubble*.

An explicit definition of market fundamentals depends on a particular model's structure; indeed, the very notion of a bubble can make no sense in the absence of a precise model detailing a markets operation. Without such a model, it is impossible both to define market fundamentals and to then isolate them from the presence, or otherwise, of a bubble.

BUBBLES AND THE EFFICIENT MARKET HYPOTHESIS

Efficient market theory (EMH) applies the theory of rational expectations to the pricing of securities. As discussed in Chapter 10, the EMH comes in three versions: the weak form, the semi-strong form and the strong form.

1 The weak form of the EMH asserts that prices fully reflect the information contained in the historical sequence of prices. Thus, investors cannot devise an investment strategy to yield abnormal profits on the basis of an analysis of past price patterns.

2   The semi-strong form of the EMH asserts that current stock prices reflect not only historical price information, but also all publicly available information relevant to a company's securities. If markets are efficient in this sense, then an analysis of balance sheets, income statements, announcements of dividend changes or stock splits or any other public information about a company (the technique of fundamental analysis) will not yield abnormal economic profits.

3   The strong form of the EMH asserts that all information that is *known* to any market participant about a company is fully reflected in market prices. Hence, not even those with privileged inside information can make use of it to secure superior investment results. There is perfect revelation of all private information in market prices.

The theory of rational expectations states that expectations will not differ from optimal forecasts (the best guesses of the future) using all available information. Rational expectations theory makes sense because it is costly for people not to have the best forecast of the future. The theory has two important implications:

1   if there is a change in the way a variable moves, there will be a change in the way expectations of this variable are formed, too; and

2   the forecast errors of expectations are unpredictable.

The lessons of the EMH are that bubbles are impossible because markets are 'efficient', that is, prices reflect all available information about an asset. Adherents of the EMH, believing that stocks are always correctly priced, tend to deny a connection between excessive speculation and subsequent economic crises. However, the necessary assumptions underlying the EMH must be simultaneously held. Thus it is necessary to examine the extent to which they do hold.

The stock market crash of 19 October 1987 discussed in Chapter 10 and again here should make us question the validity of efficient markets and rational expectations. EMH critics do not believe that a rational marketplace could have produced such a massive swing in share prices. To what degree should the stock market crash make us doubt the validity of rational expectations and efficient markets theory?

Nothing in rational expectations theory rules out large one-day changes in stock prices. A large change in stock prices can result from new information that produces a dramatic change in optimal forecasts of the future valuation of firms. Some financial economists have pointed out that there are many possible explanations for why rational explanations of the future value of firms dropped dramatically on 19 October 1987: moves in Congress to restrict corporate take-overs, the disappointing performance of the trade deficit, congressional failure to reduce the budget deficit substantially, increased fears of inflation, the decline of the dollar and increased fears of financial stress in the banking industry. Other financial economists doubt whether these explanations are enough to explain the stock market drop because none of these market fundamentals seems important enough.

One lesson from the 1987 Black Monday stock market crash appears to be that factors other than market fundamentals may have had an effect on stock prices. The crash of 1987 has therefore convinced many financial economists that the stronger version of efficient markets theory, which states that asset prices reflect the true fundamental (intrinsic) value of securities, is incorrect. They attribute a large role in the determination of stock prices to market psychology and to the institutional nature of the marketplace. However, nothing in this view contradicts the basic reasoning behind rational expectations of efficient markets theory – that market participants eliminate unexploited profit opportunities. Even though stock market prices may not always solely reflect market fundamentals, this does not mean that rational expectations do not hold. As long as the stock market crash was unpredictable, the basic lessons of the theory of rational expectations hold.

RATIONAL BUBBLES

Famous documented 'first' bubbles, Garber (1990) include the South Sea share price bubble of the 1720s and the Tulipmania bubble. In the latter case, the price of tulip bulbs rocketed between November 1636 and January 1637 only to collapse suddenly in February 1637 and by 1639 the price had fallen to around 1/200 of 1 per cent of its peak value. The increase in stock prices in the 1920s and subsequent 'crash' in 1929, the stock market crash of 1987 and the rise of the dollar between 1982 and 1985 and its subsequent fall, have also been interpreted in terms of a self-fulfilling bubble.

Keynes (1936), as mentioned earlier, is noted for his observation that stock prices may not be governed by an objective view of 'fundamentals' but by what 'average opinion expects average opinion to be'. His analogy for the forecasting of stock prices was that of trying to forecast the winner of a beauty contest. Objective beauty is not necessarily the issue; what is important is how one thinks the other judges' perception of beauty will be reflected in their voting patterns.

Rational bubbles arise because of the indeterminate aspect of solutions to rational expectations models, which for stocks is implicitly reflected in what is known as the Euler equation for stock prices. This equation states that the price you are prepared to pay today for a stock depends on the price you think you can obtain at some point in the future. The standard form of the Euler equation determines a sequence of prices but does not 'pin down' a unique price level. However, in general the Euler equation does not rule out the possibility that the price may contain an explosive bubble.

While one can certainly try and explain prolonged rises or falls in stock prices as due to some kind of irrational behaviour such as 'herding', or 'market psychology', nevertheless recent work emphasizes that such sharp movements or 'bubbles' may be consistent with the assumption of rational behaviour. Even if traders are perfectly rational, the actual stock price may contain a 'bubble element' and therefore there can be a divergence between the stock price and its fundamental value.

So proponents of rational bubbles attempt to demonstrate how the market prices of stocks may deviate, possibly substantially from their fundamental values even when agents are homogenous, rational and the market is informationally efficient. To do this they must show that the market price may equal its fundamental value plus a 'bubble term' and yet the stock will be willingly held by rational agents and no supernormal profits can be made.

It must be stressed that firm conclusions about the existence or otherwise of speculative bubbles are difficult to establish. There are severe econometric difficulties in testing for rational bubbles. Such tests critically depend on the correct specification for asset returns. Rejection of the no-bubble hypothesis may well be due to mis-specifying the underlying model of the fundamentals.

SOME BUBBLES IN HISTORY

It is instructive to examine some of the most famous 'bubbles' in history which have ended in speculative collapses. The most analyzed have been the Tulipmania in Holland in 1636, the South Sea Bubble in England, 1711–1720, and the 1929 Wall Street Crash. Recent empirical work, particularly on Tulipmania and the South Sea Bubble, Garber (1998) has cast doubts on whether these were bubbles. But it is still useful to paint the picture.

Tulipmania – Holland in 1636

The first account of tulips in Europe is from 1559 when a collector of exotic flora, Councillor Hewart, received a consignment of tulip bulbs from a friend in Constantinople, which he planted in his garden in Augsberg, Germany. His tulips drew a good deal of attention and in following years this flower became more and more popular among the upper classes, particularly in Germany and Holland, where it became the custom to order bulbs at exorbitant prices directly from Constantinople. Up to 1634 this custom became increasingly common, and from that year affluent society in Holland considered lack of a tulip collection to be proof of poor taste.

Year by year tulip bulb prices rose, finally reaching astronomic heights. According to original accounts of the peak of the tulipmania, in one deal the following price was paid for one tulip bulb of the rare *Semper Augustus* variety: 4600 florins, a new carriage, two grey mares and a complete bridle and harness.

As a fatted ox at that time cost 120 florins, 4600 florins was an awful lot of money! One single bulb of another rare variety, 'Viceroy', was sold for 24 carriage loads of grain, eight fat hogs, four cows, four barrels of ale, 1000 pounds of butter and a few tons of cheese.

In early 1636 demand for tulip bulbs had risen so drastically that people started to trade them on exchanges in a number of Dutch towns. Tulips were no longer bought only by well-to-do collectors but also by agents and speculators. At the smallest price drop they bought up, to sell later at a profit. To facilitate trading-on margin, tulip options were introduced, requiring a margin deposit of only 10–20 per cent. Ordinary people in all business sectors started to sell off assets to invest in this attractive market.

The Dutch tulip boom also drew attention from abroad and capital began to stream into the market. This capital forced up prices for land, property and luxury goods, as well as tulips, to new record heights. Fortunes grew and a growing *nouveau riche* group was added to the old upper classes. This new affluent class had earned its money from, and reinvested in, tulip bulbs. The story is told of a brewer in Utrecht who went so far as to exchange his brewery for three valuable tulip bulbs.

In September and October of 1636 market psychology began to alter and doubts began to emerge. How could one be *sure* that three tulip bulbs were worth as much as a brewery? Suppressed mirth began to be heard. Who said a tulip bulb was worth anything at all? The market was seized by panic and prices began to plummet.

Many of the *nouveau riche* had to face the fact that they owned a fortune consisting only of tulip bulbs which nobody wanted, less broker cash loans which they could not repay. The government tried to find a compromise by declaring all tulip contracts from before November 1636 as being invalid, while all subsequent contracts would be honoured at 10 per cent of original value. But prices dropped below this 10 per cent and the number of bankruptcies increased day by day. The Dutch tulipmania was followed by a depression from which it took the country many years to recover.

Garber (1989) points out that the standard version of tulipmania neglects discussion about what the market fundamental price of bulbs should have been. To form an expectation about the price of tulip bulbs, Garber collected data on bulb price patterns for various highly valued tulip bulbs. He found that the extremely high prices reported for rare bulbs and their rapid decline, reflected normal pricing behaviour in bulb markets and cannot be interpreted as evidence of market irrationality. Garber points out that serious traders ignored the market and participants in the market had almost no wealth anyway. Garber concludes that tulip prices at the time could be explained by market fundamentals and that tulipmania does not qualify as being a bubble. It must be stressed that his findings have been hotly disputed.

The South Sea Bubble

A second instructive example of bubbles was the speculation in England at the beginning of the eighteenth century. A company, later known under the name 'The South Sea Bubble', started in 1711 when the Earl of Oxford founded the South Sea Company, financed by a number of the merchants of that time. The company's full name was 'The Governor and Company of the Merchants of Great Britain to the South Seas and other parts of America for the encouragement of the Fishing'. The company acquired almost 10 million pounds of the British national debt, against a guaranteed annuity of 6 per cent, and the monopoly of all trading with Latin America.

A short time after the company's founding rumours of incredible profits from the South Sea trading arose, where English goods could be bartered for gold and silver from the 'inexhaustible' mines of Peru and Mexico. In fact, the Spanish colonial power allowed only one English ship to call per year, for which it charged one quarter of all profits and 5 per cent of turnover. On the stock exchange the South Sea stock led a quiet existence, the price often moving only two or three points over a month.

In 1717 the King of England recommended that the national debt be 'privatized' once more. The country's two large financial institutions, the Bank of England and the South Sea Company, each submitted a proposed solution and, after heated parliamentary debate, it was resolved to allow the South Sea Company to acquire a further debt liability at an interest rate of 5 per cent per year.

But in 1719 an event took place in France which was to be of great significance for the English company. A well-to-do man named John Law had founded a company in Paris, 'Compagnie d'Occident', to trade with, and colonize, the American State of Mississippi. By a series of manipulations John Law succeeded in starting a massive wave of speculation in this company's stock, the price rising from 466 francs on 9 August to 1705 francs on 2 December 1719. Buyers were French and foreigners alike, which caused the British Ambassador to request His Majesty's Government to do something to stop the massive flow of English capital to the 'Mississippi Bubble' on the French stock exchange. The Mississippi Bubble collapsed on 2 December 1719, and in the ensuing crash investors, seeking profitable opportunities, moved their funds from France to England.

The opportunity to privatize the UK national debt provided an interesting opportunity for the principal stockholders in the British South Sea Company, who now offered to take over the entire debt of the English State. On 22 January 1720 the House of Commons appointed a committee to consider the proposal. Despite many warnings, on 2 February the decision was taken to submit a bill to Parliament. Investors were delighted at this prospect of further capitalization of the company and over a few days the price rose to £176, supported by the inflow of funds from France by investors who were now seeking new profitable opportunities. During further readings of the bill new rumours started to circulate on the unbelievable profits which could be made and stocks rose further to a price of £317.

Even at this price the company's original founders and co-directors could reap a capital gain which was enormous by the standards of that time, and in a virtually inactive company. This whetted their appetites for more, and new positive rumours were circulated on 12 April and fresh stock was subscribed to for £1 million at a price of £300. The issue was subscribed twice over and a few days later stock was traded at £340. The company then declared that a 10 per cent dividend would be paid on all new and old stock and a further new subscription was invited for £1 million at a price of £400. This was also oversubscribed. The company was still almost totally inactive.

Many other companies jumped on this speculative bandwagon issuing their own shares. However on 11 June 1720 the King proclaimed a number of these companies to be 'public nuisances' and trading in their stocks was prohibited on penalty of a fine. A list of 104 prohibited companies, described by Mackay (1841) below, were banned.

Despite the government's endeavours new bubbles appeared every day and the speculation fever continued to rise. Figure 12.1 charts the progress of the South Sea bubble. The South Sea Company was traded at a price of £550 on 28 May 1720. From this already impressive level, during June the price rose above £700. In this period price movements were extremely nervous, with great periodic shifts. On a single day, 3 June, the price thus dropped before noon to £650, to rise again in the afternoon to £750. Many large investors used the high prices to take profits, which were reinvested in anything from land and commodities to real estate and other stocks. However, others bought the South Sea Company's stock, one of them the physicist, Isaac Newton. During the stock's early rises he had sold all his South Sea stock, cashing a profit of £7000. In midsummer he bought again, a transaction which would come to cost him £20,000.

At the beginning of June, South Sea stock rose again and for a short enchanted moment, on 24 June 1720, the security was traded at £1050. As only few were aware, the time was running out for investors. Those in the know were the company's original founders and its Board Chairman, who had used the earlier high prices to get rid of their own stock. At the beginning of August this ominous fact began to leak to the general public and the stock price began to fall slowly and steadily.

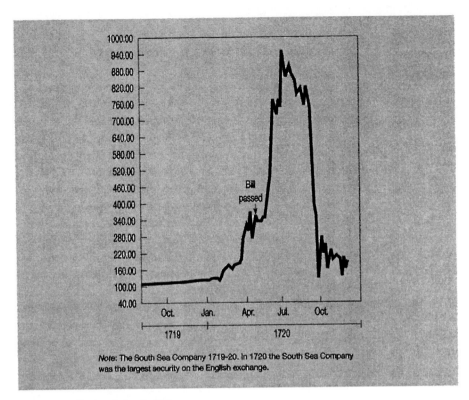

Note: The South Sea Company 1719-20. In 1720 the South Sea Company was the largest security on the English exchange.

Fig 12.1 ● The South Sea Bubble

Source: The Psychology of Finance, L. Trede. Reproduced with permission of John Wiley and Sons Ltd

On 31 August the South Sea Management announced that an annual dividend of 50 per cent would be paid for the following 12 years. This would have completely drained the company of cash and the news did not stop the investors' increasing unease. On 1 September the stock continued to fall and when it reached £725 two days later, panic broke out. The security went through the floor over the rest of the month and when the company's bank was declared bankrupt on 24 September the fall accelerated. On the last day of the month the share could be bought at a price of £150. In only three months it had fallen by 85 per cent.

The company was finally dissolved in 1855 and its stock converted to bonds. In its 140 years of existence the company never succeeded in trading in the South Seas on any noteworthy scale.

The Wall Street Crash of 1929

The 1929 Wall Street Crash was the conclusion of one of history's largest episodes of speculation. For a number of years up to 1924 the American Dow Jones Industrial Index fluctuated within a relatively narrow price interval with strong selling pressure whenever it reached 110. From 1921, when the stock market was very depressed, to 1928, industrial output rose by 4 per cent annually and by 15 per cent from 1928 to 1929. Inflation was low and new industries sprouted forth everywhere.

This rising optimism, combined with easy access to cheap money, stimulated stock investors and after a temporary reversal in 1926 almost no month passed without a rise in stocks creating a new generation of rich investors. Investment trusts increased in number as stock investments rose in popularity. From around 40 companies before 1921 the number rose to 160 at the beginning of 1927 and 300 at the end of the same year. From the beginning of 1927 to the autumn of 1929 the total assets of investment trusts increased more than tenfold and there was almost unlimited confidence in these companies.

On 24 October 1929, trading reached 12 million stocks. Nervousness, however, had set in and a panic was evident. As the situation was clearly getting out of hand, on 25 October President Hoover made the following statement: 'The fundamental business of the country, that is, production and distribution of commodities, is on a sound and prosperous basis.'

Hoover's declaration had the same reassuring effect as a pilot announcing that the engine was *not* on fire. Panic grew and in the next few days prices continued to. This culminated on 29 October when, in a wave of enforced sales, 16 million stocks were realized at any price going. The story goes that a messenger at the stock exchange got the idea of bidding a dollar per share for a lot without buyers – and got his deal. Prices did not start to stabilize until the index reached 224 on 13 November, as shown in Figure 12.2.

In 1930 prices started to fall once more, continuing to a bottom of 58 on 8 July 1932.

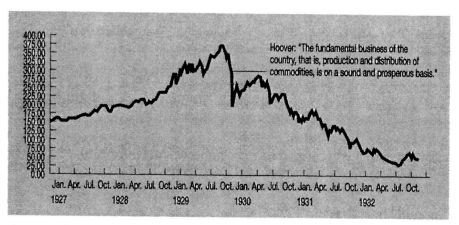

Fig 12.2 ● The 1929 Stock Market Crash

Source: The Psychology of Finance, L. Trede. Reproduced with permission of John Wiley and Sons Ltd

SPECULATIVE BUBBLES THEORY

In Chapter 10 we discussed the role that catastrophe theory can play in explaining stock market bubbles. Here we continue with the second model designed to explain large changes in stock prices, 'Speculative Bubbles Theory'. Applying the speculative bubbles theory, stock market investment is more about inflating and bursting speculative bubbles than about investors making rational long-term forecasts. Under the speculative bubble theory an asset's price can be bid up above its intrinsic value because some market participants believe that others will be willing to pay still more for it tomorrow. For a while this belief is self-sustaining and the market booms, but eventually participants lose faith that prices can rise further and the market crashes.

This theory, also named by Malkiel (2000), the 'Castles in the Air' Theory, based upon the thrills of making a killing by selling castles in the air, has long antecedents. Examples in history abound. Two of its best known examples are the Tulip Bulb Mania and the South Sea Bubble, discussed earlier. Under the Tulip Bulb Theory of 1593, the price of tulips rose to the extent that, prior to its collapse, the value of one tulip would have fed a ship's crew for a year. The South Sea Bubble of 1711 offered the rights to monopolies in the South Sea enabling fortunes to be made and lost.

McKay (1841) provides an impressive list of South Sea Bubble emulators. Companies were created to:

- design a wheel of perpetual motion
- build hospitals for bastard children
- build ships to defeat pirates
- improve the art of making soap
- extract silver from lead.

One of the most outrageous companies was one which was designed to be 'a company for carrying on an undertaking of great advantage but nobody knew what it was'. The shares of all these companies had the characteristics of speculative bubbles.

Rational speculative bubbles

Hardouvelis (1988) has argued that speculative bubbles may be triggered by an extraneous event that is unrelated to fundamental economic conditions; one group of investors buys with the expectation of a large capital gain, and others follow suit, without paying proper attention to economic factors such as future dividends or interest rates. If such behaviour persists, it may feed on itself as consecutive waves of buying increase prices. Speculative bubbles may subsequently burst very suddenly. An overvalued market is fragile and a relatively unimportant piece of 'bad' news may easily create pessimism and set off a selling wave.

The traditional method of searching for market overvaluation or speculative bubbles counts the number of unusually high returns during the suspected bubble period and assesses the likelihood that the total number of these high returns could have arisen from chance (Blanchard and Watson, 1982). An unusually high return (or a positive 'abnormal' return) is a return higher than the risk-free rate plus the usual risk premium necessary to compensate risk-averse shareholders for the uncertainty associated with their security returns. In the absence of a speculative bubble, a very large number of unusually high returns would normally occur by chance only with a small probability. Hence, a large number of unusually high returns constitutes evidence consistent with the presence of speculative bubbles.

Unfortunately, although simple, this traditional test has low statistical power to detect speculative bubbles; share prices are very volatile and their swings generate both large positive and large negative returns. The latter tend to mask any existing bubble evidence.

In order to construct a more powerful test for bubbles, it is necessary to formulate a more precise economic account of the development of the bubble. One can imagine many different scenarios of market overvaluation, but analysis restricts the possible scenarios to those in which investors know that the market is overvalued yet show no special desire to liquidate their positions and continue to buy or sell as they would in the absence of bubbles. This is a realistic working assumption for the period before October 1987. Robert Shiller (1987) provides survey evidence indicting that, before October 1987, 71.7 per cent of individual investors and 84.3 per cent of institutional investors thought that the market was overvalued at the time. Schiller argued that the crash was generated by what he calls a 'feedback loop'. After a first price decline investors sold, not based on fundamentals, but because they were worried about what was going on and about market irrationality. The drop did not stop until enough people started to have opposing feelings. (Shiller's later contributions to bubbleology are discussed further in Chapter 13.)

Explaining why investors did not get out of an overvalued market is more difficult. One could argue that the presence of highly liquid futures markets and associated trading strategies such as portfolio insurance led investors to the false belief that they could enjoy large positive returns in an upward market yet still avoid suffering a large loss if the market took a big plunge.

An alternative explanation outlined above by Hardouvelis (1988) is one that does not depend on some sort of collective irrationality. Within the economics literature this is known as the 'rational speculative bubble hypothesis'.

The 'bubble premium'

In the case of a rational speculative bubble, investors know that the bubble may crash and that they will not be able to get out once the crash starts, but they remain in the market because they believe – for whatever reason – that there is a good probability that the bubble will continue to grow, bringing them large positive returns. These returns are expected to be higher than the risk-free rate plus the usual risk premium in the absence of bubbles, and large enough to compensate them exactly for the probability of the bubble crash and a large one-time negative return. Hence, it is rational for investors to stay in the market. The expected extra return when no bubble crash occurs can be called the 'bubble premium'. The theory implies that the bubble premium is not only positive, but also increases during the lifetime of the bubble. The time trend in the bubble premium derives from the explosive nature of the bubble component of the share price. As time goes on, the bubble component of the share price grows larger and larger relative to the fundamental components. This growth implies that with the passage of time, the expected drop in the share price in the case of a bubble crash grows larger too, necessitating a larger and larger bubble premium.

The evidence points to a positive and rising bubble premium for approximately 18 months before October 1987 in the national stock markets of the USA and Japan. Overall, the evidence is consistent with the hypothesis of rational speculative bubbles (Hardouvelis, 1988).

CHAPTER 13

Behavioural finance, prospect theory and efficient markets

WHAT IS BEHAVIOURAL FINANCE?

Behavioural finance is that branch of financial economics which adopts a psychological view of the way investors take financial decisions. It investigates what happens in financial markets when some of the agents display human limitations and complications. It focuses on the way investor psychology rewards stock picking techniques which cause markets to overreact and underreact to the news affecting stock prices. Much of the momentum of behavioural finance was derived from the ongoing academic repercussions of the 1987 stock market crash. Prior to the October 1987 crash, as discussed throughout this book, the theoretical driving force behind financial markets revolved around the efficient markets hypothesis. The EMH insists on the rationality and stability of stock markets and denies that the markets engage in bouts of wild speculation. Share prices, it claims, represent the best possible estimates of companies' future earnings in the light of all publicly available information. So, under this theory, competition among well informed market participants is deemed to drive financial asset prices to a level which reflects the best possible forecast of future payment streams, with the effect that high or low share prices can always be justified as ones which have efficiently discounted all available information.

Since 1965, and particularly in the decade prior to the 1987 stock market crash, the evidence in support of the theory was impressive. Professor Jensen of Rochester University and the Harvard Business School claims the theory is the most thoroughly tested in the social sciences, with a literature comprising several hundred papers (1978).

What, one must ask, can the EMH theorist offer as an explanation for the crash? Many of the critics of the EMH claim that its proponents are clutching at straws. One has to ask whether the informed best estimates of all future dividends accruing to US companies fell by 23 per cent in that one day in October 1987? The EMH, with its emphasis on fundamental news, has been badly battered by the crash.

Financial economists are divided between those who believe that markets are efficient and those whose adherents believe, applying the new discipline of behavioural finance, that behaviour in financial markets can best be explained by psychology rather than by the principles of rational behaviour, so favoured by adherents of efficient markets. This chapter attempts to put together the arguments propounded by both EMH critics and proponents. Readers will become aware that this debate has polarized the two camps and that the debate will no doubt dominate the academic journals for some time to come.

MEAN REVERSION AND THE EFFICIENT MARKETS HYPOTHESIS

Mean reversion, sometimes called negative serial correlation, sometimes called regression to the mean, refers to the fact that markets initially overreact to news and other information, with the effect that price rises are followed by subsequent price falls (and vice versa). In discussing the issue of whether there is mean reversion in the stock market, financial economists are really asking whether stock prices are predictable. The presence of traders basing their investment strategy on the mean reversion principle are known as contrarian strategists. The principle is that investors should buy securities when prices are still falling and sell them when prices are still rising. Contrarians believe strongly that the apparent mispricing in the market will be corrected in the near future.

In discussing whether the EMH holds, it is essential to distinguish between 'informed' and 'uninformed' investors. Informed (or smart) investors (e.g. institutional investors or rich private clients) invest in costly research and aim to use their superior information to take trading positions and hence to make excess returns. Current security prices respond to the activities of the informed investors. Uninformed investors (sometimes called *noise traders*), on the other hand, do not invest in collecting information, but, by observing what is happening to security prices, they can infer the information acquired by the informed traders. In this way, all investors become informed.

It is the presence of noise traders than can lead to excess volatility and mean reversion. Fundamental values respond to information but securities prices respond to both information and noise. A big increase in noise, say as a result of the fashions and fads favoured by noise traders, can induce *excess volatility* in security prices (Shiller, 1989). It is also possible for the effect of noise to be cumulative, so that prices temporarily overshoot their long-run fundamental values before returning slowly to equilibrium. This is what is formally known as *mean reversion* (Shiller, 1989). If smart investors acquire a piece of good information about a firm, they will buy the firm's shares causing a jump in the share price. Noise traders observe the increase in price and increase their demand for the shares. This causes the price to rise even more (it is now well above fundamental values) and smart investors begin to unload their shares onto the market. The share price peaks and begins to fall. Noise traders panic and also begin to sell their shares, further depressing the price which may now undershoot the fundamental value. Smart investors begin to buy back the undervalued shares and their actions restore the share price to its fundamental value. Because noise traders buy shares if they observe share prices rising and sell shares if they observe share prices falling, they are sometimes called *positive feedback traders*. Had they adopted the contrarian strategy of selling shares while they are still rising, and buying them while they are still falling, then they would be called *negative feedback traders* (Cutler et al., 1989).

The principle that security prices make excessive short-term changes away from their fundamental value in the light of new information coming into the market, with prices later reverting to their equilibrium trend value, has been actively researched.

There is some evidence that the prices of certain stocks rise 'too high' and fall 'too low'. In 1985 at the annual meeting of the American Finance Association, economists Werner DeBondt and Richard Thaler presented a paper entitled, 'Does the Stock Market Overreact?' (1985). To test whether extreme movements of stock prices in one direction provoke regression to the mean and are subsequently followed by extreme movements in the other direction, they studied the three-year returns of over a thousand stocks from January 1926 to December 1982. They classified the stocks that had gone up by more or had fallen by less than the market average in each three-year period as 'winners', and the stocks that had gone up by less or had fallen by more than the market average as 'losers'. They then calculated the average performance of each group over the subsequent three years.

Their findings were unequivocal: 'Over the last half-century, loser portfolios . . . outperform the market by, on average, 19.6 per cent 36 months after portfolio formation. Winner portfolios, on the other hand, earn [produce returns] about 5.0 per cent less than the market' (1985).

Although DeBondt and Thaler's test methods have been subjected to some criticism, their findings have been confirmed by other analysts using different methods. When investors overreact to new information and ignore long-term trends, regression to the mean turns the average winner into a loser and the average loser into a winner. This reversal tends to develop with some delay, which is what creates the profitable opportunity. One could really say that first the market overreacts to short-term news and then underreacts while awaiting new short-term news of a different character.

The studies of this process have followed one of three approaches. Those by Poterba and Summers (1988) measure the ratio of short-term volatility to long-term volatility. If prices always follow their fundamental value, the ratio of short-term to long-term volatility will be unity. If, however, there are large short-term deviations from fundamental values which decay over time as the price reverts to its long-term equilibrium, the ratio of volatilities will be less than unity. This latter hypothesis is exactly what Poterba and Summers found for the New York Stock Exchange over the period 1926 to 1985 for all investment horizons of two years or more. In addition they found that the evidence of mean reversion was stronger in small capitalization stocks than for large capitalization stocks.

The second approach has been to look for long-term negative serial correlation. Fama and French (1988a), for example, regressed multi-year real returns (New York Stock Exchange returns adjusted for inflation) upon past multi-year returns over the period 1926 to 1985 and found negative serial correlation. Moreover the serial correlation was larger for small capitalization stocks. The presence of serial correlation, as discussed in Chapter 10, would suggest market inefficiency.

Fama and French (1988b) and Campbell and Shiller (1988) regressed stock returns on the difference between stock prices and dividends or earnings. The Fama and French study covered 1926 to 1986, while the Campbell and Shiller study covered the period 1871 to 1987. Both studies found negative serial correlation in two- and four-year returns (Fama and French) and one-, three- and ten-year returns (Campbell and Shiller).

However, there is some doubt as to the robustness of these findings, and therefore their support for market inefficiency. First, there is the problem of small sample sizes because of the long period over which mean reversion can operate. For example, the period 1926–86 is 60 years, but provides only 30 observations of two-year returns and only 15 observations of four-year returns.

In addition, as Fama and French (1988b) note, negative serial correlation does not seem to apply to the data if the period 1926–40 is removed. However, the negative serial correlation found in Fama and French (1988a) applied to both time periods.

The third approach is to search for extreme price behaviour in one period and observe the behaviour of the same securities in subsequent time periods. The studies of DeBondt and Thaler (1985 and 1987), mentioned earlier for the US market, for example, show stocks that were extreme winners or losers over a three- to five-year period show positive or negative excess returns respectively in the following period.

WHAT IS PROSPECT THEORY?

The overreaction to new information that DeBondt and Thaler reported in the behaviour of stock prices was, they argue, the result of the human tendency to give most weight to recent evidence and to lose sight of the long run. After all, they reason, we know a lot more about what is happening right now than we can ever know about what will happen at some uncertain date in the future.

The most influential research into how people manage risk and uncertainty has been conducted by Daniel Kahneman and the late Amos Tversky, based at Princeton and Stanford. Kahneman and Tversky call their concept *Prospect Theory* (1979). Prospect theory brings together several aspects of psychological research and differs in crucial respects from expected utility theory, although, equally crucially, it shares the advantage of being able to be modelled mathematically. The theory is based on the results of hundreds of experiments in which people have been asked to choose between pairs of gambles. Prospect theory discovered behaviour patterns that had never been recognized by proponents of rational decision-making. Kahneman and Tversky ascribe these patterns to two human shortcomings. First, emotion often destroys the self-control that is essential to rational decision-making. Second, people are often unable to understand fully what they are dealing with. They experience what psychologists call cognitive difficulties. People, behavioural finance proponents claim, suffer from cognitive dissonance: holding beliefs plainly at odds with the evidence, usually because the belief has been held and cherished for a long time. Psychiatrists sometimes call this 'denial'. Nature is so varied and so complex that we have a hard time drawing valid generalizations from what we observe. We use shortcuts that lead us to erroneous perceptions, or we interpret small samples as representative of what larger samples would show.

Tversky and Kahnemann (1974) demonstrate that we display risk *aversion* when we are offered a choice in one setting and then turn into risk-*seekers* when we are offered the same choice in a different setting. We tend to ignore the common components of a problem and concentrate on each part in isolation. This is one reason why Markowitz's prescription for portfolio building was so slow to find acceptance. We have trouble recognizing how much information is enough and how much is too much. We pay excessive attention to low-probability events accompanied by high drama and overlook events that happen in a routine fashion. We treat costs and uncompensated losses differently, even though their impact on wealth is identical. We start out with a purely rational decision about how to manage our risks and then extrapolate from what may be only a run of good luck. As a result, we forget about regression to the mean, overstay our positions, and end up in trouble.

Kahneman and Tversky pose the following question to show how intuitive perceptions mislead us (1984). Ask yourself whether the letter K appears more often as the first or as the third letter of English words. You will probably answer that it appears more often as the first letter. Actually, K appears as the third letter twice as often. Why the error? We find it easier to recall words with a certain letter at the beginning than words with that same letter somewhere else.

The asymmetry between the way we make decisions involving gains and decisions involving losses is one of the most striking findings of prospect theory. It is also one of the most useful.

Where significant sums are involved, most people will reject a fair gamble in favour of a certain gain – $100,000 certain is preferable to a 50-50 possibility of $200,000 or nothing. We are risk-averse, in other words.

But what about losses? Kahneman and Tversky's first paper on prospect theory (1979), describes an experiment showing that our choices between negative outcomes are mirror images of our choices between positive outcomes. In one of their experiments they first asked the subjects to choose between an 80 per cent chance of winning $4000 and a 20 per cent chance of winning nothing versus a 100 per cent chance of receiving $3000. Even though the risky choice has a higher mathematical expectation, an expected value of $3200, 80 per cent of the subjects chose the certain $3000. These people were risk-averse.

Then Kahneman and Tversky offered a choice between taking the risk of an 80 per cent chance to the participants of losing $4000 and a 20 per cent chance of breaking even versus a 100 per cent chance of losing $3000. Now 92 per cent of the respondents chose the gamble, even though its mathematical expectation of a loss of $3200 was once again larger than the certain loss of $3000. When the choice involves losses, from this evidence, we are risk-seekers, not risk-averse.

Prospect theory also claims that people regularly miscalculate probabilities. People assume that outcomes which are very probable are less likely than they really are, that outcomes which are unlikely are more likely than they are, and that extremely improbable, but still possible, outcomes have no chance at all of happening. Prospect theorists also argue that individuals tend to view decisions in isolation, rather than as part of a bigger picture.

Studies of investor behaviour in the capital markets reveal that most of what Kahneman and Tversky and their associates hypothesized in the laboratory is played out by the behaviour of investors.

BEHAVIOURAL FINANCE AND PROSPECT THEORY

Richard Thaler, responding to these flaws in the rational model, has launched a new field of study called 'behavioural finance' (1993). Behavioural finance analyzes how investors struggle to find their way through the give and take between risk and return, one moment engaging in cool calculation and the next yielding to emotional impulses. The result of this mixture between the rational and not-so-rational is a capital market that itself fails to perform consistently in the way that the theoretical models predict that it will perform.

Earlier in this chapter we discussed a paper titled 'Does the Stock Market Overreact?' which Thaler and one of his graduate students, Werner DeBondt, presented at the annual meeting of the American Finance Association in December 1985. There this paper served as an example of regression to the mean. It can also serve as an example of the failure of the theory of rational behaviour.

As an example of prospect theory, Thaler and DeBondt demonstrated that when new information arrives, investors revise their beliefs not according to the objective methods set forth by Bayes (1763), but by giving too much weight to the new information and too little to the prior and longer-term information. The essence of the Bayesian approach is to provide a mathematical rule explaining how you should change your existing beliefs in the light of new evidence. In other words it allows investors to combine new data with their existing knowledge or expertise.

The canonical example of Bayesian theory is to imagine that a new-born baby observes his or her first sunset, and wonders whether the sun will rise again. The baby assigns equal prior probabilities to both possible outcomes and represents this by placing one white and one black marble in a bag. The following day when the sun rises, the child places another white marble in the bag. The probability that a marble plucked randomly from the bag will be white (i.e. the child's degree of belief in future sunrises) has gone from a half to two-thirds. After sunrise the next day the child adds another white marble, and the probability (and thus the degree of belief goes from two-thirds to three-quarters, and so on. Gradually, the initial belief that the sun is just as likely as not to rise each morning is modified to become a near certainty that the sun will rise. In a Bayesian analysis, in other words a set of observations should be seen as something that changes opinion, rather than as a means of determining ultimate truth. This is far more subtle than the traditional way of presenting results, in which an outcome is deemed statistically significant only if there is a better than 95 per cent chance that it could not have occurred by chance.

In contrast to the Bayesian approach, however, applying prospect theory investors weight the probabilities of outcomes on the 'distribution of impressions' rather than on an objective calculation based on historical probability distributions. As a consequence, stock price systematically overshoot so far in either direction that their reversal is predictable regardless of what happens to earnings or dividends or any other objective factor.

PSYCHOLOGICAL ANCHORS FOR THE STOCK MARKET

Shiller (2000), a major critic of the efficient markets school, demonstrated that the stock market cannot be explained by standard economic models based on fundamentals. Figure 13.1 shows, for the USA, the monthly real Standard and Poor's (S&P) Composite Stock Price Index from January 1871 to January 2000 (upper curve), along with the corresponding series of real S&P Composite earnings (lower curve) for the same years. Figure 13.1 allows us to get a truly long-term perspective on the US stock market's recent levels. As Shiller demonstrates, we can see how differently the market has behaved recently as compared with the past. We see that the market has been heading up fairly uniformly ever since it bottomed out in July 1982. It is clearly the most dramatic bull market in US history. The rapid rise of prices in the years 1992 to 2000

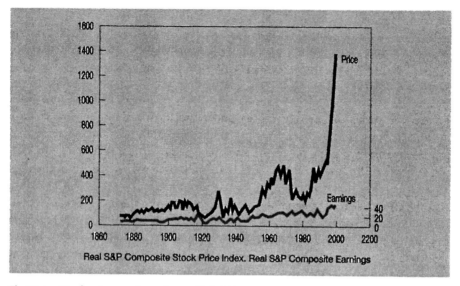

Fig 13.1 ● Stock prices and earnings, 1871–2000

Source: Irrational Exuberance, Robert J. Shiller (2000). Reproduced with permission Princeton University Press

has been most remarkable. As Shiller puts it the price index 'looks like a rocket taking off through the top of the chart'.

How can this recent explosive growth of stock prices be explained? Standard valuation models of the stock market, as discussed in Chapter 7, stress that stock prices efficiently discount future corporate earnings. However, as Figure 13.1 shows, no such growth in earnings has taken place. Earnings appear to oscillate around a slow steady growth path over the last 100 years while stock prices have risen sharply. To explain this Shiller turns to behavioural finance.

Psychological research, Shiller argues, demonstrates that there are patterns of human behaviour that suggest anchors for the market that would not be expected if markets worked entirely rationally. Shiller's argument is in line with the work of Kahnemann and Tversky, and Thaler. These patterns of human behaviour are not the result of extreme human ignorance, but rather of the character of human intelligence, reflecting its limitations as well as its strengths. Investors are striving to do the right thing, but they have limited abilities and certain natural modes of behaviour that decide their actions when an unambiguous prescription for action is lacking. Investors turn to what they best understand, some form of psychological anchoring.

Two kinds of psychological anchors are considered by Shiller: *quantitative anchors* and *moral anchors*. *Quantitative anchors* give indications for the appropriate levels of the market that some people use as indications of whether the market is over- or under-priced and whether it is a good time to buy. Moral anchors operate by determining the strength of the reason that compels people to buy stocks, a reason that they must weigh against their other uses for the wealth they already have (or could have) invested in the market. With quantitative anchors, people are weighing numbers against prices when they decide whether stocks (or other assets) are priced right. With moral anchors, people compare the intuitive or emotional strength of the argument for investing in the market against their wealth and their perceived need for money to spend now.

QUANTITATIVE ANCHORS FOR THE STOCK MARKET

Designers of questionnaires, as Shiller demonstrates, have learned that the answers people give to these questionnaires can be heavily influenced by suggestions that are given on the questionnaires themselves. For example, when people are asked to state within which of a number of ranges their income falls, their answers are influenced by the ranges given. The ranges serve as 'anchors' to which they make their answers conform.

Psychologists, Shiller illustrates, have shown that people's decisions in ambiguous situations are influenced by whatever available anchor is at hand. When you must come up with an estimate, and you are unsure what to say, you take whatever number is before you. Psychologists Amos Tversky and Daniel Kahneman demonstrated this tendency clearly in an experiment involving a wheel of fortune, i.e. a large wheel with the numbers from 1 to 100 on it, similar to those used in television game shows, that is designed to stop at a random number when it is spun (1974). Subjects were asked difficult questions whose answers were numbers between 1 and 100, with questions such as the percentage of African nations in the United Nations. They were asked first to say whatever the answer they would give was above or below the number just produced by the wheel of fortune. Then they were asked to give their own answer. The experimenters found that the answer was quite substantially influenced by the random number on the wheel. For example, if the wheel stopped at 10, the median percentage of African nations according to their subjects was 25, whereas if the wheel stopped at 65, the median percentage was 45. This experiment was particularly interesting because it was designed so that the subject clearly knew that the number produced by the wheel was purely random and, moreover, because the number produced by the wheel should have had no emotional significance for the respondents. So, what are the lessons here for investors?

In making judgements about the level of stock prices, the most likely anchor for investors is the most recently remembered price. The tendency of investors to use this anchor enforces the similarity of stock prices from one day to the next. Other possible anchors are remembered past prices. The tendency of past prices to serve as anchors may be part of the reason for the observed tendency for trends in individual stock prices to be reversed. Another Jones anchor may be the nearest milestone of a prominent index such as the Dow, the nearest round-number level, and investors' use of this anchor may help explain unusual market behaviour surrounding such levels. Past price changes may also provide an anchor, if attention is suitably drawn to them. The drop in the market in the October 1987 crash was nearly the same in percentage terms as that in the October 1929 crash, a fact to which investors' attention is often drawn.

For individual stocks, price changes may tend to be anchored to the price changes of other stocks, and price earning ratios may be anchored to other firms' price earnings levels. This kind of anchoring, Shiller suggests, may help to explain why individual stock prices move together as much as they do, and thus ultimately why stock price indexes are as volatile as they are. It may also explain why stocks of companies that are in different industries but are headquartered in the same country tend to have more similar price movements than stocks of companies that are in the same industry but are headquartered in different countries, contrary to one's expectation that the industry would define the fundamentals of the company better than the location of its headquarters. Indeed, all of the anomalies noted in financial markets, Shiller notes, have a simple explanation in terms of quantitative anchoring to convenient numbers.

MORAL ANCHORS FOR THE STOCK MARKET

With moral anchoring, the market is tied down by people's comparisons of the intuitive force of stories and reasons as to why they should hold their investments against their perceived need to consume the wealth that these investments represent. The market is not prevented from going up to arbitrarily high levels because people have no idea what is intrinsically the 'right' level or what level would be too high. Rather, if the market were to get too high, the discrepancy between the wealth many people would then have in the market and their current living standards would, when compared with their reasons for holding stocks, encourage them to sell.

Shiller gives an appreciation of the nature of this anchor with an extreme example. Suppose, counter-factually, that the psychology of the market caused the level of the stock market to rise so as to make most holders of stocks multimillionaires – on paper. Then, unless the reason for these people have to continue holding every single share is perceived to be extremely strong, they would want to start *living* a little more like multimillionaires and sell some of their stocks to be able to spend the money. Such selling would obviously bring stock prices down, since there would be no buyers, and obviously there just isn't sufficient current national income available to sustain anything like this many multimillionaires. The stock market, on this reasoning, can reach fantastic levels only if people think that they have good reasons not to test it by trying to enjoy their new-found wealth.

Underlying this notion of moral anchors, Shiller demonstrates, is the psychological principle that much of the human thinking that results in action is not quantitative, but instead takes the form of *storytelling* and *justification*. This is why, in the case of moral anchors, people are weighing a story, which has no quantitative dimension, against the observed quantity of financial wealth that they have available for consumption. Such reasoning is not well described by the usual kind of economic theory, but there is a large amount of evidence in support of the assertion that investor reasoning does take this form.

Shiller concludes that these psychological anchors for the market can attach themselves to the strangest things. Given the nature of herd behaviour and epidemics within financial markets, it would appear that psychology rather than fundamentals has an important role in explaining recent volatility in the behaviour of stock prices.

STOCK PRICES: DO THEY FOLLOW A RANDOM WALK?

Whether an economic time series follows a random walk has long been a question of great interest to financial economists. Indeed, since the publication of Louis Bachelier's thesis *Theory of Speculation* in 1900, the theoretical and empirical implications of the random walk hypothesis as a model for speculative prices have been extensively researched.

Since Keynes' (1936) now famous pronouncement that most investors' decisions 'can only be taken as a result of animal spirits – of spontaneous urge to action rather than inaction, and not as the outcome of a weighted average of benefits multiplied by quantitative probabilities', a great deal of research has been devoted to examining the efficiency of stock market price formation. In Fama's (1970) survey, the vast majority of those studies were unable to reject the 'efficient markets' hypothesis for common stocks. Although several seemingly anomalous departures from market efficiency have been well documented, many financial economists would agree with Jensen's belief that 'there is no other proposition in economics which has more solid empirical evidence supporting it than the Efficient Markets Hypothesis' (1978).

Although a precise formulation of an empirically refutable efficient markets hypothesis must obviously be model-specific, historically the majority of such tests have focused on the forecastability of common stock returns. Within this paradigm, which has been broadly categorized as the 'random walk' theory of stock prices, few studies have been able to reject the random walk model statistically. However, several recent papers have uncovered empirical evidence which suggests that stock returns contain predictable components, as discussed in Chapter 10. For example, Keim and Stambaugh (1986) find statistically significant predictability in stock prices by using forecasts based on certain predetermined variables. In addition, Fama and French (1988a) show that long holding-period returns are significantly negatively serially correlated, implying that 25 to 40 per cent of the variation of longer-horizon returns is predictable from past returns.

Some of these studies have attributed this forecastability to what has come to be known as the 'stock market over-reaction' hypothesis, referred to earlier. This is the notion that investors are subject to waves of optimism and pessimism and therefore create a kind of 'momentum' that causes prices to temporarily swing away from their fundamental values. See DeBondt and Thaler (1985, 1987); DeLong, Shleifer, Summers and Waldmann (1989) and Poterba and Summers (1988). Although such a hypothesis does imply predictability, since what goes down must come up and vice versa, a well-articulated equilibrium theory of over-reaction with sharp empirical implications has yet to be developed.

But common to virtually all existing theories of over-reaction is one very specific empirical implication: price changes must be *negatively* autocorrelated for some holding period. For example, DeBondt and Thaler (1985) write: 'If stock prices systematically overshoot, then their reversal should be predictable from past return data alone'. Therefore, the extent to which the data are consistent with stock market over-reaction, broadly defined, may be distilled into an empirically decidable question: are return reversals responsible for the predictability in stock returns?

A more specific consequence of over-reaction is the profitability of a contrarian portfolio strategy, referred to earlier, a strategy that exploits negative serial dependence in asset returns in particular. The defining characteristic of a contrarian strategy is the purchase of securities that have performed poorly in the past and the sale of securities that have performed well. Selling the 'winners' and buying the 'losers' will earn positive expected profits in the presence of negative serial correlation because current losers are likely to become future winners and current winners are likely to become future losers. Therefore, one implication of stock market over-reaction is positive expected profits from a contrarian investment rule. It is the apparent profitability of several contrarian strategies that has led many to conclude that stock markets do indeed over-react.

Lo and MacKinley, in their book *A Non-Random Walk Down Wall Street* (1999) marshal powerful evidence that the market is not completely random after all. Indeed the market has, so to speak, they claim, a memory. In the short run, broad market returns are positively correlated, like the weather. Just as a fair day is more likely to be followed by another fair one than by rain, a positive return in one week is more likely to be followed by a positive return in the next. In the long run, however, individual stock returns display negative serial correlation. Winners over the past three years are somewhat more likely to be losers over the next three years.

EFFICIENT MARKETS FIGHT BACK!

Proponents of 'behavioural finance' claim that stock prices adjust only slowly to new information, proving, they claim, that financial markets may not be efficient after all. They argue that investors often over-react or under-react to new public information, after which they slowly revise their views.

In his article 'Market efficiency, long term returns and behavioural finance', in the September 1998 *Journal of Financial Economics*, Eugene Fama of the University of Chicago and a long-time proponent of financial market efficiency claims that the growing evidence of market anomalies does *not* succeed in proving that markets are inefficient. He argues that whether these studies are considered collectively *or* individually, research on anomalies actually proves the opposite, namely that markets *are* in fact efficient. Fama also claims that many such studies are riddled with statistical and measurement problems.

Fama claims that even if one does not question the evidence of investor over- and under-reaction (which he does), when considered *collectively*, the body of research on market anomalies fails to bury the EMH. Evidence of such anomalies is insufficient proof of market inefficiency, unless *either* over-reaction *or* under-reaction is the dominant observed phenomenon. In his words, 'if over-reaction was the general result in studies of long-term returns, market efficiency would be dead'. But this, Fama claims, is *not* the case; the incidence of over-reaction is about as common as that of under-reaction, proving that markets *are* efficient, since such behaviour can be attributable to chance.

Fama's main argument is that there is no clear evidence of *systematic* over-reaction or under-reaction in the long-term return studies of market anomalies. Furthermore, long-term return *reversals* are as frequent as long-term return *continuations*.

As Table 13.1 illustrates, there is an even split among studies proving over-reaction and under-reaction, long-term return reversals and continuations. Announcement and post-announcement returns have the same sign for seasoned equity offerings, dividend initiations and omissions, share repurchases, stock splits and spin-offs (indicating under-reaction). They have opposite signs for new exchange listings, proxy fights and IPOs (indicating over-reaction). This collective evidence, Fama argues, is *perfectly consistent with efficient markets*.

Furthermore, when considered *individually*, Fama states that studies predicting the death of market efficiency hold up poorly. Even some of the better studies succeed only in explaining the specific anomalies they were *designed* to explain, but fail to describe the 'big picture'. Since 'splashy' results get more attention, he claims that researchers are motivated to find them. As a result, the evidence of anomalies is biased and the underlying studies do not represent a collection of random samples.

Table 13.1 ● Over-reaction and under-reaction to market anomalies

Event	Pre-event return	Announcement return	Post-event return
Initial public offerings	na	+	−
Seasoned equity offerings	+	−	−
Mergers (acquiring firm)	+	0	−
Dividend initiations	+	+	+
Dividend omissions	−	−	−
Earnings announcements	na	+	+
New exchange listings	+	+	−
Share repurchases	0	+	+
Proxy fights	−	+	− (or 0)
Stock splits	+	+	+
Spin-offs	+	+	+ (or 0)
(+) positive	(−) negative	(0) no reaction	(na) not available

Source: adapted from Table 1 of Fama (1998), 'Market efficiency, long-term returns and behavioural finance', Journal of Financial Economics, September 1998

Fama concedes that despite the fact that studies providing over-reaction and under-reaction are evenly split, markets could very well be inefficient if the anomalies were so *large* that they could not be attributed to chance alone. But, he claims, most studies are riddled with statistical and measurement problems and anomalies detected in many studies disappear when measured using different techniques. Fama further argues that any test of market efficiency is simultaneously a test of how stocks are priced. The two are inseparable, hence results cannot be attributed to market efficiency alone, especially if the underlying stock pricing model is incomplete. This problem tends to be more acute in studies based on long-term returns – typical for research on anomalies – because any error in the stock pricing model is compounded over a longer period of time.

Fama claims that studies of long-term returns are also sensitive to the way the tests are done. For example, many studies compare their results to the returns of a buy-and-hold strategy, based on *equal-weighting* of returns. Fama argues that this tends to create the *illusion* of an anomaly. The reason is that the commonly-used capital asset pricing model (CAPM) is inappropriate in pricing small-capitalization stocks; hence, studies using an equal-weighting of returns are more likely to have contaminated results than those based on *value-weighting* (where smaller stocks carry less weight). Hence, the observed IPO anomalies may be attributable not to over-reaction, but to the mispricing of IPOs, which tend to involve smaller stocks.

Fama states that some studies that identify anomalies using data covering a specific period fail when applied to different timeframes (e.g. stock splits). In other studies, evidence of anomalies is statistically insignificant (e.g. share repurchases), or disappears when stocks are adjusted for size (e.g. dividend omissions and initiations). In summary, Fama states that 'if a reasonable change in the method of estimating abnormal returns causes an anomaly to disappear, the anomaly is on shaky footing, and it is reasonable to suggest that it is an illusion'. Most anomalies are largely limited to small stocks, which Fama claims are typically under-priced using standard asset pricing models. The post-earnings-announcement drift is one of the few *bona fide* anomalies, which he claims is above suspicion.

Fama concludes that any new theory on how investors behave and markets operate should explain the full range of observed results. It should not be a *piecemeal* attempt at explaining one specific anomaly.

CHAPTER 14

Some puzzles in financial economics

INTRODUCTION

Financial markets have been characterized by tremendous growth in recent years. This growth has been shadowed by intensive academic research, particularly concerning the pricing of financial assets. Valuation models for pricing financial assets were discussed in Chapters 6 and 7. In this chapter we discuss the extent to which these models can accurately explain the principal characteristics of recent financial market behaviour, both on the part of investors and on the part of the markets themselves. Many standard models break down when applied to the actual behaviour of financial markets. The question marks raised, normally referred to as 'puzzles', are the subject matter of this chapter. The puzzles discussed here are:

- the equity risk premium puzzle
- the international diversification puzzle
- the asset allocation puzzle.

THE EQUITY RISK PREMIUM PUZZLE

The equity risk premium puzzle revolves around the fact that there is an enormous discrepancy between the returns on stocks and those from fixed income securities. Since 1926 the annual real return on US stocks has been about 7 per cent, while the real return on Treasury bills has been less than 1 per cent. This differential favouring equities is referred to as 'the equity premium'. As demonstrated by Mehra and Prescott (1985), the combination of a high equity premium and a low risk-free rate, is difficult to explain with plausible levels of investor risk aversion. Mehra and Prescott estimate that investors would have to have coefficients of relative risk aversion in excess of 30 to explain the historical equity premium, whereas previous estimates and theoretical arguments suggest that the actual figure is close to 1.0.

The robustness of the equity premium has been addressed by Siegel (1991, 1992) who examines the returns since 1802. As we discussed in Chapter 7, Siegel finds that real equity returns have been remarkably stable. For example, over the three time periods 1802–1870, 1871–1925 and 1926–1990, real compound equity returns were 5.7, 6.6 and 6.4 per cent. However, returns on short-term government bonds have fallen dramatically, the figures for the same three time periods being 5.1, 3.1 and 0.5 per cent. Thus, there was no equity premium in the first two-thirds of the nineteenth century (because bond returns were high), but over the last 120 years stocks have had a significant edge.

The reason why this is referred to as the equity premium is that it is practically impossible to explain the co-existence of the 6 per cent equity return with the historical short-term or risk-free real rate of return of (just under) 1 per cent, at least using the standard model of investor behaviour. The degree of risk aversion needed to reconcile these two figures is implausibly high.

In their model Mehra and Prescott (1988) assume that the utility of consumption in a given year does not depend on consumption in other years and that there is constant relative risk aversion.

The relevant parameter in their model is the coefficient of relative risk aversion, referred to as A, whose interpretation is that if consumption falls by 1 per cent, then the marginal value of a dollar of income increases by A per cent. In their model, Mehra and Prescott found that to explain the historic equity risk premium, as was mentioned earlier, A needed to be between 30 and 40, which was deemed to be much too high.

To see why this is so, consider a gamble where there is a 50 per cent chance to double your wealth, and a 50 per cent chance to have your wealth fall by half. If A = 30, then you have the absurd implication of being willing to pay 49 per cent of your wealth to avoid the 50 per cent chance of losing half your wealth. The Mehra and Prescott paper has been enormously influential, and has spawned a whole new body of literature on this issue.

CAN THEORETICAL MODELS EXPLAIN THE EQUITY RISK PREMIUM?

Various models have been put forward to explain the need for such a high equity premium. We will examine four of them here.

1 Effect of a borrowing constraint

Constanides, Donaldson and Mehra (1998) consider an economy in which consumers are subject to a borrowing constraint. The bulk of the future income of the young agents is derived from wages forthcoming in their middle age. The stock market does potentially offer a good hedge against these uncertain wages, and young agents would be better off if they could borrow while they were young to invest in equities. However, the borrowing constraint prevents them from doing so. It is the middle-aged who hold a diversified portfolio of bonds and equities, as the uncertainty about their future wages has diminished and they no longer need equities to hedge their bets. Clearly such a model delivers a rather higher equity risk premium than one without a borrowing constraint.

2 Myopic loss aversion

Bernartzi and Thaler (1995) make three key assumptions.

1 Agents are assumed to derive utility from returns, not the overall level of assets.

2 Investors display 'loss aversion', i.e. losses are assumed to hurt significantly more than the pleasure yielded from gains.

3 Even long-term investors are assumed to evaluate their portfolios frequently.

They find that they can explain the size of the historical (*ex post*) equity risk premium by using the previously estimated parameters of prospect theory. See Kahneman and Tversky (1979), discussed in Chapter 13. Their work assumes that investors evaluate their portfolios annually. Their result is of particular interest since their assumptions appear to be quite plausible in the light of commonly observed behaviour.

3 A liquidity-based asset pricing model (LAPM)

In some interesting new work, Holstrom and Tirole (1998) consider the implications of an alternative approach to asset prices based on industrial and financial corporations' desire to hoard liquidity to fulfil future cash needs. They refer to this as a liquidity-based asset pricing model (LAPM). For simplicity, they assume that consumers are risk neutral, so that shares and bonds alike would trade at par in the standard CAPM. However, in the LAPM, US Treasury securities offer better insurance against shortfalls in corporate earnings and other liquidity needs than shares do, and this fact can generate an equity risk premium (so households hold equities, firms hold bonds).

4 Disasters have not occurred to the US economy

Jorion and Goetzmann (1995) conjecture that the equity premium may be due to the fact that disasters have largely bypassed the US economy. Their theory is based on the fact that at the beginning of the 1920s there were active stock markets in many countries, including France, Russia, Germany, Japan and Argentina. But the stock markets of all these countries were interrupted by war, hyper-inflation or political turmoil.

Presumably, Jorion and Goetzmann go on to argue, investors thought there was some probability that the USA would be disrupted as well. But this event has not occurred, so historical equity returns have not reflected it. The large equity premium in the USA may be tied to investors' recognition of the possibility of economic disruption and stock market interruption that never materialized.

Investors generally are risk averse. Risk-averse stock market investors want a high return on investments in normal times to compensate them for the risk of extreme losses that would occur if the stock market crashed or was interrupted by war or political turmoil. The USA has not experienced the extreme financial market disruptions that many other countries have. Perhaps, Jorion and Goetzmann suggest, US investors have, by the luck of the draw, been rewarded for catastrophic events that did not occur.

PROSPECT THEORY AND THE EQUITY PREMIUM PUZZLE

People betting on horse races back long shots over favourites far more often than they should. Prospect theory suggests this is because they attach too low a probability to likely outcomes and too high a probability to quite unlikely ones. Gamblers also tend to shift their bets away from favourites towards long shots as the day's racing nears its end. Because of the commission taken by the bookmakers, by the time later races are run many racegoers have lost some money. For many of them, a successful bet on an outsider could probably turn a losing day into a winning one. Mathematically and rationally this should not matter. The last race of the day is no different from the first race of the next day. But most racegoers close their 'mental account' at the end of each racing day, and they hate to leave the track a loser.

Applying this reasoning to the equity premium puzzle provides an explanation of the equity premium puzzle. American stocks have long delivered higher returns to investors than seems justified by the difference in riskiness of equities and bonds. Orthodox financial economists largely ascribe this simply to the fact that investors have less appetite for risk than expected. But prospect theory suggests that if investors, rather like race goers, are averse to losses during any given year, this might justify such a high equity premium. Annual losses on shares are much more frequent than annual losses on bonds, so investors demand a much higher premium for holding shares to compensate for the greater risk of suffering a loss in any given year.

What will happen to the equity premium?

According to Ibbotson Associates, a research firm, the equity premium has averaged around seven percentage points since 1926. Economists fall into three camps about where it will go in future: those who think it will remain high, those who think it will be smaller, because investors have a more sensible view of the riskiness of shares; and those who agree it will be smaller, but think this will come as a nasty shock, following a stock market crash.

Those who think the equity premium will remain high have to explain how company profits can grow fast enough to justify current share prices. According to Jeremy Siegel (1995), an economist at Wharton, to deliver an equity premium of seven points (above the returns on Treasury bonds) without further increases in price earnings ratios, real per-share corporate earnings would have to grow by about 9 per cent a year – more than five times as fast as the average since 1871 and double the growth rate since the Second World War. This implies that within 50 years the average returns generated each year by American shares would exceed America's GDP!

Those who reckon that future earnings growth will be faster in future tend to believe in the 'new economy' – that low inflation and new technology will produce faster economic growth and profitability. Robert Hall, an economist at Stanford University (2000) has looked at this from a novel angle. What if today's share prices accurately value the capital of American companies? Because the ratio of share prices to the replacement cost of physical capital (factories, machines and so on) – a ratio known as Tobin's q which we discussed in Chapter 7 – is at a record high, that would imply there has been a huge increase in intangible assets, such as new technology and human capital. Hall thinks this is plausible, but only if returns on capital were to have risen to an average of 17 per cent a year during the 1990s. That is well above the post-war average of 10 per cent – although not so far above the 13 per cent average of the 1950s.

What about the impact of lower inflation on share prices? Franco Modigliani and Richard Cohn (1979) caused a stir by arguing that shares were much too cheap because investors had ignored the effect of inflation on the real value of liabilities such as debt, and so were undervaluing firms with large borrowings. A study by Jay Ritter and Richard Warr of the University of Florida (1999) finds that as inflation has fallen, there has been less of such 'money illusion', and that this alone explains a large part of the rise in equities since 1979. But it does not suggest that share prices will continue to rise as fast as they have done recently. High equity returns may merely reflect the one-off transition from high to low inflation.

Those who do not believe in the 'new economy' reckon instead that the equity premium will be much lower in future. Some financial economists are untroubled by this. For years, the profession has been trying to solve the 'equity-premium puzzle' – namely that the equity premium was much higher than seemed to be justified by the riskiness of shares. Might it now have solved itself, because investors show that they expect equity premiums to be at least as high as they have been in the past.

The other explanation for current share prices is that investors are indeed being irrational. Economists who believe this point to evidence from psychology that, for instance, people give too much weight to recent experience – share prices have been going up, so investors expect them to go on doing so. These ideas were discussed in Chapter 13. Combined with demographic factors – such as the baby-boomer generation investing for retirement – this could send share prices soaring even further above 'rational' levels. If so, these academics should not be surprised. John Maynard Keynes, another economist who knew about the stock market, once noted that 'there is nothing so dangerous as the pursuit of a rational investment policy in an irrational world' (Keynes, 1936).

THE INTERNATIONAL DIVERISIFICATION PUZZLE

The international diversification puzzle, sometimes referred to as the 'home bias' puzzle, revolves around the choice of international assets by domestic investors. It is widely agreed that investors hold too little of their financial wealth in foreign securities. In the past, this could be explained by the general lack of international financial integration and national barriers to capital flows. However, the growth and integration of capital markets over the past 20 years have not led to similarly dramatic portfolio reallocations. For example, Kenneth French and James Poterba (1991) report that US investors hold about 94 per cent of their financial assets in the form of US securities. For Japan, the United Kingdom, and Germany, the portfolio share of domestic assets in each case exceeds 85 per cent. While recent years have witnessed an increase in international diversification, holdings of domestic assets are still far too high to be consistent with the standard theory of portfolio choice.

Baxter and Jerman (1997) argue even further that the divergence between diversified portfolios and observed portfolios is much larger than is currently thought. This claim is motivated by the observation that, for a nation as a whole, the largest component of wealth consists of non-traded human capital. Labour's share in US national income is about 60 per cent. Baxter and Jerman use this as a rough benchmark of the share of human capital in total wealth. Their main finding is that the returns to human capital and physical capital are very highly correlated within countries, even though the growth rates of labour and capital income are not highly correlated. They go on to show that a substantial short position in domestic marketable assets is consequently required to hedge human capital risk. As a result, individuals wishing to hold a diversified world portfolio should establish a short position in domestic marketable assets.

How can the international diversification puzzle be explained?

Explanations for this puzzle revolve around the fact that investors are either prevented from arbitraging differences between domestic and foreign assets or that the gains from doing so may not be large enough.

The standard international CAPM model states that the required returns on foreign deposits relative to domestic deposits depend positively upon the measure of relative risk-aversion and the variability of returns captured by the covariance between excess returns and the return on the portfolio. The returns depend negatively upon the covariance between excess returns and the returns on the portfolio. It was in applying this model that French and Poterba (1991) found that US, Japanese, French and British investors had a much stronger preference for domestic equity holdings than is suggested by the CAPM model.

How good is the international CAPM model?

It is necessary to ask here whether the CAPM model is in fact a good description of the world. Dumas and Solnik (1993) found that the international CAPM is not rejected by the data. Although other models have provided mixed results, the international CAPM does appear to have some predictive content for international equity returns.

Is the international risk diversifiable with domestic assets?

It is important to know whether it is possible to capture the returns by investing overseas by investing in some domestic assets? If so, then domestic residents may hold a disproportionately large component of domestic assets simply because they can gain the same diversification benefits with particular domestic securities as with foreign assets.

One possible group of domestic returns that may be correlated with foreign returns corresponds to the equity of domestic multinational corporations. Since much of their earnings come from abroad, it might seem that their returns more closely match the returns on foreign stock markets than those of other domestic companies. Jacquillat and Solnik (1978) ask whether the stocks of domestic multinational firms have this diversification potential by regressing the returns of their stocks on the returns of stock indexes for a set of countries. They find that the coefficients on their own domestic stock index (the traditional market 'betas') are close to one. Therefore, domestic multinational stocks are not much different in providing diversification benefits than the strategy of simply holding the domestic market portfolio.

Segmented equity markets and government restrictions

One explanation for the puzzle may be that domestic investors face barriers to acquiring foreign equities. The inability to obtain or hold foreign equities at the same cost as foreign residents may be the result of government restrictions such as taxes, or may reflect more subtle constraints. In the extreme case of complete capital market immobility, investors may be forced to hold only their own countries' equities. More realistically, domestic investors are likely to face some restrictions, if only those of information and transactions costs, that potentially impede capital flows, with the likely outcome that portfolios of domestic residents are biased toward domestic equities.

Taken together, the evidence suggests that government restrictions can be important for explaining why the portfolios of domestic residents in developing countries may face barriers to investing in overseas equities. On the other hand, this argument is more difficult to make for the developed countries that do not face these restrictions. The US investor demonstrates a strong 'home bias' in equity holdings with developed countries, yet it does not impose significant restrictions on capital account movements.

In a recently published paper, Obstfeld and Rogoff (2000) explain the home bias in equity holdings puzzle by examining differences in prices between goods prices for importers and exporters. Even though they assume that securities can be traded cost-free, trade in the goods from which the securities are derived still incurs costs. With assumed trading costs of 25 per cent, their simulation generates portfolios with home biases very like those in the real world. Whether the assumed trading costs really do explain the home bias problem has opened up a whole new research area for financial economists.

THE ASSET ALLOCATION PUZZLE

How should investors' attitudes toward risk influence the composition of their portfolios? A simple and elegant answer to this question comes from the mutual-fund separation theorem. This theorem, a building block of the most basic capital asset pricing model (CAPM), was discussed in Chapter 8. According to the theorem, more risk-averse investors should hold more of their portfolios in the risk-less asset. The composition of risky assets, however, should be the same for all investors.

Canner, Mankiw and Weil (1997) show that popular financial advisers appear not to follow the mutual-fund separation theorem and this phenomenon has become known as the 'asset allocation puzzle'. When financial advisers are asked to allocate portfolios among stocks, bonds and cash, they recommend more complicated strategies than indicated by the theorem. Moreover, these strategies differ from the theorem in a systematic way. According to these advisers, more risk-averse investors should hold a higher ratio of bonds to stocks. This advice contradicts the conclusion that all investors should hold risky assets in the same proportion, hence the puzzle.

Theoretical background

The capital asset pricing model is based on the work of William F. Sharpe (1964), John Lintner (1965) and Jan Mossin (1966). This model, discussed in detail in Chapter 9, shows how rational investors should combine risky assets with a given distribution of returns. It rests on the following important assumptions.

1 All assets can be freely traded.

2 Investors operate over a one-period planning horizon.

3 Investors can hold long or short positions in all assets.

4 Investors are indifferent between any two portfolios with identical means and variances.

The fourth assumption can be replaced with the assumption that asset returns are normal, so that the mean and variance fully characterize the distribution of returns.

5 A risk-less asset exists.

In this case, the risk-less asset and a single mutual fund of risky assets are sufficient to generate all efficient portfolios. Under these conditions, all investors should hold risky assets in the same proportions. In particular, every investor should hold the same ratio of bonds to stocks. To achieve the desired balance of risk and return, investors simply vary the fraction of their portfolios made up of the risk-less asset.

To illustrate this principle, consider a world with three assets: an index fund of stocks; an index fund of bonds; and risk-less cash. Suppose the means and variance-covariance matrix of annual real returns for bonds and stock from 1926 to 2000 represents the distribution of future returns. In addition, suppose that cash offers a risk-less real return equal to the mean real return on Treasury bills over the same period. Straightforward calculations show that under these assumptions, all mean-variance efficient portfolios should hold bonds and stocks in a ratio of 0.33:1. For example, the portfolio composed of 60 per cent stocks, 20 per cent bonds and 20 per cent cash is mean-variance efficient: there is some quadratic objective function for which this portfolio is optimal. Other investors will hold other portfolios, depending on their preferences toward risk. But all investors should hold portfolios with a 0.33:1 ratio of bonds to stocks with differing amounts of cash. This is illustrated in Table 14.1.

Table 14.1 ● Mean variant efficient portfolios

	Stocks (%)	Bonds (%)	Cash (%)
Average risk investor	60	20	20
Risk-loving investor	72	24	4
Risk-averse investor	45	15	40

Now we know the theory, what advice do professional advisers provide?

Canner, Mankiw and Weil (1997) collated investment advice from four well-known financial advisers. See Table 14.2. These findings were then plotted out against the CAPM predictions in Figure 14.1. In Table 14.2 each of the advisers presents recommended allocations among stocks bonds and cash (money market instruments) for three investors with different preferences towards risk (low, average, high). The last column gives the recommended ratio of bonds to stocks, which the authors use to measure the composition of risky assets. The advisers all provide consistent advice. The recommended ratio of bonds to stocks falls as the investors become more willing to take on risk.

Table 14.2 ● Asset allocations recommended by financial advisers

		Per cent of Portfolio			
Adviser and investor type		Cash	Bonds	Stocks	Ratio of bonds to stocks
A.	Fidelity				
	Conservative	50	30	20	1.50
	Moderate	20	40	40	1.00
	Aggressive	5	30	65	0.46
B.	Merrill Lynch				
	Conservative	20	35	45	0.78
	Moderate	5	40	55	0.73
	Aggressive	5	20	75	0.27
C.	Jane Bryant Quinn				
	Conservative	50	30	20	1.50
	Moderate	10	40	50	0.80
	Aggressive	0	0	100	0.00
D.	The New York Times				
	Conservative	20	40	40	1.00
	Moderate	10	30	60	0.50
	Aggressive	0	20	80	0.25

Source: Canner, Mankiw and Weil (1997)

Figure 14.1 shows a scatter plot of the recommended portfolios. The horizontal axis shows the fraction of the portfolio made up of stocks. This fraction is a good proxy for tolerance toward risk. The vertical axis shows the ratio of

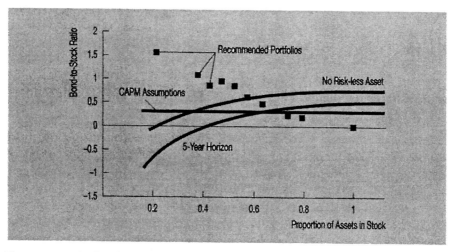

Fig 14.1 ● Optimal and recommended portfolios

bonds to stocks. The set of optimal portfolios according to the separation theorem is the horizontal line labelled 'CAPM Assumptions'. Figure 14.1 suggests that textbook theory does not well describe the behaviour of actual investors (or at least investment advisers).

How can this divergence between the model and the real world be explained?

Perhaps the theory is too simple. Life is, in fact, more complicated than theory would indicate. Perhaps popular advice on portfolio allocation is simply wrong. Maybe the underlying assumptions behind the CAPM are unrealistic. Answers to those questions remain inconclusive. Explaining popular advice to investors, using models of fully rational investors, remains an important puzzle for financial economists.

CHAPTER 15

Derivatives markets and financial economics

- What are derivatives?
- What are options?
- Where do option prices come from?
- What are the factors influencing the price of futures?
- How are options priced?
- Determinants of the value of a call option

WHAT ARE DERIVATIVES?

Derivatives are contracts which give one party a claim on an underlying asset (derived from the cash value of an underlying asset) at some point in the future, and bind a counterparty to meet a corresponding liability. The contract might describe an amount of currency, a security, a physical commodity, a stream of payments or a market index. It might bind both parties equally, or offer one party an option to exercise it or not. It might provide for assets or obligations to be swapped. It might be a bespoke derivative combining several elements. Whether derivatives are traded on exchanges or not, their market price will depend in part on the movement of the price of the underlying asset since the contract was created.

The rapid growth of derivatives trading around the world in recent years has been propelled by the internationalization of capital markets in general, by technological advances in computers and telecommunications, and by the increasingly fierce competition among big banks and securities houses to devise and sell products.

Where did derivatives come from?

Trading in derivative contracts has a long history. The first recorded accounts of derivative contracts can be traced back to the philosopher Thales of Miletus in ancient Greece, who, during the winter, negotiated what were essentially call options on oil presses for the spring olive harvest. De la Vega reported in 1688 that options and futures, or 'time bargains' as they were then known, were trading on the Amsterdam Bourse soon after it was opened. Evidence also suggests that futures contracts for rice were traded in Japan in the seventeenth and eighteenth centuries.

The first formalized futures exchange in the USA was the Chicago Board of Trade, which opened in 1848 with 82 members. In March 1851, the first futures contract was recorded. The contract called for the delivery of 3000 bushels of corn in June at a price of one cent per bushel below the March price. Listed stock options began trading in April 1973 on the Chicago Board Options Exchange (CBOE). Other exchanges began offering stock call options in 1975 and put options in 1977.

The recent revolution in option pricing theory also dates to 1973 with the publications by Fischer Black and Myron Scholes of their classic paper on option valuation. Since the publication of that paper the valuation of options and various other derivative contracts has been one of the primary areas of research among financial economists.

Some terminology relating to derivatives

Derivatives are often described as being complex instruments which defy understanding for the mathematically unsophisticated. Despite their intimidating appearance they are, in fact, constructed from simple elements, known to the financial markets for literally centuries.

Take the most basic of derivative transactions, a *forward contract*. One party agrees to buy, say, $1 million in three months' time, at a price fixed today in sterling terms. The mathematics of the transaction are well within the capacity of a pocket calculator. If prevailing interest rates are higher for the dollar than for sterling, somebody who wants to buy dollars forward for payment in sterling will be quoted a price lower than the one that is prevailing for transactions that are settled immediately.

Futures contracts differ from forward contracts by virtue of being traded on official exchanges. To make trading easier, their terms will be standard ones set by the appropriate exchange; they will be for a fixed quantity (of bonds, or pork bellies, or whatever instrument is being traded) and will run for a fixed period.

Options are a form of forward contracts in which the buyer can decide whether to exercise a right to buy (or sell) the underlying asset within an agreed time. The seller of the option then has to work out how to price the probability that the option will or will not be exercised. As discussed in detail in Chapter 2, only in 1973 did two American financial economists, Myron Scholes and Fischer Black, provide a plausible answer to the option pricing problem by devising a mathematical model with several inputs, the most important of which was the volatility of the price of the underlying asset.

Swaps complete the simple taxonomy. Albeit on a rather larger scale, an interest-rate swap works just as if, for sound financial reasons, Person A with a fixed-rate mortgage, and Person B with a floating-rate mortgage of the same size, agree to assume responsibility for one another's interest payments. Person A will take over the floating-rate payments and person B will take over the fixed-rate payments. In real life, big borrowers may swap interest-rate or currency obligations because they disagree over interest-rate trends, or because they find it cheaper to borrow money in foreign markets. A Japanese company wanting long-term Japanese yen may find it cheaper to borrow US dollars, then swap them into yen.

Table 15.1 provides formal definitions of the principal derivatives contracts traded: forwards, futures, options and swaps.

Table 15.1 ● Derivatives defined

Term	Definition
Forward contract	A contract to buy or sell a specified amount of a designated commodity, currency, security, or financial instrument at a known date in the future and at a price set at the time the contract is made. Forward contracts are negotiated between the contracting parties and are not traded on organized exchanges.
Futures contract	A contract to buy or sell a specified amount of a designated commodity, currency, security, or financial instrument at a known date in the future and at a price set at the time the contract is made. Futures contracts are traded on organized exchanges and are thus standardized. The contracts are marked to market daily, with profits and losses settled in cash at the end of the trading day.
Option contract	A contract that gives its owner the right, but not the obligation, to buy or sell a specified asset at a stipulated price, called the strike or exercise price. Contracts that give owners the right to buy are referred to as *call* options and contracts that give the owner the right to sell are called *put* options. Options include both standardized products that trade on organized exchanges and customized contracts between private parties.
Swap contract	A private contract between two parties to exchange cash flows in the future according to some prearranged formula. The most common type of swap is the 'plain vanilla' interest rate swap, in which the first party agrees to pay the second party cash flows equal to interest at a predetermined fixed rate on a notional principal. The second party agrees to pay the first party cash flows equal to interest at a floating rate on the same notional principal. Both payment streams are denominated in the same currency. Another common type of swap is the currency swap. This contract calls for the counterparties to exchange specific amounts of two different currencies at the outset, which are repaid over time according to a pre-arranged formula that reflects amortization and interest payments.

WHAT ARE OPTIONS?

An option is a contract between two parties that gives the buyer the right, but not the obligation, to buy or sell a specific quantity of a commodity or instrument at an agreed price for a specified period. The option buyer pays the seller a premium for the privilege of being able to buy or sell the instrument, at a fixed price, without having the commitment to do so.

To take an example, consider an option to buy gold at US $400 per ounce. Let us say the market price of gold is currently US $395. The option buyer pays the option seller a premium of US $3.50. The option buyer has the right, but not the obligation to buy gold at US $400. It will be profitable for the option buyer to exercise this right if the price of gold rises above US $403.50.

However, if the price of gold falls in the market, then the option buyer has no commitment to buy gold at US $400, and the option buyer can then allow the option to expire unexercised, and purchase gold at the cheaper market price.

Options are one of the most powerful derivatives contracts and it is important to become familiar with the terminology of the option market. A summary of the principal terms is illustrated below.

1 The option buyer becomes the *holder*. The option seller is called the *writer*.

2 A *call* option gives the owner the right to buy a specified quantity of a commodity at an agreed price over a given period.

3 A *put* option gives the owner the right to sell a specified quantity of a commodity at an agreed price over a given period.

4 The *premium* is the price paid for the option.

5 The *strike price* or *exercise price* is the rate at which the option may be exercised; in other words, it is the price which has been agreed under the option contract.

6 The *expiry date* is the final date on which the option can be exercised.

7 A *European-style* option can be exercised only on the expiry date, whereas an American-style option can be exercised at any date prior to and including the expiry date. (Note that these terms have no geographical significance.)

Exchange-traded versus over-the-counter options

Options may be traded on exchanges, i.e. in a physical location, or on the over-the-counter (OTC) market, in which dealing takes place between two counterparties, usually over the telephone.

Exchange-traded options have the following characteristics:

(a) fixed expiry dates, generally at three-monthly intervals for the third Wednesday in March, June, September and December;

(b) maturities of generally up to two years;

(c) strike/exercise prices at fixed intervals;

(d) fixed contract sizes;

(e) standardization of contracts. This means that markets tend to be liquid. In other words, bid-offer spreads (the difference between the buying and selling price) tend to be narrow, and large orders can usually be transacted fairly easily;

(f) trading is closely monitored. The clearing house of the exchange acts as the counterparty to every trade, thus the credit risk, i.e. the risk of default on a trade, is standardized and limited;

(g) prices are publicly quoted, i.e. trading takes place by open outcry between traders on the floor of the exchange. Prices are reported by information vendors such as Bloomberg and Reuters, and prices and volumes are reported in the financial press.

Over-the-counter options have the following characteristics.

1 Strike prices, contract sizes and maturity are all subject to negotiation.

2 They can be longer term than exchange-traded options – some banks will write them for up to ten years.

3 The holder has a direct credit risk on the writer. The writer has no credit risk on the holder provided the premium is paid up front.

4 The price at which the option is dealt is known only to the counterparties.

WHERE DO OPTION PRICES COME FROM?

In order to understand option prices it is essential to understand two key concepts, arbitrage and forwards/futures markets. Arbitrage is discussed below. Forwards and futures are financial instruments that relate present and future prices, and they are critical in understanding option pricing.

Arbitrage

Arbitrage is a powerful market force that helps to establish the value of many financial instruments. When discussing arbitrage it is important to distinguish between deterministic arbitrage and statistical arbitrage.

What is deterministic arbitrage?

Deterministic arbitrage is the classic technique of simultaneously buying and selling the same or equivalent products at different prices to achieve a risk-less profit. For example, what do we do if gold trades at $400 in New York and $410 in London? The answer is quite simple: we buy low and sell high. Specifically, we buy low for $400 in New York, and we sell high at $410 in London – and we make $10 risk-lessly. By 'risk-lessly' we mean there is no risk of prices moving against us. If we can execute these two trades simultaneously, there is no gold price risk, and we can be confident of a profit as long as other factors do not intervene.

One of the best ways to illustrate arbitrage opportunities is to use examples based on simple raffles. Raffles define and clarify some of the ideas of profit and probability we discuss further in this chapter.

Let's assume that a daily raffle sells *exactly* 100 tickets each morning. At the end of the day, one of these 100 tickets is chosen, and the holder of that ticket wins $1000. What is the fair price or expected value of one ticket? To solve this problem, we divide the $1000 prize by 100 tickets for a fair price of $10.

If we pay $10 for the ticket and we do not win, we will not feel we were cheated because we paid too much. We will attribute it to, say, the luck of the draw. Similarly, if we win, we will be ecstatic, but we will not think we bought a cheap ticket because, by the accident of probability, we won the prize.

When we divide the value of the prize by the number of tickets, we are able to derive the fair value or, in statistical terminology, the *expected value* or *mean value* of each ticket, in line with our discussion in Chapter 4.

What do we do if tickets sell for $9 instead of $10? At $9, the ticket is cheap – so cheap that it is worth buying every ticket in the raffle. When the winning number is drawn at the end of the day we stand to make a risk-less profit of $100. If we hold all the tickets, we win the $1000 prize – having paid only $900. We can arbitrage a deterministic $100 profit – meaning we are certain to make that $100 – as long as the person who created the raffle does not disappear after collecting our money.

What do we do if tickets sell for $11? Because $11 is too much to pay for a ticket, we want to sell raffle tickets instead of buying them if we can. We might hold our own raffle selling tickets at $10.50. After selling 100 tickets, we will take in $1050. The prize we have to pay the raffle winner is $1000, so we have $50 left in our pockets. If any raffle ticket sells for less than fair value it is worth buying it. If it is overvalued it is worth selling it.

The effect of these raffle scenarios is similar to the effect of gold trading at $400 in New York and at $410 in London. When there are many buyers of gold in New York, their demand forces the price up. When there are many sellers of gold in London, their supply forces the price down. Nobody can say exactly where the price will end up, but we presume it will finish up somewhere between $400 and $410. Eventually, we know that the price will equilibrate to a fair value – the same price to buyers and sellers in all markets. The *fair value* of gold does not necessarily mean this is the price gold will trade at – it means it is the *efficient market* value or the expected value. Locking in a sure profit by taking advantage of mispricing is known as deterministic arbitrage.

What is statistical arbitrage?

Let us assume for purposes of illustration that raffle tickets sell for less than their fair value. Now let us look at a different, but related, kind of arbitrage: statistical arbitrage.

What do we do if raffle tickets sell for $9 but we are permitted to buy only one ticket a day? Do we:

1 never buy a ticket;

2 buy a ticket once in a while; or

3 buy a ticket every day?

In this case, the ticket should be selling for $10 but only costs $9, so we have a $1 'edge', or expected profit per ticket. If we buy only one ticket a day, we are engaged in statistical arbitrage.

We do not have a certain profit if we cannot buy all the tickets in an under-priced raffle. We have to decide what is the best thing to do in an uncertain situation. In fact, the correct choice for someone who can accept the risk of a string of losses before winning the prize is not one, two, or even three tickets. The full answer is: buy one ticket every day until the universe ends. What do we expect to happen after buying a ticket every day until the end of time? We expect our fortune to grow without limit!

The key word in this scenario is *expect*. We are not certain to win this money, but we expect to win this money. We expect to earn an average of $1 a day on this raffle, because our edge, the expected value of our position, is $1. We expect to make that edge on average after repeated trials. This is called sta-tistical arbitrage because it is not certain or determined that we will make this profit – but we expect to make this profit over time.

What do we expect to happen after 100 days when we have spent $900 on raffle tickets? We expect to win one time. Are we assured of winning one time? Absolutely not – we could lose every time or we could win 2, 3, or even 99 times.

What do we expect to happen after 1000 days? There will be 1000 winners after 1000 days. With 1000 winners and a 1 in 100 chance of winning each day, we expect to win 10 times. We may not win 10 times – we may win only 8 times, or we may win 12 times. In fact, there is about a 70 per cent chance that we will win between 7 and 13 times. If we play 1000 times, we will be very surprised if we do not win at all – because the probability of not winning at all in 1000 tries is extremely small, if the raffle is fair.

The more times we play, the closer we should come to the number of times we expect to win and to the average of $1 a day we expect to make. If we play 1,000,000 times, we expect to make close to $1,000,000 – our profit might fall a few hundred dollars short of $1,000,000 or rise a few hundred dollars beyond $1,000,000, but that is a fairly small percentage variation compared to the percentage variation we might see after 100 days.

After 1,000,000 raffles, we expect to win about 10,000 times (1/100 of 1,000,000). Statisticians tell us we have about a 70 per cent chance of winning between 9,900 and 10,100 times. The larger number of raffles brings us closer to our expected average of 1 win for every 100 times. The longer the period, the closer we expect to come to the average payoff. To apply these principles to the pricing of derivatives we now need to turn to probability distributions.

Probability distributions

Suppose gold is trading at $400 an ounce today. What price will gold be in one year? If we ask many different people this question, we will probably get many different answers. Some people will be very pessimistic, predicting a dramatic drop in gold prices. Others will be very optimistic, predicting a large rise in gold prices. A number of people will fall in between the two extremes. After we accumulate all of the responses, we will get a picture of where people think gold is going to trade in a year. The picture might look something like Figure 15.1.

The numbers at the top of each bar represent the percentage of people who predict that the price of gold will reach that price category in a year. Our first bar, centred at $350 an ounce, indicates that 3 per cent of the people surveyed think gold will be around $350; about 7 per cent of the people think it will be around $375; 12 per cent predict a price near $400, and so forth. Many people are clustered in the middle – around $450.

This picture is called a *distribution* and was discussed in Chapter 4. A distribution is characterized by its *mean* or average – its expected value. A distribution will always be centred at the expected value.

When we add up and average the different responses from the people surveyed, we find that, for this particular example, the mean is centred around $450. (The mean calculated from the actual responses is $453.50.) On average, the people in this group feel that the future price of gold, that is the price of gold a year from now, should be approximately $450.

A distribution is also characterized by its width or dispersion, which is sometimes expressed as the *standard deviation* or the *volatility*. You can see in this

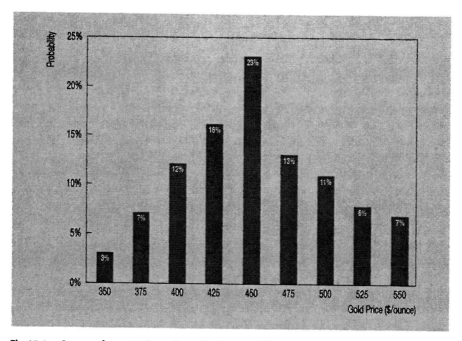

Fig 15.1 ● Survey of expectations about the future gold price

distribution that, even though it is centred around $450, there is a great deal of variation in the responses. Some people estimate a price as low as $350, and some people estimate a price as high as $550. The standard deviation measures the dispersion in the distribution, and for our gold price survey distribution this measure of dispersion is around $50.

The mean and the standard deviation are two important quantitative characteristics of the distribution. Many distributions we encounter in nature and in the financial markets have a particular shape called a *normal* or *bell-shaped* distribution. Returns for commodities, such as gold, or for currencies or stocks or bonds have underlying distributions that often are approximately normal. A normal distribution is characterized in part by its symmetry about the mean and by the fact that it is high in the middle and low at the ends. We will assume, for purposes of the illustration which follows, that gold prices are approximately normally distributed.

The normal distribution has some very useful characteristics, again discussed in Chapter 4 and illustrated in Figure 15.2. In a normal distribution of gold price forecasts, we have 68 per cent confidence that the future price will be within one standard deviation of the mean. In our forecast distribution, the mean is about $450, and the standard deviation is about $50. Assuming this distribution is normal, we are 68 per cent confident that the future price will fall somewhere between $400 and $500 ($450 minus $50 and $450 plus $50). Adding the percentage responses in the price range between $400 and $500 on our bar chart in Figure 15.1, we find that about 75 per cent of our forecasters feel that the future price will be within one standard deviation of the mean.

From the normal distribution we know that we have 95 per cent confidence that the future price will be within two standard deviations of the mean in a normal distribution. Two standard deviations down from the mean is about $350, and two standard deviations up from the mean is about $550 so we have about 95 per cent confidence that the future price of gold will be somewhere between $350 and $550. In our forecast distribution, all the responses are within that interval.

Finally, we are 99 per cent confident that the future price will be within three standard deviations of the mean in a normal distribution. Three standard deviations from the mean is $150. We are 99 per cent confident, or almost completely confident, that the future price of gold will be within a range of $300 to $600, that is $150 down from the mean and $150 up from the mean. These properties of the normal distribution provide powerful assistance in the pricing of derivatives.

Who are the market participants in the derivatives markets?

In order to understand how to apply these arbitrage principles and ultimately to understand how option prices are determined, we need to examine the

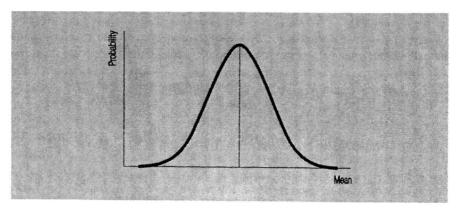

Fig 15.2 ● A normal distribution

actions of the different participants in the markets. In this case we choose the gold market but any other market could easily have been chosen.

The expected future price of gold is important to anyone who uses the gold *spot* markets, that is the markets for immediate delivery or receipt of gold, and to the gold futures and forward markets, the markets for delivery at some future time period. These users would include:

● investors

● long speculators

● short speculators

● long hedgers

● short hedgers

● arbitrageurs.

It is useful to describe each of these market participants, discuss what motivates their market behaviour, and look at how their actions affect the spot and the future or forward price of an underlying commodity or security.

Let's look first at investors. Investors think that gold is a good investment, a gold bug in the terminology of the market. They want to buy gold and hold it long term. When investors buy gold, they force up the spot price of gold. When the spot price of gold rises, the future or forward price tends to rise as well.

Long speculators are not long-term investors, but they think gold is going up and would like to take a position that is going to be profitable if they are right. They can accomplish this in a couple of different ways. First, they can buy spot gold. If gold goes up in a short period of time, they can sell that gold at a higher price and make a profit.

Alternatively, they can buy a future or forward contract on gold. Their purchase of forward gold tends to make the future or forward price go up; and, just as demand for spot gold tends to raise future or forward prices, demand for forward gold tends to raise spot prices. As we will see later, when long speculators buy a future or a forward, they do not have to pay out much money. When investors buy spot gold, say 100 ounces at $400, they have to pay $40,000, immediately.

Short speculators think that the gold price is going down. They are very pessimistic about the outlook for gold. Like investors and long speculators, short speculators have two choices. They can sell gold spot, or they can sell a future or forward contract on gold.

If short speculators happen to own gold, they can simply sell it. Alternatively, if they are in a position to borrow gold relatively easily and sell it short, i.e. to sell gold they do not physically own, they might do that. But if they do not have direct access to gold, they will probably find it easier to sell a future or forward contract on gold.

Short speculators affect the price of spot gold. The effect on the spot price is clear if the short speculators own gold and want to shift their investment to something else. If they are not trading in the spot market, the direct effect of their sale will be on the forward or future price, making it trade at a lower price.

A long hedger is someone who needs gold a year from now. A long hedger might be a dentist or a jeweller – someone who has all the gold he or she needs right now but who wants to be assured of the gold price a year from now. There is no advantage in buying the gold now and spending a large sum of money to store and insure it. A long hedger will probably want to buy a future or forward contract on gold, which will tend to push up the future or forward price.

A short hedger might be a gold producer, busy digging gold out of the ground. A short hedger does not have much gold right now, but expects to have a large store of gold to sell in a year's time. The short hedger wants to make sure his or her hard work pays off and that the gold can be sold at a good price. The short hedgers cannot sell spot gold because they do not have it. However, they can sell a future or forward contract on gold now. Short hedgers are likely to affect the future of forward price, and since they are selling, their actions will tend to make the future or forward price trade lower.

Our last market participant, the gold arbitrageur, is the most important in some ways. Arbitrageurs have no opinion about gold's value and no opinion on the likely direction of gold prices, but they are very aware of gold price relationships. Even if an arbitrageur did have a personal opinion about the value of gold or the direction of gold prices, his or her opinion would not affect his or her financial transactions. An arbitrageur's, actions in the marketplace tie the actions of all other market participants together. An arbitrageur makes sure the spot price of gold and the future or forward price of gold are in their proper relationship. If the prices are not appropriate relative to one another, an arbitrageur will try to profit by buying in the cheap market and selling in the expensive market. The actions of arbitrageurs are extremely important in seeing that spot prices and future prices are kept in line.

The arbitrageur's role and the pricing of futures markets

One of the reasons for emphasizing the role of the arbitrageur in a discussion of options is that arbitrageurs are an important factor in determining the spot/forward price relationship, and the first step in finding the value of an option is finding the value of future or forward prices.

If gold is trading at $400 today, at what price will someone agree today to buy or sell it one year in the future? We used a survey, Figure 15.1, to forecast the price of gold in a year, but there is a rational, deterministic relationship between the spot price and the forward price of gold that does not rely on an opinion survey or on anyone's gold price forecast, it simply applies the arbitrage ideas discussed above.

Suppose that the carry cost of gold, that is, the cost of borrowing money, the cost of buying the gold and financing it for a year, is 10 per cent. Assume the spot gold price is $400. Holding the gold position will cost us 10 per cent for a year, because if we had to borrow the $400 to buy the gold we would have had to pay interest at 10 per cent. To own gold a year from now, it will cost us more than $400 now. In fact as shown by Equation (1), it will cost us $440.

Future or forward price of gold
Spot price of gold + cost of carry = future or forward price of gold (1)
$400 + (10% × $400) = $440

If the present value of gold is $400, the future value of gold in one year should be $440. By future value, we do not necessarily mean the price gold will sell for in the future; it is the value that the future gold price has today because of the cost of carrying gold for a year.

Present value, spot value and *the cash market* refer to the same thing. We have been talking about spot gold, but we can also talk about the spot value, current market value or cash value of a stock, a bond, or some other *underlying* commodity or financial instrument, to broaden the futures pricing principles.

Future value is the value of the future or the forward. There is a difference between futures and forwards, but the difference is in how they are traded, not in how they are valued. At this point we will treat futures and forwards as though they were interchangeable. Later, we will discuss the practical differences between futures markets and forward markets.

WHAT ARE THE FACTORS INFLUENCING THE PRICE OF FUTURES?

Traders in any commodity, say a wheat buyer (bread maker), or a wheat seller (wheat farmer), fearing wheat price volatility, are anxious to use a cash market hedge to hedge wheat price risk. A futures contract is a derivative of this spot market hedge. A seller of wheat will not wish the price to fall in the future when a sale is anticipated. A buyer of wheat will not wish the price to rise when a purchase is anticipated. If an agreement is made to deliver a quantity and grade of wheat in three months' time, how might the seller of the wheat arrange affairs so that there is no price risk? If they remain in an open position, i.e. not owning the wheat, there is no knowing what the price of wheat will be in three months' time. Therefore a cash market hedge can be constructed as follows. Wheat will already be held or can be purchased at today's spot price. Take today's spot price which is known and add to this the *cost of carrying* the wheat for three months. These carry costs will be:

● storage;

● insurance;

● transport costs involved in making delivery to a named place; and

● financing costs of the operation over the three months, i.e. interest foregone, or interest paid on funds used to purchase the commodity.

This gives us the following relationship between the spot and futures price:

spot wheat price plus the cost of carry =   agreed price of wheat in three
                                            months' time (i.e. futures price)

Such a strategy will fix the price of wheat for both parties in three months' time. Regardless of what happens to the spot price during the three months, the agreed price will be received or paid.

Futures price

A price in the futures agreement or contract has to be agreed. The question arises what must/should this price be?

The price, as indicated above, 'should' be today's spot price adjusted by the cost of carry for three months. If you agree this price with your counterparty this will become the entry price, as it is known. If the entry price is not 'correct', then an arbitrage can be made, as illustrated below, using the cash market hedge described above and the simultaneous mispriced futures agreement.

If the entry price of the futures contract (remember this will give the seller of wheat the right to sell the wheat at this agreed, entry price in three months' time) is greater than spot plus cost of carry then an arbitrage profit is possible. In this example, the futures price is said to be 'rich' to the cash price, so on the principle that you sell that which is overpriced (the future) and buy that which is underpriced (commodity at spot), it follows that:

> if future (entry) price > spot plus cost of carry
> (e.g. \$10   > \$8 + \$1.50)

then arbitrageurs in the spot market will take a long position, i.e. purchase wheat at the spot rate, and carry this for three months.

> Their total outlay   = spot price plus the cost of carry
> i.e. \$9.50   = \$8 + \$1.50

In the futures market they will take a short position, i.e. sell a futures contract. In three months' time they will sell the goods held over the three months at a total outlay of:

original spot (\$8) plus cost of carry (\$1.50), for a sum greater than this (\$10), as enabled by the futures contract held, because:

> future contract price > spot price plus cost of carry
> i.e. \$10   > \$8 + \$1.50

This arbitrage process is called a *cash and carry transaction*. In this example a risk-free profit is being made. The arbitrage opportunity will be eroded and disappear as such transactions are made. Demand at the spot price will raise the spot price so that this, when added to the cost of carry, equals the futures price. At the same time there will be a greater demand for short positions in futures and this will drive down the futures price. In both markets the tendency will be to equalize prices. If the futures price equals the spot price plus full carrying cost, then the futures price will be a *full carry price*.

If the futures price is 'cheap', then arbitrageurs buy what is cheap (the futures market) and sell that which is expensive (the spot price). This arbitrage again 'should' result in a *full carry futures price*.

At the end of either of these transactions, the futures entry price should equal the spot price plus the cost of carry.

The principle emerges therefore that spot and future prices differ due to the principle of cost of carry. However, at maturity spot and futures will be identical. If they are not identical it will be possible, a fraction of time before maturity, to take a futures position and an opposite cash market position, arbitrage and profit from the difference. A simple example illustrates this.

Say the futures price is \$10 and the spot price is \$8. Selling a futures contract (right to deliver at \$10) and buying in the spot market at \$8 obviously gives a profit of \$2 per unit quantity.

If prices are identical at maturity, but differ at the beginning of the period, it follows that even if the spot price were to remain constant (highly unlikely) the futures price would gradually have to change as the contract approached maturity. To illustrate this we must first define what, in the derivatives market, is known as 'basis'.

What is basis?

Basis is the difference between the forward or future value and the spot value. For many products, the basis is defined as the cost minus the benefit of holding the underlying security. This gives the following relationship:

basis = cost of transaction – benefit from the transaction

In our gold futures pricing example, we considered only the financial cost of carrying gold at 10 per cent, because there are no economic of financial benefits from owning gold. (It might give you a feeling of comfort to own gold, but we are not counting that.) In some other products, there are benefits to holding financial instruments as well as costs.

Should we now consider the futures markets for stocks we must again consider the cost of carry, that is, the cost of the money to buy the stock, but we must now also consider the possible benefit of holding stocks, i.e. the possibility of receiving a cash dividend. Not all stocks pay dividends, but if they do, the dividend is a benefit.

In currency markets, the cost of carrying a foreign currency is the investor's domestic interest rate. If US dollar-based investors want euros, they have to give up dollars to buy the euros. When they give up the dollars, they either take them out of an interest-bearing account, which means they lose the interest income, or they borrow the dollars from a bank and pay domestic interest. Either way they have a carry cost in the domestic currency, and that is the dollar cost. On the other hand, when they get the euros, they can invest them in a euro account and earn interest at euro rates. The interest on the euro account is a benefit of owning the euros.

Let us now turn to the bond market. Traders or portfolio managers often have to borrow money to carry bonds. They borrow money in the *repo (repurchase agreement) market*, posting the bonds as *collateral* for the loan. The *repo rate* is the term used for the interest rate charged on such a loan. On the other hand, while they own the bond they are entitled to any coupon interest that accumulates. For a bond, the repo rate is the carry cost of the bond, and the coupon interest is the benefit.

The basis in each of these examples consists of the cost of holding the instrument or commodity minus the benefit of owning the underlying instrument or commodity from the spot date to the forward date.

What is the basis for different instruments?

- For gold, the basis is simply the interest cost of carrying the gold.

- For a stock, the basis is the interest cost of carrying the stock minus the dividends earned from the stock.

- For a currency, the basis is the cost of the interest on the domestic currency minus the benefit of the interest earned on the foreign currency.

- For a bond, the basis is the cost of borrowing at the repo rate minus the benefit of the coupon payment.

Spot versus forward arbitrage

Applying the idea of basis to arbitrage examples will help clarify some spot and forward pricing relationships. Suppose that gold is trading for $400, and the forward price, which we said earlier should be trading at $440, is trading at $450. It will cost us $400 plus 10 per cent of $400 to buy gold and carry it for one year. That means we can buy gold today by borrowing money from the bank, and in one year we have to repay the bank $440. With the gold forward trading today for $450, we can sell it and make a profit. In one year, we do two more transactions:

Deliver gold for	$450	an ounce to complete the forward contract
Repay bank	−$440	an ounce
Net difference	$10	profit

With a spot price of $400 and a forward price of $450, we can buy gold today and sell it forward, making a certain profit of $10 per ounce. This is a risk-less profit, an arbitrage profit, which is made by simultaneously buying and selling equivalent instruments.

Let us look at this transaction from a different perspective. It may seem as though we bought gold, but because we bought gold by borrowing money and carrying it for a year, we effectively bought the forward, paying $440 an ounce to own gold in one year. Simultaneously, we sold the actual forward, the one that is tradable, for $450. These are equivalent instruments, and they should be priced identically. When equivalent instruments do not trade at the same price an arbitrage profit can be made.

Suppose that spot gold is trading at $400 and forward gold is trading at $420 – lower than the $440 forward price we calculated earlier. Forward gold at $420 sounds like a bargain – let's buy the forward and simultaneously sell the spot to make a certain profit of $20.

If we do not own gold, we must borrow it and sell it for $400, or sell short spot gold. We can then invest the $400 from the sale of the gold. The bank will pay us 10 per cent interest, and we will have $440 in the bank a year later. Then, we will do two more transactions to close out the arbitrage:

Withdraw money from the bank	$440	an ounce
Accept delivery of forward gold at	−$420	an ounce
Net difference	$20	profit

We have to return the gold we borrowed, and our profit may be reduced if we have to pay a fee for borrowing the gold. In the first example, the gold forward was expensive compared to the $440 it would cost us to buy gold and carry it for a year. So we sold forward gold, bought spot gold, and carried it for a year. In the second example, the gold forward was cheap, so we bought forward gold, sold spot gold, and earned interest on a bank deposit.

In both cases, we arbitraged a profit with no price risk. In fact, we exchanged price risk for basis risk. It is important to emphasize that, in both cases, forward transactions were agreed on at the beginning of the period, and actual transactions were done at the end of the period.

Regardless of what any investor thinks the price of gold will be in a year, the actions of arbitrageurs – the people who monitor the relationships between the spot and the forward – will ensure that the spot price and the forward price have the appropriate cash and carry relationship to each other.

That does not mean the arbitrageurs determine the value of the spot or the value of the forward. While hedgers, speculators and investors affect the spot price or the forward price, arbitrageurs ensure that the cash and carry relationship between the spot and forward is preserved. We have emphasized this relationship because knowing how to value futures and forwards relative to the spot price is the first step toward knowing how to value options.

What are forward market contracts?

A forward contract is an agreement between two parties made independently of any organized exchange market. Nobody other than the parties to the forward agreement needs to be involved – there are no formal rules outside the agreement between the two parties. The forward contract is a stand-alone, customized contract. It can be based on any amount of any good. It can be written for settlement at any time and at any price. It can be, as an extreme example, for delivery of 37,000 gallons of vodka in 52 days at $2 a gallon. The terms can be virtually anything as long as both parties agree to them.

One party agrees to sell the vodka at the contract price, and the other party agrees to buy it at that price. Since the contract can be for any amount of any good, at any time, and at any price and since each party depends on the other party to meet contractual obligations, the forward contract *cannot* be traded freely with other potential counterparties. Forwards are not *fungible*; that is, one forward contract is not interchangeable with another contract that has similar terms, and the present value of the forward contract is not easily converted to a cash market value.

Each party has to be able to trust that the other party will uphold his or her side of the agreement, because the two counterparties are exposed to each other's ability and willingness to perform on the contract. There is *credit risk* associated with a forward contract, which must be controlled. This is based in the fact that you cannot be sure that the counterparty will deliver as agreed. The credit risk is often controlled by banks, which act as *intermediaries*, assuring the performance of their clients. A very important point to remember about forward contracts is that no money is exchanged by the parties until the actual exchange of goods or financial instruments at *settlement*. There is normally no interim cash flow.

What are futures contracts?

A futures contract, in contrast to a forward, is an agreement between two parties made through their agents on an organized futures exchange. The parties who trade on the exchange can represent themselves or they can represent customers. There are specific rules and regulations that set the terms of the contract and the procedures for trading. The contract is for a specific amount of a specific good to be delivered at a specific time determined by the exchange, and the price discovery is sometimes, but not always, determined by *open outcry* in a *trading pit*, that is, by people yelling and screaming prices at each other in a crowded room.

This is the way prices are discovered and goods are exchanged in many efficient markets. Increasingly, markets now use computer systems, known as screen-based trading, which expose bids and offers to a large number of potential traders at many locations, but the principle of bringing bids and offers together is the same.

Several features of futures markets are worth noting.

- First, a futures contract is always for a specific amount of a specific good. We cannot set out our own contract amount, say 37,000 gallons of vodka. If the vodka contract set by the exchange is 20,000 gallons, we can trade any number of contracts, but each contract must be for 20,000 gallons. And we must specify the type of vodka – it must be Finlandia vodka or Stolichnaya vodka, or, more likely, simply 80-proof vodka. Since all terms are determined in the futures contract, the contracts can be retraded freely with other counterparties. We can buy the contract from one person, sell the contract to another, and wash our hands of the commitment. We can eliminate our obligation, because, with futures, the organized futures exchange handling the transaction takes the other side of the contract.

- The futures exchange is the ultimate counterparty for all futures trades, so the only credit risk is the creditworthiness of the exchange, which is normally very low. Once a trade is completed, the transaction is passed to some type of exchange clearing corporation. The futures contract buyers and sellers have an agreement with the clearing corporation. Ultimately, if a trader takes delivery rather than offset the contract, i.e. reversing it, the exchange will select someone who is short the contract to make delivery. The party making delivery does not have to be the party who sold the contract originally. After the trade settles, the original parties to the trade lose any direct tie to each other based on the trade. No credit intermediary is necessary, but margin must be deposited to ensure each party meets its obligations.

The exchange clearing corporation has to stand behind the creditworthiness of its members, so it asks everyone for a deposit. Customers make a deposit with their broker, known as margin, and the broker passes the deposit to the clearing corporation. Futures margin is a good faith deposit, demonstrating ability and willingness to meet contractual obligations. Table 15.2 illustrates the advantages and disadvantages of futures and forward contracts.

Table 15.2 ● The advantages and disadvantages of futures and forwards

		Futures Markets		*Forward Markets*
Default risk	+	Low	−	Greater than for futures
Transaction costs/ commissions	+	Low	−	Higher than for futures
Standardization	+	Contracts are liquid; allows for secondary market	−	No secondary market
	−	Imperfect hedge	+	Tailor made hedge
Interest rate risk	−	Daily cash flows from marking to market must be deposited at unknown interest rates		Not applicable
Contract sizes and underlying currencies	−	Limited number of contracts and underlying securities makes hedging with futures less effective	+	Tailor made
Maturities	−	Short maturity only	+	Slightly longer to much longer maturities than for futures

HOW ARE OPTIONS PRICED?

The method used to price options depends on the type of option being priced. As can be seen from Table 15.3 the two pricing models are the binomial model used for American options, which was designed by Cox, Ross and Rubinstein,

Table 15.3 ● European versus American options

Type of Option	Exercise Date	Pricing Model
American option	Any time up to maturity	Cox, Rubinstein and Ross
European option	At maturity date	Black-Scholes

and the Black-Scholes option pricing model, used for pricing European options. As we show below, the binomial model can also be used to price European options.

The key to valuing options is to design a risk-free portfolio in which the value does not change when there is a change in the underlying asset. This risk-free element is achieved by designing a portfolio which replicates, i.e. one in which the pay-offs of the portfolio exactly match the pay-offs of the option. A good example of this is achieved by applying the binomial model.

The binomial model

One-period binomial model – the role of the replicating portfolio

To illustrate the binomial model it is necessary to look at what effect a fall or rise in price of the underlying stock should have on the option price. Our first example is a European call option on a stock, and an assumption that the stock is currently valued at €100. In this example an option to purchase this stock expires in one year and the strike or exercise price is €100. The annual risk-free interest rate is 5 per cent, so that borrowing €1 today will mean having to pay back €1.05 one year from now. For simplicity, the assumption here is that there are only two possible outcomes when the option expires – the stock price can be either €120 (an up state) or €80 (a down state). Note that the value of the call option will be €20 if the up state occurs and €0 if the down state occurs as shown below. See Figure 15.3. In other words, if the price falls to €80 the option becomes valueless.

Since there are only two possible states in the future it is possible to replicate the value of the option in each of these states by forming a portfolio of the stock and risk-free asset. If Δ, an unknown number of shares of the stock are purchased and M dollars are borrowed at the risk-free rate, the stock portion of the portfolio is worth $120 \times \Delta$ in the up state and $80 \times \Delta$ in the down state, while $1.05 \times M$ will have to be paid back in either of the two states. Thus, to match, or replicate, the value of the portfolio to the value of the option in the two possible states, it must be the case that:

$$€120 \times \Delta - 1.05 \times M = €20 \text{ (up state)} \qquad (2)$$

and

$$€80 \times \Delta - 1.05 \times M = €0 \text{ (down state)} \qquad (3)$$

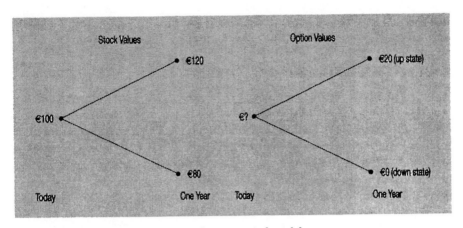

Fig 15.3 • Stock and option values in the one-period model

Rearranging the formulae from Equations (2) and (3) gives us a value for Δ:

€40 Δ = 20
and therefore Δ = 0.05.

Inserting Δ = 0.5 in equation (2) gives us:

€120 × 0.5 – 1.05M = €20
€40 = 1.05M
So M = €38.10

The resulting system of two equations with two unknowns Δ and M, *solved above*, gives us Δ = 0.5, and M is approximately €38.10. Therefore, one would need to buy 0.5 shares of the stock and borrow €38.10 at the risk-free rate in order for the value of the portfolio to be €20 and €0 in the up and down states respectively. Equivalently, selling 0.5 shares of the stock and lending €38.10 at the risk-free rate would mean pay-offs from that portfolio of €20 and €0 in the up and down states respectively, which would completely offset the pay-offs from the option in those states. This is a powerful finding as it enables us to replicate the risk free portfolio and price the options accordingly. It is also worth noting that the current value of the option must equal the current value of the portfolio, which is 100 × Δ – M =100 × 0.5 – M = €11.90. In other words, a call option on the stock is equivalent to a long position in the stock financed by borrowing at the risk-free rate.

The variable Δ is called the delta of the option. In the previous example, if C_u and C_d denote the values of the call option in the up and down states, with S_u and S_d denoting the price of the stock in the up and down states respectively, then it can be verified that $\Delta = (C_u - C_d)/(S_u - S_d)$. The delta of an option reveals how the value of the option is going to change with a change in the stock price. For example, knowing Δ, C_d, and the difference between the stock prices in the up and down states makes it possible to know how much the option is going to be worth in the up state, that is, C_u, is also known.

The two-period binomial model

A model in which a year from now there are only two possible states of the world is certainly not realistic, but construction of a multiperiod model can alleviate this problem. The one-period model assumes a replicating portfolio for a call option on a stock currently valued at €100 with a strike price of €100 and which expires in a year. However, let us now assume the year is divided into two six-month periods and the value of the stock can either increase or decrease by 10 per cent in each period. The semi-annual risk-free interest rate is 2.47 per cent, which is equivalent to an annual compounded rate of 5 per cent. The states of the world for the stock values are given in Figures 15.4. and 15.5. Given this structure, how does one build a portfolio of the stock and the risk-free asset to replicate the option? The calculation is similar to the one above except that it is done recursively, starting one period before the option expires and working backwards to find the current position.

In the case in which the value of the stock over the first six months increases by 10 per cent to €110 (that is, the up state six months from now), the value of the option in the up state is found by forming a replicating portfolio containing Δ_u shares of the stock financed by borrowing M_u euros at the risk-free rate. Over the next six months, the value of the stock can either increase another 10 per cent to €121 or decline 10 per cent to €99, so that the option at expiration will be worth either €21 or €0. Since the replicating portfolio has to match the values of the option, regardless of whether the stock price is €121 or €99, the Equations (4) and (5) must be satisfied:

$$€121 \times \Delta_u - 1.0247 \times M_u = €21 \tag{4}$$

and

$$€99 \times \Delta_u - 1.0247 \times M_u = €0 \tag{5}$$

Solving these equations results in $\Delta_u = 0.9545$ and $M_u = 92.22$. Thus the value of the replicating portfolio is $110 \times \Delta_u - M_u = €12.78$. If, instead, six months from now the stock declines 10 per cent in value, to €90 (the down state), the stock price at the expiration of the option will either be €99 or €81, which is always less than the exercise price. Thus the option is worthless a year from now if the down state is realized six months from now, and consequently the value of the option in the down state is zero. Given the two possible values of the option six months from now, it is now possible to derive the number of shares of the stock that one needs to buy and the amount necessary to borrow to replicate the option pay-offs in the up and down state six months from now. Since the option is worth €12.78 and €0 in the up and down states respectively, it follows that:

$$€110 \times \Delta - 1.0247 \times M = €12.78 \tag{6}$$

and

$$€90 \times \Delta - 1.0247 \times M = €0 \tag{7}$$

Solving Equations (6) and (7) results in $\Delta = 0.6389$ and $M = €56.11$. Thus the value of the option price today is $100 \times \Delta - M = €7.77$. The values of the stock option are shown graphically in Figures 15.4 and 15.5.

A feature of this replicating portfolio is that it is always self-financing. Once it is set up, no further external cash inflows or outflows are required in the future. For example, if the replicating portfolio is set up by borrowing €56.11 and buying 0.6389 shares of the stock and in six months the up state is realized, the initial portfolio is liquidated. The sale of the 0.6389 shares of stock at €110 per share nets €70.28. Repaying the loan with interest, which amounts to €57.50, leaves €12.78. The new replicating portfolio requires borrowing €92.22. Combining this amount with the proceeds of €12.78 gives €105, which is exactly enough to buy the required $0.9545 \, \Delta_u$ shares of stock at €110 per share. Replicating portfolios always have this property: liquidating the current portfolio nets exactly enough money to form the next portfolio. Thus the portfolio can be set up today, rebalanced at the end of each period with no infusions of external cash, and at expiration should match the pay-off of the option, no matter which states of the world occur.

In the replicating portfolio presented above, the option expires either one or two periods from now, but the same principle applies for any number of periods. Given, in this example, that there are only two possible states over each period, a self-financing replicating portfolio can be formed at each date and state by trading in the stock and a risk-free asset. As the number of periods

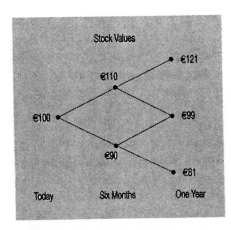

Figure 15.4 • Stock values in the two-period model

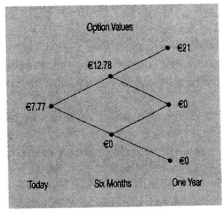

Figure 15.5 • Option values in the two-period model

increases, the individual periods get shorter so that more and more possible states of the world exist at expiration. In the limit, continuums of possible states and periods exist so that the portfolio will have to be continuously rebalanced. The Black-Scholes-Merton model discussed below is the limiting case of these models with a limited number of periods.

DETERMINANTS OF THE VALUE OF A CALL OPTION

The value of a call option is determined by the following six factors.

1 **The price of the underlying asset**
   The value of a call option is positively related to the price of the underlying security. The higher the value of the underlying asset, the greater the value of the call option. This is not surprising as a call buyer has bought the right to buy at a fixed price. The more the underlying asset rises, the more the call option is worth, and vice versa.

2 **The exercise price**
   The value of a call option is inversely related to the exercise price. The lower the exercise price, the higher the value of the call option. Other things being equal, a lower exercise price means that the call option is more in-the-money. Again, this is not surprising as this is what the call option owner has to pay when he or she exercises the option.

3 **The time until expiration**
   The value of a call option is a positive function of time until expiration. The longer the time until expiration, the greater the value of the call option. The reason for this is that the call owner has more time to allow his or her option to get in-the-money.

The first three determinants of call option value are illustrated by Table 15.4. Look across any row of the table; the value of the call option decreases as the exercise price increases. Look down any column; as time to maturity increases the value of the call option also increases.

4 **The price volatility of the underlying asset**
   The greater the volatility of the underlying asset, the higher the value of the call option, since pay-offs to a call buyer are asymmetric. If the underlying asset does poorly, the call buyer loses everything. If the underlying asset does well, the call buyer does very well. Greater dispersion in the possible value of the underlying asset implies bigger call option pay-offs on the upside but the same pay-off (loss of everything) on the downside, making a call option more valuable. Obviously asset prices can fall as well as rise, but if they fall, the call option holder has the option not to exercise his or her option.

Table 15.4 ● The impact of maturity and exercise price on call option prices

| | Price of Underlying Asset = $110 | | |
| | Exercise Price | | |
Maturity (months)	$90	$100	$110
3	$30	$16	$4
6	$34	$19	$6.50
9	$37	$21.50	$8.50

The impact of volatility upon call option value is illustrated by the two-security example in Table 15.5. Assume two securities with the following possible prices at expiration. Each of these securities has the same mean of $100, but Security 2 has greater dispersion of outcomes. An option on Security 2 is more valuable because of this dispersion. To see the point, consider the case of call options with exercise prices of $100 on each security. The pay-offs on these options are shown in Table 15.6.

Table 15.5 ● Two-security example of volatility

Security 1

Prices at expiration	$90	$100	$110
Probability	1/3	1/3	1/3
	Mean price = ($90)(1/3) + ($100)(1/3) + ($110)(1/3) = $100		

Security 2

Prices at expiration	$80	$100	$120
Probability	1/3	1/3	1/3
	Mean price = ($80)(1/3) + ($100)(1/3) + ($120)(1/3) = $100		

Table 15.6 ● Value of a call option

Call Option on Security 1

Prices of underlying asset	$90	$100	$110
Value of call option	$0	$0	$10
Probability	1/3	1/3	1/3
	Mean value = ($0)(1/3) + ($0)(1/3) + ($10)(1/3) = $3.33		

Call Option on Security 2

Prices of underlying asset	$80	$100	$120
Value of call option	$0	$0	$20
Probability	1/3	1/3	1/3
	Mean value = ($0)(1/3) + ($0)(1/3) + ($20)(1/3) = $6.67		

The call option on Security 2 in Table 15.6 clearly has a greater value. If the options are out-of-the-money or at-the-money, both options expire worthless. If the options are in-the-money, Security 2 has a higher pay-off and, therefore, must be worth more.

5 **The risk-free interest rate**
The higher the interest rate, the greater the value of a call option. This is based on the fact that if a call buyer has bought the option rather than the underlying asset, then the funds saved can then be invested at the now higher interest rate.

6 **Dividends or interest on the underlying asset**
The higher the cash payments on the underlying asset, the lower the value of a call option. The total return on an asset is the cash payment (dividends or coupon interest) plus price appreciation. For a given total rate of return, higher cash payments on an asset imply lower returns from price increases. Since the call buyer gains only if the price of the underlying asset increases, higher cash payments on the underlying asset tend to reduce the capital gains and the value of the call option.

From put-call parity, the price of a put can be shown to depend upon the call price, the price of the underlying asset, and the present value of the exercise price. It follows that the preceding six determinants of call prices also affect put prices. There are two major differences for put options. First, as the price of the underlying security increases, the value of the put goes down. That is, the value of a put is inversely related to the price of the underlying security. Second, a higher exercise price increases the value of the put. The value of a put option is directly related to the exercise price.

Table 15.7 provides an illustration of how both call options and put options on stocks respond to the factors influencing their price.

Table 15.7 ● Factors affecting option prices

Variable Increases	Call Price	Put Price
Stock price	Increases	Decreases
Time to expiry	Increases	Increases
Stock volatility	Increases	Increases
Risk-free rate	Increases	Decreases
Exercise price	Decreases	Increases
Dividend	Decreases	Increases

Black-Scholes model

The binomial model discussed earlier, assumes a discrete-time stationary binomial stochastic process for security price movements. In the limit, as the discrete-time period becomes infinitely small, this stochastic process becomes a *diffusion process* (also called a *continuous-time random walk*, an *Ito process*, or *geometric Brownian motion*). This was the process assumed by Black and Scholes (1973) in their derivation of the option pricing formula, discussed in Chapter 3. As with the binomial model, Black and Scholes begin by constructing a risk-less hedge portfolio, long in the underlying security and short in the call options. This portfolio generates the risk-less rate of return, but the internal dynamics of the portfolio are driven by the diffusion process for the security price. The structure of the hedge portfolio can be put into a form that is identical to the heat equation in physics. Once this was recognized, the solution to the equation was easily derived.

In the case of a European call option with no cash payments on the underlying asset and with a certain, continuously compounded interest rate, Black and Scholes demonstrated that the value of a call option is an explicit function of the first five factors mentioned in Table 15.7. The Black-Scholes model is shown in Equation (7):

$$C = PN(d_1) - Ee^{-rt} N(d_2) \tag{7}$$

where

C = the price of a call option
P = the current price of the underlying
E = the exercise price
e = the base of natural logarithms
r = the continuously compounded interest rate
t = the remaining life of the call option

$N(d_1)$ and $N(d_2)$ are the cumulative probabilities from the normal distribution of getting the values d_1 and d_2, where d_1 and d_2 are as follows:

$$d_1 = \frac{\ln(P/E) + (r + 0.5\sigma^2)t}{\sigma\sqrt{t}}$$

$$d_2 = d_1 - \sigma\sqrt{t}$$

σ = the standard deviation of the continuously compounded rate of return on the underlying asset.

The term e^{-rt} is the present value of \$1 received t periods from the present. It is the continuously compounded equivalent of what we have called d, the present value of \$1.

To understand the Black-Scholes model better, consider the case where $N(d_1)$ and $N(d_2)$ are both equal to 1. This is equivalent to assuming complete certainty. Then the model becomes Equation (8):

$$C = P - Ee^{-rt} \qquad (8)$$

$N(d_1)$ and $N(d_2)$ represent cumulative probabilities from the normal distribution. Figure 15.6 illustrates these cumulative probabilities, which must be numbers between 0 and 1. If they are less than 1.0, there is some uncertainly about the level of the stock price at option expiration. From the definition of d_1, d_2 must be smaller than d_1. Assume that we know that $N(d_1)$ is 0.75 and $N(d_2)$ is 0.25. Then the Black-Scholes model becomes Equation (9):

$$C = (0.75)P - (0.25)Ee^{-rt} \qquad (9)$$

The Black-Scholes function is shown in Figure 15.7.

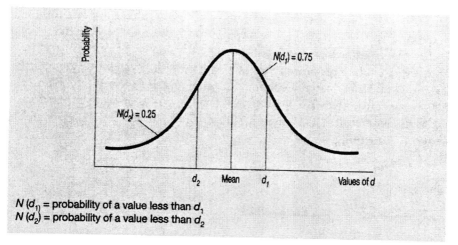

$N(d_1)$ = probability of a value less than d_1
$N(d_2)$ = probability of a value less than d_2

Fig 15.6 ● Cumulative normal distribution

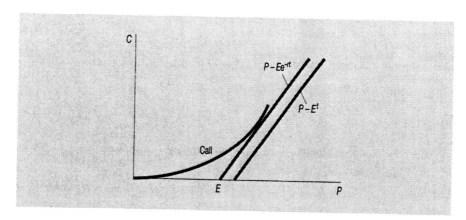

Fig 15.7 ● Black-Scholes model

Since the Black-Scholes model requires no cash payments and interest rate certainty, it cannot be applied to debt instruments. However, the Black-Scholes models can be applied to common stocks without dividends. The model can be adapted for common stocks that pay dividends.

One of the attractions of the Black-Scholes model is that most of the inputs are readily observable. The standard deviation of the return on the underlying asset is not directly observable. However, this can be estimated from past data, if the standard deviation is relatively stable over time.

CHAPTER 16

Recent developments in financial economics

WHERE IS THE MARKET GOING? UNCERTAIN FACTS AND NOVEL THEORIES

Over the last century, the stock market in the USA has yielded impressive returns to its investors. For example, in the postwar period, stock returns have averaged eight percentage points above Treasury bills. Will stocks continue to give such impressive returns in the future? Are long-term average stock returns a fundamental feature of advanced industrial economies? Or are they the opposite of the old joke on Soviet agriculture – 100 years of good luck? If not pure good luck, perhaps they result from features of the economy that will disappear as financial markets evolve.

How does the recent rise in the stock market affect our view of future returns? Do high prices now mean lower returns in the future? Or have stocks finally achieved Irving Fisher's brilliantly mistimed 1929 prediction of a 'permanently high plateau'? If stocks have reached a plateau, is it a rising plateau, or is the market likely to bounce around its current level for many years, not crashing but not yielding returns much greater than those of bonds?

These questions are on all of our minds as we allocate our pension plan monies. They are also important to many public policy questions. For example, many proposals to reform social security emphasize the benefits of moving to a funded system based on stock market investments. But this is a good idea only if the stock market continues to provide the kind of returns in the future that it has in the past.

In this chapter, I summarize the academic, and if I dare say so, scientific, evidence on these issues. I start with the statistical analysis of past stock returns. The long-term average return is in fact rather poorly measured. The standard statistical confidence interval extends from 3 per cent to 13 per cent. Furthermore, average returns have been low following times of high stock prices, such as the present. Therefore, the statistical evidence suggests a period of quite low average returns, followed by slow reversion to a poorly measured long-term average, and it cautions us that statistical analysis alone leaves lots of uncertainty.

Then, I survey economic theory to see if standard models that summarize a vast amount of other information shed light on stock returns. Standard models do not predict anything like the historical equity premium. After a decade of effort, a range of drastic modifications to the standard models can account for the historical equity premium. But it remains to be seen whether the drastic modifications and a high equity premium, or the standard models and a low equity premium will triumph in the end. In sum, economic theory gives one further reason to fear that long-term average excess returns will not return to 8 per cent, and it details the kind of beliefs one must have about the economy to reverse that pessimistic view.

However, I conclude with a warning that low average returns do not imply one should change one's portfolio. Someone has to hold every stock on the market. An investor should only hold less stocks than average if that investor is different from the average investor in some identifiable way, such as risk exposure, attitude or information.

AVERAGE RETURNS AND RISK

The most obvious place to start thinking about future stock returns is a statistical analysis of past stock returns.

Average real returns

Table 16.1 presents several measures of average real returns on stocks and bonds in the postwar period. The value weighted NYSE portfolio shows an impressive annual return of 9 per cent after inflation. The S&P 500 is similar. The equally weighted NYSE portfolio weights small stocks more than the value weighted portfolio. Small stock returns have been even better than the market on average, so the equally weighted portfolio has earned more than 11 per cent. Bonds by contrast seem a disaster. Long-term government bonds earned only 1.8 per cent after inflation, despite a standard deviation (11 per cent) more than half that of stocks (about 17 per cent). Corporate bonds earned a slight premium over government bonds, but at 2.1 per cent are still unappealing compared to stocks. Treasury bills earned only 0.8 per cent on average after inflation.

Table 16.1 ● Annual real returns 1947–96

	VW	S&P500	EW	GB	CB	TB
			per cent			
Average return $E(R)$	9.1	9.5	11.0	1.8	2.1	0.8
Standard deviation $\sigma(R)$	16.7	16.8	22.2	11.1	10.7	2.6
Standard error $\sigma(R) \sqrt{T}$	2.4	2.4	3.0	1.6	1.5	0.4

Notes: VW = value weighted NYSE, EW = equally weighted NYSE, GB = ten-year government bond, CB = corporate bond, TB = three-month Treasury bills. All less CPI inflation.

Source: All data for this and subsequent figures and tables in this chapter are from the Center for Research on Security Prices (CRSP) at the University of Chicago

A reward for risk

Table 16.1 highlights a crucially important fact. *High average returns are only earned as a compensation for risk.* High stock returns cannot be understood merely as high 'productivity of the American economy' (or high marginal productivity of capital) or impatience by consumers. Such high productivity or impatience would lead to high returns on bonds as well. To understand average stock returns, and to assess whether they will continue at these levels, it is not necessary to understand why the economy gives such high returns to saving – it doesn't – but why it gives such high compensation for *bearing risk*. The risk is substantial. A 17 per cent standard deviation means the market is quite likely to decline 9 – 17 = 8% or rise 9 + 17 = 26% in a year. (More precisely, there is about a 30 per cent probability of a decline bigger than –8 per cent or a rise bigger than 26 per cent.)

Risk at short and long horizons

It is a common fallacy to dismiss this risk as 'short-run price fluctuation' and to argue that stock market risk declines in the long run.

The most common way to fall into this trap is to confuse the *annualized* or average return with the actual return. For example, the two-year log or continuously compounded return is the sum of the one-year returns, $r_{0\to2} = r_{0\to1} + r_{1\to2}$. Then, if returns were independent over time, like coin flips, the mean and variance would scale the same way with horizon: $E(r_{0\to2}) = 2E(r_{0\to1})$ and $\sigma^2(r_{0\to2}) = 2\sigma^2(r_{0\to1})$. Investors who cared about mean and variance would invest the same fraction of their wealth in stocks for any return horizon. The variance of *annualized* returns does stabilize; $\sigma(1/2\ r_{0\to2}) = 1/2\sigma^2(r_{0\to1})$. But the investor cares about the total, not annualized return. An example may clarify the distinction. Suppose you are betting $1 on a coin flip. This is a risky bet, you will either gain or lose $1. If you flip the coin 1000 times, the average number of heads (annualized returns) will almost certainly come out quite near 50 per cent. However, the risk of the bet (total return) is much larger: it only takes an average number of heads equal to 0.499 (that is, 499/1000) to lose a dollar; if the average number of heads is 0.490, still very close to 0.5, you lose $10. Just as we care about dollars, not the fraction of heads, we care about total returns, not annualized rates.

To address the short-run price fluctuation fallacy directly, Table 16.2 shows that mean returns and standard deviations scale with horizon just about as this independence argument suggests, out to five years.

(In fact, returns are not exactly independent over time. Estimates in Fama and French [1988a] and Poterba and Summers [1988] suggest that the variance grows a bit less slowly than the horizon for the first five to ten years, and then grows with horizon as before, so stocks are in fact a bit safer for long horizons than the independence assumption suggests. However, this qualification does not rescue the annualized return fallacy. Also bear in mind that long-horizon statistics are measured even less well than annual statistics; there are only five non-overlapping ten-year samples in the postwar period.)

The stock market is like a coin flip, but it is a biased coin flip. Thus, even though mean and variance may grow at the same rate with horizon, the probability that one loses money in the stock market does decline over time. (For example, for the normal distribution, tail probabilities are governed by $E(r)/\sigma(r)$, which grows at the square root of horizon.) However, portfolio advice is not based on pure probabilities of making or losing money; but on measures such as the mean and variance of return. Based on such measures, there is not much presumption that stocks are dramatically safer for long-run investments.

I cannot stress enough that the high average returns come only as compensation for risk. Our task below is to understand this risk and people's aversion to it. Many discussions, including those surrounding the move to a funded social security system, implicitly assume that one gets the high returns without taking on substantial risk. What happens to a funded social security system if the market goes down?

Table 16.2 ● How risk and return vary with investment horizon

Horizon h	$E(R^e)$	$\sigma(R^e)$	$\dfrac{1}{\sqrt{h}}\dfrac{E(R^e)}{\sigma(R^e)}$		
(years)	h	$\sqrt{h}$			
1	8.6	17.1	0.50		
2	9.1	17.9	0.51		
3	9.2	16.8	0.55		
5	10.5	21.9	0.48		

Notes: R^e = value weighted return less T-bill rate. Column one shows average excess return divided by horizon. Column two shows standard deviation of excess return divided by square root of horizon. Column three shows Sharpe ratio divided by square root of horizon. All statistics in per cent.

Means versus standard deviations – Sharpe ratio

Figure 16.1 presents mean returns versus their standard deviations. In addition to the portfolios listed in Table 16.1, I include ten portfolios of NYSE stocks sorted by size. This picture shows that average returns alone are not a particularly useful measure. By taking on more risk, one can achieve very high average returns. In the picture, the small stock portfolio earns over 15 per cent per year average real return, though at the cost of a huge standard deviation. Furthermore, one can form portfolios with even higher average returns by leveraging – borrowing money to buy stocks – or investing in securities such as options that are very sensitive to stock returns. Since standard deviation (and

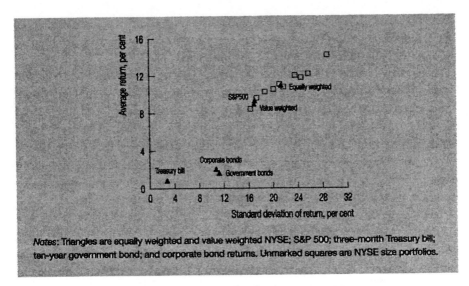

Notes: Triangles are equally weighted and value weighted NYSE; S&P 500; three-month Treasury bill; ten-year government bond; and corporate bond returns. Unmarked squares are NYSE size portfolios.

Fig 16.1 ● Mean versus standard deviation of real returns, 1947–96

beta or other risk measures) grow exactly as fast as mean return, the extra mean return gained in this way exactly corresponds to the extra risk of such portfolios. When considering economic models, it is easy to get them to produce higher mean returns (along with higher standard deviations) by considering claims to leveraged capital.

In sum, *excess returns* of stocks over Treasury bills are more interesting than the level of returns. This is the part of return that is a compensation for risk, and it accounts for nearly all of the amazingly high average stock returns. Furthermore, the *Sharpe ratio* of mean excess return to standard deviation, or the slope of a line connecting stock returns to a risk-free interest rate in Figure 16.1, is a better measure of the fundamental characteristic of stocks than the mean excess return itself, since it is invariant to leveraging. The stock portfolios listed in Table 16.1 all have Sharpe ratios near 0.5.

Standard errors

The average returns and Sharpe ratios look impressive. But are these true or just chance? One meaning of chance is this. Suppose that the average excess return really is low, say 3 per cent. How likely is it that a 50-year sample has an average excess return of 8 per cent? Similarly, if the next 50 years are 'just like' the last 50, in the sense that the structure of the economy is the same but the random shocks may be different, what is the chance that the average return in the *next* 50 years will be as good as it was in the last 50?

Since we only see one sample, these questions are really unanswerable at a deep level. Statistics provides an educated guess in the *standard error.*

Assuming that each year's return is statistically independent, our best guess of the standard deviation of the *average* return is $\sigma / \sqrt{T}$, where σ is the standard deviation of annual returns and T is the data size.

This formula tells us something important: *stock returns are so volatile that it is very hard to statistically measure average returns*. Table 16.1 includes standard errors of stock returns measured in the last 50 years, and Table 16.3 shows standard errors for a variety of horizons. The confidence interval, mean +/–2 standard deviations, represents the 95 per cent probability range. As the table shows, even very long-term averages leave a lot of uncertainty about mean returns. For example, with 50 years of data, an 8 per cent average excess return is measured with a 2.4 percentage point standard error. Thus, the confidence interval says that the true average excess return is between $8 - 2 \times 2.4 =$ 3% and $8 + 2 \times 2.4 = 13\%$ with 95 per cent probability.[1] This is a wide band of uncertainty about the true market return, given 50 years of data. One can also see that five- or ten-year averages are nearly useless; it takes a long time to statistically discern that the average return has increased or decreased. As a cold winter need not presage an ice age, so even a decade of bad returns need not change one's view of the true underlying average return.

The standard errors are also the standard deviations of average returns over the next T years, and Table 16.3 shows that there is quite a lot of uncertainty about those returns. For example, if the true mean excess return is and will continue to be 8 per cent, the five-year standard error of 7.6 per cent is almost as large as the mean. This means that there is still a good chance that the next five-year return will average less than the Treasury bill rate.

On the other hand, though the average return on stocks is not precisely known, the 2.4 per cent standard error means that we can confidently reject the view that the true mean excess return was zero or even 2–3 per cent. The argument that *all* the past equity premium was luck doesn't hold up well against this simple statistical argument.

Table 16.3 ● Standard error of average return at various horizons

Horizon T (years)	Standard error $\sigma/\sqrt{T}$ (percentage points)
5	7.6
10	5.4
25	3.8
50	2.4

Note: Returns assumed to be statistically independent with standard deviation $\sigma = 17$ per cent.

Selection and crashes

Two important assumptions behind the standard error calculation, however, suggest ways in which the postwar average stock return might still have been largely due to luck. Argentina and the USA looked very similar at the middle of the last century. Both economies were under-developed relative to Britain and Germany and had about the same per capita income. If Argentina had experienced the USA's growth and stock returns, and vice versa, this chapter would be written in Spanish from the Buenos Aires Federal Reserve Bank, with high Argentine stock returns as the subject.

The statistical danger this story points to is *selection* or *survival* bias. If you flip one coin ten times, the chance of seeing eight heads is low. But if you flip ten coins ten times, the chance that the coin with the greatest number of heads exceeds eight heads is much larger. Does this story more closely capture the 50-year return on US stocks? Brown, Goetzmann and Ross (1995) present a strong case that the uncertainty about true average stock returns is much larger than $\sigma/\sqrt{T}$ suggests. As they put it, 'Looking back over the history of the London or the New York stock markets can be extraordinarily comforting to an investor – equities appear to have provided a substantial premium over bonds, and markets appear to have recovered nicely after huge crashes. ... Less comforting is the past history of other major markets: Russia, China, Germany and Japan. Each of these markets has had one or more major interruptions *that prevent their inclusion in long term studies*' [my emphasis].

In addition, think of the things that didn't happen in the last 50 years. There were no banking panics, no depressions, no civil wars, no constitutional crises, the cold war was not lost, and no missiles were fired over Berlin, Cuba, Korea or Vietnam. If any of these things had happened, there undoubtedly would have been a calamitous decline in stock values. The statistical problem is *non-normality*. Taking the standard deviation from a sample that did not include rare calamities, and calculating average return probabilities from a normal distribution may understate the true uncertainty. But investors, aware of that uncertainty, discount prices and hence leave high returns on the table.

We can cast the issue in terms of fundamental beliefs about the economy. Was it clear to people in 1945 (or 1871, or whenever the sample starts) and throughout the period that the average return on stocks would be 8 per cent greater than that of bonds? If so, one would expect them to have bought more stocks, even considering the risk described by the 17 per cent year-to-year variation. But perhaps it was not in fact obvious in 1945, that rather than slipping back into depression, the USA would experience a half century of growth never before seen in human history. If so, much of the equity premium was unexpected good luck.

TIME VARYING EXPECTED RETURNS

Regressions of returns on price/dividend ratios

We are not only concerned with the *average* return on stocks but whether returns are expected to be unusually low at a time of high prices, such as the present. The first and most natural thing one might do to answer this question is to look at a regression forecast. To this end, Table 16.4 presents regressions of returns on the price/dividend (P/D) ratio.

Table 16.4 ● OLS regressions of excess returns and dividend growth on VW P/D ratio

Horizon k (years)	$R_{t \to t+k} = a + b(P_t/D_t)$			$D_{t+k}/D_t = a + b(P_t/D_t)$		
	b	σ(b)	R^2	b	σ(b)	R^2
1	−1.04	(0.33)	0.17	−0.39	(0.18)	0.07
2	−2.04	(0.66)	0.26	−0.52	(0.40)	0.07
3	−2.84	(0.88)	0.38	−0.53	(0.43)	0.07
5	−6.22	(1.24)	0.59	−0.99	(0.47)	0.15

Notes: $R_{t \to t+k}$ indicates the k year return on the value weighted NYSE portfolio less the k year return from continuously reinvesting in Treasury bills; b = regression slope coefficient (defined by the regression equation above); σ(b) = standard error of regression coefficient. Standard errors in parentheses use GMM to correct for heteroscedasticity and serial correlation.

The regression at a one-year horizon shows that excess returns are in fact predictable from P/D ratios, though the 0.17 R^2 is not particularly remarkable. However, at longer and longer horizons, the slope coefficients increase and larger and larger fractions of return variation can be forecasted. At a five-year horizon, 60 per cent of the variation in stock returns can be forecasted ahead of time from the P/D ratio. (Fama and French, 1988b, is a famous early source for this kind of regression.)

One can object to dividends as the divisor for prices. However, price divided by just about anything sensible works about as well, including earnings, book value and moving averages of past prices. There seems to be an additional business-cycle component of expected return variation that is tracked by the term spread or other business cycle forecasting variables, including the default spread and investment-capital ratio, the T-bill rate, the ratio of the T-bill rate to its moving average, and the dividend/earnings ratio. (See Fama and French, 1989, for term and default spreads, Campbell, 1987, for term spread, Cochrane, 1991c, for investment-capital ratios, Lamont, 1997, for dividend/earnings, and Ferson and Constantinides, 1991, for an even more exhaustive list with references.) However, price ratios such as P/D are the most important forecasting variables, especially at long horizons, so I focus on the

P/D ratio to keep the analysis simple. In a similar fashion, *cross-sectional* variation in expected returns can be very well described by the P/D ratio or (better) the ratio of market value to book value, which contains the price in its numerator. Portfolios of 'undervalued' or 'value' stocks with low price ratios outperform portfolios of 'overvalued' or 'growth' stocks with high price ratios. (See Fama and French, 1993.)

Slow moving P/D and P/E

Figure 16.2 presents P/D and price/earnings (P/E) ratios over time. This graph emphasizes that price ratios are very *slow moving* variables. This is why they forecast long-horizon movements in stock returns.

The rise in forecast power with horizon is not a separate phenomenon. It results from the ability to forecast one period returns and the slow movement in the P/D ratio.[2] As an analogy, if it is 10 degrees below zero in Chicago (low P/D ratio), one's best guess is that it will warm up a degree or so per day. Spring does come, albeit slowly. However, the weather varies a lot; it can easily go up or down 20 degrees in a day, so this forecast is not very accurate (low R^2). But the fact that it is 10 degrees below zero signals that the temperature will rise a bit on average per day for many days. By the time we look at a six-month horizon, we forecast a 90 degree rise in temperature. The daily variation of 20 degrees is still there, but the change in temperature (90 degrees) that can be forecasted is much larger relative to the daily variation, implying a high R^2.

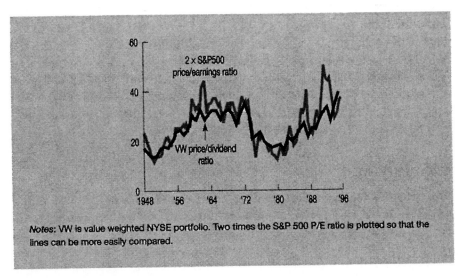

Notes: VW is value weighted NYSE portfolio. Two times the S&P 500 P/E ratio is plotted so that the lines can be more easily compared.

Fig 16.2 ● P/D and P/E ratios

The slow movement in the P/D ratio also means that the ability to forecast returns is not the fabled alchemists' stone that turns lead into gold. A high P/D ratio means that prices will grow more slowly than dividends for a long time until the P/D ratio is re-established, and vice versa. Trading on these signals – buying more stocks in times of low prices, and less in times of high prices – can raise (unconditional) average returns a bit, but not much more than 1 per cent for the same standard deviation. If there were a 50 per cent R^2 at a daily horizon, one could make a lot of money; but not so at a five-year horizon.

The slow movement of the P/D ratio also means that on a purely *statistical* basis, one can cast doubt on whether the P/D ratio really forecasts returns. What we really know, looking at Figure 16.2 (Figure 16.4 also makes this point), is that low prices relative to dividends and earnings in the 1950s preceded the boom market of the early 1960s; that the high P/D ratios of the mid-1960s preceded the poor returns of the 1970s; and that the low price ratios of the mid-1970s preceded the current boom. We also know that price ratios are very high now. In any real sense, there really are three data points. I do not want to survey the extensive statistical literature that formalizes this point, but it is there. Most importantly, it shows that the t-statistics one might infer from regressions such as Table 16.4 are inflated; with more sophisticated tests, return predictability actually has about a 10 per cent probability value before one starts to worry about fishing and selection biases.

What about repurchases? P/E and other forecasts

Is the P/D ratio still a valid signal? Perhaps increasing dividend repurchases mean that the P/D ratio will not return to its historical low values; perhaps it has shifted to a new mean so today's high ratio is not bad for returns. To address this issue, Figure 16.2 plots the S&P 500 P/E ratio along with the P/D ratio. The two measures line up well. The P/E ratio forecasts returns almost as well as the P/D ratio. The P/E ratio, price/book value and other ratios are also at historic highs, forecasting low returns for years to come. Yet they are of course immune to the criticism that the dividend–earnings relationship might be fundamentally different from the past.

Return forecasts

What do the regressions of Table 16.4 say, quantitatively, about future returns? Figure 16.3 presents one-year returns and the P/D ratio forecast. Figure 16.4 presents five-year returns and the P/D ratio forecast. I include in-sample and out-of-sample forecasts in Figures 16.3 and 16.4. To form the out-of-sample forecasts, I paired the regressions from Table 16.4 with an autoregression of P/D_t,

$$P/D_{t+1} = \mu + \rho\, P/D_t + \delta_{t+1}.$$

Then, for example, since my data run to the end of 1996, the forecast returns for 1997 and 1998 are:

$$E(R_{1997}) = a + b(P/D_{1996})$$
$$E(R_{1998}) = a + b(\mu + \rho\, P/D_{1996}),$$

and so on.[3]

The one-year return forecast is extraordinarily pessimistic. It starts at a −8 per cent excess return for 1997, and only very slowly returns to the estimated unconditional mean excess return of 8 per cent. In ten years, the forecast is still −5 per cent, in 25 years it is −1.75 per cent, and it is still only 2.35 per cent in 50 years. The five-year return forecasts are similarly pessimistic.

Of course, this forecast is subject to lots of uncertainty. There is uncertainty about what actual returns will be, given the forecasts. This will always be true. If one could precisely forecast the direction of stock prices, stocks would cease to be risky and would cease to pay a risk premium. There is also a great deal of uncertainty about the forecasts themselves.

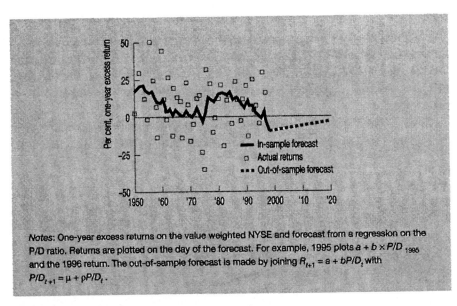

Notes: One-year excess returns on the value weighted NYSE and forecast from a regression on the P/D ratio. Returns are plotted on the day of the forecast. For example, 1995 plots $a + b \times P/D_{1995}$ and the 1996 return. The out-of-sample forecast is made by joining $R_{t+1} = a + bP/D_t$ with $P/D_{t+1} = \mu + \rho P/D_t$.

Fig 16.3 ● Actual and forecast one-year excess returns

The forecasts attempt to measure *expected returns*, the quantity that investors must trade off against unavoidable risk in deciding how attractive an investment is, and they undoubtedly measure expected returns with error.

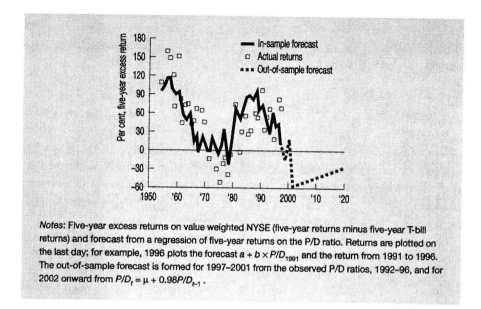

Fig 16.4 • Actual and forecast five-year excess returns

The plots of actual returns on top of the in-sample, one-year-ahead forecasts in Figures 16.3 and 16.4 give one measure of the forecast uncertainty. One can see that year-to-year returns are quite likely to vary a lot given the forecast. Five-year returns track the forecast more closely, but here the chance of over-fitting is greater.

To get a handle on how reliable or robust the pessimistic forecast is, Figure 16.5 gives a scatterplot of one-year returns and their forecasts based on P/D,

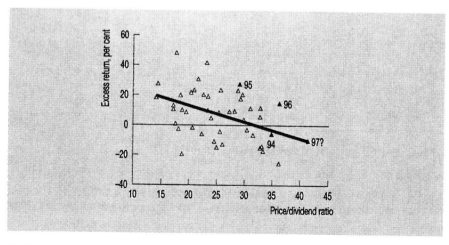

Fig 16.5 • One-year excess returns versus one-year ahead forecast from P/D

together with the fitted regression line. The scatterplot indicates that the regression results are not spurious, or the result of a few outlying years.

The point marked '97?' is the P/D ratio at the end of 1996 together with the forecast return for 1997. We see immediately one source of trouble with the point forecast: the P/D ratio has never in the postwar period been as high as it is now. Extending historical experience to never-before seen values is always dangerous. One is particularly uncomfortable with a prediction that the market should earn *less* than the T-bill rate, given the strong theoretical presumption for a positive expected excess return.[4] One could easily draw a downward sloping line through the points, flattening out on the right, predicting a zero excess return for P/D ratios above 30 to 35, and never predicting a negative excess return. A nonlinear regression that incorporates this idea will fit about as well as the linear regression I have run. However, the scatterplot does not demand such a nonlinear relation either, so this is largely a matter of choice. In sum, while the scatterplot does suggest that the current forecast should be low, it does not give robust evidence that the forecast excess return should be negative.

What about the last few years of high returns?

The P/D ratios also pointed to low returns in 1995 and 1996. Anyone who took that advice missed out on a dramatic surge in the market, and some fund managers who took that advice are now unemployed. Doesn't this mean that the P/D signal should no longer be trusted?

To answer this criticism, look at the figures again. They make clear that the returns for 1995 and 1996 and even another 20 per cent or so return for 1997 are not so far out of line, despite a pessimistic P/D forecast, that we should throw away the regression based on the previous 47 years of experience. To return to the analogy, if it is 10 degrees below zero in Chicago, that means spring is coming. But we can easily have a few weeks of 20 degree below weather before Spring finally arrives. The graphs make vivid how large a 17 per cent standard deviation really is, and to what extent the forecasts based on the P/D ratio mark long-term tendencies that are still subject to lots of short-term swings rather than accurate forecasts of year-to-year booms or crashes.

Another source of uncertainty about the forecast is how persistent the P/D ratio really is. If, for example, the P/D ratio had no persistence, then the low return forecast would only last a year. After that, it would return to the unconditional mean of 9 per cent (8 per cent over Treasury bills). Now, given a true value $\rho = 0.98$ in $P/D_t = \mu + \rho P/D_{t-1} + \delta_t$, the median ordinary least squares (OLS) estimate is 0.90, as I found in sample. That is why Figure 16.3 uses the value $\rho = 0.98$. However, given this true value, the OLS estimate lies between 0.83 and 0.94 only 50 per cent of the time and between 0.66 and 1.00 for 95 per cent of the time. Thus, there is a huge range of uncertainty over the true

FINANCIAL ECONOMICS

value of ρ. The best thing that could happen to the forecast is if the P/D ratio were really less persistent than it seems. In this case, the near-term return forecast would be unchanged, but the long-term return forecast would return to 9 per cent much more quickly.

VARIANCE DECOMPOSITION

When prices are high relative to dividends (or earnings, cash flow, book value, or some other divisor), one of three things must be true.

1 Investors expect dividends to rise in the future.

2 Investors expect returns to be low in the future. Future cash flows are discounted at a lower than usual rate, leading to higher prices.

3 Investors expect prices to keep rising forever, in a 'bubble'.

This is not a theory, it is an accounting identity like $1=1$: If the P/D ratio is high, either dividends must rise, prices must decline, or the P/D ratio must never return to its historical average. Which of the three options holds for our stock market?

Historically, *virtually all variation in P/D ratios has reflected varying expected returns*. At a simple level, Table 16.4 makes this point with regressions of long-horizon dividend growth on P/D ratios to match the regressions of returns on P/D ratios. The dividend-growth coefficients are much smaller, typically one standard error from zero, and the R^2 values are tiny. Worse, the *signs* are wrong. To the extent that a high P/D ratio forecasts any change in dividends, it seems to forecast a small *decline* in dividends.

To be a little more precise, the identity:

$$1 = R_{t+1}^{-1} R_{t+1} = R_{t+1}^{-1} \frac{P_{t+1} + D_{t+1}}{P_t}$$

yields, with a little algebra, the approximate identity:

$$p_t - d_t = \text{const.} + \sum_{j=1}^{\infty} \rho^j (\Delta d_{t+j} - r_{t+j}) + \tag{1}$$
$$\lim_{j \to \infty} \rho^j (P_{t+j} - d_{t+j}),$$

where $\rho = P/D/(1 + P/D)$ is a constant of approximation, slightly less than one and lowercase letters denote logarithms (Campbell and Shiller, 1988). Equation (1) gives a precise meaning to my earlier statement that a high P/D ratio *must* be followed by high dividend growth Δd, low returns r, or a bubble.

Bubbles do not appear to be the reason for historical P/D ratio variation. Unless the P/D ratio grows faster than $1/\rho^j$, there is no bubble. It is hard to believe that P/D ratios can grow *forever*. Empirically, P/D ratios do not seem to have a trend or unit root over time.[5]

This still leaves two possibilities: are high prices signals of high dividend growth or low returns? To address this issue, equation 1 implies[6] P/D ratios can *only* vary if they forecast changing dividend growth or if they forecast changing returns.

$$var(p_t - d_t) = cov(p_t - d_t, \sum_{j=1}^{\infty} \rho^j \Delta d_{t+j}) - \tag{2}$$

$$cov(p_t - d_t, \sum_{j=1}^{\infty} \rho^j r_{t+j}).$$

Equation (2) has powerful implications. At first glance, it would seem a reasonable approximation that returns cannot be forecasted (the 'random walk' hypothesis) and neither can dividend growth. But if this were the case, the P/D ratio would have to be a *constant*. Thus, the fact that the P/D ratio varies *at all* means that either dividend growth or returns can be forecasted.

This observation solidifies one's belief in P/D ratio forecasts of returns. Yes, the statistical evidence that P/D ratios forecast returns is weak. But P/D ratios *have* varied. The choice is, P/D ratios forecast returns *or* they forecast dividend growth. They have to forecast something. Given this choice and Table 16.3, it seems a much firmer conclusion that they forecast returns.

Table 16.5 presents some estimates of the price-dividend variance decomposition (Equation (2)), taken from Cochrane (1991b). As one might suspect from Table 16.4, Table 16.5 shows that in the past *almost all variation in P/D ratios has been due to changing return forecasts*. (The rows of Table 16.5 do not add up to exactly 100 per cent because Equation (2) is an approximation. The elements do not have to be between 0 and 100 per cent. For example, –34, 138 occurs because high prices seem to forecast lower dividend growth. Therefore they must and do forecast really low returns. The real and nominal rows differ because P/D forecasts inflation in the sample.)

Table 16.5 ● Variance decomposition of VW P/D ratio

	Dividends	Returns
Real	–34	138
Standard error	(10)	(32)
Nominal	30	85
Standard error	(41)	(19)

Notes: VW = value weighted NYSE. Table entries are the percentage of the variance of the price/dividend ratio attributable to dividend and return forecasts, $100 \times cov(p_t - d_t, \sum_{j=1}^{15} \rho^j \Delta d_{t+j})/var(p_t - d_t)$ and similarly for returns.

So much for history. What does it mean? Again, we live at a moment of historically unprecedented P/D, P/E and other multiples. Perhaps *this time* high prices reflect high long-run dividend growth. If so, the prices have to reflect an unprecedented expectation of future dividend growth: the P/D ratio is about double its long-term average, so the level of dividends has to double, above and beyond its usual growth. However, if this time is at all like the past, high prices reflect low future returns.

The bottom line

Statistical analysis suggests that the long-term average return on broad stock market indexes is 8 per cent greater than the T-bill rate, with a standard error of about 3 per cent. High prices are related to low subsequent excess returns. Based on these patterns, the expected excess return (stock return less T-bill rate) is near zero for the next five years or so, and then slowly rising to the historical average. The large standard deviation of excess returns, about 17 per cent, means that actual returns will certainly deviate substantially from the expected return. Finally, one always gets more expected return by taking on more risk.

ECONOMICS: UNDERSTANDING THE EQUITY PREMIUM

Statistical analysis of past returns leaves a lot of uncertainty about future returns. Furthermore, it is hard to believe that average excess returns are 8 per cent without knowing *why* this is so. Perhaps most important, no statistical analysis can predict if the future will be like the past. Even if the true expected excess return was 8 per cent, did that result from fundamental or temporary features of the economy? Thus, we need an economic understanding of stock returns.

Economic theory and modelling is often portrayed as an ivory tower exercise, out of touch with the real world. Nothing could be further from the truth, especially in this case. Many superficially plausible stories have been put forth to explain the historically high return on stocks and the time-variation of returns. Economic models or theories make these stories explicit, check whether they are internally consistent, see if they can quantitatively explain stock returns, and check that they do not make wildly counterfactual predictions in other dimensions, for example, requiring wild variation in risk-free rates or strong persistent movements in consumption growth. Few stories survive this scrutiny.

We have a vast experience with economic theory; a range of model economies have formed the backbone of our understanding of economic growth and dynamic micro, macro and international economics for close to 25 years. Does a large equity premium make sense in terms of such standard economics? Did people in 1947, and throughout the period, know that stocks were going to yield 8 per cent over bonds on average, yet were rationally unwilling to hold more stocks because they were afraid of the 17 per cent standard deviation or some other measure of stocks' risk? If so, we have 'explained' the equity premium. If so, statistics from the past may well describe the future, since neither people's preferences nor the riskiness of technological opportunities seems to have changed dramatically. But what if it makes no sense that people should be so scared of stocks? In this case, it is much more likely that the true premium is small, and the historical returns were in fact just good luck.

The answer is simple: standard economic models utterly fail to produce anything like the historical average stock return or the variation in expected returns over time. After ten years of intense effort, there is a range of drastic modifications to standard models that can explain the equity premium and return predictability and (harder still) are not inconsistent with a few obvious related facts about consumption and interest rates. However, these models are truly drastic modifications; they fundamentally change the description of the source of risk that commands a premium in asset markets. Furthermore, they have not yet been tested against the broad range of experience of the standard models. These facts must mean one of two things. Either the standard models are wrong and will change drastically, or the phenomenon is wrong and will disappear.

I first show how the standard model utterly fails to account for the historical equity premium (Sharpe ratio). The natural response is to see if perhaps we can modify the standard model. I consider what happens if we simply allow a very high level of risk aversion. The answer here, as in many early attempts to modify the standard model, is unsatisfactory. While one can explain the equity premium, easy explanations make strongly counterfactual predictions regarding other facts. The goal is to explain the equity premium in a manner consistent with the level and volatility of consumption growth (both about 1 per cent per year), the predictability of stock returns described above, the relative lack of predictability in consumption growth, the relative constancy of real risk-free rates over time and across countries, and the relatively low correlation of stock returns with consumption growth. This is a tough assignment, which is only now starting to be accomplished.

Then I survey alternative views that do promise to account for the equity premium, without (so far) wildly counterfactual predictions on other dimensions. Each modification is the culmination of a decade-long effort by a large number of researchers. (For literature reviews, see Kocherlakota, 1996, and Cochrane and Hansen, 1992.) The first model maintains the complete and frictionless market simplification, but changes the specification of how people feel about consumption over time, by adding *habit persistence* in a very special way that produces a strong *precautionary saving* motive. The second model abandons the perfect markets simplification. Here, uninsurable individual-level risks are the key to the equity premium. I will also discuss a part of an emerging view that the equity premium and time-variation of expected returns result from the fact that few people hold stocks. This view is not flushed out yet to a satisfactory model, but does give some insight.

Both modifications answer the basic question, 'Why are consumers so afraid of stocks?' in a similar way, and give a fundamentally different answer from the standard model's view that expected returns are driven by risks to wealth or consumption. The modifications both say that consumers are really afraid of stocks because stocks pay off poorly in *recessions*. In one case a recession means a time when consumption has recently fallen, no matter what its level. In the second case a recession is a time of unusually high cross-sectional (though not aggregate) uncertainty. In both cases the raw risk to wealth is not a particularly important part of the story.

The standard model

To say anything about dynamic economics, we have to say something about how people are willing to trade consumption in one moment and set of cir- cumstances (state of nature) for consumption in another moment and set of circumstances. For example, if people were always willing to give up a dollar of consumption today for $1.10 in a year, then the economy would feature a steady 10 per cent interest rate. It also might have quite volatile consumption, as people accept many such opportunities. If people did not care what the cir- cumstances were in which they would get $1.10, then all expected returns would be equal to the interest rate (risk neutrality). Of course, this is an ex- treme example. There certainly comes a point at which such willingness to substitute consumption becomes strained. If someone were going to consume $1000 this year but $10,000 next year, it might take a bit more than a 10 per cent interest rate to get him or her to consume even less this year.

To capture these ideas about people's willingness to substitute consumption, we use a *utility function* that gives a numerical 'happiness' value for every pos- sible stream of future consumption:

$$U = E\int_{t=0}^{\infty} e^{-\rho t} u(C_t)dt. \tag{3}$$

E denotes expectation; C_t denotes consumption at date t; ρ is the subjective discount factor; and $e^{-\rho t}$ captures the fact that consumers prefer earlier con- sumption to later. The function $u(.)$ is increasing and concave, to reflect the idea that people always like more consumption, but at a diminishing rate. The function $u(C) = C^{1-\gamma}$ is a common specification, with γ between 0 and 5. $\gamma = 0$ or $u(C) = C$ corresponds to *risk neutrality*, a constant interest rate ρ, and a perfect willingness to substitute across time. $\gamma = 1$ corresponds to $u(C) = \ln(C)$, which is a very attractive choice since it implies that each doubling of consumption adds the same amount of happiness. For most asset pricing prob-

lems, writing the utility function over an infinite lifespan is a convenient simplification that makes little difference to the results. Economic models are
often written in discrete time, in which case the utility function is:

$$U = E \sum_{t=0}^{\infty} e^{-\rho t} u(C_t).$$

Dynamic economics takes this representation of people's preferences and
mixes it with a representation of technological opportunities for production
and investment. For example, the simplest model might specify that output is
made from capital, $Y = f(K)$, output is invested or consumed, $Y = C+I$, and
capital depreciates but is increased by investment, $K_{t+1} = (1 - \delta)K_t + I_t$, in discrete time. To study business cycles, one adds detail, including at least labour,
leisure and shocks. To study monetary issues, one adds some friction that
induces people to use money, and so on.

Despite the outward appearance of tension, this is a great unifying moment
for macroeconomics. Practically all issues relating to business cycles, growth,
aggregate policy analysis, monetary economics and international economics are
studied in the context of variants of this simple model. The remaining differences concern details of implementation.

Since this basic economic framework explains such a wide range of phenomena, what does it predict for the equity risk premium? Give the opportunity to
buy assets such as stocks and bonds to a consumer whose preferences are
described by Equation (3), and figure out what the optimal consumption and
portfolio decision is. (The appendix includes derivations of all equations.) The
following conditions describe the optimal choice:

$$r^f = \rho + \gamma E(\Delta c) \tag{4}$$
$$E(r) - r^f = \gamma \, cov(\Delta c, r) = \gamma \sigma \, (\Delta c) \sigma(r) corr(\Delta c, r), \tag{5}$$

where

   Δc denotes the proportional change in consumption
   r denotes a risky asset return
   r^f denotes the risk-free rate
   cov denotes covariance
   $corr$ denotes correlation

and

$$\gamma \equiv - \frac{Cu''(C)}{u'(C)}$$

is a measure of *curvature* or *risk aversion*. Higher γ means that more consumption gives less pleasure very quickly; it implies that people are less willing to
substitute less consumption now for more consumption later and to take risks.

Equation (5) expresses the most fundamental idea in finance. It says that the average excess return on any security must be proportional to the *covariance* of that return with marginal utility and, hence, consumption growth. This is because people value financial assets that can be used to smooth consumption over time and in response to risks. For example, a 'risky' stock, one that has a high standard deviation $\sigma(r)$, may nonetheless command no greater average return $E(r)$ than the risk-free rate if its return is uncorrelated with consumption growth $corr(\Delta c, r) = 0$. If it yields any more, the consumer can buy just a little bit of the security, and come out ahead because the risk is perfectly diversifiable. Readers familiar with the capital asset pricing model (CAPM) will recognize the intuition; replacing wealth or the market portfolio with consumption gives the most modern and general version of that theory.

The equity premium puzzle

To evaluate the equity premium, I transform Equation (5) to:

$$\frac{E(r) - r^f}{\sigma(r)} = \gamma \sigma (\Delta c)\, corr(\Delta c, r). \tag{6}$$

The left-hand side is the Sharpe ratio. As I showed above, the (unconditional) Sharpe ratio is about 0.5 for the stock market, and it is robust to leveraging or choice of assets. The right-hand side of Equation (6) says something very important. A high Sharpe ratio or risk premium must be the result of:

1 high aversion to risk, γ, or

2 lots of risk, $\sigma(\Delta c)$.

Furthermore, it can only occur for assets whose returns are correlated with the risks. This basic message will pervade the following discussion of much-generalized economic models. If the right-hand side of Equation (6) is low, then the consumer should invest more in the asset with return r. Doing so will make the consumption stream more risky and more correlated with the asset return. Thus, as the consumer invests more, the right-hand side of Equation (6) will approach the left-hand side.

The right-hand side of Equation (6) is a prediction of what the Sharpe ratio should be. It does not come close to predicting the historical equity premium. The standard deviation of aggregate consumption growth is about 1 per cent or 0.01. The correlation of consumption growth with stock returns is a bit harder to measure since it depends on horizon and timing issues. Still, for horizons of a year or so, 0.2 is a pretty generous number. $\gamma \simeq 1$ or 2 is standard; $\gamma = 10$ is a very generous value. Putting this all together, $10 \times 0.01 \times 0.2 = 0.02$ rather than 0.5. At a 20 per cent standard deviation, a 0.02 Sharpe ratio implies an average excess return for stocks of $0.02 \times 20 = 0.4\%$ (40 basis points) rather than 8 per cent.

This devastating calculation is the celebrated 'equity premium puzzle' of Mehra and Prescott (1985), as reinterpreted by Hansen and Jagannathan (1991). The failure is quantitative not qualitative, as Kocherlakota (1996) points out. Qualitatively, the right-hand side of Equation (6) does predict a positive equity premium. The problem is in the numbers. This is a strong advertisement for quantitative rather than just qualitative economics.

Can we change the numbers?

The correlation of consumption growth with returns is the most suspicious ingredient in this calculation. While the correlation is undeniably low in the short run, a decade-long rise in the stock market should certainly lead to more consumption. In fact, the low correlation is somewhat of a puzzle in itself: standard (one-shock) models typically predict correlations of 0.99 or more. Marshall and Daniel (1997) find correlations in the data up to 0.4 at a two-year horizon, and by allowing lags. But even plugging in a correlation of $corr(\Delta c, r) = 1$, $\sigma(\Delta c) = 0.01$ and $\gamma < 10$ implies a Sharpe ratio less than 0.1, or one-fifth the sample value.

A large literature has tried to explain the equity premium puzzle by introducing frictions that make T-bills 'money-like', which artificially drive down the interest rate (for example, Aiyagari and Gertler, 1991). The highest Sharpe ratio occurs in fact when one considers short-term risk-free debt and money, since the latter pays no interest. Perhaps the same mechanism can be invoked for the spread between stocks and bonds. However, a glance at Figure 16.1 shows that this will not work. High Sharpe ratios are pervasive in financial markets. One can recover a high Sharpe ratio from stocks alone, or from stocks less long-term bonds.

Time-varying expected returns

The consumption-based view with $u'(C) = C^{-\gamma}$ also has trouble explaining the fact that P/D ratios forecast stock returns. Consider the conditional version of Equation (6):

$$\frac{E_t(r) - r^f_t}{\sigma_t(r)} = \gamma \sigma_t(\Delta c) corr_t(\Delta c, r), \tag{7}$$

where E_t, σ_t, $corr_t$ represent conditional moments. I showed above that the P/D ratio gives a strong signal about mean returns, $E_t(r)$. It does not, however, give much information about the standard deviation of returns. Figure 16.5 does suggest a slight increase in return standard deviation along with the higher mean return when P/D ratios decline – the leverage effect of Black (1976). However, the increase in standard deviation is much less than the increase in mean return. Hence, the Sharpe ratio of mean to standard deviation varies over time and increases when prices are low.

How can we explain variation in the Sharpe ratio? Looking at Equation (7), it could happen if there were times of high and low consumption volatility, variation in $\sigma_t(\Delta c)$. But that does not seem to be the case; there is little evidence that aggregate consumption growth is much more volatile at times of low prices than high prices. The conditional correlation of consumption growth and returns could vary a great deal over time, but this seems unlikely, or more precisely like an unfathomable assumption on which to build the central understanding of time-varying returns.

What about the CAPM?

Finance researchers and practitioners often express disbelief (and boredom) with consumption-based models such as the above. Even the CAPM performs better: expected returns of different portfolios such as those in Figure 16.1 line up much better against their covariances with the market return than against their covariances with consumption growth. Why not use the CAPM or other, better-performing finance models to understand the equity premium?

The answer is that the CAPM and related finance models are *useless* for understanding the market premium. The CAPM states that the expected return of a given asset is proportional to its 'beta' times the expected return of the market,

$$E\left(R^i\right) = R^f + \beta_{i,m}[E(R^m) - R^f].$$

This is fine if you want to think about an individual stock's return given the market return. But the average market return – the thing we are trying to explain, understand and predict – is a *given* to the CAPM. Similarly, multifactor models explain average returns on individual assets, *given* average returns on 'factor mimicking portfolios', including the market. Option pricing models explain option prices, *given* the stock price. To understand the market premium, there is no substitute for economic models such as the consumption-based model outlined above and its variants.

Highly curved power utility

Since we have examined all the other numbers on the right-hand side of Equation (6), perhaps we should raise curvature γ. This is a central modification. All of macroeconomics and growth theory considers values of γ no larger than 2–3. To generate a Sharpe ratio of 0.5, $\gamma = 250$ is needed in Equation (6). Even if *corr* = 1, γ must still equal 50. What's wrong with $\gamma = 50$ to 250? Although a high curvature γ explains the equity premium, it runs quickly into trouble with other facts.

Consumption and interest rates

The most basic piece of evidence for low γ is the relationship between consumption growth and interest rates. Real interest rates are quite stable over time (see the standard deviation in Table 16.1) and roughly the same the world over, despite wide variation in consumption growth over time and across countries. A value of $\gamma = 50$ to 250 implies that consumers are essentially unwilling to substitute consumption over time; equivalently that variation in consumption growth must be accompanied by huge variations in interest rates that we do not observe.

Look again at the first basic relationship between consumption growth and interest rates, Equation (4), reproduced here:

$$r_t^f = \rho + \gamma E_t(\Delta c) \tag{4}$$

High values of γ are troublesome even in understanding the level of interest rates. Average consumption growth and real interest rates are both about 1 per cent. Thus, $\gamma = 50$ to 250 requires $\rho = -0.5$ to -2.5, or a -50 per cent to -250 per cent subjective discount rate. That's the wrong sign: people should prefer current to future consumption, not the other way around (Weil, 1989).[7]

The absence of much interest rate variation across time and countries is an even bigger problem. People save more and defer consumption in times of high interest rates, so consumption growth rises when interest rates are higher. However, $\gamma = 50$ means that a country with consumption growth one per centage point higher than normal must have real interest rates 50 percentage points higher than normal, and consumption one percentage point lower than normal must have real interest rates 50 percentage points lower than normal, implying huge negative interest rates – consumers pay financial intermediaries 48 per cent to keep their money. This just does not happen.

This observation can also be phrased as a conceptual experiment, suitable for thinking about one's own preferences or for survey evidence on others' preferences. For example, what does it take to convince someone to skip a vacation? Take a family with $50,000 per year income, consumption equal to income, which spends $2500 (5 per cent) on an annual vacation. If interest rates are good enough, though, the family can be persuaded to skip this year's vacation and go on two vacations next year. What interest rate does it take to persuade the family to do this? The answer is $(\$52,500/\$47,500)^\gamma - 1$. For $\gamma = 250$ that is an interest rate of 3×10^{11}. For $\gamma = 50$, we still need an interest rate of 14,800 per cent. I think most of us would defer the vacation for somewhat lower interest rates.

The standard use of low values for γ in macroeconomics is also important for delivering realistic quantity dynamics in macroeconomic models, including relative variances of investment and output, and for delivering reasonable speeds of adjustment to shocks.

Risk aversion

Economists have also shied away from high curvature γ on the basis that people do not seem that risk averse. After examining the argument, I conclude that there are fewer solid reasons to object to high risk aversion than to object to high aversion to intertemporal substitution via the consumption-interest rate relationships I examined above.

Surveys and thought experiments

Since Sharpe ratios are high for many assets, much analysis of risk aversion comes from simple thought experiments rather than data. For example, how much would a family pay per year to avoid a bet that led with equal probability to a y increase or decrease in annual consumption for the rest of their lives? Table 16.6 presents some calculations of how much our family with $50,000 per year of income and consumption would pay to avoid various bets of this form.[8] For bets that are reasonably large relative to wealth, high γ means that families are willing to pay almost the entire amount of the bet to avoid taking it. For example, in the lower right-hand corner, the family with $\gamma = 250$ would rather pay $9889 for sure than take a 50 per cent chance of a $10,000 loss. This prediction is surely unreasonable, and has led most authors to rule out risk aversion coefficients over ten. Survey evidence for this kind of bet also finds low risk aversion, certainly below $\gamma = 5$ (Barsky, Kimball, Juster and Shapiro, 1997), and even negative risk aversion if the survey is taken in Las Vegas.

Table 16.6 ● Amount family would pay to avoid an even bet

Bet	Risk Aversion γ				
	2	10	50	100	250
$10	$0.00	$0.01	$0.05	$0.10	$0.25
100	0.20	1.00	4.99	9.94	24
1,000	20	99	435	665	863
10,000	2000	6921	9430	9718	9889

Notes: I assume the family has a constant $50,000 per year consumption and an even chance of winning or losing the indicated net, per year.

Yet the results for small bets are not so unreasonable. The family might reasonably pay 5 cents to 25 cents to avoid a $10 bet. We are all risk neutral for small enough bets. For small bets,

$$\frac{\text{amount willing to pay to avoid bet}}{\text{size of bet}} \approx \gamma \frac{\text{size of bet}}{\text{consumption}}.$$

Thus, for any γ, the amount one is willing to pay is an arbitrarily small fraction of the bet for small enough bets. For this reason, it is easy to cook numbers of conceptual experiments like Table 16.6 by varying the size of the bet and the presumed wealth of the family. Significantly, I only used *local* curvature above; γ represented the derivative $\gamma = -Cu''(C)/u'(C)$. In asking how much the family would pay to avoid a \$10,000 bet, we are asking for the response to a very, very non-local event.

The main lesson of conceptual experiments and laboratory and survey evidence of simple bets is that people's answers to such questions routinely violate expected utility. This observation lowers the value of this source of evidence as a measurement of risk aversion. As a similar cautionary note, Barsky *et al.* report that whether an individual partakes in a wide variety of risky activities correlates poorly with the level of risk aversion inferred from a survey. In the end, surveys about hypothetical bets that are far from the range of everyday experience are hard to interpret.

Microeconomic evidence

Microeconomic observations might be a more useful measure of risk aversion, that is, evidence from people's actual behaviour in their daily activities. For example, the numbers in Table 16.6 could be matched with insurance data. People are willing to pay substantially more than actuarially fair values to insure against car theft or house fires. What is the implied risk aversion? But even if there are other markets whose prices reflect less risk aversion than stocks, this leaves open the question: if people are risk-neutral in other markets, why do they become risk-averse in the stockbroker's office? Perhaps the risk aversion people display in the stock broker's office should be the fact and the (possibly) low risk aversion displayed in other offices should be the puzzle.

Portfolio calculations

A common calibration of risk aversion comes from simple portfolio calculations (see Friend and Blume, 1975). Following the principle that the last dollar spent should give the same increase in happiness in any alternative use, the marginal value of wealth should equal the marginal utility of consumption,[9] $V_W(W,.) = u_c(C)$. Therefore, if we assume returns are independent over time and no other variables are important for the marginal value of wealth, $V_W(W)$, Equation (6) can also be written as

$$\frac{E(r) - r^f}{\sigma(r)} = \frac{-WV_{WW}}{V_W} \sigma(\Delta w) corr(\Delta w, r). \tag{8}$$

The quantity $-WW_{WW}/V_W$ is in fact a better measure of risk aversion than $-Cu_{cc}/u_c$, since it represents aversion to bets over wealth rather than bets over consumption; most bets observed are paid off in dollars. For a consumer who invests entirely in stocks, $\sigma(\Delta w)$ is the standard deviation of the stock return and $corr(\Delta w, r) = 1$. To generate a Sharpe ratio of 0.5, it seems that we only need risk aversion equal to 3,

$$\frac{-WV_{WW}}{V_W} = \frac{0.5}{0.17} \cong 3.$$

The Achilles heel of this calculation is the hidden simplifying assumption that returns are independent over time, so no variables other than wealth show up in V_W. If this were the case, consumption would move one-for-one with wealth, and $\sigma(\Delta c) = \sigma(\Delta w)$. If wealth doubles and nothing else has changed, the consumer would double consumption. The calculation, therefore, hides a model with the drastically counterfactual implication that consumption growth has a 17 per cent standard deviation!

The fact that consumption has a standard deviation so much lower than that of stock returns suggests that returns are not independent over time (as is already known from the return on P/D regressions) and/or that other state variables must be important in driving stock returns. If some other state variable, z, is allowed – representing subsequent expected returns, labour income, or some other measure of a consumer's overall opportunities – the substitution $V_W(W, z) = u_c(C)$ in Equation (6) adds another term to Equation (8),

$$\frac{E(r) - r^f}{\sigma(r)} = \frac{-WV_{WW}}{V_W} \sigma(\Delta w) corr(\Delta w, r)$$

$$+ \frac{zW_{Wz}}{V_W} \sigma(z) corr(z, r).$$

The Sharpe ratio may be driven not by consumers' risk aversion and the wealth-riskiness of stocks, but by stocks' exposure to other risks.

In the current context, this observation just tells us that portfolio-based calibrations of risk aversion do not work, because they implicitly assume independent returns and, hence, consumption growth as volatile as returns. Below, I introduce plausible candidates for the variable z that can help us to understand high Sharpe ratios. The fact that consumption is so much less volatile than shock returns indicates that the other state variables must account for the bulk of the equity premium.

Overall, the evidence against high risk aversion is not that strong, and it is at least a possibility to consider. This argument does not rescue the power utility model with $\gamma = 50$ to 250 – that ship sank on the consumption-interest rate shoals. However, other models with high risk aversion can be contemplated.

New utility functions and state variables

If changing the parameter γ in $u'(C) = C^{-\gamma}$ does not work, perhaps we need to change the *functional form*. Changing the form of $u(C)$ is not a promising avenue. As I have stressed by using a continuous time derivation, only the derivatives of $u(C)$ really matter; hence quite similar results are achieved with other functional forms. A more promising avenue is to consider other arguments of the utility function, or *nonseparabilities*.

Perhaps how people feel about eating more today is affected not just by how much they are already eating, but by other things, such as how much they ate yesterday or how much they worked today. Then, the covariance of stock returns with these other variables will also determine the equity premium. Fundamentally, consumers use assets to smooth marginal utility. Perhaps today's marginal utility is related to more than just today's consumption.

Such a modification is a fundamental change in how we view stock market risk. For example, perhaps more leisure raises the marginal utility of consumption. Stocks are then feared because they pay off badly in recessions when employment is lower and leisure is higher, not because consumers are particularly averse to the risk that stocks decline *per se*. Formally, our fundamental Equation (6) is derived from

$$E_t(r) - r_t^f = cov_t(\Delta u_c, r),$$

and substituting $u_c = \partial u(c)/\partial c$. If I substitute $u_c = \partial u(c,x)/\partial c$ instead, then u_c will depend on other variables x as well as c, and

$$E(r) - r^f = \gamma\, cov(\Delta c, r) + \frac{u_{cx}}{u_c}\, cov(x, r).$$

Since the first covariance does not account for much premium, we will have to rely heavily on the latter term to explain the premium.

There is a practical aim to generalizing the utility function as well. As illustrated in the last section, one parameter γ did two things with power utility: it controlled how much people are willing to substitute consumption over time (consumption and interest rates) and it controlled their attitudes toward risk. The choice $\gamma = 50$ to 250 was clearly a crazy representation of how people feel about consumption variation over time, but perhaps not so bad a representation of risk aversion. Maybe a modification of preferences can disentangle the two attitudes.

State separability and leisure

With the latter end in mind, Epstein and Zin (1989) started an avalanche of academic research on utility functions that relax state-separability. The expectation E in the utility function of Equation (3) sums over states of nature, for example:

$$U = prob(\text{rain}) \times u(C \text{ if it rains}) + prob(\text{shine}) \times u(C \text{ if it shines}).$$

'Separability' means that one adds utility across states, so the marginal utility of consumption in one state is unaffected by what happens in another state. But perhaps the marginal utility of a little more consumption in the sunny state of the world is affected by the level of consumption in the rainy state of the world.

Epstein and Zin and Hansen, Sargent and Tallarini (1997) propose recursive utility functions of the form:

$$U_t = C_t^{1-\gamma} + e^{-\rho} f\left[E_t f^{-1}(U_{t+1})\right].$$

If $f(x) = x$, this expression reduces to power utility. These utility functions are not state-separable, and do conveniently distinguish risk aversion from intertemporal substitution among other modifications. However, this research is only starting to pay off in terms of plausible models that explain the facts (Campbell, 1996, is an example) so I will not review it here.

Perhaps leisure is the most natural extra variable to add to a utility function. It is not clear *a priori* whether more leisure enhances the marginal utility of consumption (why bother buying a boat if you are at the office all day and cannot use it?) or vice versa (if you have to work all day, it is more important to come home to a really nice big TV), but we can let the data speak on this matter. However, explicit versions of this approach have not been very successful to date. (Eichenbaum, Hansen and Singleton, 1988, for example.) On the other hand, recent research has found that adding labour income growth as an extra *ad hoc* factor can be useful in explaining the cross-section of average stock returns (Jagannathan and Wang, 1996; Reyfman, 1997). Though not motivated by an explicit utility function, the facts in this research may in the future be interpretable as an effect of leisure on the marginal utility of consumption.

Force of habit

Nonseparabilities over *time* have been more useful in empirical work. Anyone who has had a large pizza dinner knows that yesterday's consumption can have an impact on today's appetite. Might a similar mechanism apply over a longer time horizon? Perhaps people get accustomed to a standard of living, so a fall in consumption hurts after a few years of good times, even though the same level of consumption might have seemed very pleasant if it arrived after years of bad times. This view at least explains the perception that recessions are awful events, even though a recession year may be just the second or third best year in human history rather than the absolute best. Law, custom and social insurance insure against falls in consumption as much as low levels of consumption.

Following this idea, Campbell and Cochrane (1997) specify that people slowly develop habits for higher or lower consumption. Technically, they replace the utility function $u(C)$ with

$$u\,(C-X) = (C-X)^{1-\eta}, \tag{9}$$

where X represents the level of habits. In turn, habit X adjusts slowly to the level of consumption.[10] (I use the symbol η for the power, because curvature and risk aversion no longer equal η.) This specification builds on a long tradition in the microeconomic literature (Duesenberry, 1949; and Deaton, 1992) and recent asset-pricing literature (Constantinides, 1990; Ferson and Constantinides, 1991; Heaton, 1995; and Abel, 1990).

When a consumer has such a habit, local curvature depends on how far consumption is above the habit, as well as the power η,

$$\gamma_t \equiv \frac{-C_t u_{cc}}{u_c} = \eta \frac{C_t}{C_t - X_t}.$$

As consumption falls toward habit, people become much less willing to tolerate further falls in consumption; they become very risk averse. Thus, a low power coefficient η (Campbell and Cochrane use $\eta = 2$) can still mean a high and time-varying curvature.

Recall our fundamental Equation (6) for the Sharpe ratio:

$$\frac{E_t(r) - r_t^f}{\sigma_t(r)} = \gamma_t \sigma_t(\Delta c)\,corr_t(\Delta c, r).$$

High curvature γ_t means that the model can explain the equity premium, and curvature that varies over time, as consumption rises in booms and falls toward habit in recessions, means that the model can explain a time-varying and countercyclical (high in recessions, low in booms) Sharpe ratio, despite constant consumption volatility, $\sigma_t(\Delta c)$, and correlation, $corr_t(\Delta c, r)$.

So far so good, but doesn't raising curvature imply high and time-varying interest rates? In the Campbell-Cochrane model, the answer is no. The reason is precautionary saving. Suppose times are bad and consumption is low relative to habit. People want to borrow against future, higher consumption and this should drive up interest rates. However, people are also much more risk averse in bad times; they want to save more in case tomorrow might be even worse. These two effects balance.

The precautionary saving motive also makes the model more plausibly consistent with variation in consumption growth across time and countries. The interest rate in the model adds a precautionary savings motive term to Equation 4:

$$r^f = \rho + \eta E(\Delta c) - \frac{1}{2}\left(\frac{\eta}{\bar{S}}\right)^2 \sigma^2(\Delta c),$$

where $\bar{S}$ denotes the steady state value of $(C-X)/C$, about 0.05. The power coefficient, $\eta = 2$, controls the relationship between consumption growth and interest rates, while the curvature coefficient, $\gamma = \eta \, C/(C-X)$, controls the risk premium. Thus, this habit model allows high risk aversion with low aversion to intertemporal substitution and is consistent with the consumption and interest rate data and a sensible value of ρ.

Campbell and Cochrane create a simple artificial economy with these preferences. Consumption growth is independent over time and real interest rates are constant. They calculate time series of stock prices and interest rates in the artificial economy and subject them to the standard statistical analysis reviewed above. The artificial data replicate the equity premium (0.5 Sharpe ratio). The ability to forecast returns from the P/D ratio and the P/D variance decomposition are both quite like the actual data. The standard deviation of returns rises a bit when prices decline, but less than the rise in mean returns, so a low P/D ratio forecasts a higher Sharpe ratio. Artificial data from the model also replicate much of the low observed correlation between consumption growth and returns, and the CAPM and *ad hoc* multifactor models perform better than the power utility consumption-based model in the artificial data.

The model also provides a good account of P/D fluctuations over the last century, based entirely on the history of consumption. However, it does not account for the currently high P/D ratio. This is because the model generates a high P/D ratio when consumption is very high relative to habit and, therefore, risk aversion is low. Measured consumption has been increasing unusually slowly in the 1990s.

Like other models that explain the equity premium and return predictability, this one does so by fundamentally changing the story of why consumers are afraid of holding stocks. From Equation (9), the marginal utility of consumption is proportional to:

$$u_c = C_t^{-\eta} \left(\frac{C_t - X_t}{C_t} \right)^{-\eta}.$$

Thus, consumers dislike low consumption as before, but they are also afraid of recessions, times when consumption, whatever its level, is low relative to the recent past as described by habits. Consumers are afraid of holding stocks not because they fear the wealth or consumption volatility *per se*, but because bad stock returns tend to happen in recessions, times of a recent belt-tightening.

This model fulfills a decade-long search kicked off by Mehra and Prescott (1985). It is a complete-markets, frictionless economy that replicates not only the equity premium but also the predictability of returns, the nearly constant interest rate, and the near-random walk behaviour of consumption.

Habit models with low risk aversion

The individuals in the Campbell-Cochrane model are highly risk-averse. They would respond to surveys about bets on wealth much as the $\gamma = 50$ column of

Table 16.6. The model does not give rise to a high equity premium with low risk aversion; it merely disentangles risk aversion and intertemporal substitution so that a high risk aversion economy can be consistent with low and constant interest rates, and it generates the predictability of stock returns.

Constantinides (1990) and Boldrin, Christiano and Fisher (1995) explore habit persistence models that can generate a large equity premium without large risk aversion. That is, they create artificial economies in which consumers simultaneously shy away from stocks with a very attractive Sharpe ratio of 0.5, yet would happily take bets with much lower rewards.

Suppose a consumer wins a bet or enjoys a high stock return. Normally, the consumer would instantly raise consumption to match the new higher wealth level. But consumption is addictive in these models: too much current consumption will raise the future habit level and blunt the enjoyment of future consumption. Therefore, the consumer increases consumption slowly and predictably after the increase in wealth. Similarly, the consumer would borrow to slowly decrease consumption after a decline in wealth, avoiding the pain of a sudden loss at the cost of lower long-term consumption.

The fact that the consumer will choose to spread out the consumption response to wealth shocks means that the consumer is not averse to wealth bets. If consumption responds little to a wealth shock, then marginal utility of consumption, $u_c(C)$, also responds little, as does the marginal value of wealth, $V_W(W,\cdot) = u_c$. Risk aversion to wealth bets is measured by the change of marginal utility when wealth changes $(\partial \ln V_W / \delta \ln W = -WV_{WW}/V_W)$.

The argument is correct, but shows the problem with these models. The change in consumption in response to wealth is not eliminated, it is simply deferred. Thus, these models have trouble with long-run behaviour of consumption and asset returns.

If consumption growth is considered independent over time (formally, an endowment economy), which is a good approximation to the data, the model must feature strong interest rate variation to keep consumers from trying to adapt consumption smoothly to wealth shocks. For example, consumers all want to save if wealth goes up, thereby slowly increasing consumption. For consumption growth to remain unpredictable, we must have a strong decline in the interest rate at the same time as the wealth increase. Of course, interest rates are in fact quite stable and, if anything, slightly positively correlated with stock returns.

Alternatively, interest rates may be fixed to be constant over time as in Constantinides (1990) (formally, linear technologies). But then there is no force to stop consumers from slowly and predictably raising consumption after a wealth shock. Thus, such models predict counterfactually that consumption growth is positively auto-correlated over time, and that long-run consumption growth shares the high volatility of long- and short-run wealth.

The Campbell-Cochrane habit model avoids these long-run problems with precautionary savings. In response to a wealth shock, consumers with the Campbell-Cochrane version of habit persistence would also like to save more for intertemporal substitution reasons, but they also feel less risk averse and so want to save less for precautionary savings reasons. The balance means that consumption can be a random walk with constant interest rates, consistent with the data. However, it means that consumption does move right away, so u_c and V_W are affected by the wealth shock, and the consumers are highly risk averse. In this model, wealth (stock prices) comes back toward consumption after a shock, so that long-run wealth shares the low volatility of long- and short-run consumption, and high stock prices forecast low subsequent returns.

A finance perspective

To get a high equity premium with low risk aversion, we need to find some crucial characteristic that separates stock returns from wealth bets. This is a difficult task. After all, what are stocks if not a bet? The answer must be some additional state variable. Having a stock pay off badly must tell you additional bad news that losing a bet does not; therefore, people shy away from stocks even though they would happily take a bet with the same mean and variance.

In the context of perfect-markets models without leisure or other goods, the only real candidates for extra state variables are variables that describe changes in expected returns. If stock prices rise, the consumer learns something important that is not learned from winning a bet: the consumer learns that future stock returns are going to be lower. The trouble is the sign of this relationship. Lower returns in the future are bad news.[11] Stocks act as a hedge for this bad news; they go *up* just at the time one gets bad news about future returns. This consideration makes stocks *more* desirable than pure bets. Thus, considering time variation in expected returns requires even *more* risk aversion to explain the equity premium.

Consistency with individual consumption behaviour

The low risk aversion models face one more important hurdle: microeconomic data. Suppose an individual receives a wealth shock (wins the lottery), not shared by everyone else. For aggregate wealth shocks, we could appeal to interest rate variation to avoid the prediction that consumption would grow slowly and predictably. However, interest rates can't change in response to an individual wealth shock. Thus, we are stuck with the prediction that the individual's consumption will increase slowly and predictably. The huge literature on individual consumption (see Deaton, 1992, for survey and references) almost unanimously finds the opposite. People who receive windfalls consume too much, too soon, and have typically spent it all in a few years. The literature abounds with 'liquidity constraints' to explain the 'excess sensitivity' of consumption. The Campbell-Cochrane model avoids the prediction of slowly increasing consumption by specifying an *external* habit; each person's habit responds to everyone else's consumption, related to the need to 'keep up with the Joneses', as advocated by Abel (1990). Though the external specification has little impact on aggregate consumption and prices, it means that individual consumption responds fully and immediately to individual wealth shocks, because there is no need for individuals to worry about habit formation. The downside is, again, high risk aversion.

In the end, there is currently no representative agent model with low risk aversion that is consistent with the equity premium, the stability of real interest rates, nearly unpredictable consumption growth, and return predictability of the correct sign.

HETEROGENEOUS AGENTS AND IDIOSYNCRATIC RISKS

In the above discussion, I did not recognize any difference between people. Everyone is different, so why bother looking at representative agent or complete market models? While making an assumption such as 'all people are identical' seems obviously foolish, it is not foolish to hope that we can use aggregate behaviour to make sense of aggregate data, without explicitly taking account of the differences between people. While differences are there, one hopes they are not relevant to the basic story. However, seeing the difficulties that representative agent models face, perhaps it is time to see if the (aggregate) equity premium does in fact surface from differences between people rather than common behaviour.

The empirical hurdle

Idiosyncratic risk explanations face a big empirical challenge. Look again at the basic Sharpe ratio Equation (6):

$$\frac{E(r) - r^f}{\sigma(r)} = \gamma \sigma(\Delta c) corr(\Delta c, r). \tag{6}$$

This relationship should hold for every (any) consumer or household. At first sight, thinking about individuals seems promising. After all, individual consumption is certainly more variable than aggregate consumption at 1 per cent per year, so we can raise $\sigma(\Delta c)$. However, this argument fails quantitatively. First, it is inconceivable that we can raise $\sigma(\Delta c)$ enough to account for the equity premium. For example, even if individual consumption has a standard deviation of 10 per cent per year, and maintaining a generous limit $\gamma < 10$, we still predict a Sharpe ratio no more than $10 \times 0.1 \times 0.2 = 0.2$. To explain the 0.5 Sharpe ratio with risk aversion $\gamma = 10$, we have to believe that individual consumption growth has a 25 per cent per year standard deviation; for a more traditional $\gamma = 2.5$, we need 100 per cent per year standard deviation. Even 10 per cent per year is a huge standard deviation of consumption growth. Remember, we are considering the risky or uncertain part of consumption growth. Predictable increases or decreases in consumption due to age and life-cycle effects, expected raises and so on, do not count. We are also thinking of the flow of consumption (nondurable goods, services) not the much more variable purchases of durable goods, such as cars and houses.

More fundamentally, the addition of idiosyncratic risk lowers the correlation between consumption growth and returns, which lowers the predicted Sharpe ratio. Idiosyncratic risk is, by its nature, idiosyncratic. If it happened to everyone, it would be aggregate risk. Idiosyncratic risk cannot therefore be correlated with the stock market, since the stock market return is the same for everyone.

For a quantitative example, suppose that individual consumption of family $i, \Delta c^i$, is determined by aggregate consumption, Δc^a, and idiosyncratic shocks (such as losing your job), ε^i,

$$\Delta c^i = \Delta c^a + \varepsilon^i.$$

For the risk ε^i to average to zero across people, we must have $E(\varepsilon^i) = 0$ and $E(\varepsilon^i | \Delta c^a) = E(\varepsilon^i | r) = 0$. Then, the standard deviation of individual consumption growth does increase with the size of idiosyncratic risk:

$$\sigma^2(\Delta c^i) = \sigma^2(\Delta c^a) + \sigma^2(\varepsilon^i).$$

But the correlation between individual consumption growth and aggregate returns declines in exact proportion as the standard deviation $\sigma(\Delta c^i)$ rises:

$$\frac{E(r) - r^f}{\sigma(r)} = \gamma \frac{cov(\Delta c^a + \varepsilon^i, r)}{\sigma(r)} = \gamma \frac{cov(\Delta c^a, r)}{\sigma(r)}.$$

Therefore, *the equity premium is completely unaffected by idiosyncratic risk.*

The theoretical hurdles

The theoretical challenge to idiosyncratic risk explanations is even more severe. We can easily construct models in which consumers are given lots of idiosyncratic income risk. But it is very hard to keep consumers from insuring themselves against those risks, producing a very steady consumption stream and a low equity premium.

Start by handing out income to consumers; call it 'labour income' and make it risky by adding a chance of being fired. Left to their own devices, consumers would come up with unemployment insurance to share this risk, so we have to close down or limit markets for labour income insurance. Then, consumers who lose their jobs will borrow against future income to smooth consumption over the bad times, achieving almost the same consumption smoothness. We must shut down these markets too.

However, nothing stops our borrowing-constrained consumers from saving. They build up a stock of durable goods, government bonds or other liquid assets that they can draw down in bad times and again achieve a very smooth consumption stream (Telmer, 1993; and Lucas, 1994). To shut down this avenue for consumption-smoothing, we can introduce large transactions costs and ban from the model the simple accumulation of durable goods. Alternatively, we can make idiosyncratic shocks permanent, because borrowing and saving can only insure against transitory income. If losing your job means losing it forever, there is no point in borrowing and planning to pay it back when you get a new job.

Heaton and Lucas (1996a) put all these ingredients together, calibrating the persistence of labour income shocks from microeconomic data. They also allow the cross-sectional variance of shocks to increase in a downturn, a very helpful ingredient suggested by Mankiw (1986) that I discuss in detail in the next section. Despite all of these ingredients, their model explains at best one-half of the observed excess average stock return (and this much only with no net debt). It also predicts counterfactually that interest rates are as volatile as stock returns, and that individuals have huge (10 per cent to 30 per cent, depending on specification) consumption growth uncertainty.

A model that works

Constantinides and Duffie (1996) construct a model in which idiosyncratic risk can be tailored to generate any pattern of aggregate consumption and asset prices; it can generate the equity premium, predictability, relatively constant interest rates, smooth and unpredictable aggregate consumption growth, and so forth. Furthermore, it requires no transactions costs, borrowing constraints, or other frictions, and the individual consumers can have any nonzero value of risk aversion.

As mentioned earlier, if consumers are given idiosyncratic income that is correlated with the market return, they will trade away that risk. Constantinides and Duffie therefore specify that the *variance* of idiosyncratic risk rises when the market declines. Variance cannot be traded away. In addition, if marginal utility were linear, an increase in variance would have no effect on the average level of marginal utility. The interaction of cross-sector variance correlated with the market and nonlinear marginal utility produces an equity premium.

The Constantinides-Duffie model and the Campbell-Cochrane model are quite similar in spirit, though the Constantinides-Duffie model is built on incomplete markets and idiosyncratic risks, while the Campbell-Cochrane model is in the representative-agent frictionless and complete market tradition.

First, both models make a similar, fundamental change in the description of stock market risk. Consumers do not fear the loss of wealth of a bad market return so much as they fear a bad return in a recession, in one model a time of heightened labour market risk and in the other a fall of consumption relative to the recent past. This recession state variable or risk factor drives most expected returns.

Second, both models require high risk aversion. While Constantinides and Duffie's proof shows that one can dream up a labour income process to rationalize the equity premium for any risk aversion coefficient, I argue below that even vaguely plausible characterizations of actual labour income uncertainty will require high risk aversion to explain the historical equity premium.

Third, both models provide long-sought demonstrations that it is possible to rationalize the equity premium in their respective class of models. This is particularly impressive in Constantinides and Duffie's case. Many researchers (myself included) had come to the conclusion that the effort to generate an equity premium from idiosyncratic risk was hopeless.

The open question in both cases is empirical. The stories are consistent; are they right? For Constantinides and Duffie, does actual individual labour income behave as their model requires in order to generate the equity premium? The empirical work remains to be done, but here are some of the issues.

A simple version of the model

Each consumer i has power utility,

$$U = E \sum_t e^{-\rho t} C_{it}^{1-\gamma}.$$

Individual consumption growth, C_{it}, is determined by an independent, idiosyncratic normal $(0,1)$ shock, η_{it},

$$\ln \left(\frac{C_{it}}{C_{i,t-1}} \right) = \eta_{it} y_t - \frac{1}{2} y_t^2, \tag{10}$$

where y_t is the cross-sectional standard deviation of consumption growth at any moment in time. y_t is specified so that a *low* market return, R_t, gives a high cross-sectional variance of consumption growth:

$$y_t = \sigma \left[\ln \left(\frac{C_{it}}{C_{it-1}} \right) \Big| R_t \right] \tag{11}$$

$$= \sqrt{\frac{2}{\gamma(\gamma+1)}} \sqrt{\ln \frac{1}{R_t} + \rho}.$$

Since η_{it} determines consumption *growth*, the idiosyncratic shocks are permanent, which I argued above was important to keep consumers from smoothing them away.

Given this structure, the individual is exactly happy to consume C_{it} and hold the stock (we can call C_{it} income I_{it} and prove the optimal decision rule is to set $C_{it} = I_{it}$.). The first-order condition for an optimal consumption-portfolio decision:

$$1 = E_{t-1}\left[e^{-\rho}\left(\frac{C_{it}}{C_{it-1}}\right)^{-\gamma} R_{t+1}\right]$$

holds, exactly.[12]

The general model

The actual Constantinides-Duffie model is much more general than the above example. They show that the idiosyncratic risk can be constructed to price exactly a large collection of assets, not just one return as in the example, and they allow uncertainty in aggregate consumption. Therefore, they can tailor the idiosyncratic risk to exactly match the Sharpe ratio, return forecastability and consumption-interest rate facts as outlined above.

In the general model, Constantinides and Duffie define:

$$y_t = \sqrt{\frac{2}{\gamma(\gamma+1)}} \sqrt{\ln m_t + \rho + \gamma\ln\frac{C_t}{C_{t-1}}}, \tag{12}$$

where m_t is a strictly positive discount factor[13] that prices all assets under consideration. That is, m_t satisfies:

$$1 = E_{t-1}[m_t R_t] \text{ for all } R_t. \tag{14}$$

Then, they let:

$$C_{it} = \delta_{it} C_{it}$$
$$\delta_{it} = \delta_{it-1} \exp\left[\eta_{it} y_t - \frac{1}{2} y_t^2\right].$$

Following exactly the same argument in the text, we can now show that:

$$1 = E_{t-1}\left[e^{-\rho}\left(\frac{C_{it}}{C_{it-1}}\right)^{-\gamma} R_{t+1}\right]$$

for all the assets priced by m.

Microeconomic evaluation and risk aversion

Like the Campbell-Cochrane model, this model could be either a new view of stock market (and macroeconomic) risk or just a theoretically interesting existence proof. The first question is whether the microeconomic picture painted by this model is correct, or even plausible. Is idiosyncratic risk large enough? Does idiosyncratic risk really rise when the market falls, and enough to account for the equity premium? Do people really shy away from stocks because stock returns are low at times of high labour market risk?

This model does not change the empirical puzzle discussed earlier. To get power utility consumers to shun stocks, they still must have tremendously volatile consumption growth or high risk aversion. The point of this model is to show how consumers can get stuck with high consumption volatility in equilibrium, already a difficult task.

More seriously than volatility itself, consumption growth variance also represents the amount by which the distribution of individual consumption and income spreads out over time, since the shocks must be permanent and independent across people. The 10 per cent to 50 per cent volatility ($\sigma(\Delta c)$) that is required to reconcile the Sharpe ratio with low risk aversion means that the distribution of consumption (and income) must also *spread out* by 10 per cent to 50 per cent per year.

Constantinides and Duffie show how to avoid the implication that the overall distribution of income spreads out, by limiting inheritance and repopulating the economy each year with new generations that are born equal. But the distribution of consumption must still spread out within each generation to achieve the equity premium with low risk aversion. Is this plausible? Deaton and Paxson (1994) report that the cross-sectional variance of log consumption within an age cohort rises from about 0.2 at age 20 to 0.6 at age 60. This means that the cross-sectional standard deviation of consumption rises from $\sqrt{0.2} = 0.45$ or 45 per cent at age 20 to $\sqrt{0.6} = 0.77$ or 77 per cent at age 60 (77 per cent means that an individual one standard deviation better off than the mean consumes 77 per cent more than the mean consumer). This works out to about 1 per cent per year, not 10 per cent or so.

Finally, the cross-sectional uncertainty about individual income must not only be large, it must be higher when the market is lower. This risk factor is after all the central element of Constantinides and Duffie's explanation for the market premium. Figure 16.6 shows how the cross-sectional standard deviation of consumption growth varies with the market return and risk aversion in my simple version of Constantinides and Duffie's model. If we insist on low ($\gamma = 1$ to 2) risk aversion, the cross-sectional standard deviation of consumption growth must be extremely sensitive to the level of the market return. Looking at the $\gamma = 2$ line for example, is it plausible that a year with 5 per cent market return would show a 10 per cent cross-sectional variation in consumption growth, while a mild 5 per cent decline in the market is associated with a 25 per cent cross-sectional variation?

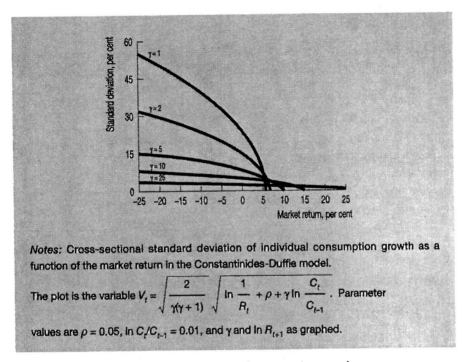

Notes: Cross-sectional standard deviation of individual consumption growth as a function of the market return in the Constantinides-Duffie model.

The plot is the variable $V_t = \sqrt{\dfrac{2}{\gamma(\gamma+1)}} \sqrt{\ln\dfrac{1}{R_t} + \rho + \gamma \ln\dfrac{C_t}{C_{t-1}}}$. Parameter

values are $\rho = 0.05$, $\ln C_t/C_{t-1} = 0.01$, and γ and $\ln R_{t+1}$ as graphed.

Fig 16.6 ● Cross-sectional standard deviation of consumption growth

Source: Illustrated London News (drawing of the Brooklands track by Melton Prior)

The Heaton and Lucas (1996a) model can be regarded as an empirical assessment of these issues. Rather than constructing a labour income process that generates an equity premium, they calibrated the labour income process from microeconomic data. They found less persistence and less increase in cross-sectional variation with a low market return than specified by Constantinides and Duffie, which is why their model predicts a low equity premium with low risk aversion. Of course, this view is at best preliminary evidence. They did not test the exact Constantinides-Duffie specification as a special case, nor did they test whether one can reject the Constantinides-Duffie specification.

All of these empirical problems are avoided if we allow high risk aversion rather than a large risk to drive the equity premium. The $\gamma = 25$ line in Figure 16.6 looks possible; a $\gamma = 50$ line would look even better. With high risk aversion, we do not need to specify highly volatile individual consumption growth, spreading out of the income distribution, or dramatic sensitivity of the cross-sectional variance to the market return. As in any model, a high equity premium must come from a large risk, or from large risk aversion. Labour market risk correlated with the stock market does not seem large enough to account for the equity premium without high risk aversion.

Segmented markets

All these models try to answer the basic question, if stocks are so attractive, why have people not bought more of them? So far, I have tried to find representations of people's preferences or circumstances, or a description of macroeconomic risk, in which stocks aren't that attractive after all. Then the high Sharpe ratio is a compensation for risk.

Instead, we could argue that stocks really are attractive, but a variety of market frictions keep people from buying them. This approach yields some important insights. First of all, stock ownership has been quite concentrated. The vast majority of American households have not directly owned any stock or mutual funds. One might ask whether the consumption of people who do own stock lines up with stock returns. Mankiw and Zeldes (1991) find that stockholders do have consumption that is more volatile and more correlated with stock returns than non-stockholders. But it is still not volatile and correlated enough to satisfy the right-hand side of Equation (6) with low risk aversion.

Heaton and Lucas (1996b) look at individual asset and income data. They find that the richest households, who own most of the stocks, also get most of their income from proprietary business income. This income is likely to be more correlated with the stock market than is individual labour income. Furthermore, they find that among rich households, those with more proprietary income hold fewer stocks in their portfolios. This paints an interesting picture of the equity premium: in the past most stocks were held by rich people, and most rich people were proprietors whose other income (and consumption) was quite volatile and covaried strongly with the market. This is a hard crowd to sell stocks to, so they have required a high risk premium. The Campbell-Cochrane and Constantinides-Duffie models specify that stock market risk is spread as evenly as possible through the population, whereas if the risk is shared among a small group of people, higher rewards will have to be offered to offset that risk.

These views are still not sorted out quantitatively. We don't know why rich stockholders don't buy even more stocks, given low risk aversion and the tyrannical logic of Equation (6). We don't know why only rich people held stocks in the first place: the literature shows that even quite high transactions' costs and borrowing constraints should not be enough to deter people with low risk aversion from holding stocks.

If these segmented market views of the past equity premium are correct, they suggest that the future equity premium will be much lower. Transaction costs are declining through financial deregulation and innovation. The explosion in tax-deferred pension plans and no-load mutual funds means more and more people own stocks, spreading risks more evenly, driving up prices, and driving down prospective returns. Equation (6) will hold much better for the average consumer in the future. One would expect to see a lower equity premium. One would also expect consumption that is more volatile and more closely correlated with the stock market, which will result in a fundamental change in the nature and politics of business cycles.

TECHNOLOGY AND INVESTMENT

So far, I have tried to rationalize stock returns from the consumer's point of view: does it make sense that consumers should not have tried to buy more stocks, driving stock returns down toward bond returns? I can ask the same questions for the firm: do firms' investment decisions line up with stock prices as they should?

The relative prices of apples and oranges are basically set by technology, the relative number of apples versus oranges that can be grown on the same acre of land. We do not need a deep understanding of consumers' desires to figure out what the price should be. If technology is (close to) linear, it will determine relative prices, while preferences will determine quantities. Does this argument work for stocks?

Again, there is a standard model that has served well to describe quantities in growth, macroeconomics and international economics. The standard model consists of a production function by which output, Y, is made from capital, K, and labour, L, perhaps with some uncertainty, θ, together with an accumulation equation by which investment I turns into new capital in the future. In equations, together with the most common functional forms:

$$Y_t = f(K_t, L_t, \theta_t) = \theta_t K_t^\alpha L_t^{1-\alpha} \tag{15}$$
$$K_{t+1} = (1-\delta)K_t + I_t$$
$$Y_t = C_t + I_t.$$

It was well known already in the 1970s that this standard, 'neoclassical' model would be a disaster at describing asset pricing facts. It predicts that stock prices and returns should be extremely stable. To see this, invest an extra dollar, reap the extra output that the additional capital will produce, and then invest a bit less next year. This action gives a physical or investment return. For the technology described in Equation (15), the investment return is:

$$R_{t+1}^I = 1 + f_k (K_{t+1}, L_{t+1}) - \delta \tag{16}$$

$$= 1 + \alpha \frac{Y_{t+1}}{K_{t+1}} - \delta.$$

With the share of capital $\alpha \approx 1/3$, an output-capital ratio $Y/K \approx 1/3$, and depreciation $\delta \approx 10\%$, we have $R^I \approx 6\%$, so average equity returns are easily within the range of plausible parameters. The trouble lies with the variance. Capital is quite smooth, so even if output varies 3 per cent in a year, the investment return only varies by 1 per cent, far below the 17 per cent standard deviation of stock returns. The basic problem is the absence of price variation. The capital accumulation equation shows that installed capital, K_t, and uninstalled capital, I_t, are perfect substitutes in making new capital, K_{t+1}. Therefore, they must have the same price – the price of stocks relative to consumption goods must be exactly 1.0.

The obvious modification is that there must be some difference between installed and uninstalled capital. The most natural extra ingredient is an adjustment cost or irreversibility: it is hard to get any work done on the day the furniture is delivered, and it is hard to take paint back off the walls and sell it. To recognize these sensible features of investment, we can reduce output during periods of high investment or make negative investment costly by modifying Equation (15) to:

$$Y_t = f(K_t, L_t, \theta_t) - c(I_t, \cdot). \tag{17}$$

The dot reminds us that other variables may influence the adjustment or irreversibility cost term. A common specification is:

$$Y_t = \theta_t K_t^\alpha L_t^{1-\alpha} - \frac{a}{2} \frac{I_t^2}{K_t}.$$

Now, there is a difference between installed and uninstalled capital, and the price of installed capital can vary. Adding an extra unit of capital tomorrow via extra investment costs $1 - \partial c(\cdot)/\partial I$ units of output today, while an extra unit of capital would give $(1-\delta)$ units of capital tomorrow. Hence the price of capital in terms of output is:

$$P_t = \frac{1-\delta}{1 - \partial c / \partial i} \approx 1 + \frac{\partial c}{\partial I} - \delta \tag{18}$$

$$= 1 + a \frac{I_t}{K_t} - \delta,$$

where the last equality uses the quadratic functional form. (This is the q theory of investment. With an asymmetric c function, this is the basis of the theory of irreversible investment. Abel and Eberly [1996] give a recent synthesis with references.)

Equation (18) shows that stock prices are expected to be high when investment is high, or firms are expected to issue stock and invest when stock prices are high. The investment return is now:

$$R^I_{t+1} = (1-\delta)\ \frac{1 + f_k(t+1) - c_k(t+1) + c_i(t+1)}{1 + c_i(t)} \tag{19}$$

$$= (1-\delta)\ \frac{1 + \alpha\ \dfrac{Y_{t+1}}{K_{t+1}} - \dfrac{a}{2}\ \dfrac{I^2_{t+1}}{K^2_{t+1}} + a\ \dfrac{I_{t+1}}{K_{t+1}}}{1 + a\ \dfrac{i_t}{K_t}}$$

$$\approx 1 + \alpha\ \frac{Y_{t+1}}{K_{t+1}} - \delta + a\left(\frac{I_{t+1}}{K_{t+1}} - \frac{I_t}{K_t}\right).$$

Comparing Equation (19) with Equation (16), the investment return contains a new term proportional to the change in investment. Since investment is quite volatile, this model can be consistent with the volatility of the market return. In Equation (18), the last term adds price changes to the model of the investment return.

How does all this work? Figure 16.7 presents the investment-output ratio along with the value weighted P/D ratio. (The results are almost identical using an investment-capital ratio with capital formed from depreciated past investment.) Equation (18) suggests that these two series should move

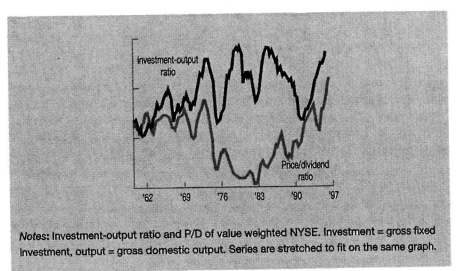

Notes: Investment-output ratio and P/D of value weighted NYSE. Investment = gross fixed investment, output = gross domestic output. Series are stretched to fit on the same graph.

Fig 16.7 ● **Value weighted portfolio P/D and investment**

together. The cyclical movements in investment and stock prices do line up pretty well. The longer-term variation in P/D is not mirrored in investment: this simple model does not explain why investment stayed robust in the late 1970s despite dismal stock prices. However, the recent surge in the market is matched by a surge in investment.

This kind of model has been subject to an enormous formal empirical effort, which pretty much confirms the figure. First, the model is consistent with a good deal of the cyclical variation in investment and stock returns, both forecasts and *ex post*. (See, for example, Cochrane, 1991c.) It does not do well with longer-term trends in the P/D ratio. Second, early tests relating investment to interest rates that imposed a constant risk premium did not work (Abel, 1983). The model only works at all if one recognizes that most variation in the cost of capital comes from time-varying expected stock returns with relatively constant interest rates. Third, the model in Equation (18) taken literally allows no residual. If prices deviate one iota from the right-hand side of Equation (18), then the model is statistically rejected – we can say with perfect certainty that it is not a literal description of the data-generating mechanism. There is a residual in actual data of course, and the residual can be correlated with other variables such as cash flow that suggest the presence of financial frictions (Fazzari, Hubbard and Peterson, 1988). Finally, the size of the adjustment cost, a, is the subject of the same kind of controversy that surrounds the size of the risk aversion coefficient, γ. From Equation (19) and the fact that investment growth has standard deviation of about 10 per cent, $a \approx 2$ is needed to rationalize the roughly 20 per cent standard deviation of stock returns. With $I/Y \approx 15\%$ and $Y/K \approx 33\%$, and hence $I/K \approx 1/20$, a value $a \approx 2$ means that adjustment costs relative to output are

$$\frac{a}{2} \frac{I}{K} \frac{I}{Y} = \frac{2}{2} \left(\frac{1}{20}\right) \times 15\% = 0.75\%,$$

which does not seem unreasonable. However, estimates of a based on regressions, Euler equations, or other techniques often result in much higher values, implying that implausibly large fractions of output are lost to adjustment costs.

This model does not yet satisfy the goal of determining the equity premium by technological considerations alone. Current specifications of technology allow firms to transform resources over time but not across states of nature. If the firm's own stock is undervalued, it can issue more and invest. However, if the interest rate is low, there is not much one can say about what the firm should do without thinking about the price of residual risk, and hence a preference approach to the equity premium. Technically, the marginal rate of transformation across states of nature is undefined.

Implications of the recent surge in investment and stock prices

The association between stock returns and investment in Figure 16.7 verifies that at least one connection between stock returns and the real economy works in some respects as it should. This argues against the view that stock market swings are due entirely to waves of irrational optimism and pessimism. It also verifies that the flow of money into the stock market does at least partially correspond to new real assets and not just price increases on existing assets.

In particular, the surge in stock prices since 1990 has been accompanied by a surge in investment. If expected stock returns and the cost of capital are low, then investment should be high. Statistically, high investment-output or investment-capital ratios also forecast low stock returns (Cochrane, 1991c). Thus, high investment provides additional statistical and economic evidence for the view that expected stock returns are quite low.

GENERAL EQUILIBRIUM

To really understand the equity premium, we need to combine the utility function and production function modifications to construct complete, explicit economic models that replicate the asset pricing facts. This effort should also preserve, if not enhance, our understanding of the broad range of dynamic microeconomic, macroeconomic, international and growth facts underpinning the standard models. The task is challenging. Anything that affects the relationship between consumption and asset prices will affect the relationship between consumption and investment. Asset prices mediate the consumption-investment decision and that decision lies at the heart of any dynamic macroeconomic model. We have learned a bit about how to go about this task, but have developed no completely satisfactory model as yet.

Jermann (1997) tried putting habit persistence consumers in a model with a neoclassical technology like Equation (15), which is almost completely standard in business-cycle models. The easy opportunities for intertemporal transformation provided by that technology meant that the consumers used it to dramatically smooth consumption, destroying the prediction of a high equity premium. To generate the equity premium, Jermann added an adjustment cost technology like Equation (17), as the production-side literature had proposed. This modification resulted in a high equity premium, but also large variation in risk-free rates.

Boldrin, Christiano and Fisher (1995) also add habit-persistence preferences to real business cycle models with frictions in the allocation of resources to two sectors. They generate about one-half of the historical Sharpe ratio. They find some quantity dynamics are improved over the standard model. However, their model still predicts highly volatile interest rates and persistent consumption growth.

To avoid the implications of highly volatile interest rates, I suspect we will need representations of technology that allow easy transformation across time but not across states of nature, analogous to the need for easy intertemporal substitution but high risk aversion in preferences. Alternatively, the Campbell-Cochrane model above already produces the equity premium with constant interest rates, which can be interpreted as a linear production function. Models with this kind of precautionary savings motive may not be as severely affected by the addition of an explicit production technology.

Hansen, Sargent and Tallarini (1997) use non-state-separable preferences similar to those of Epstein and Zin in a general equilibrium model. They show that a model with standard preferences and a model with non-state-separable preferences can predict the same path of quantity variables (such as output, investment and consumption) but differ dramatically on asset prices. This example offers some explanation of how the real business cycle and growth literature could spend 25 years examining quantity data in detail and miss all the modifications to preferences that we seem to need to explain asset pricing data. It also means that asset price information is crucial to identifying preferences and calculating welfare costs of policy experiments. Finally, it offers hope that adding the deep modifications necessary to explain asset pricing phenomena will not demolish the success of standard models at describing the movements of quantities.

PORTFOLIO IMPLICATIONS

The standard economic models, which have been used with great success to describe growth, macroeconomics, international economics and even dynamic microeconomics, do not predict the historical equity premium, let alone the predictability of returns. After ten years of effort, a range of deep modifications to the standard models show promise in explaining the equity premium as a combination of high risk aversion and new risk factors. Those modifications are now also consistent with the broad facts about consumption, interest rates and predictable returns. However, the modifications have so far only been aimed at explaining asset pricing data. We have not yet established whether the deep modifications necessary to explain asset market data retain the models' previous successes at describing quantity data.

The modified models are drastic revisions to the macroeconomic tradition. In the Campbell-Cochrane model, for example, strong time-varying precautionary savings motives balance strong time-varying intertemporal substitution motives. Uncertainty is of first-order importance in this model; linearizations near the steady state and dynamics with the shocks turned off give dramatically wrong predictions about the model's behaviour. The costs of business cycles are orders of magnitude larger than in standard models. In the Constantinides-Duffie model, one has to explicitly keep track of microeconomic heterogeneity in order to say anything about aggregates.

The new models are also a drastic revision to finance. We are used to thinking of aversion to wealth risk, as in the CAPM, as a good starting place or first-order approximation. But this view cannot hold. To justify the equity premium, people must be primarily averse to holding stocks because of their exposure to some other state variable or risk factor, such as recessions or changes in the investment opportunity set. To believe in the equity premium, one has to believe that these stories are sensible.

Finally, every quantitatively successful current story for the equity premium still requires astonishingly high risk aversion. The alternative, of course, is that the long-run equity premium is much smaller than the average postwar 8 per cent excess return. The standard model was right after all, and historically high US stock returns were largely due to luck or some other transient phenomenon.

Faced with the great difficulty economic theory still has in digesting the equity premium, I think the wise observer shades down the estimate of the future equity premium even more than suggested by the statistical uncertainty documented above.

Summary

In sum, the long-term average stock return may well be lower than the postwar 8 per cent average over bonds, and currently high prices are a likely signal of unusually low expected returns. It is tempting to take a sell recommendation from this conclusion. There is one very important caution to such a recommendation. *On average, everyone has to hold the market portfolio.* The average person does not change his or her portfolio at all. For every individual who keeps money out of stocks, someone else must have a very long position in stocks. Prices adjust until this is the case. Thus, one should only hold less stocks than the average person if one is different from everyone else in some crucial way. It is not enough to be bearish, one must be more bearish than everyone else.

In the economic models that generate the equity premium, every investor is exactly happy to hold his or her share of the market portfolio, no more and no less. The point of the models is that the superficial attractiveness of stocks is balanced by a well-described source of risk, so that people are just willing to hold them. Similarly, the time variation in the equity premium does not necessarily mean one should attempt to time the market, buying more stocks at times of high expected returns and vice versa. Every investor in the Campbell-

Cochrane model, for example, holds exactly the same portfolio all the time, while buy and sell signals come and go. In the peak of a boom they are not feeling very risk averse, and put their money in the market despite its low expected returns. In the bottom of a bust, they feel very risk averse, but the high expected returns are just enough to keep their money in the market.

To rationalize active portfolio strategies, such as pulling out of the market at times of high price ratios, you have to ask, who is there who is going to be more in the market than average now? And, what else are you going to do with the money?

More formally, it is easy to crank out portfolio advice, solutions to optimal portfolio problems given objectives like the utility function in Equation (3). Assuming low risk aversion, and no labour income or other reason for time-varying risk exposure or risk aversion, solutions typically suggest large portfolio shares in equities and a strong market timing approach, sometimes highly leveraged and sometimes (now) even short. (See Barberis, 1997; Brandt, 1997.) If everyone followed this advice, however, the equity premium and the predictable variation in expected returns would disappear. Everyone trying to buy stocks would simply drive up the prices; everyone trying to time the market would stabilize prices. Thus, the majority of investors must be solving a different problem, deciding on their portfolios with different considerations in mind, so that they are always just willing to hold the outstanding stocks and bonds at current prices. Before going against this crowd, it is wise to understand why the crowd seems headed in a different direction.

Here, a good macroeconomic model of stock market risk could be extremely useful. The models describe why average consumers are so afraid of stocks and why that fear changes over time. Then, individuals in circumstances that make them different from everyone else can understand why they should behave differently from the crowd. If you have no habits or are immune to labour income shocks, in other words if you are unaffected by the state variables or risk factors that drive the stock market premium, by all means go your own way. However, the current state of the art is not advanced enough to provide concrete advice along these lines.

The last possibility is that one thinks one is smarter than everyone else, and that the equity premium and predictability are just patterns that are ignored by other people. This is a dangerous stance to take. *Someone* must be wrong in the view that he or she is smarter than everyone else. Furthermore, this view also suggests that the opportunities are not likely to last. People do learn. The opinions in this article are hardly a secret. We could interpret the recent run-up in the market as the result of people finally figuring out how good an investment stocks have been for the last century, and building institutions that allow wide participation in the stock market. If so, future returns are likely to be much lower, but there is not much one can do about it but sigh and join the parade.

Notes

[1] More formally, we can only reject hypotheses that the true return is less than 3 per cent or greater than 13 per cent with 95 per cent probability.

[2] A bit more formally, if you start with a regression of log returns on the P/D ratio, $r_{t+1} = a + b\ p/d_t + \varepsilon_{t+1}$, and a similar autoregression of the P/D ratio, $p/d_t = \mu + \rho\ p/d_{t-1} + \delta_t$, then you can calculate the implied long-horizon regression statistics. The fact that ρ is a very high number implies that long-horizon return regression coefficients and R^2 rise with the horizon, as in the table. See Hodrick (1992) and Cochrane (1991a) for calculations.

[3] The OLS regression estimate of ρ, is 0.90. However, this estimate is severely downward biased. In a Monte Carlo replication of the regression, a true coefficient $\rho = 0.90$ resulted in an estimate $\hat{\rho}$, with a mean of 0.82, a median of 0.83 and a standard deviation of 0.09. Assuming a true coefficient of 0.98 produces an OLS estimator $\hat{\rho}_{OLS}$, with median 0.90. I therefore adjust for the downward bias of the OLS estimate by using $\hat{\rho} = 0.98$.

[4] To generate a negative expected excess return, we have to believe that the market return is negatively conditionally correlated with the state variables that drive excess returns, for example consumption growth. This is theoretically possible, but seems awfully unlikely.

[5] Craine (1993) does a formal test of price/dividend stationarity and connects the test to bubbles. My statements are a superficial dismissal of a large literature. A lot of careful attention has been paid to the bubble possibility, but the current consensus seems to be that bubbles, as I have defined them here, do not explain price variation.

[6] Eliminate the last term, multiply both sides by $(p_t - d_t) - E\ (p_t - d_t)$ and take expectations.

[7] Several ways around this argument do exist. Kocherlakota (1990) defends a preference for later consumption. Kandel and Stambaugh (1991) note that the argument hinges critically on the definition of Δc. If we define Δc as the proportional change in consumption $\Delta c = (C_{t+\Delta t} - C_t)/C_t$ as I have (or, more properly, $\Delta c = dC/C$ in continuous time; see Appendix 16.1), then we obtain Equation (4). However, if we define Δc as the change in log consumption, $\Delta c = \ln (C_{t+\Delta t}/C_t)$ or more properly $\Delta c = d(\ln C)$, we obtain an additional term, $r^f = \rho + \gamma E(\Delta c) - 1/2\gamma^2\sigma^2 (\Delta c)$. For $\gamma < 100$ or so, the choice does not matter. The last term is small, since $E(\Delta c) \approx \sigma(\Delta c) \approx 0.01$. However, since γ is squared, the second term can be large with $\gamma = 250$, and can take the place of a negative ρ in generating a 1 per cent interest rate with 1 per cent consumption growth. What's going on? The model $u\ell(C) = C^{-250}$ is extraordinarily sensitive to the probability of consumption declines. The second model gives slightly higher weight to those probabilities. Rather than rescue the model with $\gamma = 250$, in my evaluation, this example shows how special it is: It says that

interest rates as well as all asset prices depend only on the probabilities assigned to extremely rare events.

[8] I specify bets on annual consumption to sidestep the objection that most bets are bets on wealth rather than bets on consumption. As a first-order approximation, consumers will respond to lost wealth by lowering consumption at every date by the same amount. More sophisticated calculations yield the same qualitative results.

[9] The value function is formally defined as the achieved level of expected utility. It is a function of wealth because the richer you are, the happier you can get, if you spend your wealth wisely. The value can also be a function of other variables such as labour income or expected returns that describe the environment. Thus:

$$V(W_t, .) = \max_{\{c_{t+s}\}} E_t \int_{s=0}^{\infty} e^{-\rho s} u(c_{t+s}) ds \ s.t. \ \text{(constraints)}.$$

The dot reminds us that there can be other arguments to the value function. $V_W = u_c$ is the 'envelope' condition, and follows from this definition.

[10] Precisely, define the 'surplus consumption ratio', $S = (C - X)/C$, and denote $s = \ln S$. Then s adapts to consumption following a discrete-time 'square root process'

$$s_{t+1} - s_t = -(1 - \phi)(s_t - \bar{s}) + \left[\frac{1}{\bar{S}} \ \sqrt{1 - 2(s - \bar{s})} - 1 \right] (c_{t+1} - c_t - g).$$

Taking a Taylor approximation, this specification is locally the same as allowing log habit x to adjust to consumption:

$$x_{t+1} \approx \text{const.} + \phi x_t + (1 - \phi) c_{t+1}.$$

Campbell and Cochrane specify that habits are 'external': Your neighbour's consumption raises your habit. This is a simplification, since it means that each consumption decision does not take into account its habit-forming effect. They argue that this assumption does not greatly affect aggregate consumption and asset price implications, though it is necessary to reconcile the unpredictability of individual consumption growth.

[11] Technically, this assertion depends on the form of the utility function. For example, with log utility, consumers don't care about future returns. In this statement I am assuming risk aversion greater than 1. See Campbell (1996).

[12] To prove this assertion, just substitute for C_{it} and take the expectation:

$$1 = E_{t-1} \exp \left[-\rho - \gamma \eta_{it} y_t + \frac{1}{2} \gamma y_t^2 + \ln R_{t+1} \right].$$

Since η is independent of everything else, we can use $E[f(\eta y)] = E[f(\eta y)|y)]$. Now, with η normal, $E\left(\exp\left[-\gamma \eta_{it} y_t\right]|y_t\right) = \exp\left[\frac{1}{2} \gamma^2 y_t^2\right]$. Therefore, we have

$$1 = E_{t-1} \exp \left[-\rho + \frac{1}{2} \gamma^2 y_t^2 + \frac{1}{2} \gamma y_t^2 + \ln R_{t+1} \right]$$

$$1 = E_{t-1} \exp \left[-\rho + \frac{1}{2} \gamma(\gamma+1) \left(\frac{2}{\gamma(\gamma+1)} \right) \left(\ln \frac{1}{R_t} + \rho \right) + \ln R_{t+1} \right]$$

$$1 = E_{t-1} 1.$$

[13] There is a possibility that the square root term in Equations (11) and (12) might be negative. Constantinides and Duffie rule out this possibility by assuming that the discount factor m satisfies:

$$\ln m_t \geq -\rho - \gamma \ln \frac{C_t}{C_{t-1}} \tag{13}$$

in every state of nature, so that the square root term is positive.

We can sometimes construct such discount factors by picking parameters a, b in $m_t = \max [a + bR_t, e^{-\rho} (C_t/C_{t-1})^{-\gamma}]$ to satisfy Equation (14). However, neither this construction nor a discount factor satisfying Equation (13) is guaranteed to exist for a given set of assets. The restriction in Equation (13) is a tighter form of the familiar restriction that $m_t \geq 0$ is equivalent to the absence of arbitrage in the assets under consideration. Presumably, this restriction is what rules out markets for individual labour income risks in the model. The example $m = 1/R$ that I use is a positive discount factor that prices a single asset return $1 = E(R^{-1}R)$, but does not necessarily satisfy the restriction in Equation (13). For high R, we can have very negative $\ln 1/R$. This is why the lines in Figure 16.6 run into the horizontal axis at high R.

References

Abel, Andrew B. (1983) 'Optimal investment under uncertainty', *American Economic Review*, 73 (1), 228–233.

Abel, Andrew B. (1990) 'Asset prices under habit formation and catching up with the Joneses', *American Economic Review Papers and Proceedings*, 80 (2), 38–42.

Abel, Andrew B. and Eberly, Janice C. (1996) 'Optimal investment with costly reversibility', *Review of Economic Studies*, 63, 581–594.

Aiyagari, S. Rao and Gertler, Mark (1991) 'Asset returns with transactions costs and undiversifiable individual risk', *Journal of Monetary Economics*, 27 (3), 311–331.

Barberis, Nicholas (1997) 'Investing for the long run when returns are predictable', University of Chicago, Center for Research on Security Prices, working paper No. 439.

Barsky, Robert B., Kimball, Miles S., Juster, F. Thomas and Shapiro, Matthew D. (1997) 'Preference parameters and behavioural heterogeneity: An experimental approach in the health and retirement survey', National Bureau of Economic Research, working paper No. 5213.

Bernardo, Antonio and Ledoit, Olivier (1996) 'Gain, loss and asset pricing', University of California at Los Angeles, Anderson Graduate School of Management, working paper No. 16-96.

Black, Fischer (1976) 'Studies of stock price volatility changes', *Proceedings of the 1976 Meetings of the Business and Economic Statistics Section, American Statistical Association*, 177–181.

Boldrin, Michele, Christiano, Lawrence J. and Fisher, Jonas D.M. (1995) 'Asset pricing lessons for modeling business cycles', NBER, working paper No. 5262.

Brandt, Michael (1997) 'Estimating portfolio and consumption choice: A conditional Euler equations approach', University of Chicago, Ph.D. dissertation.

Brown, Stephen J., Goetzmann, William N. and Ross, Stephen A. (1995) 'Survival', *Journal of Finance*, 50 (3), 853–873.

Campbell, John Y. (1987) 'Stock returns and the term structure', *Journal of Financial Economics*, 18, 373–399.

Campbell, John Y. (1996) 'Understanding risk and return', *Journal of Political Economy*, 104, 298–345.

Campbell, John Y. and Cochrane, John H. (1997) 'By force of habit: A consumption-based explanation of aggregate stock market behaviour', University of Chicago, working paper. [Revision of National Bureau of Economic Research, working paper No. 4995, dated 1 January 1995.]

Campbell, John Y. and Shiller, Robert J. (1988) 'The dividend–price ratio and expectations of future dividends and discount factors', *Review of Financial Studies*, 1, 195–227.

Cochrane, John H. (1991) 'Volatility tests and efficient markets: A review essay', *Journal of Monetary Economics*, 27, 463–485.

Cochrane, John H. (1991) 'Explaining the variance of price–dividend ratios', *Review of Financial Studies*, 15, 243–280.

Cochrane, John H. (1991), 'Production-based asset pricing and the link between stock returns and economic fluctuations', *Journal of Finance*, 41, 207–234.

Cochrane, John H. and Hansen, Lars Peter (1992) 'Asset pricing lessons for macroeconomics', in Blanchard, O. and Fischer, Stanley (eds.), in *1992 NBER Macroeconomics Annual*.

Constantinides, George M. (1989) 'Theory of valuation: Overview', in Bhattahcharya, S. and Constantinides, G. M. (eds.), *Theory of Valuation: Frontiers of Modern Financial Theory, Volume I*.

Constantinides, George M. (1990) 'Habit formation: A resolution of the equity premium puzzle', *Journal of Political Economy*, 98, 519–543.

Constantinides, George M. and Duffie, Darrell (1996) 'Asset pricing with the heterogeneous consumers,' *Journal of Political Economy*, 104, 219–240.

Craine, Roger (1993) 'Rational bubbles: A test', *Journal of Economic Dynamics and Control*, 17, 829–846.

Deaton, Angus S. (1992) *Understanding Consumption*, New York: Oxford University Press.

Deaton, Angus and Paxson, Christina (1994) 'Intertemporal choice and inequality', *Journal of Political Economy*, 102, 437–467.

Duesenberry, James S. (1949) *Income, Saving, and the Theory of Consumer Behavior*, Cambridge, M.A: Harvard University Press.

Eichenbaum, Martin, Hansen, Lars Peter and Singleton, Kenneth J. (1988) 'A time series analysis of representative agent models of consumption and leisure choice under uncertainty', *Journal of Business and Economic Statistics*, 103, 51–78.

Epstein, Larry G. and Zin, Stanley E. (1989) 'Substitution, risk aversion and the temporal behavior of asset returns', *Journal of Political Economy*, 99, 263–286.

Fama, Eugene F. and French, Kenneth R. (1988) 'Permanent and temporary components of stock prices', *Journal of Political Economy*, 96, 246–273.

Fama, Eugene F. and French, Kenneth R. (1988) 'Dividend yields and expected stock returns', *Journal of Financial Economics*, 22, 3–27.

Fama, Eugene F. and French, Kenneth R. (1989) 'Business conditions and expected returns on stocks and bonds', *Journal of Financial Economics*, 25, 23–49.

Fama, Eugene F. and French, Kenneth R. (1993) 'Common risk factors in the returns on stocks and bonds,' *Journal of Financial Economics*, 33, 3–56.

Fazzari, Steven M., Hubbard, Robert Glenn, Glenn, Robert and Petersen, Bruce C. (1988) 'Financing constraints and corporate investment', *Brookings Papers on Economic Activity*.

Ferson, Wayne E. and Constantinides, George (1991) 'Habit persistence and durability in aggregate consumption: Empirical tests', *Journal of Financial Economics*, 29, 199–240.

Friend, I. and Blume, M. (1975) 'The demand for risky assets', *American Economic Review*, 55, 900–922.

Hansen, Lars Peter and Jagannathan, Ravi (1991) 'Restrictions on intertemporal marginal rates of substitution implied by asset returns', *Journal of Political Economy*, 99, 225–262.

Hansen, Lars Peter, Sargent, Thomas J. and Tallarini, Thomas D. (1997) 'Robust permanent income and pricing', University of Chicago, manuscript.

Heaton, John C. (1995) 'An empirical investigation of asset pricing with temporally dependent preference specifications', *Econometrica*, 63, 681–717.

Heaton, John and Lucas, Deborah J. (1996a) 'Evaluating the effects of incomplete markets on risk sharing and asset pricing', *Journal of Political Economy*, 104, 443–487.

Heaton, John and Lucas, Deborah, J. (1996b) Saving behavior and portfolio choice: Which risks matter?' Northwestern University, working paper.

Hodrick, Robert (1992) 'Dividend yields and expected stock returns: Alternative procedures for inference and measurement', *Review of Financial Studies*, 5 (3), 357–386.

Jagannathan, Ravi and Wang, Z. (1996) 'The conditional CAPM and the cross-section of expected returns', *Journal of Finance*, 51, 3–53. [Updated in *Staff Report*, No. 208, Federal Reserve Bank of Minneapolis, 1997.]

Jermann, Urban (1997) 'Asset pricing in production economies,' *Journal of Monetary Economics*.

Kandel, Shmuel and Stambaugh, Robert F. (1990) 'Expectations and volatility of consumption and asset returns', *Review of Financial Studies*, 3 (2), 207–232.

Kandel, Shmuel and Stambaugh, R. F. (1991) 'Asset returns and intertemporal preferences', *Journal of Monetary Economics*, 27, 39–71.

Kocherlakota, Narayanna R. (1990) 'On the "discount" factor in growth economies', *Journal of Monetary Economics*, 25, 43–47.

Kocherlakota, Narayanna R. (1996) 'The equity premium: It's still a puzzle', *Journal of Economic Literature*, 34, 42–71.

Lamont, Owen (1991) 'Earnings and Expected Returns', National Bureau of Economic Research, working paper No. 5671.

Lucas, Deborah J. (1994) 'Asset pricing with undiversifiable income risk and short sales constraints: Deepening the equity premium puzzle', *Journal of Monetary Economics*, 34, 325–341.

Mankiw, N. Gregory (1996) 'The equity premium and the concentration of aggregate shocks', *Journal of Financial Economics*, 17, 211–219.

Mankiw, N. Gregory and Zeldes, Stephen P. (1991) 'The consumption of stockholders and non-stockholders', *Journal of Financial Economics*, 29, 97–112.

Marshall, David and Daniel, Kent (1997) 'The equity premium puzzle and the risk-free rate puzzle at long horizons', *Macroeconomic Dynamics*, 1 (1), 452–484.

Mehra, Rajnish and Prescott, Edward (1985) 'The equity premium puzzle', *Journal of Monetary Economics*, 15, 145–161.

Merton, Robert C. (1973) 'An intertemporal capital asset pricing model', *Econometrica*, 41, 867–887.

Poterba, James and Summers, Lawrence J. (1988) 'Mean reversion in stock prices', *Journal of Financial Economics*, 22, 27–59.

Reyfman, Alexander (1997) 'Labour market risk and expected asset returns', University of Chicago, Ph.D. dissertation, Ch. 3.

Rietz, Thomas A. (1988) 'The equity risk premium: A solution', *Journal of Monetary Economics*, 22, 117–131.

Shiller, Robert J. (1982) 'Consumption, asset markets, and macroeconomic fluctuations', *Carnegie Rochester Conference Series on Public Policy*, 17, 203–238.

Telmer, Chris I. (1993) 'Asset pricing puzzles and incomplete markets', *Journal of Finance*, 48, 1803–1832.

Weil, Philippe (1989) 'The equity premium puzzle and the risk-free rate puzzle', *Journal of Monetary Economics*, 24, 401–421.

Derivations

VARIANCE DECOMPOSITION

Massaging an identity,

$$1 = R_{t+1}^{-1} R_{t+1}$$

$$1 = R_{t+1}^{-1} \frac{P_{t+1} + D_{t+1}}{P_t}$$

$$\frac{P_t}{D_t} = R_{t+1}^{-1} \frac{P_{t+1} + D_{t+1}}{D_t}$$

$$\frac{P_t}{D_t} = R_{t+1}^{-1} \left(\frac{P_{t+1}}{D_{t+1}} + 1 \right) \frac{D_{t+1}}{D_t}$$

$$\frac{P_t}{D_t} = \sum_{j=1}^{\infty} \prod_{k=1}^{j} R_{t+k}^{-1} \frac{D_{t+k}}{D_{t+k-1}} + \lim_{j \to \infty} \left(\prod_{k=1}^{j} R_{t+k}^{-1} \right) \frac{P_{t+j}}{D_{t+j}} \tag{20}$$

This equation shows how price-dividend ratios are exactly linked to subsequent returns, dividend growth or a potential bubble. It is convenient to approximate this relation. We can follow Cochrane (1991b) and take a Taylor expansion now, or follow Campbell and Shiller (1986) and Taylor and expand the first equation in (20) to:

$$p_t - d_t = \Delta d_{t+1} - r_{t+1} + \rho(p_{t+1} - d_{t+1})$$

and then iterate to:

$$p_t - d_t = \sum_{j=1}^{\infty} \rho^j (\Delta d_{t+j} - r_{t+j}) + \lim_{j \to \infty} \rho^j (p_{t+j} - d_{t+j}).$$

Consumption-portfolio equations

I develop the consumption-portfolio problem in continuous time. This leads to a number of simplifications that can also be derived as approximations or specializations to the normal distribution in discrete time. A security has price P, dividend Ddt and thus instantaneous rate of return $dP/P + D/Pdt$. The utility function is:

$$E_t \int e^{-\rho s}\, u(C_{t+s})ds.$$

The first-order condition for an optimal consumption-portfolio choice is:

$$u'(C_t)P_t = E_t \int e^{-\rho s}\, u'(C_{t+s})D_{t+s}ds + E_t \left[e^{-\rho k}\, u'(C_{t+k})P_{t+k} \right].$$

Letting the time interval shrink to zero, we have:

$$0 = E_t\left[d(\Lambda P)\right] + D_t dt$$

where:

$$\Lambda_t \equiv e^{-\rho t}\, u'(C_t).$$

Expanding the second moment, and dividing by ΛP:

$$0 = E_t \left(\frac{dP}{P} \right) + \frac{D}{P}\, dt + E_t \left(\frac{d\Lambda}{\Lambda} \right) + E_t \left[\frac{d\Lambda}{\Lambda}\, \frac{dP_t}{P_t} \right].$$

Applying this basic condition to a risk-free asset:

$$r_t^f\, dt = -E_t \left[\frac{d\Lambda}{\Lambda} \right] = \rho dt - E_t \left[\frac{du'(C)}{u'(C)} \right] = \rho dt - \frac{Cu''(C)}{u'(C)}\, E_t \left[\frac{dC}{C} \right]$$

$$r_t^f\, dt = \rho dt + \gamma E_t \left[\frac{dC}{C} \right].$$

For any other asset:

$$0 = E_t \left(\frac{dP}{P} \right) + \frac{D}{P}\, dt - r_t^f dt = -E_t \left[\frac{d\Lambda}{\Lambda}\, \frac{dP_t}{P_t} \right].$$

Using Ito's lemma on Λ, we have:

$$E_t \left[\frac{d\Lambda}{\Lambda}\, \frac{dP_t}{P_t} \right] = \frac{Cu''(C)}{u'(C)}\, E_t \left(\frac{dC}{C}\, \frac{dP}{P} \right).$$

Finally, using the symbols:

$$r = \frac{dP}{P} + \frac{D}{P}\, dt, r^f = r^f\, dt,$$

$$\gamma = \frac{-Cu''(C)}{u'(C)}, \Delta c = \frac{dC}{C}$$

we have the following equation,

$$E_t(r) - r^f = -\gamma \operatorname{cov}_t[\Delta c, r] = -\gamma \sigma_t(\Delta c)\sigma_t(r)\rho_t(\Delta c, r).$$

I drop the t subscript in the text where it is not important to keep track of the difference between conditional and unconditional moments.

RISK AVERSION CALCULATIONS

What is the amount x that a consumer is willing to pay every period to avoid a bet that either increases consumption by y every period or decreases it by the same amount? The answer is found from the condition:

$$\sum_j \delta^j u(C-x) = \frac{1}{2}\sum_j \delta^j u(C+y) + \frac{1}{2}\sum_j \delta^j u(C-y).$$

Using the power functional form:

$$(C-x)^{1-\gamma} = \frac{1}{2}(C+y)^{1-\gamma} + \frac{1}{2}(C-y)^{1-\gamma},$$

and solving for x:

$$x = C - \left[\frac{1}{2}(C+y)^{1-\gamma} + \frac{1}{2}(C-y)^{1-\gamma}\right]^{\frac{1}{1-\gamma}}.$$

This equation is easier to solve in ratio form; the fraction of consumption that the family would pay is related to the fractional wealth risk by:

$$\frac{x}{C} = 1 - \left[\frac{1}{2}\left(1 + \frac{y}{C}\right)^{1-\gamma} + \frac{1}{2}\left(1 - \frac{y}{C}\right)^{1-\gamma}\right]^{\frac{1}{1-\gamma}}.$$

This equation is the basis for the calculations in Table 16.5.
    For small risks, we can approximate:

$$u(C-x) = \frac{1}{2}\left[u(C+y) + u(C-y)\right]$$

$$-u'(C)x \approx \frac{1}{2}u''(C)y^2$$

$$\frac{x}{C} \approx \frac{-Cu''(C)}{u'(C)}\left(\frac{y}{C}\right)^2 = \gamma\left(\frac{y}{C}\right)^2$$

$$\frac{x}{C} \approx \gamma\left(\frac{y}{C}\right)^2$$

$$\frac{x}{y} \approx \gamma\left(\frac{y}{C}\right).$$

CHAPTER 17

What is different about the new financial economics?

INTRODUCTION AND SUMMARY

The last 15 years have seen a revolution in the way financial economists understand the investment world. We once thought that stock and bond returns were essentially unpredictable. Now we recognize that stock and bond returns have a substantial predictable component at long horizons. We once thought that the capital asset pricing model (CAPM) provided a good description of why average returns on some stocks, portfolios, funds or strategies were higher than others. Now we recognize that the average returns of many investment opportunities cannot be explained by the CAPM, and 'multifactor models' are used in its place. We once thought that long-term interest rates reflected expectations of future short-term rates and that interest rate differentials across countries reflected expectations of exchange rate depreciation. Now we see time-varying risk premiums in bond and foreign exchange markets as well as in stock markets. We once thought that mutual fund average returns were well explained by the CAPM. Now we see that funds can earn average returns not explained by the CAPM, that is, unrelated to market risks, by following a variety of investment 'styles'.

In this chapter, I survey these new facts, and I show how they are variations on a common theme. Each case uses price variables to infer market expectations of future returns; each case notices that an offsetting adjustment (to dividends, interest rates or exchange rates) seems to be absent or sluggish. Each case suggests that financial markets offer rewards in the form of average returns for holding risks related to recessions and financial distress, in addition to the risks represented by overall market movements. In the next chapter: 'Recent developments in modern portfolio theory', I survey and interpret recent advances in portfolio theory that address the question, What should an investor do about all these new facts?

First, a slightly more detailed overview of the facts then and now. Until the mid-1980s, financial economists' view of the investment world was based on three bedrocks.

1 The CAPM is a good measure of risk and thus a good explanation of the fact that some assets (stocks, portfolios, strategies or mutual funds) earn higher average returns than others. The CAPM states that assets can only earn a high average return if they have a high 'beta', which measures the tendency of the individual asset to move up or down with the market as a

whole. Beta drives average returns because beta measures how much adding a *bit* of the asset to a diversified portfolio increases the volatility of the *portfolio*. Investors care about portfolio returns, not about the behaviour of specific assets.

2   Returns are unpredictable, like a coin flip. This is the *random walk* theory of stock prices. Though there are bull and bear markets; long sequences of good and bad *past* returns; the expected *future* return is always about the same. *Technical analysis* that tries to divine future returns from patterns of past returns and prices is nearly useless. Any apparent predictability is either a statistical artifact which will quickly vanish out of sample or cannot be exploited after transaction costs.

Bond returns are not predictable. This is the *expectations model* of the term structure. If long-term bond yields are higher than short-term yields – if the yield curve is upward sloping – this does not mean that you expect a higher return by holding long-term bonds rather than short-term bonds. Rather, it means that short-term interest rates are expected to rise in the future. Over one year, the rise in interest rates will limit the capital gain on long-term bonds, so they earn the same as the short-term bonds over the year. Over many years, the rise in short rates improves the rate of return from rolling over short-term bonds to equal that of holding the long-term bond. Thus, you expect to earn about the same amount on short-term or long-term bonds at any horizon.

Foreign exchange bets are not predictable. If a country has higher interest rates than are available in the USA for bonds of a similar risk class, its exchange rate is expected to depreciate. Then, after you convert your investment back to dollars, you expect to make the same amount of money holding foreign or domestic bonds.

In addition, stock market volatility does not change much through time. Not only are returns close to unpredictable, they are nearly identically distributed as well. Each day, the stock market return is like the result of flipping the same coin, over and over again.

3   Professional managers do not reliably outperform simple indexes and passive portfolios once one corrects for risk (beta). While some do better than the market in any given year, some do worse, and the outcomes look very much like luck. Funds that do well in one year are not more likely to do better than average the next year. The average actively managed fund performs about 1 per cent *worse* than the market index. The more actively a fund trades, the lower the returns to investors.

Together, these views reflect a guiding principle that asset markets are, to a good approximation, *informationally efficient* (Fama, 1970, 1991). Market prices already contain most information about fundamental value and, because the business of discovering information about the value of traded assets is extremely competitive, there are no easy quick profits to be made, just as there are not in any other well-established and competitive industry. The only way to earn large returns is by taking on additional risk.

These views are not ideological or doctrinaire beliefs. Rather, they summarize the findings of a quarter of a century of careful empirical work. However, every one of them has now been extensively revised by a new generation of empirical research. The new findings need not overturn the cherished view that markets are reasonably competitive and, therefore, reasonably efficient. However, they do substantially enlarge our view of what activities provide rewards for holding risks, and they challenge our understanding of those risk premiums.

Now, we know that:

1 There are assets whose average returns cannot be explained by their beta. Multifactor extensions of the CAPM dominate the description, performance attribution, and explanation of average returns. Multifactor models associate high average returns with a tendency to move with other risk factors in addition to movements in the market as a whole. (See Figure 17.1.)

2 Returns are predictable. In particular: variables including the dividend/price (d/p) ratio and term premium can predict substantial amounts of stock return variation. This phenomenon occurs over business cycle and longer horizons. Daily, weekly and monthly stock returns are still close to unpredictable, and technical systems for predicting such movements are still close to useless.

The CAPM uses a *time-series* regression to measure beta, β, which quantifies an asset's or portfolio's tendency to move with the market as a whole:

$$R_t^i - R_t^f = a_i + \beta_{im} (R_t^m - R_t^f) + \varepsilon_{t}^{i}; \quad (1)$$

$t = 1,2 \dots T$ for each asset i.

Then, the CAPM predicts that the expected excess return should be proportional to beta:

$$E(R_t^i - R_t^f) = \beta_{im}\lambda_m \text{ for each } i. \quad (2)$$

λ_m gives the 'price of beta risk' or 'market risk premium' – the amount by which expected returns must rise to compensate investors for higher beta. Since the model applies to the market return as well, we can measure λ_m via

$$\lambda_m = E(R_t^m - R_t^f).$$

Multifactor models extend this theory in a straightforward way. They use a time-series *multiple* regression to quantify an asset's tendency to move with multiple risk factors F^A, F^B, etc.

$$R_t^i - R_t^f = a_i + \beta_{im} (R_t^m - R_t^f) + \beta_{iA}F_t^A + \beta_{iB}F_t^B$$
$$+ \dots + \varepsilon_{t}^{i}; \ t = 1,2 \dots T \text{ for each asset } i. \quad (3)$$

Then, the multifactor model predicts that the expected excess return is proportional to the betas

$$E(R_t^i - R_t^f) = \beta_{im}\lambda_m + \beta_{iA}\lambda_A + \beta_{iB}\lambda_B + \dots$$
$$\text{for each } i. \quad (4)$$

The residual or unexplained average return in either case is called an alpha,

$$\alpha_i = E(R_t^i - R_t^f) - (\beta_{im}\lambda_m + \beta_{iA}\lambda_A + \beta_{iB}\lambda_B + \dots).$$

Fig 17.1 ● The CAPM and multifactor models

Bond returns are predictable. Though the expectations model works well in the long run, a steeply upward sloping yield curve means that expected returns on long-term bonds are higher than on short-term bonds for the next year. These predictions are not guarantees – there is still substantial risk – but the tendency is discernible.

Foreign exchange returns are predictable. If you put your money in a country whose interest rates are higher than usual relative to the USA, you expect to earn more money even after converting back to dollars. Again, this prediction is not a guarantee – exchange rates do vary, and a lot, so the strategy is risky.

Volatility does change through time. Times of past volatility indicate future volatility. Volatility also is higher after large price drops. Bond market volatility is higher when interest rates are higher, and possibly when interest rate spreads are higher as well.

3   Some mutual funds seem to outperform simple indexes, even after controlling for risk through market betas. Fund returns are also slightly predictable: past winning funds seem to do better than average in the future, and past losing funds seem to do worse than average in the future. For a while, this seemed to indicate that there is some persistent skill in active management. However, multifactor models explain most fund persistence: funds earn persistent returns by following fairly mechanical *styles*, not by persistent skill at stock selection.

Again, these statements are not dogma, but a cautious summary of a large body of careful empirical work. The strength and usefulness of many results are hotly debated, as are the underlying reasons for many of these new facts. But the old world is gone.

THE CAPM AND MULTIFACTOR MODELS
The CAPM

The CAPM proved stunningly successful in a quarter of a century of empirical work. Every strategy that seemed to give high average returns turned out to have a high beta, or a large tendency to move with the market. Strategies that one might have thought gave high average returns (such as holding very volatile stocks) turned out not to have high average returns when they did not have high betas.

Figure 17.2 presents a typical evaluation of the CAPM. I examine ten portfolios of NYSE stocks sorted by size (total market capitalization), along with a portfolio of corporate bonds and long-term government bonds. As the vertical axis shows, there is a sizeable spread in average returns between large stocks

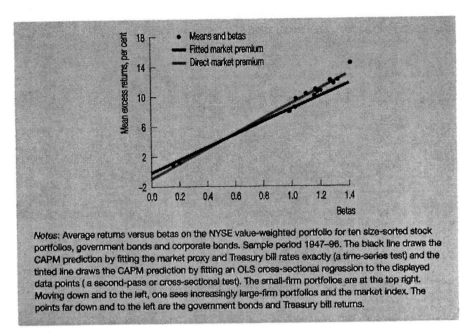

Notes: Average returns versus betas on the NYSE value-weighted portfolio for ten size-sorted stock portfolios, government bonds and corporate bonds. Sample period 1947–96. The black line draws the CAPM prediction by fitting the market proxy and Treasury bill rates exactly (a time-series test) and the tinted line draws the CAPM prediction by fitting an OLS cross-sectional regression to the displayed data points (a second-pass or cross-sectional test). The small-firm portfolios are at the top right. Moving down and to the left, one sees increasingly large-firm portfolios and the market index. The points far down and to the left are the government bonds and Treasury bill returns.

Fig 17.2 ● CAPM – Mean excess returns versus beta, version 1

(lower average return) and small stocks (higher average return) and a large spread between stocks and bonds. The figure plots these average returns against market betas. You can see how the CAPM prediction fits: portfolios with higher average returns have higher betas.

In fact, Figure 17.2 captures one of the first significant *failures* of the CAPM. The smallest firms (the far right portfolio) seem to earn an average return a few per cent too high given their betas. This is the celebrated 'small-firm effect' (Banz, 1981), and this deviation is statistically significant. Would that all failed economic theories worked so well! However, the plot shows that this effect is within the range that statisticians can argue about. Estimating the slope of the line by fitting a cross-sectional regression (average return against beta), shown in the tinted line, rather than forcing the line to go through the market and Treasury bill return, shown in the black line, halves the small-firm effect. Figure 17.3 uses the equally weighted portfolio as market proxy, and this change in specification eliminates the small-firm effect, making the line of average returns versus betas if anything too shallow rather than too steep.

Why we expect multiple factors

In retrospect, it is surprising that the CAPM worked so well for so long. The assumptions on which it is built are very stylized and simplified. Asset pricing theory recognized at least since Merton (1973, 1971) the theoretical possibil-

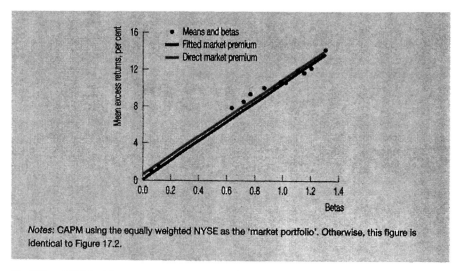

Notes: CAPM using the equally weighted NYSE as the 'market portfolio'. Otherwise, this figure is identical to Figure 17.2.

Fig 17.3 ● CAPM – Mean excess returns versus beta, version 2

ity, indeed probability, that we should need *factors, state variables* or *sources of priced risk*, beyond movements in the market portfolio to explain why some average returns are higher than others. (See Figure 17.1 for details of the CAPM and multifactor models.)

Most importantly, *the average investor has a job.* The CAPM (together with the use of the NYSE portfolio as the market proxy) simplifies matters by assuming that the average investor only cares about the performance of his or her investment portfolio. While there are investors like that, for most of us eventual wealth comes both from investment and from earning a living. Importantly, events like recessions hurt the majority of investors. Those who don't actually lose jobs get lower salaries or bonuses. A very limited number of people actually do better in a recession.

With this fact in mind, compare two stocks. They both have the same sensitivity to market movements. However, one of them does well in recessions, while the other does poorly. Clearly, most investors prefer the stock that does well in recessions, since its performance will cushion the blows to their other income. If lots of people feel that way, they bid up the price of that stock, or, equivalently, they are willing to hold it at a lower average return. Conversely, the procyclical stock's price will fall or it must offer a higher average return in order to get investors to hold it.

In sum, we should expect that procyclical stocks that do well in booms and worse in recessions will have to offer higher average returns than countercyclical stocks that do well in recessions, even if the stocks have the same market beta. We expect that *another dimension of risk* – covariation with recessions – will matter in determining average returns.[1]

What kinds of additional factors should we look for? Generally, asset pricing theory specifies that assets will have to pay high average returns if they do poorly in 'bad times'– times in which investors would particularly like their investments not to perform badly and are willing to sacrifice some expected return in order to ensure that this is so. Consumption (or, more generally, marginal utility) should provide the purest measure of bad times. Investors consume less when their income prospects are low or if they think future returns will be bad. Low consumption thus *reveals* that this is indeed a time at which investors would especially like portfolios not to do badly, and would be willing to pay to ensure that wish. Alas, efforts to relate asset returns to consumption data are not (yet) a great success. Therefore, empirically useful asset pricing models examine more direct measures of good times or bad times. Broad categories of such indicators are as follows:

1 The market return. The CAPM is usually included and extended. People are unhappy if the market crashes.

2 Events, such as recessions, that drive investors' noninvestment sources of income.

3 Variables, such as the p/d ratio or slope of the yield curve, that forecast stock or bond returns (called 'state variables for changing investment opportunity sets').

4 Returns on other well-diversified portfolios.

One formally justifies the first three factors by stating assumptions under which each variable is related to average consumption. For example:

1 if the market as a whole declines, consumers lose wealth and will cut back on consumption;

2 if a recession leads people to lose their jobs, then they will cut back on consumption; and,

3 if you are saving for retirement, then news that interest rates and average stock returns have declined is bad news, which will cause you to lower consumption. This last point establishes a connection between predictability of returns and the presence of additional risk factors for understanding the cross-section of average returns. As pointed out by Merton (1971), one would give up some average return to have a portfolio that did well when there was bad news about future market returns.

The fourth kind of factor – additional portfolio returns – is most easily defended as a proxy for any of the other three. The fitted value of a regression of any pricing factor on the set of all asset returns is a portfolio that carries exactly the same pricing information as the original factor – a *factor-mimicking* portfolio.

It is vital that the extra risk factors affect the *average* investor. If an event makes investor A worse off and investor B better off, then investor A buys assets that do well when the event happens and investor B sells them. They transfer the risk of the event, but the price or expected return of the asset is unaffected. For a factor to affect prices or expected returns, it must affect the average investor, so investors collectively bid up or down the price and expected return of assets that covary with the event rather than just transferring the risk without affecting equilibrium prices.

Inspired by this broad direction, empirical researchers have found quite a number of specific factors that seem to explain the variation in average returns across assets. In general, empirical success varies inversely with theoretical purity.

Small and value/growth stocks

The size and book to market factors advocated by Fama and French (1996) are one of the most popular additional risk factors.

Small-cap stocks have small market values (price times shares outstanding). Value (or high book/market) stocks have market values that are small relative to the value of assets on the company's books. Both categories of stocks have quite high average returns. Large and growth stocks are the opposite of small and value and seem to have unusually low average returns. (See Fama and French, 1993, for a review.) The idea that low prices lead to high average returns is natural.

High average returns are consistent with the CAPM, if these categories of stocks have high sensitivity to the market, high betas. However, small and especially, value stocks, seem to have abnormally high returns even after accounting for market beta. Conversely, growth stocks seem to do systematically worse than their CAPM betas suggest. Figure 17.4 shows this value–size puzzle. It is just like Figure 17.2, except that the stocks are sorted into portfolios based on size and book/market ratio[2] rather than size alone. The highest portfolios have *three* times the average excess return of the lowest portfolios, and this variation has nothing at all to do with market betas.

In Figure 17.5, I connect portfolios of different sizes within the same book/market category (panel A). Variation in *size* produces a variation in average returns that is positively related to variation in market betas, as shown in Figure 17.2. In panel B, I connect portfolios that have different book/market ratios within size categories. Variation in book/market ratio produces a variation in average return that is *negatively* related to market beta. Because of this value effect, the CAPM is a disaster when confronted with these portfolios.

To explain these facts, Fama and French (1993, 1996) advocate a multifactor model with the market return, the return of small less big stocks (SMB), and the return of high book/market less low book/market stocks (HML) as

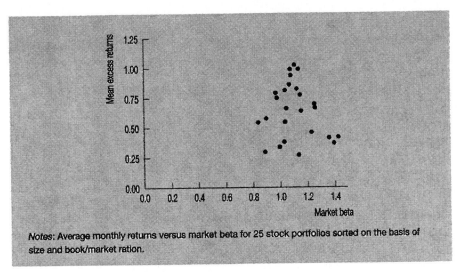

Notes: Average monthly returns versus market beta for 25 stock portfolios sorted on the basis of size and book/market ration.

Fig 17.4 • Mean excess returns versus market beta, Fama–French portfolios

three factors. They show that variation in average returns of the 25 size and book/market portfolios can be explained by varying loadings (betas) on the latter two factors.

Figure 17.6 illustrates Fama and French's results. As in Figure 17.5, the vertical axis is the average returns of the 25 size and book/market portfolios. Now, the horizontal axis is the predicted values from the Fama–French three-factor model. The points should all lie on a 45 degree line if the model is

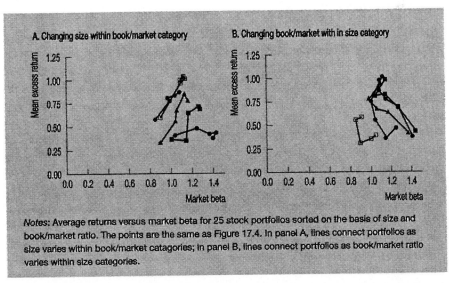

Notes: Average returns versus market beta for 25 stock portfolios sorted on the basis of size and book/market ratio. The points are the same as Figure 17.4. In panel A, lines connect portfolios as size varies within book/market catagories; in panel B, lines connect portfolios as book/market ratio varies within size categories.

Fig 17.5 • Mean excess returns versus market beta, varying size and book/market ratio

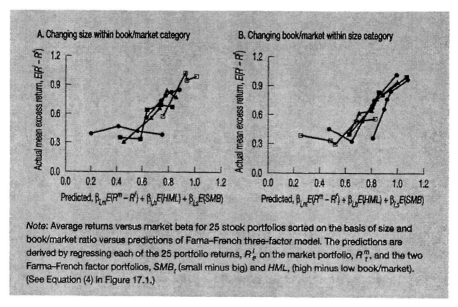

Note: Average returns versus market beta for 25 stock portfolios sorted on the basis of size and book/market ratio versus predictions of Fama–French three-factor model. The predictions are derived by regressing each of the 25 portfolio returns, R_i^i, on the market portfolio, R^m, and the two Fama–French factor portfolios, SMB_t (small minus big) and HML_t (high minus low book/market). (See Equation (4) in Figure 17.1.)

Fig 17.6 ● Mean excess return versus three-factor model predictions

correct. The points lie much closer to this prediction in Figure 17.6 than in Figures 17.4 and 17.5. The worst fit is for the growth stocks (lowest line, panel A), for which there is little variation in average return despite large variation in size beta as one moves from small to large firms.

What are the size and value factors?

One would like to understand the real, macroeconomic, aggregate, nondiversifiable risk that is proxied by the returns of the HML and SMB portfolios. Why are investors so concerned about holding stocks that do badly at the times that the HML (value less growth) and SMB (small-cap less large-cap) portfolios do badly, even though the market does not fall? The answer to this question is not yet totally clear.

Fama and French (1995) note that the typical value stock has a price that has been driven down due to financial distress. The stocks of firms on the verge of bankruptcy have recovered more often than not, which generates the high average returns of this strategy.[3] This observation suggests a natural interpretation of the value premium: in the event of a credit crunch, liquidity crunch or flight to quality, stocks in financial distress will do very badly, and this is precisely when investors least want to hear that their portfolio is losing money. (One cannot count the 'distress' of the individual firm as a risk factor. Such distress is idiosyncratic and can be diversified away. Only aggregate events that average investors care about can result in a risk premium.)

Heaton and Lucas's (1997) results add to this story for the value effect. They note that the typical stockholder is the proprietor of a small, privately held business. Such an investor's income is, of course, particularly sensitive to the kinds of financial events that cause distress among small firms and distressed value firms. Therefore, this investor would demand a substantial premium to hold value stocks and would hold growth stocks despite a low premium.

Liew and Vassalou (1999), among others, link value and small-firm returns to macroeconomic events. They find that in many countries, counterparts to HML and SMB contain supplementary information to that contained in the market return for forecasting gross domestic product (GDP) growth. For example, they report a regression:

$$GDP_{t \to t+4} = \alpha + 0.065 \, MKT_{t-4 \to t} + 0.058 \, HML_{t-4 \to t} + \varepsilon_{t+4},$$

where $GDP_{t \to t+4}$ denotes the following year's GDP growth and $MKT_{t-4 \to t}$ and $HML_{t-4 \to t}$ denote the previous year's return on the market index and HML portfolio. Thus, a 10 per cent HML return raises the GDP forecast by 0.5 percentage points. (Both coefficients are significant with t-statistics of 3.09 and 2.83, respectively.)

The effects are still under investigation. Figure 17.7 plots the cumulative return on the HML and SMB portfolios; a link between these returns and obvious macroeconomic events does not jump out. Both portfolios have essentially no correlation with the market return, though HML does seem to move inversely with large market declines. HML goes down more than the market in some business cycles, but less in others.

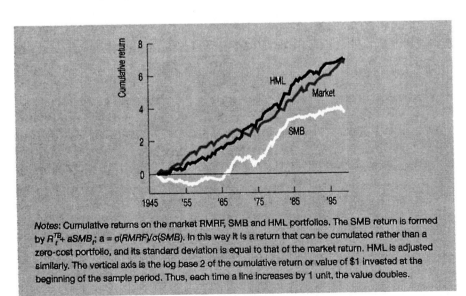

Notes: Cumulative returns on the market RMRF, SMB and HML portfolios. The SMB return is formed by $R_t^{TB} + aSMB_t$; $a = \sigma(RMRF)/\sigma(SMB)$. In this way it is a return that can be cumulated rather than a zero-cost portfolio, and its standard deviation is equal to that of the market return. HML is adjusted similarly. The vertical axis is the log base 2 of the cumulative return or value of $1 invested at the beginning of the sample period. Thus, each time a line increases by 1 unit, the value doubles.

Fig 17.7 • Cumulative returns on market portfolios

On the other hand, one can ignore Fama and French's motivation and regard the model as an *arbitrage pricing* theory (APT) following Ross (1976). If the returns of the 25 size and book/market portfolios could be *perfectly* replicated by the returns of the three-factor portfolios – if the R^2 values in the time-series regressions of the 25 portfolio on the three factors were 100 per cent – then the multifactor model would have to hold exactly, in order to preclude arbitrage opportunities. To see this, suppose that one of the 25 portfolios – call it portfolio A – gives an average return 5 per cent above the average return predicted by the Fama–French model, and its R^2 is 100 per cent. Then, one could short a combination of the three-factor portfolios, buy portfolio A, and earn a completely risk-less profit. This logic is often used to argue that a *high* R^2 should imply an *approximate* multifactor model. If the R^2 were only 95 per cent, then an average return 5 per cent above the factor model prediction would imply that the strategy long portfolio A and short a combination of the three-factor portfolios would earn a very high average return with very little, though not zero, risk – a very high Sharpe ratio.

In fact, the R^2 values of Fama and French's (1993) time-series regressions are all in the 90 per cent to 95 per cent range, so extremely high risk prices for the residuals would have to be invoked for the model *not* to fit well. Conversely, given the average returns from HML and SMB and the failure of the CAPM to explain those returns, there would be near-arbitrage opportunities if value and small stocks did not move together in the way described by the Fama–French model.

One way to assess whether the three factors proxy for real macroeconomic risks is by checking whether the multifactor model prices additional portfolios, especially portfolios whose *ex post* returns are not well explained by the factors (portfolios that do not have high R^2 values in time-series regressions). Fama and French (1996) find that the SMB and HML portfolios comfortably explain strategies based on alternative price multiples (price/earnings, book/market), five-year sales growth (this is the only strategy that does not form portfolios based on price variables), and the tendency of five-year returns to reverse. All of these strategies are not explained by CAPM betas. However, they all also produce portfolios with high R^2 values in a time-series regression on the HML and SMB portfolios. This is good and bad news. It might mean that the model is a good APT, and that the size and book/market characteristics describe the major sources of priced variation in all stocks. On the other hand, it might mean that these extra ways of constructing portfolios just haven't identified other sources of priced variation in stock returns. (Fama and French, 1996, also find that HML and SMB do not explain *momentum*, despite high R^2 values. I discuss this anomaly below.) The portfolios of stocks sorted by industry in Fama and French (1997) have lower R^2 values, and the model works less well.

A final concern is that the size and book/market premiums seem to have diminished substantially in recent years. The sharp decline in the SMB portfolio return around 1980 when the small-firm effect was first popularized is obvious in Figure 17.7. In Fama and French's (1993) initial samples, 1960–90, the HML cumulative return starts about one-half (0.62) below the market and ends up about one-half (0.77) above the market. On the log scale of the figure, this corresponds to Fama and French's report that the HML average return is about double (precisely, $2^{0.62+0.77} = 2.6$ times) that of the market. However, over the entire sample of the plot, the HML portfolio starts and ends at the same place and so earns almost exactly the same as the market. From 1990 to now, the HML portfolio loses about one-half relative to the market, meaning an investor in the market has increased his or her money one and a half times as much as an HML investor. (The actual number is 0.77 so the market return is $2^{0.77} = 1.71$ times better than the HML return.)

Among other worries, if the average returns decline right after publication it suggests that the anomalies may simply have been overlooked by a large fraction of investors. As they move in, prices go up further, helping the apparent anomaly for a while. But once a large number of investors have moved in to include small and value stocks in their portfolios, the anomalous high average returns disappear.

However, average returns are hard to measure. There have been previous 10- to 20-year periods in which small stocks did very badly, for example the 1950s, and similar decade-long variations in the HML premium. Also, since SMB and HML have a beta of essentially zero on the market, *any* upward trend is a violation of the CAPM and says that investors can improve their overall mean–variance trade-off by taking on some of the HML or SMB portfolio.

Macroeconomic factors

I focus on the size and value factors because they provide the most empirically successful multifactor model and have attracted much industry as well as academic attention. Several authors have used macroeconomic variables as factors. This procedure examines directly whether stock performance during bad macroeconomic times determines average returns. Jagannathan and Wang (1996) and Reyfman (1997) use labour income; Chen, Roll and Ross (1986) look at industrial production and inflation among other variables; and Cochrane (1996) looks at investment growth. All these authors find that average returns line up with betas calculated using the macroeconomic indicators. The factors are theoretically easier to motivate, but none explains the value and size portfolios as well as the (theoretically less solid, so far) size and value factors.

Merton's (1973, 1971) theory says that variables which predict market returns should show up as factors that explain cross-sectional variation in average returns. Campbell (1996) is the lone test I know of to directly address this question. Cochrane (1996) and Jagannathan and Wang (1996) perform related tests in that they include 'scaled return' factors, for example, market return at t multiplied by d/p ratio at $t - 1$; they find that these factors are also important in understanding cross-sectional variation in average returns.

The next step is to link these more fundamentally determined factors with the empirically more successful value and small-firm factor portfolios. Because of measurement difficulties and selection biases, fundamentally determined macroeconomic factors will never approach the empirical performance of portfolio-based factors. However, they may help to explain which portfolio-based factors really work and why.

PREDICTABLE RETURNS

The view that risky asset returns are largely unpredictable, or that prices follow 'random walks', remains immensely successful (Malkiel, 1990, is a classic and readable introduction). It is also widely ignored.

Unpredictable returns mean that if stocks went up yesterday, there is no exploitable tendency for them to decline today because of 'profit taking' or to continue to rise today because of 'momentum'. 'Technical' signals, including analysis of past price movements trading volume, open interest and so on are close to useless for forecasting short-term gains and losses. As I write, value funds are reportedly suffering large outflows because their stocks have done poorly in the last few months, leading fund investors to move money into blue-chip funds that have performed better (New York Times Company, 1999). Unpredictable returns mean that this strategy will not do anything for investors' portfolios over the long run except rack up trading costs. If funds are selling stocks, then contrarian investors must be buying them, but unpredictable returns mean that this strategy cannot improve performance either. If one cannot systematically make money, one cannot systematically lose money either.

As discussed in the introduction, researchers once believed that stock returns (more precisely, the excess returns on stocks over short-term interest rates) were completely unpredictable. It now turns out that average returns on the market and individual securities *do* vary over time and that stock returns *are* predictable. Alas for would-be technical traders, much of that predictability comes at long horizons and seems to be associated with business cycles and financial distress.

Market returns

Table 17.1 presents a regression that forecasts returns. Low prices – relative to dividends, book value, earnings, sales or other divisors – predict higher subsequent returns. As the R^2 values in Table 17.1 show, these are long-horizon effects: annual returns are only slightly predictable and month-to-month returns are still strikingly unpredictable, but returns at five-year horizons seem very predictable. (Fama and French, 1989, is an excellent reference for this kind of regression.)

The results at different horizons are reflections of a single underlying phenomenon. If daily returns are very slightly predictable by a slow-moving variable, that predictability adds up over long horizons. For example, you can predict that the temperature in Chicago will rise about one-third of a degree per day in Spring. This forecast explains very little of the day-to-day variation in temperature, but tracks almost all of the rise in temperature from January to July. Thus, the R^2 rises with horizon.

Precisely, suppose that we forecast returns with a forecasting variable x, according to:

$$R_{t+1} - R_{t+1}^{TB} = a + bx_t + \varepsilon_{t+1} \tag{1}$$

$$x_{t+1} = c + \rho x_t + \delta_{t+1}. \tag{2}$$

Small values of b and R^2 in Equation (1) and a large coefficient ρ in Equation (2) imply mathematically that the long-horizon regression as in Table 17.1 has a large regression coefficient b and large R^2.

This regression has a powerful implication: stocks are in many ways like bonds. Any bond investor understands that a string of good past returns that pushes the price up is bad news for subsequent returns. Many stock investors see a string of good past returns and become elated that we seem to be in a 'bull market', concluding future stock returns will be good as well. The regression reveals the opposite: a string of good past returns which drives up stock prices is bad news for subsequent stock returns, as it is for bonds.

Table 17.1 ● OLS regression of excess returns on price/dividend ratio

Horizon k	b	Standard error	R^2
1 year	−1.04	0.33	0.17
2 years	−2.04	0.66	0.26
3 years	−2.84	0.88	0.38
5 years	−6.22	1.24	0.59

Notes: OLS regressions of excess returns (value-weighted NYSE–Treasury bill rate) on value-weighted price/dividend ratio.

$$R_{t \to t+k}^{VW} - R_{t \to t+k}^{TB} = a + b(P_t/D_t) + \varepsilon_{t+k}.$$

$R_{t \to t+k}$ indicates the k year return. Standard errors use GMM to correct for heteroskedasticity and serial correlation.

Long-horizon return predictability was first documented in the volatility tests of Shiller (1981) and LeRoy and Porter (1981). They found that stock prices vary far too much to be accounted for by changing expectations of subsequent cash flows; thus changing discount rates or expected returns must account for variation in stock prices. These volatility tests turn out to be almost identical to regressions such as those in Table 17.1 (Cochrane, 1991).

Momentum and reversal

Since a string of good returns gives a high price, it is not surprising that individual stocks that do well for a long time (and reach a high price) subsequently do poorly, and stocks that do poorly for a long time (and reach a low price, market value or market to book ratio) subsequently do well. Table 17.2, taken from Fama and French (1996) confirms this hunch. (Also, see DeBont and Thaler, 1985, and Jegadeesh and Titman, 1993.)

The first row in Table 17.2 tracks the average monthly return from the *reversal* strategy. Each month, allocate all stocks to ten portfolios based on performance from year –5 to year –1. Then, buy the best-performing portfolio and short the worst-performing portfolio. This strategy earns a hefty –0.74 per cent monthly return.[4] Past long-term losers come back and past winners do badly. Fama and French (1996) verify that these portfolio returns are explained by their three-factor model. Past winners move with value stocks, and so inherit the value stock premium. (To compare the strategies, the table always buys the winners and shorts the losers. In practice, of course, you buy the losers and short the winners to earn +0.71 per cent monthly average return.)

The second row of Table 17.2 tracks the average monthly return from a *momentum* strategy. Each month, allocate all stocks to ten portfolios based on

Table 17.2 ● Average monthly returns, reversal and momentum strategies

Strategy	Period	Portfolio formation (months)	Average return, 10–1 (monthly %)
Reversal	July 1963–Dec. 1993	60–13	–0.74
Momentum	July 1963–Dec. 1993	12–2	+1.31
Reversal	Jan. 1931–Feb. 1963	60–13	–1.61
Momentum	Jan. 1931–Feb. 1963	12–2	+0.38

Notes: Each month, allocate all NYSE firms to ten portfolios based on their performance during the 'portfolio formation months' interval. For example, 60–13 forms portfolios based on returns from 5 years ago to 1 year, 1 month ago. Then buy the best-performing decile portfolio and short the worst-performing decile portfolio.

Source: Fama and French (1996, Table 6)

performance in the last *year*. Now, the winners continue to win and the losers continue to lose, so that buying the winners and shorting the losers generates a positive 1.31 per cent monthly return.

Momentum is not explained by the Fama–French (1996) three-factor model. The past losers have low prices and tend to move with value stocks. Hence, the model predicts that they should have high average returns, not low average returns.

Momentum stocks move together, as do value and small stocks, so a 'momentum factor' works to 'explain' momentum portfolio returns (Carhart, 1997). This step is so obviously ad hoc (that is, an APT factor that will only explain returns of portfolios organized on the same characteristic as the factor rather than a proxy for macroeconomic risk) that most people are uncomfortable adding it. We obviously do not want to add a new factor for every anomaly.

Is momentum really there, and if so, is it exploitable after transaction costs? One warning is that it does not seem stable over subsamples. The third and fourth lines in Table 17.2 show that the momentum effect essentially disappears in the earlier data sample, while reversal is even stronger in that sample.

Momentum is really just a new way of looking at an old phenomenon, the small apparent predictability of monthly individual stock returns. A tiny regression R^2 for forecasting monthly returns of 0.0025 (0.25 per cent) is more than adequate to generate the momentum results of Table 17.2. The key is the large standard deviation of individual stock returns, typically 40 per cent or more on an annual basis. The average return of the best performing decile of a normal distribution is 1.76 standard deviations above the mean,[5] so the winning momentum portfolio went up about 80 per cent in the previous year and the typical losing portfolio went down about 60 per cent. Only a small amount of continuation will give a 1 per cent monthly return when multiplied by such large past returns. To be precise, the monthly individual stock standard deviation is about $40\%/\sqrt{12} \approx 12\%$. If the R^2 is 0.0025, the standard deviation of the predictable part of returns is $\sqrt{0.0025} \times 12\% \approx 0.6\%$. Hence, the decile predicted to perform best will earn $1.76 \times 0.6\% \approx 1\%$ above the mean. Since the strategy buys the winners and shorts the losers, an R^2 of 0.0025 implies that one should earn a 2 per cent monthly return by the momentum strategy.

We have known at least since Fama (1965) that monthly and higher frequency stock returns have slight, statistically significant predictability with R^2 about 0.01. Campbell, Lo and MacKinlay (1997, Table 2.4) provide an updated summary of index autocorrelations (the R^2 is the squared autocorrelation), part of which I show in Table 17.3. Note the correlation of the equally weighted portfolio, which emphasizes small stocks.[6]

However, such small, though statistically significant, high-frequency predictability has thus far failed to yield exploitable profits after one takes into

Table 17.3 ● First-order autocorrelation, CRSP value-weighted and equally weighted index returns

Frequency	Portfolio	Correlation ρ_1
Daily	Value-weighted	0.18
	Equally weighted	0.35
Monthly	Value-weighted	0.043
	Equally weighted	0.17

Note: Sample 1962–94.

Source: Campbell, Lo and MacKinlay (1997)

account transaction costs, thin trading of small stocks, and high short-sale costs. The momentum strategy for exploiting this correlation may not work in practice for the same reasons. Momentum does require frequent trading. The portfolios in Table 17.2 are re-formed every month. Annual winners and losers will not change that often, but the winning and losing portfolio must be turned over at least once per year. In a quantitative examination of this effect, Carhart (1997) concludes that momentum is not exploitable after transaction costs are taken into account. Moskowitz and Grinblatt (1999) note that most of the apparent gains from the momentum strategy come from short positions in small illiquid stocks. They also find that a large part of momentum profits come from short positions taken in November. Many investors sell losing stocks toward the end of December to establish tax losses. By shorting illiquid losing stocks in November, an investor can profit from the selling pressure in December. This is also an anomaly, but it seems like a glitch rather than a central principle of risk and return in asset markets.

Even if momentum and reversal are real and as strong as indicated by Table 17.2, they do not justify much of the trading based on past results that many investors seem to do. To get the 1 per cent per month momentum return, one buys a portfolio that has typically gone up 80 per cent in the last year, and shorts a portfolio that has typically gone down 60 per cent. Trading between stocks and fund categories such as value and blue-chip with smaller past returns yields at best proportionally smaller results. Since much of the momentum return seems to come from shorting small illiquid stocks, mild momentum strategies may yield even less. And we have not quantified the substantial risk of momentum strategies.

BONDS

The venerable expectations model of the term structure specifies that long-term bond yields are equal to the average of expected future short-term bond yields (see Figure 17.8). For example, if long-term bond yields are higher than short-term bond yields – if the yield curve is upward sloping – this means that short-term rates are expected to rise in the future. The rise in future short-term rates means that investors can expect the same rate of return whether they hold a long-term bond to maturity or roll over short-term bonds with initially low returns and subsequent higher returns.

As with the CAPM and the view that stock returns are independent over time, a new round of research has significantly modified this traditional view of bond markets.

Table 17.4 calculates the average return on bonds of different maturities. The expectations hypothesis seems to do pretty well. Average holding period returns do not seem very different across bond maturities, despite the increasing standard deviation of longer-maturity bond returns. The small increase in average returns for long-term bonds, equivalent to a slight average upward slope in the yield curve, is usually excused as a 'liquidity premium'. Table 17.4 is just the tip of an iceberg of successes for the expectations model. Especially

---

Let $p_t^{(N)}$ denote the log of the N year discount bond price at time t. The N period continuously compounded yield is defined by

$$y_t^{(N)} = -\frac{1}{N} p_t^{(N)}.$$

The continuously compounded holding period return is the selling price less the buying price, $hpr_{t+1}^{(N)} = p_{t+1}^{(N-1)} - p_t^{(N)}$. The forward rate is the rate at which an investor can contract today to borrow money $N-1$ years from now, and repay that money N years from now. Since an investor can synthesize a forward contract from discount bonds, the forward rate is determined from discount bond prices by:

$$f_t^{(N)} = p_t^{(N-1)} - p_t^{(N)}.$$

The 'spot rate' refers, by contrast with a forward rate, to the yield on any bond for which the investor take immediate delivery. Forward rates are typically higher than spot rates when the yield curve rises, since the yield is the average of intervening forward rates:

$$y_t^{(N)} = \frac{1}{N} \left(f_t^{(1)} + f_t^{(2)} + f_t^{(3)} + \ldots + f_t^{(N)} \right).$$

The expectations hypothesis states that the expected log or continuously compounded return should be the same for any bond

strategy. This statement has three mathematically equivalent expressions.

1. The forward rate should equal the expected value of the future spot rate:

$$f_t^{(N)} = E_t \left(y_{t+N-1}^{(1)} \right).$$

2. The expected holding period return should be the same on bonds of any maturity:

$$E_t \left(hpr_{t+1}^{(N)} \right) = E_t \left(hpr_{t+1}^{(M)} \right) = y_t^{(1)}.$$

3. The long-term bond yield should equal the average of the expected future short rates:

$$y_t^{(N)} = \frac{1}{N} E_t \left(y_t^{(1)} + y_{t+1}^{(1)} + \ldots + y_{t+N-1}^{(1)} \right).$$

The expectations hypothesis is often amended to allow a constant risk premium of undetermined sign in these equations. Its violation is then often described as evidence for a 'time-varying risk premium'.

The expectations hypothesis is not quite the same thing as risk-neutrality, because the expected log return is not equal to the log expected return. However, the issues here are larger than the difference between the expectations hypothesis and strict risk-neutrality.

Fig 17.8 • Bond definitions and expectations hypothesis

Table 17.4 ● Zero-coupon bond returns

Maturity N	Average holding period return	Standard error	Standard deviation
1	5.83	0.42	2.83
2	6.15	0.54	3.65
3	6.40	0.69	4.66
4	6.40	0.85	5.71
5	6.36	0.98	6.58

Note: Continuously compounded one-year holding period returns on zero-coupon bonds of varying maturity. Annual data from CRSP 1953–97.

in times of significant inflation and exchange rate instability, the expectations hypothesis has done a very good first-order job of explaining the term structure of interest rates.

However, if there are times when long-term bonds are expected to do better and other times when short-term bonds are expected to do better, the unconditional averages in Table 17.4 could still show no pattern. Similarly, one might want to check whether a forward rate that is *unusually high* forecasts an unusual *increase* in spot rates.

Table 17.5 updates Fama and Bliss's (1987) classic regression tests of this idea. Panel A presents a regression of the change in yields on the forward-spot spread. (The forward-spot spread measures the slope of the yield curve.) The expectations hypothesis predicts a slope coefficient of 1.0, since the forward rate should equal the expected future spot rate. If, for example, forward rates are lower than expected future spot rates, traders can lock in a borrowing position with a forward contract and then lend at the higher spot rate when the time comes.

Instead, at a one-year horizon we find slope coefficients near zero and a negative adjusted R^2. Forward rates one year out seem to have no predictive power whatsoever for changes in the spot rate one year from now. On the other hand, by four years out, we see slope coefficients within one standard error of 1.0. Thus, the expectations hypothesis seems to do poorly at short (one-year) horizons, but much better at longer horizons.

If the expectations hypothesis does not work at one-year horizons, then there is money to be made – one must be able to foresee years in which short-term bonds will return more than long-term bonds and vice versa, at least to some extent. To confirm this implication, panel B of Table 17.5 runs regressions of the one-year excess return on long-term bonds on the forward-spot spread. Here, the expectations hypothesis predicts a coefficient of zero: no signal (including the forward-spot spread) should be able to tell you that this is

Table 17.5 ● Forecasts based on forward-spot spread

	A.		Change in yields			B.		Holding period returns		
N	Intercept	Standard error, intercept	Slope	Standard error, slope	Adjusted R^2	Intercept	Standard error, intercept	Slope	Standard error, slope	Adjusted R^2
1	0.10	0.3	−0.10	0.36	−0.020	−0.1	0.3	1.10	0.36	0.16
2	−0.01	0.4	0.37	0.33	0.005	−0.5	0.5	1.46	0.44	0.19
3	−0.04	0.5	0.41	0.33	0.013	−0.4	0.8	1.30	0.54	0.10
4	−0.30	0.5	0.77	0.31	0.110	−0.5	1.0	1.31	0.63	0.07

Notes: OLS regressions, 1953–97 annual data. Panel A estimates the regression $y_{t+n}^{(1)} - y_t^{(1)} = a + b \, (f_t^{(N+1)} - y_t^{(1)})$ $+ \, \varepsilon_{t+N}$ and panel B estimates the regression $hpr_{t+1}^{(N)} - y_t^{(1)} = a + b \, (f_t^{(N+1)} - y_t^{(1)}) + \varepsilon_{t+1}$, where $y_t^{(M)}$ denotes the N-year bond yield at date t; $f_t^{(M)}$ denotes the N-period ahead forward rate; and $hpr_{t+1}^{(N)}$ denotes the one-year holding period return at date $t+1$ on an N-year bond. Yields and returns in annual percentages.

a particularly good time for long bonds versus short bonds, as the random walk view of stock prices says that no signal should be able to tell you that this is a particularly good or bad day for stocks versus bonds. However, the coefficients in panel B are all about 1.0. A high forward rate does not indicate that interest rates will be higher one year from now; it seems to indicate that investors will earn that much more by holding long-term bonds.[7]

Of course, there is risk. The R^2 values are all 0.1–0.2, about the same values as the R^2 from the d/p regression at a one-year horizon, so this strategy will often go wrong. Still, 0.1–0.2 is not zero, so the strategy does pay off more often than not, in violation of the expectations hypothesis. Furthermore, the forward-spot spread is a slow-moving variable, typically reversing sign once per business cycle. Thus, the R^2 builds with horizon as with the d/p regression, peaking in the 30 per cent range (Fama and French, 1989).

FOREIGN EXCHANGE

Suppose interest rates are higher in Germany than in the USA. Does this mean that one can earn more money by investing in German bonds? There are several reasons that the answer might be no. First, of course, is default risk. Governments have defaulted on bonds in the past and may do so again. Second, and more important, is the risk of devaluation. If German interest rates are 10 per cent and US interest rates are 5 per cent, but the euro falls 5 per cent relative to the dollar during the year, you make no more money holding the German bonds despite their attractive interest rate. Since lots of investors are making this calculation, it is natural to conclude that an interest rate differential across countries on bonds of similar credit risk should reveal an expectation of currency devaluation. The logic is exactly the same as that of the expectations hypothesis in the term structure. Initially attractive yield or interest rate differentials should be met by an offsetting event so that you make no more money on average in one maturity or currency versus another.[8]

As with the expectations hypothesis in the term structure, the expected depreciation view still constitutes an important first-order understanding of interest rate differentials and exchange rates. For example, interest rates in east Asian currencies were very high on the eve of the recent currency tumbles, and many banks were making tidy sums borrowing at 5 per cent in dollars to lend at 20 per cent in local currencies. This suggests that traders were anticipating a 15 per cent devaluation, or a smaller chance of a larger devaluation, which is exactly what happened. Many observers attribute high nominal interest rates in troubled economies to 'tight monetary policy' aimed at defending the currency. In reality, high nominal rates reflect a large probability of inflation and devaluation – loose monetary policy – and correspond to much lower real rates.

Still, does a 5 per cent interest rate differential correspond to a 5 per cent expected depreciation, or does some of it represent a high expected return from holding debt in that country's currency? Furthermore, while expected depreciation is clearly a large part of the interest rate story in high-inflation economies, how does the story play out in economies like the USA and Germany, where inflation rates diverge little but exchange rates still fluctuate a large amount?

The first row of Table 17.6 (from Hodrick, 2000, and Engel, 1996) shows the average appreciation of the dollar against the indicated currency over the sample period. The dollar fell against the deutschemark, yen and Swiss franc, but appreciated against the pound sterling. The second row gives the average interest rate differential – the amount by which the foreign interest rate exceeds the US interest rate.[9] According to the expectations hypothesis, these two numbers should be equal – interest rates should be higher in countries whose currencies depreciate against the dollar.

The second row shows roughly the expected pattern. Countries with steady long-term inflation have steadily higher interest rates and steady depreciation. The numbers in the first and second rows are not exactly the same, but exchange rates are notoriously volatile so these averages are not well measured. Hodrick (2000) shows that the difference between the first and second rows is not statistically different from zero. This fact is analogous to the evidence in Table 17.4 that the expectations hypothesis works well *on average* for US bonds.

As in the case of bonds, however, we can ask whether times of *temporarily* higher or lower interest rate differentials correspond to times of above- and below-average depreciation as they should. The third and fifth rows of Table 17.6 update Fama's (1984) regression tests. The number here should be +1.0 in each case – one percentage point extra interest differential should correspond to one percentage point extra expected depreciation. On the contrary, as

Table 17.6 • Forward discount puzzle

	Deutsche-mark	Pound sterling	Yen	Swiss franc
Mean appreciation	−1.8	3.6	−5.0	−3.0
Mean interest differential	−3.9	2.1	−3.7	−5.9
b, 1975–89	−3.1	−2.0	−2.1	−2.6
R^2	0.026	0.033	0.034	0.033
b, 1976–96	−0.7	−1.8	−2.4	−1.3
b, 10-year horizon	0.8	0.6	0.5	−

Notes: The first row gives the average appreciation of the dollar against the indicated currency, in per cent per year. The second row gives the average interest differential – foreign interest rate less domestic interest rate, measured as the forward premium – the 30-day forward rate less the spot exchange rate. The third to sixth rows give the coefficients and R^2 in a regression of exchange rate changes on the interest differential:

$$s_{t+1} - s_t = a + b\,(r_t^f - r_t^d) + \varepsilon_{t+1},$$

where

s = log spot exchange rate,
r_f = foreign interest rate, and
r^d = domestic interest rate.

Source: Hodrick (2000), Engel (1996) and Meredith and Chinn (1998)

Table 17.6 shows, a higher than usual interest rate abroad seems to lead to further *appreciation*. This is the *forward discount puzzle*. See Engel (1996) and Lewis (1995) for recent surveys of the avalanche of academic work investigating whether this puzzle is really there and why.

The R^2 values shown in Table 17.6 are quite low. However, like d/p and the term spread, the interest differential is a slow-moving forecasting variable, so the return forecast R^2 builds with horizon. Bekaert and Hodrick (1992) report that the R^2 rises to the 30 per cent to 40 per cent range at six-month horizons and then declines. That's high, but not 100 per cent; taking advantage of any predictability strategy is quite risky.

The puzzle does *not* say that one earns more by holding bonds from countries with higher interest rates than others. Average inflation, depreciation and interest rate differentials line up as they should. The puzzle *does* say that one earns more by holding bonds from countries whose interest rates are *higher than usual* relative to US interest rates (and vice versa). The fact that the 'usual' rate of depreciation and interest differential changes through time will, of course, diminish the out-of-sample performance of these trading rules.

One might expect that exchange rate depreciation works better for long-run exchange rates, as the expectations hypothesis works better for long-run interest rate changes. The last row of Table 17.6, taken from Meredith and Chinn (1998) verifies that this is so. Ten-year exchange rate changes are correctly forecast by the interest differentials of ten-year bonds.

MUTUAL FUNDS

Studying the returns of funds that follow a specific strategy gives us a way to assess whether that strategy works in practice, after transaction costs and other trading realities are taken into account. Studying the returns of actively managed funds tells us whether the time, talent and effort put into picking securities pays off. Most of the literature on evaluating fund performance is devoted to the latter question.

A large body of empirical work, starting with Jensen (1969), finds that actively managed funds, on average, underperform the market index. I use data from Carhart (1997), whose measures of fund performance account for *survivor bias*. Survivor bias arises because funds that do badly go out of business. Therefore, the average fund that is alive at any point in time has an artificially good track record.

As with the stock portfolios in Figure 17.2, the fund data in Figure 17.9 show a definite correlation between beta and average return: funds that did well took on more market risks. A cross-sectional regression line is a bit flatter than the line drawn through the Treasury bill and market return, but this is a typical result of measurement error in the betas. (The data are annual, and many funds are only around for a few years, contributing to beta measurement error.) The average fund underperforms the line connecting Treasury bills and the market index by 1.23 per cent per year (that is, the average alpha is –1.23 per cent).

The wide dispersion in fund average returns in Figure 17.9 is a bit surprising. Average returns vary across funds almost as much as they do across individual stocks. This fact implies that the majority of funds are *not* holding well-diversified portfolios that would reduce return variation, but rather are loading up on specific bets.

Initially, the fact that the *average* fund underperforms the market seems beside the point. Perhaps the average fund is bad, but we want to know whether the good funds are any good. The trouble is, we must somehow distinguish skill from luck. The only way to separate skill from luck is to group funds based on some *ex ante* observable characteristic, and then examine the average performance of the group. Of course, skilful funds should have done better, on average, in the past, and should continue to do better in the future. Thus, if there is skill in stock picking, we should see some persistence in fund performance. However, a generation of empirical work found no persistence at all. Funds that did well in the past were no more likely to do well in the future.

Since the average fund underperforms the market, and fund returns are not predictable, we conclude that active management does not generate superior performance, especially after transaction costs and fees. This fact is surprising. Professionals in almost any field do better than amateurs. One would expect that a trained experienced professional who spends all day reading about markets and

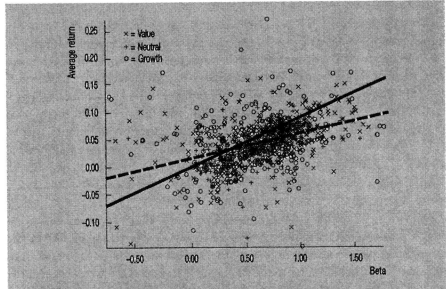

Notes: Average returns of mutual funds over the Treasury bill rate versus their market betas. Sample consists of all funds with average total net assets greater than $25 million and more than 25 per cent of their assets in stocks, in the Carhart (1996) database. Data sample 1962–96. The average excess return is computed as $E(R^i - R^f) = a_i + \beta_i \times 9\%$. a_i and β_i are computed from a time-series regression of fund annual excess returns on market annual excess returns over the life of the fund. The o, + and x labels in the figure sort funds into thirds based on their regression coefficient h on the Fama–French value (HML) portfolio. The breakpoints are $h = -0.084, 0.34$. The dashed line gives the fit of a cross-sectional ordinary least squares regression of a_i on β_i; the solid line connects the Treasury bill (β and excess return = 0) and the market return (β = 1, excess return = 9%).

Fig 17.9 • Average returns of mutual funds versus market betas

stocks should be able to outperform simple indexing strategies. Even if entry into the industry is so easy that the *average* fund does not outperform simple indexes one would expect a few stars to outperform year after year, as good teams win championship after championship. Alas, the contrary fact is the result of practically every investigation, and even the anomalous results document very small effects.

Funds and value

Given the value, small-firm and predictability effects, the idea that funds cluster around the market line is quite surprising. All of these new facts imply inescapably that there are simple, mechanical strategies that can give a risk/reward ratio greater than that of buying and holding the market index. Fama and French (1993) report that the HML portfolio alone gives nearly double the market Sharpe ratio – the same average return at half the standard deviation. Why don't funds cluster around a risk/reward line significantly above the market's?

Of course, we should not expect *all* funds to cluster around a higher risk/reward trade-off. The average investor holds the market, and if funds are large enough, so must the average fund. Index funds, of course, will perform like the index. Still, the typical actively managed fund advertises high mean and, perhaps, low variance. No fund advertises cutting average returns in half to spare investors exposure to nonmarket sources of risk. Such funds, apparently aimed at mean–variance investors, should cluster around the highest risk/reward trade-off available from mechanical strategies (and more, if active management does any good). Most troubling, funds who *say* they follow value strategies don't outperform the market either. For example, Lakonishok, Shleifer and Vishny (1992, Table 3) find that the average value fund underperforms the S&P500 by 1 per cent just like all the others.

We can resolve this contradiction if we think that fund managers were simply unaware of the possibilities offered by our new facts, and so (despite the advertising) were not really following them. That seems to be the implication of Figure 17.9, which sorts funds by their HML beta. One would expect the high-HML beta funds to outperform the market line. But the cut-off for the top one-third of funds is only a HML beta of 0.3, and even that may be high (many funds don't last long, so betas are poorly measured; the distribution of measured betas is wider than the actual distribution). Thus, the 'value funds' were really not following the 'value strategy' that earns the HML returns; if they were doing so they would have HML betas of 1.0. Similarly, Lakonishok, Shleifer and Vishny's (1992) documentation of value funds' underperformance reveals that their market beta is close to 1.0. These results imply that value funds are not really following a value strategy, since their returns correlate with the market portfolio and not the value portfolio.

Interestingly, the number of value and small-cap funds (as revealed by their betas, not their marketing claims) is increasing quickly. Before 1990, 14 per cent of funds had measured SMB betas greater than 1.0, and 12 per cent had HML betas greater than 1.0. In the full sample, both numbers have *doubled* to 22 per cent and 23 per cent. This trend suggests that funds will, in the future, be much less well described by the market index.

The view that funds were unaware of value strategies, and are now moving quickly to exploit them, can explain why most funds still earn near the market return, rather than the higher value return. However, this view contradicts the view that the value premium is an equilibrium risk premium, that is, that everyone knew about the value returns but chose not to invest all along because they feared the risks of value strategies. If it is not an equilibrium risk premium, it won't last long.

Persistence in fund returns

The fund counterpart to momentum in stock returns has been more extensively investigated than the value and size effects. Fund returns have also been
found to be persistent. Since such persistence can be interpreted as evidence
for persistent skill in picking stocks, it is not surprising that it has attracted a
great deal of attention, starting with Hendricks, Patel and Zeckhauser (1993).

Table 17.7, taken from Carhart (1997), shows that a portfolio of the best-performing one-thirtieth of funds last year outperforms a portfolio of the
worst-performing one-thirtieth of funds by 1 per cent per month (column 2).
This is about the same size as the momentum effect in stocks, and similarly
results from a small autocorrelation plus a large standard deviation in individual
fund returns. This result verifies that mutual fund performance is persistent.

Table 17.7 • Portfolios of mutual funds formed on previous year's return

Last year rank	Average return	CAPM alpha	4-factor alpha
	(---------------------- per cent ------------------)		
1/30	0.75	0.27	−0.11
1/10	0.68	0.22	−0.12
5/10	0.38	−0.05	−0.14
9/10	0.23	−0.21	−0.20
10/10	0.01	−0.45	−0.40
30/30	−0.25	−0.74	−0.64

Notes: Each year, mutual funds are sorted into portfolios based on the previous year's return. The rank
column gives the rank of the selected portfolio. For example, 1/30 is the best performing portfolio when
funds are divided into 30 categories. Average return gives the average monthly return in excess of the T-bill
rate of this portfolio of funds for the following year. Four-factor alpha gives the average return less the
predictions of a multifactor model that uses the market, the Fama–French HML and SMB portfolios, and
portfolio PR1YR which is long NYSE stocks that did well in the last year and short NYSE stocks that did
poorly in the last year.

Source: Carhart (1997)

Perhaps the funds that did well took on more market risks, raising their betas
and, hence, average returns in the following year. The third column in Table
17.7 shows that this is not the case. The cross-sectional variation in fund
average returns has nothing to do with market betas. Just as in the case of individual stock returns, we have to understand fund returns with multifactor
models, if at all.

The last column of Table 17.7 presents alphas (intercepts, the part of average return not explained by the model) from a model with four factors – the market, the Fama–French HML and SMB factors, and a momentum factor, PR1YR, that is long NYSE stocks that did well in the last year and short NYSE stocks that did poorly in the last year. In general, one should object to the inclusion of so many factors and such ad-hoc factors. However, this is a *performance attribution* rather than an *economic explanation* use of a multi-factor model. We want to know whether fund performance, and persistence in fund performance in particular, is due to persistent stock-picking skill or to mechanical strategies that investors could just as easily follow on their own, without paying the management costs associated with investing through a fund. For this purpose, it does not matter whether the 'factors' represent true, underlying sources of macroeconomic risks.

The alphas in the last column of Table 17.7 are almost all about 1 per cent to 2 per cent per year negative. Thus, Carhart's model explains that the persistence in fund performance is due to persistence in the underlying stocks, not persistent stock-picking skill. These results support the old conclusion that actively managed funds underperform mechanical indexing strategies. There is some remaining puzzling persistence, but it is all in the large *negative* alphas of the bottom one-tenth to bottom one-thirtieth of performers, which lose money year after year. Carhart also shows that the persistence of fund performance is due to momentum in the underlying stocks, rather than momentum funds. If, by good luck, a fund happened to pick stocks that went up last year, the portfolio will continue to go up a bit this year.

In sum, the new research does nothing to dispel the disappointing view of active management. However, we discover that passively managed 'style' portfolios can earn returns that are not explained by the CAPM.

Catastrophe insurance

A number of prominent funds have earned very good returns (and others, spectacular losses) by following strategies such as *convergence trades* and implicit *put options*. These strategies may also reflect high average returns as compensation for nonmarket dimensions of risk. They have not been examined at the same level of detail as the value and small-cap strategies, so I offer a possible interpretation rather than a documented one.

Convergence trades take strong positions in very similar securities that have small price differences. For example, a 29.5-year Treasury bond typically trades at a slightly higher yield (lower price) than a 30-year Treasury bond. (This was the most famous bet placed by LTCM. See Lewis, 1999.) A convergence trade puts a strong short position on the expensive security and a strong long position on the cheap security. This strategy is often mislabelled an 'arbitrage'.

However, the securities are similar, not identical. The spread between 29.5- and 30-year Treasury bonds reflects the lower liquidity of the shorter maturity and the associated difficulty of selling it in a financial panic. It is possible for this spread to widen. Nonetheless, panics are rare, and the average returns in all the years when they do not happen may more than make up for the spectacular losses when they do.

Put options protect investors from large price declines. The *volatility smile* in put option prices reflects the surprisingly high prices of such options, compared with the small probability of large market collapses (even when one calibrates the probability directly, rather than using the log-normal distribution of the Black–Scholes formula). Writers of out-of-the-money puts collect a fee every month; in a rare market collapse they will pay out a huge sum, but if the probability of the collapse is small enough, the average returns may be quite good.

All of these strategies can be thought of as *catastrophe insurance* (Hsieh and Fung, 1999). Most of the time they earn a small premium. Once in a great while they lose a lot, and they lose a lot in times of financial catastrophe, when most investors are really anxious that the value of their investments does not evaporate. Therefore, it is economically plausible that these strategies can earn positive average returns, even when we account for stock market risk via the CAPM and we correctly measure the small probabilities of large losses.

The difficulty in empirically estimating the true average return of such strategies, of course, is that rare events are rare. Many long samples will give a false sense of security because 'the big one' that justifies the premium happened not to hit.

The value, yield curve and foreign exchange strategies I survey above also exhibit features of catastrophe insurance. Value stocks may earn high returns because distressed stocks will all go bankrupt in a financial panic. Buying bonds of countries with high interest rates leaves one open to the small chance of a large devaluation, and such devaluation is especially likely to happen in a global financial panic. Similarly, buying long-term bonds in the depth of a recession when the yield curve is upward sloping may expose one to a small risk of a large inflation.

If these interpretations bear out, they also suggest that the premiums – the average returns from holding stocks sensitive to HML or from following the bond and foreign exchange strategies – may be overstated in the data. The markets have had an unusually good 50 years, and devastating financial panics have not happened.

IMPLICATIONS OF THE NEW FACTS

While the list of new facts appears long, similar patterns show up in every case. Prices reveal slow moving market expectations of subsequent returns, because potential offsetting events seem sluggish or absent. The patterns suggest that investors can earn substantial average returns by taking on the risks of recession and financial stress. In addition, there is a small positive autocorrelation of high-frequency returns.

The effects are not completely new. We have known since the 1960s that high-frequency returns are slightly predictable, with R^2 of 0.01 to 0.1 in daily to monthly returns. These effects were dismissed because there didn't seem to be much one could do about them. A 51/49 bet is not very attractive, especially if there is any transaction cost. Also, the increased Sharpe ratio (mean excess return/standard deviation) from exploiting predictability is directly related to the forecast R^2, so a tiny R^2, even if exploitable, did not seem important. Now, we have a greater understanding of the potential importance of these effects and their economic interpretations.

For price effects, we now realize that the R^2 rises with horizon when the forecasting variables are slow-moving. Hence, a small R^2 at short horizons can mean a really substantial R^2 in the 30 per cent to 50 per cent range at longer horizons. Also, the nature of these effects suggests the kinds of additional sources of priced risk that theorists had anticipated for 20 years. For momentum effects, the ability to sort stocks and funds into momentum-based portfolios means that very small predictability times portfolios with huge past returns gives important subsequent returns, though it is not totally clear that this amplification of the small predictability really does survive transaction costs.

Price-based forecasts

If expected returns rise, prices are driven down, since future dividends or other cash flows are discounted at a higher rate. A 'low' price, then, can *reveal* a market expectation of a high expected or required return.[10]

Most of our results come from this effect. Low price/dividend, price/earnings or price/book value signal times when the market as a whole will have high average returns. Low market value (price times shares) relative to book value signals securities or portfolios that earn high average returns. The 'small-firm' effect derives from low prices – other measures of size such as number of employees or book value alone have no predictive power for returns (Berk, 1997). The 'five-year reversal' effect derives from the fact that five years of poor returns lead to a low price. A high long-term bond yield means that the price of long-term bonds is 'low' and this seems to signal a time of good long-term bond returns. A high foreign interest rate means a low price on foreign bonds, and this seems to indicate good returns on the foreign bonds.

The most natural interpretation of all these effects is that the expected or required return – the risk premium – on individual securities as well as the market as a whole varies slowly over time. Thus we can track market expectations of returns by watching price/dividend, price/earnings or book/market ratios.

Absent offsetting events

In each case, an apparent difference in yield should give rise to an offsetting movement, but does not seem to do so. Something *should* be predictable so that returns are *not* predictable, and it is not. Figure 17.10 provides a picture of the results in Table 17.5. Suppose that the yield curve is upward sloping as in panel A. What does this mean? If the expectations model were true, the forward rates plotted against maturity would translate one for one to the forecast of future spot rates in panel B, as plotted in the black line marked 'Expectations model'. A high long-term bond yield relative to short-term bond yields should not mean a higher expected long-term bond return. Subsequent

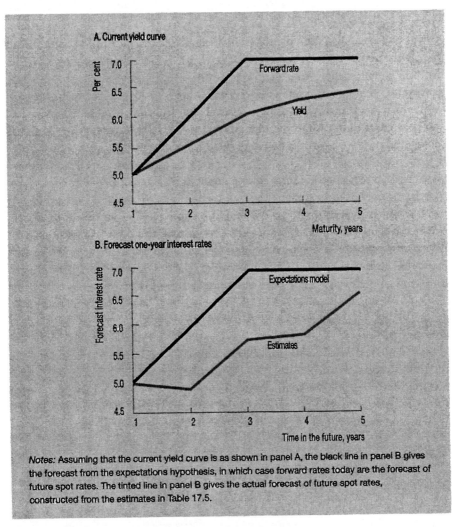

Notes: Assuming that the current yield curve is as shown in panel A, the black line in panel B gives the forecast from the expectations hypothesis, in which case forward rates today are the forecast of future spot rates. The tinted line in panel B gives the actual forecast of future spot rates, constructed from the estimates in Table 17.5.

Fig 17.10 ● Yield curve and forecast one-year interest rates

short rates should rise, cutting off the one-period advantage of long-term bonds and raising the multi-year advantage of short-term bonds.

In Figure 17.10, panel B, the line marked 'Estimates' shows the actual forecast of future spot interest rates from the results in Table 17.5. The essence of the phenomenon is *sluggish adjustment* of the short rates. The short rates do eventually rise to meet the forward rate forecasts, but not as quickly as the forward rates predict they should. Short-term yields *should* be forecastable so that returns are *not* forecastable. In fact, yields are almost unforecastable, so, mechanically, bond returns are. The roughly 1.0 coefficients in panel B of Table 17.5 mean that a 1 percentage point increase in the forward rate translates into a 1 percentage point increase in expected return. It seems that old fallacy of confusing bond *yields* with their expected *returns* for the first year contains a grain of truth.

In the same way, a high dividend yield on a stock or portfolio should mean that dividends grow more slowly over time, or, for individual stocks, that the firm has taken on more market risk and will have a higher market beta. These tendencies seem to be completely absent. Dividend/price ratios do not seem to forecast dividend growth and, hence (mechanically) they forecast returns. The one-year coefficient in Table 17.1 is very close to 1.00, meaning that a 1 percentage point increase in the dividend yield translates into a 1 percentage point increase in return. It seems that the old fallacy of confusing increased dividend yield with increased total return does contain a grain of truth.

A high foreign interest rate relative to domestic interest rates should not mean a higher expected return. We should see, on average, an offsetting depreciation. But here, the coefficients are even larger than 1.0. An interest rate differential seems to predict a further *appreciation*. It seems that the old fallacy of confusing interest rate differentials across countries with expected returns, forgetting about depreciation, also contains a grain of truth.

Economic interpretation

The price-based predictability patterns suggest a premium for holding risks related to recession and economy-wide financial distress. Stock and bond predictability are linked: the term spread (forward-spot or long yield–short yield) forecasts stock returns as well as bond returns (Fama and French, 1989). Furthermore, the term spread is one of the best variables for forecasting business cycles. It rises steeply at the bottom of recessions and is inverted at the top of a boom. Return forecasts are high at the bottom of a business cycle and low at the top of a boom. Value and small-cap stocks are typically distressed. Empirically successful economic models of the recession and distress premiums are still in their infancy (Campbell and Cochrane, 1999, is a start), but the story is at least plausible and the effects have been expected by theorists for a generation.

To make this point come to life, think concretely about what you have to do to take advantage of the predictability strategies. You have to buy stocks or long-term bonds at the bottom, when stock prices are low after a long and depressing bear market, in the bottom of a recession or the peak of a financial panic. This is a time when few people have the guts or the wallet to buy risky stocks or risky long-term bonds. Looking across stocks rather than over time, you have to invest in value or small-cap companies, with years of poor past returns, poor sales, or on the edge of bankruptcy. You have to buy stocks that everyone else thinks are dogs. Then, you have to sell stocks and long-term bonds in good times, when stock prices are high relative to dividends, earnings, and other multiples and the yield curve is flat or inverted so that long-term bond prices are high. You have to sell the popular growth stocks, with good past returns, good sales and earnings growth.

You have to sell now, and the stocks that you should sell are the blue-chips that everyone else seems to be buying. In fact, the market timing strategies said to sell long ago; if you did so, you would have missed much of the run-up in the Dow past the 6000 point. Value stocks too have missed most of the recent market run-up. However, this shouldn't worry you – a strategy that holds risks uncorrelated with the market must underperform the market close to half of the time.

If this feels uncomfortable, what you're feeling is risk. If you're uncomfortable watching the market pass you by, perhaps you *don't* really only care about long-run mean and variance; you also care about doing well when the market is doing well. If you want to stay fully invested in stocks, perhaps you too feel the time-varying aversion to or exposure to risk that drives the average investor to stay fully invested despite low prospective returns.

This line of explanation for the foreign exchange puzzle is still a bit farther off (see Engel, 1996, for a survey; Atkeson, Alvarez and Kehoe, 1999, offer a recent stab at an explanation). The strategy leads investors to invest in countries with high interest rates. High interest rates are often a sign of monetary instability or other economic trouble, and thus may mean that the investments are more exposed to the risks of global financial stress or a global recession than are investments in the bonds of countries with low interest rates, which are typically enjoying better times.

Return correlation

Momentum and persistent fund performance explained by a momentum factor are different from the price-based predictability results. In both cases, the underlying phenomenon is a small predictability of high-frequency returns. The price-based predictability strategies make this predictability important by showing that, with a slow-moving forecasting variable, the R^2 builds over horizon. Momentum, however, is based on a fast-moving forecast variable – the previous year's return. Therefore, the R^2 declines rather than building with horizon. Momentum makes the small predictability of high-frequency returns significant in a different way, by forming portfolios of extreme winners and losers. The large volatility of returns means that the extreme portfolios will have extreme past returns, so only a small continuation of past returns gives a large current return.

It would be appealing to understand momentum as a reflection of slowly time-varying average expected returns or risk premiums, like the price-based predictability strategies. If a stock's average return rises for a while, that should make returns higher both today and tomorrow. Thus, a portfolio of past winners will contain more than its share of stocks that performed well because their average returns were higher, along with stocks that performed well due to luck. The average return of such a portfolio should be higher tomorrow as well.

Unfortunately, this story has to posit a substantially different view of the underlying process for varying expected returns than is needed to explain everything else. The trouble is that a surprise increase in expected returns means that prices will fall, since dividends are now discounted at a greater rate. This is the phenomenon we have relied on to explain why *low* price/dividend, price/earnings, book/market, value, and size forecast *higher* subsequent returns. Therefore, *positive* correlation of *expected* returns typically yields a *negative* correlation of *realized* returns. To get a positive correlation of realized returns out of slow expected return variation, you have to imagine that an increase in average returns today is either highly correlated with a decrease in expected future dividend growth or with a decrease in expected returns in the distant future (an impulse response that starts positive but is negative at long horizons). Campbell, Lo and MacKinlay (1997) provide a quantitative exposition of these effects.

Furthermore, momentum returns have not yet been linked to business cycles or financial distress in even the informal way that I suggested for price-based strategies. Thus, momentum still lacks a plausible economic interpretation. To me, this adds weight to the view that it isn't there, it isn't exploitable, or it represents a small illiquidity (tax-loss selling of small illiquid stocks) that will be quickly remedied once a few traders understand it.

Remaining doubts

The size of all these effects is still somewhat in question. It is always hard to measure average returns of risky strategies. The standard formula $\sigma/\sqrt{T}$ for the standard error of the mean, together with the high volatility σ of any strategy, means that one needs 25 years of data to even start to measure average returns. With $\sigma = 16$ per cent (typical of the index), even $T = 25$ years means that one standard error is $16/5 \cong 3$ per cent per year, and a two-standard error confidence interval runs plus or minus 6 percentage points. This is not much smaller than the average returns we are trying to measure. In addition, all of these facts are highly influenced by the small probability of rare events, which makes measuring average returns even harder.

Finally, viewed the right way, we have very few data points with which to evaluate predictability. The term premium and interest rate differentials only change sign with the business cycle, and the dividend/price ratio only crosses its mean once every generation. The history of interest rates and inflation in the US is dominated by the increase, through two recessions, to a peak in 1980 and then a slow decline after that.

Many of the anomalous risk premiums seem to be declining over time. Figure 17.7 shows the decline in the HML and SMB premiums, and the same may be true of the predictability effects. The last three years of high market returns have cut the estimated return predictability from the dividend/price ratio in *half*. This fact suggests that at least some of the premium the new strategies yielded in the past was due to the fact that they were simply overlooked.

Was it really clear to average investors in 1947 or 1963 (the beginning of the data samples) that stocks would earn 9 per cent over bonds, and that the strategy of buying distressed small stocks would double even that return for the same level of risk? Would average investors have changed their portfolios with this knowledge? Or would they have stayed put, explaining that these returns are earned as a reward for risk that they were not willing to take? Was it clear that buying stocks at the bottom in the mid-1970s would yield so much more than even that high average return? If we interpret the premiums measured in sample as true risk premiums, the answer must be yes. If the answer is no, then at least some part of the premium was luck and will disappear in the future.

Since the premiums are hard to measure, one is tempted to put less emphasis on them. However, they are crucial to our interpretation of the facts. The CAPM is perfectly consistent with the fact that there are additional sources of *common* variation. For example, it was long understood that stocks in the same industry move together; the fact that value or small stocks also move together need not cause a ripple. The surprise is that investors seem to earn an average return premium for holding these additional sources of common movement, whereas the CAPM predicts that (given beta) they should have no effect on a portfolio's average returns.

The behaviour of funds also suggests the 'over-looked strategy' interpretation. As explained earlier, fund returns still cluster around the market line. It turns out that very few fund returns actually followed the value or other return-enhancing strategies. However, the number of small, value and related funds – funds that actually do follow the strategies – has increased dramatically in recent years. It might be possible to explain this in a way consistent with the idea that investors knew the premiums were there all along, but such an argument is obviously strained.

CONCLUSION

In sum, it now seems that investors can earn a substantial premium for holding dimensions of risk unrelated to market movements, such as recession-related or distress-related risk. Investors earn these premiums by following strategies, such as value and growth, market-timing possibilities generated by return predictability, dynamic bond and foreign exchange strategies, and maybe even a bit of momentum. The exact size of the premiums and the economic nature of the underlying risks is still a bit open to question, but researchers are unlikely to go back to the simple view that returns are independent over time and that the CAPM describes the cross section.

The next question is, What should investors do with this information? The next chapter addresses that question.

Notes

[1] The market also tends to go down in recessions; however recessions can be unusually severe or mild for a given level of market return. What counts here is the severity of the recession for a given market return. Technically, we are considering betas in a multiple regression that includes both the market return and a measure of recessions. See Figure 17.1.

[2] I thank Gene Fama for providing me with these data.

[3] The rest of the paragraph is my interpretation, not Fama and French's. They focus on the firm's financial distress, while I focus on the systematic distress, since idiosyncratic distress cannot deliver a risk price.

[4] Fama and French do not provide direct measures of standard deviations for these portfolios. One can infer, however, from the betas, R^2 values and standard deviation of the market and factor portfolios that the standard deviations are roughly one to two times that of the market return, so Sharpe ratios of these strategies are comparable to that of the market return in sample.

[5] We are looking for:

$$E(r|r \geq x) = \frac{\int_x^\infty rf(r)dr}{\int_x^\infty f(r)dr},$$

where x is defined as the top one-tenth cut-off,

$$\int_x^\infty f(r)dr = \frac{1}{10}.$$

With a normal distribution, $x = 1.2816\sigma$ and $E(r|r \geq x) = 1.755\sigma$.

[6] The index autocorrelations suffer from some upward bias since some stocks do not trade every day. Individual stock autocorrelations are generally smaller, but are enough to account for the momentum effect.

[7] Panel B is really not independent evidence, since the coefficients in panels A and B of Table 17.5 are mechanically linked. For example, $1.14 + (-0.14) = 1.0$, and this holds as an accounting identity. Fama and Bliss (1987) call them 'complementary regressions'.

[8] As with bonds, the expectations hypothesis is slightly different from pure risk neutrality since the expectation of the log is not the log of the expectation. Again, the size of the phenomena we study swamps this distinction.

[9] The data are actually the spread between the forward exchange rate and the spot exchange rate, but this quantity must equal the interest rate differential in order to preclude arbitrage.

[10] This effect is initially counterintuitive. One might suppose that a higher average return would attract investors, raising prices. But the higher prices, for a given dividend stream, must reduce subsequent average returns. High average returns persist, in equilibrium, when investors fear the increased risks of an asset and try to sell, lowering prices.

References

Atkeson, A., Alvarez, F. and Kehoe, P. (1999) 'Volatile exchange rates and the forward premium anomaly: A segmented asset market view', University of Chicago, working paper.

Banz, R. W. (1981) 'The relationship between return and market value of common stocks', *Journal of Financial Economics*, 9 (1), 3–18.

Bekaert, G. and Hodrick, R.J. (1992) 'Characterizing predictable components in excess returns on equity and foreign exchange markets', *Journal of Finance*, 47 (2), 467–509.

Berk, J. (1997) 'Does size really matter?' *Financial Analysts Journal*, 53, 12–18.

Campbell, John Y (1996) 'Understanding risk and return', *Journal of Political Economy*, 104 (2), 298–345.

Campbell, John Y. and Cochrane, J.H. (1999) 'By force of habit: A consumption-based explanation of aggregate stock market behaviour', *Journal of Political Economy*, 107 (2), 205–251.

Campbell, John Y., Lo, A.W. and MacKinlay, A.C. (1997) *The Econometrics of Financial Markets*, Princeton, NJ: Princeton University Press.

Carhart, Mark M. (1997) 'On persistence in mutual fund performance', *Journal of Finance*, 52 (1), 57–82.

Chen, Nai-Fu, Roll, R. and Ross, S.A. (1986) 'Economic forces and the stock market', *Journal of Business*, 59 (3), 383–403.

Cochrane, John H. (1997) 'Where is the market going? Uncertain facts and novel theories', *Economic Perspectives*, Federal Reserve Bank of Chicago, 21 (6), 3–37.

Cochrane, John H. (1996) 'A cross-sectional test of an investment-based asset pricing model', *Journal of Political Economy*, 104 (3), 572–621.

Cochrane, John H. (1991) 'Volatility tests and efficient markets: Review essay', *Journal of Monetary Economics*, 27 (3), 463–485.

Daniel, K., Hirshleifer, D. and Subrahmanyam, A. (1998) 'Investor psychology and security market under- and overreactions', *Journal of Finance*, 3 (6), 1839–1885.

DeBondt, Werner F.M. and Thaler, R.H. (1985) 'Does the stock market overreact?' *Journal of Finance*, 40 (3), 793–805.

Engel, Charles (1996) 'The forward discount anomaly and the risk premium: A survey of recent evidence', *Journal of Empirical Finance*, 3, 123–192.

Fama, Eugene F. (1991) 'Efficient markets II', *Journal of Finance*, 46 (5), 1575–1617.

Fama, E.F. (1984) 'Forward and spot exchange rates', *Journal of Monetary Economics*, 14 (3), 319–338.

Fama, E.F. (1970) 'Efficient capital markets: A review of theory and empirical work', *Journal of Finance*, 25 (2), 383–417.

Fama, E.F. (1965) 'The behaviour of stock market prices', *Journal of Business*, 38 (1), 34–105.

Fama, Eugene F. and Bliss, Robert R. (1987) 'The information in long-maturity forward rates', *American Economic Review*, 77 (4), 680–692.

Fama, Eugene F. and French, Kenneth R. (1997) 'Industry costs of equity', *Journal of Financial Economics*, 43 (2), 153–193.

Fama, E.F. and French, K.R. (1996) 'Multifactor explanations of asset pricing anomalies', *Journal of Finance*, 51 (1), 55–84.

Fama, E.F. and French, K.R. (1995) 'Size and book-to-market factors in earnings and returns', *Journal of Finance*, 50 (1), 131–155.

Fama, E.F. and French, K.R. (1993) 'Common risk factors in the returns on stocks and bonds', *Journal of Financial Economics*, 33 (1), 3–56.

Fama, E.F. and French, K.R. (1989) 'Business conditions and expected returns on stocks and bonds', *Journal of Financial Economics*, 25 (1), 23–49.

Heaton, John and Lucas, Deborah (1997) 'Portfolio choice and asset prices: The importance of entrepreneurial risk', Northwestern University, manuscript.

Hendricks, D., Patel, J. and Zeckhauser, R. (1993) 'Hot hands in mutual funds: Short-term persistence of performance', *Journal of Finance*, 48 (1), 93–130.

Hodrick, Robert (2000) *International Financial Management*, Englewood Cliffs, NJ: Prentice-Hall, forthcoming.

Hsieh, David and Fung, William (1999) 'Hedge fund risk management', Duke University, working paper.

Jagannathan, Ravi and Wang, Zhenyu (1996) 'The conditional CAPM and the cross-section of expected returns', *Journal of Finance*, 51 (1), 3–53.

Jegadeesh, Narasimham and Titman, Sheridan (1993) 'Returns to buying winners and selling losers: Implications for stock market efficiency', *Journal of Finance*, 48 (1), 65–91.

Jensen, Michael C. (1969) 'The pricing of capital assets and evaluation of investment portfolios', *Journal of Business*, 42 (2), 167–247.

Lakonishok, Josef, Shleifer, Andrei and Vishny, Robert W. (1992) 'The structure and performance of the money management industry', *Brookings Papers on Economic Activity: Microeconomics 1992*, Washington, DC, 339–391.

LeRoy, Stephen F. and Porter, Richard D. (1981) 'The present-value relation: Tests based on implied variance bounds', *Econometrica*, 49 (3), 555–574.

Lewis, Karen, K. (1995) 'Puzzles in international financial markets', in Grossman, G. and Rogoff, K. (eds.), *Handbook of International Economics*, 1913–1971.

Lewis, Michael (1999) 'How the eggheads cracked', *New York Times Magazine*, 24 January, 24–42.

Liew, Jimmy and Vassalou, Maria (1999) 'Can book-to-market, size and momentum be risk factors that predict economic growth?' Columbia University, working paper.

MacKinlay, A. Craig (1995) 'Multifactor models do not explain deviations from the CAPM', *Journal of Financial Economics*, 38 (1), 3–28.

Malkiel, Burton (1990) *A Random Walk Down Wall Street*, New York: Norton.

Markowitz, H. (1952) 'Portfolio selection', *Journal of Finance*, 7 (1), 77–99.

Meredith, Guy and Chinn, Menzie D. (1998) 'Long-horizon uncovered interest rate parity', National Bureau of Economic Research, working paper No. 6797.

Merton, Robert C. (1973) 'An intertemporal capital asset pricing model', *Econometrica*, 41 (5), 867–887.

Merton, Robert C. (1971) 'Optimum consumption and portfolio rules in a continuous time model', *Journal of Economic Theory*, 3 (4), 373–413.

Merton, Robert C. (1969) 'Lifetime portfolio selection under uncertainty: The continuous time case', *Review of Economics and Statistics*, 51 (4), 247–257.

Moskowitz, Tobias and Grinblatt, Mark (1999) 'Tax loss selling and return autocorrelation: New evidence', University of Chicago, working paper.

Moskowitz, T. and Grinblatt, M. (1998) 'Do industries explain momentum?' University of Chicago, CRSP working paper, No. 480.

New York Times Company (1999) 'Mutual funds report: What's killing the value managers?' *New York Times*, 4 April, Section 3, p. 29.

Reyfman, Alexander (1997) 'Labor market risk and expected asset returns', University of Chicago, Ph.D. thesis.

Ross, S. A. (1976) 'The arbitrage theory of capital asset pricing', *Journal of Economic Theory*, 13 (3), 341–360.

Samuelson, Paul A. (1969) 'Lifetime portfolio selection by dynamic stochastic programming,' *Review of Economics and Statistics*, 51 (3), 239–246.

Sargent, Thomas J. (1993) *Bounded Rationality in Macroeconomics*, Oxford: Oxford University Press.

Shiller, Robert J. (1981) 'Do prices move too much to be justified by subsequent changes in dividends?' *American Economic Review*, 71 (3), 421–436.

CHAPTER 18

Recent developments in modern portfolio theory

OVERVIEW

Chapter 17 summarized the revolution in how financial economists view the world. Briefly, there are strategies that result in high averate returns without large 'betas', or a tendency to move with the market as a whole. Multifactor models have supplanted to Capital Asset Pricing Model in describing these phenomena. Stock and bond returns, once thought to be independent over time, turn out to be predictable at long horizons. All of these phenomena seem to reflect a premium for holding macroeconomic risks associated with the business cycle, and for holding assets that do poorly in times of financial distress. They also all reflect the information in prices – high prices lead to low returns and low prices lead to high returns.

The world of investment opportunities has also changed. Where once investors faced a fairly straightforward choice between managed funds, index funds and relatively expensive trading on their own account, they now must choose among a bewildering variety of fund 'styles', including 'value', 'growth', 'balanced', 'income', 'global', 'emerging market' and 'convergence', as well as more complex claims of active fund managers with all sorts of customized styles and strategies, and the temptation to trade on their own via the internet. (Msn.com's latest advertisement suggests that one should sign up in order to 'check the hour's hottest stocks'. Does a beleaguered investor really have to do that to earn a reasonable return?) The advertisements of investment advisory services make it seem important to tailor an investment portfolio from this bewildering set of choices to the particular circumstances, goals and desires of each investor.

What should an investor do? To answer this question, there is now an important current of academic research that investigates how portfolio theory should adapt to our new view of the world. In this chapter, I summarize this research, and I try to distil its advice for investors. In particular, which of the bewildering new investment 'styles' should investors follow? Should they attempt to time stock, bond or foreign exchange markets, and if so how much? To what extent and how should an investment portfolio be tailored to the specific circumstances of an individual investor? Finally, what can we say about the future investment environment? What kind of products will be attractive to investors in the future, and how should public policy react to these financial innovations?

THE TRADITIONAL VIEW OF PORTFOLIO THEORY

Before surveying how new facts have *changed* portfolio advice, it's useful to remind ourselves what the traditional portfolio advice *is*, and why. Also, as the new facts have really extended rather than overturned the old facts, the new advice has really just extended traditional advice in important ways. The traditional academic portfolio theory, starting from Markowitz (1952) and expounded in every finance textbook, remains one of the most beautiful, surprising, useful and enduring bits of economics developed in the last 50 years.

Advice: a two-fund theorem

The traditional advice is to split your investments between a money-market fund and a broad-based, passively managed stock fund. That fund should concentrate on minimizing fees and transaction costs, period. It should avoid the temptation to actively manage its portfolio, trying to chase the latest hot stock. An index fund or other approximation to the 'market portfolio' that passively holds a bit of every stock is ideal.

Figure 18.1 summarizes the analysis behind this advice. The indifference curves capture the fact that investors want portfolios with greater mean return and lower return variance – portfolios that are higher up and to the left – and that they are willing to accept more volatile portfolios if they get a higher average return.

The *mean-variance frontier* gives the minimum possible variance of a portfolio return for each level of mean portfolio return. It summarizes a set of available portfolios. We construct this frontier in two steps, the curved mean-variance frontier of all risky assets, and then the straight frontier that includes a risk-free rate. Investors should all hold portfolios on the mean-variance frontier, as shown. Furthermore, every portfolio on the frontier can be formed as a combinations of the risk-free asset and the market portfolio. Therefore every investor need only hold different proportions of these *two funds*.

Bad portfolio advice

The portfolio advice is not so remarkable for what it does say, which given the setup is fairly straightforward, as it is for what it does not say. Compared with common sense and much industry practice, it is radical advice.

One might have thought that investors willing to take on a little more risk in exchange for the promise of better returns should weight their portfolios to riskier stocks, or to 'value', 'growth', 'small-cap', or other riskier fund styles.

Conversely, one might have thought that investors who are willing to forego some return for more safety should weight their portfolios to safer stocks, or to 'Blue-chip', 'large-cap', 'income', 'capital preservation', or other safer fund styles. Certainly, some professional advice in deciding which style is suited for an investor's risk tolerance, if not a portfolio professionally tailored to each investor's circumstances, seems only sensible and prudent. The advertisements that promise 'we listen' 'we build the portfolio that's right for *you*' cater to this natural and sensible-sounding idea.

Figure 18.1 proves that nothing of the sort is true. All stock portfolios lie on or inside the curved risky asset frontier. Hence, investors who want more return and are willing to take more risk than the market portfolio will do better by borrowing to invest in the market – including the large-cap, income and otherwise safe stocks – than they will by holding a portfolio of riskier stocks. Investors who want something less risky than the market portfolio will do better by splitting their investments between the market and a money-market fund than they will by holding only safe stocks, even though their stock portfolios will then contain some of the small-cap, value or otherwise risky stocks. Everyone holds the same market portfolio; the only decision is how much of it to hold.

The 'two-fund' theorem in principle still allows for a good deal of customized portfolio formation and active management if investors or managers have different *information* or *beliefs*. If you know (say) that small-cap stocks are ready for a rebound, then the optimal (or 'tangency') portfolio that reflects this knowledge will be more heavily weighted toward small-cap stocks than the market portfolio held by the average investor. All the analysis of Figure 18.1 goes through, but this specially-constructed tangency portfolio goes in the place indicated by the market portfolio in Figure 18.1. However, the empirical success of market efficiency, and the poor performance of professional managers relative to passive indexation, strongly suggests that these attempts will not pay off. For this reason, the standard advice is to hold passively-managed funds that concentrate on minimizing transaction costs and fees, rather than a carefully constructed 'tangency portfolio' that reflects an investor's or manager's special insights. However, a quantitative portfolio management industry tries hard to mix information or beliefs about the behaviour of different securities with the theory of Figure 18.1 (for example, see Black and Litterman, 1991).

Second, the 'two-fund' theorem leaves open the possibility that the investors' *horizon* matters as well as their risk aversion. What could be more natural than the often repeated advice that 'long-term' investors can afford to ride out all the market's 'short-term volatility', while 'short-term' investors should avoid stocks

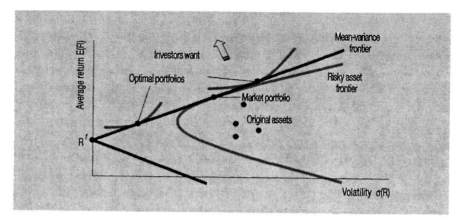

Fig 18.1 ● Mean-variance frontier, optimal portfolios and two-fund theorem

because they may have to sell at the bottom rather than wait for the inevitable recovery after a price drop? The fallacy lies in the 'inevitable recovery'. If returns are close to independent over time (like a coin flip), and prices are close to a random walk, a price drop makes it *no* more likely that prices will rise more in the future. Therefore, if returns are independent over time and stocks follow 'random walks', stocks are *not* safer in the long run, and the stock/bond allocation is independent of investment horizon.

This proposition can be shown to be precisely true in several popular mathematical models of the portfolio decision. If returns are independent over time, then the mean and variance of continuously compounded returns rises in proportion to the horizon: the mean and variance of ten year returns are ten times those of one year returns, so the ratio of mean to variance is the same at all horizons. More elegantly, Merton (1969) and Samuelson (1969) showed that investors with a constant relative risk aversion utility who can continually rebalance their portfolios between stocks and bonds, will always choose the same stock/bond proportion regardless of investment horizon when returns are independent over time.

Taking the advice

This advice has had a sizeable impact on portfolio practice. Before the early 1970s, when this advice became standard in academia, passively managed index funds were practically unknown. They have exploded in size since then. The remaining actively managed funds clearly feel the need to defend active management in the face of the advice to hold passive index funds and the fact that active managers selected on any *ex ante* basis underperform indices *ex post*, where the proposition that professional active management and stock selection could outperform blindly holding an index seemed self-evident before 1970.

The one input to the optimal portfolio advice is risk tolerance, and many providers of investment services have started thinking about how to measure risk tolerance using a series of questionnaires. This is the trickiest part of the conventional advice, in part since conventional measures of risk tolerance often seem quite out of whack with risk aversion displayed in asset markets. (This is the 'equity premium puzzle'; see Cochrane, 1997.) However, the basic question is whether you are more risk tolerant or less risk tolerant than the average investor. This question is fairly easy to conceptualize, and can lead to a solid qualitative, if not quantitative, answer.

One might object to the logical inconsistency of providing portfolio advice based on a view of the world in which everyone is already following such advice. (This is what allowed us to identify the mean-variance frontier with the market portfolio.) However, this logic is only wrong if other investors are *systematically* wrong. If some investors hold too much of a certain stock, but others hold too little of it, market valuations are unaffected and the advice to hold the market portfolio is still valid.

NEW PORTFOLIO THEORY

3.1 Multiple factors: An N-fund theorem

Figure 18.2 shows how the simple two-fund theorem of Figure 18.1 changes if there are multiple sources of priced risk. (This section is a graphical version of Fama's 1996 analysis. Much of the theory was first worked out by Merton 1969, 1971a, 1971b.)

To keep the figure simple I consider one additional factor, and for concreteness think of an additional recession factor. Now, investors care about three attributes of their portfolios:

1 they want higher average returns;

2 they want lower standard deviations or overall risk; and

3 they want portfolios that do not tend to go down in recessions.

Investors are willing to accept a portfolio with a little lower mean return or a little higher standard deviation of return if the portfolio does not do poorly in recessions. In the context of Figure 18.2, this means that investors are happier with portfolios that are higher up (more mean), more to the left (less standard deviation) and also farther out (lower recession sensitivity). The indifference *curves* of Figure 18.1 become indifference *surfaces*. The left-hand panel of Figure 18.2 shows one such surface curving upwards.

As with Figure 18.1, we next think about what is available. We can now calculate a frontier of portfolios based on their mean, variance and recession sensitivity. This frontier is the *multifactor efficient* frontier. Typical investors then pick a point as shown in the left-hand panel of Figure 18.2, which gives them the best possible portfolio – trading off mean, variance and recession sensitivity – that is available. Investors want to hold multifactor efficient, rather than mean-variance efficient, portfolios. As the mean-variance frontier of Figure 18.1 is a hyperbola, this frontier is a revolution of a hyperbola. This appendix summarizes the mathematics behind this figure.

The right-hand panel of Figure 18.2 adds a risk-free rate. As the mean-variance frontier of Figure 18.1 was the minimal V emanating from the risk-free rate that includes the hyperbolic risky frontier, now the multifactor efficient frontier is the minimum *cone* that includes the hyperbolic risky multifactor efficient frontier, as shown.

As every point of the mean-variance frontier of Figure 18.1 can be reached by some combination of two funds – a risk-free rate and the market portfolio – now every point on the multifactor efficient frontier can be reached by some combination of *three* multifactor efficient funds. The most convenient set of portfolios is, the risk-free rate (money-market security), the market portfolio (the risky portfolio held by the average investor), and one additional multifactor efficient portfolio on the tangency region as shown in the right-hand panel

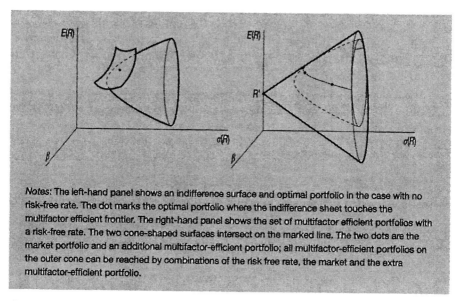

Notes: The left-hand panel shows an indifference surface and optimal portfolio in the case with no risk-free rate. The dot marks the optimal portfolio where the indifference sheet touches the multifactor efficient frontier. The right-hand panel shows the set of multifactor efficient portfolios with a risk-free rate. The two cone-shaped surfaces intersect on the marked line. The two dots are the market portfolio and an additional multifactor-efficient portfolio; all multifactor-efficient portfolios on the outer cone can be reached by combinations of the risk free rate, the market and the extra multifactor-efficient portfolio.

Fig 18.2 ● Portfolio theory in a multifactor world

of Figure 18.2. (It is especially convenient to take this third portfolio to be a zero-cost portfolio such as HML.)

Investors now may differ in their desire or ability to take on recession-related risk as well as in their tolerance for overall risk. Thus, some will want portfolios that are farther in and out, while others will want portfolios that are farther to the left and right. They can achieve these varied portfolios by different weights in the *three* multifactor efficient portfolios, or *three funds*.

Implications for mean-variance investors

The mean-variance frontier still exists – it is the projection of the cone shown in Figure 18.2 on the mean-variance plane. As you can see from the figure, average investors are willing to trade some mean or variance in order to reduce the recession-sensitivity of their portfolios. The average investor must hold the market portfolios, so *the market return is no longer on the mean-variance frontier.*

Suppose, however, that *you* are an investor who is only concerned with mean and variance – one who is not exposed to the recession risk, or the risks associated with any other factor, and you only want to get the best possible mean return for given standard deviation. If so, you still want to solve the mean-variance problem of Figure 18.2. Thus, the important implication of a multifactor world for you, is that *you should no longer hold the market portfolio.*

A mean-variance efficient portfolio can still be achieved just as in Figure 18.1 by a combination of a money market fund and a single *tangency portfolio*, lying on the upper portion of the curved risky-asset frontier. The tangency portfolio now takes stronger positions than the market portfolio in factors such as value or recession-sensitive stocks that the 'average' investor fears.

Predictable returns

The fact that returns are in fact somewhat predictable modifies the standard portfolio advice in three ways. It introduces horizon effects, it allows market timing strategies, and it introduces multiple factors via hedging demands.

Horizon effects

Recall that when stock returns are independent over time (like coin flips), then the allocation between stocks and bonds does not depend at all on the investment horizon, since mean returns (reward) and the variance of returns (risk) both increase in proportion to the investment horizon. But if returns are predictable, the mean and variance may no longer scale the same way with horizon. If a high return today implies a high return tomorrow – positive serial correlation – then the variance of returns will increase with horizon faster than does the mean return. If a high return today implies a lower return tomorrow –

negative serial correlation or 'mean reversion' – then the variance of long-horizon returns is lower than the variance of one-period returns times the horizon. In this case, stocks are more attractive for the long run.[1] For example, if the second coin flip is always the opposite of the first coin flip, then two coin flips are much less risky than they would be if each flip were independent, and a 'long-run coin flipper' is more likely to take the bet.

Which case is true? Overall, the evidence suggests that stock prices do tend to come back slowly and partially after a shock, so return variances at horizons of five years and more are about one half to two-thirds as large as short-horizon variances suggest. Direct measures of the serial correlation of stock returns, or equivalent direct measures of the mean and variance of long-horizon returns, depend a lot on the time-period studied and the econometric method. Multivariate methods give somewhat stronger evidence. Intuitively, the price/dividend ratio does not explode. Hence, the long-run variance of prices must be the same as the long-run variance of dividends, and this extra piece of information helps to measure the long-run variance of returns. (I used this idea in Cochrane and Sbordone, 1986, and Cochrane, 1994. Campbell, Lo and MacKinlay (1997) have a nice summary of these issues and the extensive literature.)

How big are the horizon effects? Barberis (1999) calculates optimal portfolios for different horizons when returns are predictable. Figure 18.3 presents some of his results.

We start with a very simple setup: the investor allocates his or her portfolio between stocks and bonds and then holds it without rebalancing for the indicated horizon. The objective is to maximize the expected utility of wealth at the indicated horizon. The flat line in Figure 18.3 shows the standard result: if returns are not predictable, then the allocation to stocks does not depend on horizon.

The top, dashed line in Figure 18.3 adds the effects of return predictability on the investment calculation. The optimal allocation to stocks increases sharply with horizon, from about 40 per cent allocation to stocks for a monthly horizon to 100 per cent allocation to stocks at a ten-year horizon. To quantify the effects of predictability, we need a mathematical model of predictability, and Barberis takes the simplest model:

$$R_{t+1} - R_{t+1}^{TB} = a + bx_t + \varepsilon_{t+1} \tag{1}$$
$$x_{t+1} = c + \rho x_t + \delta_{t+1}, \tag{2}$$

using the dividend price ratio for the forecasting variable x. (Whether one includes returns in the right-hand side makes little difference.) Barberis estimates significant mean-reversion: in Barberis' regressions, the implied standard deviation of ten year returns is 23.7 per cent, just more than half of the 45.2 per cent value implied by the standard deviation of monthly returns. Stocks are indeed safer in the long run, and the greater allocation to stocks for a long-run investor reflects this fact.

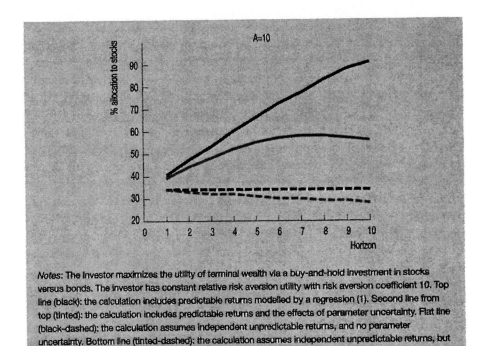

Notes: The investor maximizes the utility of terminal wealth via a buy-and-hold investment in stocks versus bonds. The investor has constant relative risk aversion utility with risk aversion coefficient 10. Top line (black): the calculation includes predictable returns modelled by a regression (1). Second line from top (tinted): the calculation includes predictable returns and the effects of parameter uncertainty. Flat line (black-dashed): the calculation assumes independent unpredictable returns, and no parameter uncertainty. Bottom line (tinted-dashed): the calculation assumes independent unpredictable returns, but adds parameter uncertainty. All distributions are conditional on a d/p ratio equal to its historical mean.

Fig 18.3 • Per cent allocation to stocks for different investment horizons

Source: Barberis (1999)

Uncertainty in predictability

This calculation ignores the fact that we really don't know how predictable returns really are. One could address this fact by calculating standard errors for portfolio computations; and such standard errors do indicate substantial uncertainty. However, standard error uncertainty is symmetric – returns might be more predictable than we think, or they might be less predictable. This measure of uncertainty would say that we are just as likely to want an even greater long-run stock allocation as we are to shade the advice back to a constant allocation.

Intuitively, however, uncertainty about predictability should lead us to shade the advice back towards the standard advice. Standard errors don't capture the uncertainties behind this (good) intuition.

First, the predictability results we have settled on certainly result to some extent from data-dredging. Thousands of series were examined, and we have settled on the one or two that seem to predict returns best in sample. The predictability will obviously be worse out of sample, and good portfolio advice should account for this bias. Standard errors take the set of forecasting variables and the functional form as given.

Second, while keeping intact the list of forecasting variables and functional forms intact, the portfolio calculation assumes that the *investor* knows the return forecasting process perfectly; the standard errors only reflect the fact that *we* don't know the return forecasting process, so we are unsure about what the investor wants to do. But investors are likely to be just as unsure as we are about the exact extent of return predictability.[2] What we would like to do is to solve a portfolio problem in which the investors treat uncertainty about the forecastability of returns as part of the risk that they face, along with the risks represented by the error terms of the statistical model. Kandel and Stambaugh (1996) and Barberis (1998) tackle this important problem.

Figure 18.3 also gives Barberis' calculations of the effects of parameter uncertainty on the stock/bond allocation problem. The lowest, dotted line considers a simple case. The investor knows, correctly, that returns are independent over time (not predictable) but the investors isn't sure about the mean return. Without parameter uncertainty, this situation gives rise to the constant stock allocation – the flat line. Adding parameter uncertainty *lowers* the allocation to stocks for long horizons; it declines from 34 per cent to about 28 per cent at a ten-year horizon.

The reason is simple. If the investor sees a few good years of returns after making the investment, this raises his or her estimate of the actual mean return, and thus raises his or her estimate of the returns over the rest of the investment period. Conversely, a few bad years lowers the investor's estimate of the mean return for the remaining years. Thus, learning about parameters induces a positive correlation between early returns and later returns. Positive correlation makes long-horizon returns more than proportionally risky, and reduces the optimal allocation to stocks.

The second line from top in Figure 18.3 shows the effects of parameter uncertainty on the investment problem, when we allow return predictability as well. As the figure shows, uncertainty about predictable returns cuts the increase in stock allocation from one to ten years in *half*. In addition to the positive correlation of returns due to learning about their mean mentioned above, uncertainty about the true amount of predictability adds to the risk (including parameter risk) of longer horizon returns.

Even this calculation assumes that the investor knows a lot of things perfectly, so the actual amount one can optimally gain by exploiting long-horizon mean reversion is likely to be substantially lower. The dividend/price ratio was selected, in sample, among hundreds of potential forecasting variables. The model imposes a linear specification, where the actual predictability is undoubtedly better modelled by some unknown nonlinear function. In particular, the linear specification implies negative expected stock returns at many points in the sample, and one might not want to take this specification seriously for portfolio advice. The dividend-price ratio is strongly autocorrelated, and estimates of this autocorrelation are subject to 'unit root' econometric problems. For this reason, long-horizon return properties inferred from a VAR are often more dramatic and apparently more precisely measured than direct long-horizon estimates.

Market timing

Market-timing strategies are the most obvious implication of return predictability. If there are times when expected returns are high and other times when they are low, investors might well want to hold more stocks when expected returns are high, and fewer when expected returns are low. Exactly how *much* market timing one should do is of course the crucial question. This is a technically challenging question which several authors have recently addressed.

The benefits of market timing

Much of the difficulty with return predictability (as with other dynamic portfolio questions) lies in computing the optimal strategy – exactly how should one adjust one's portfolio as the return prediction signals change on each date? Gallant, Hansen and Tauchen (1990) show a clever way to measure the potential benefits of market timing without actually calculating the market-timing strategy.

The mean-standard deviation trade-off or *Sharpe ratio* – the slope of the frontier graphed in Figure 18.1 – is a convenient summary of any strategy. If the risk-free rate is constant and known, it turns out that *the square of the maximum*

A statistical model, such as the regression (1) tells us the distribution of future returns once we know the parameters θ, $f(R_{t+1}|\theta)$. We'd really like to evaluate uncertainty by the distribution of returns conditional only on the return history available to make guesses about the future, $f(R_{t+1}|x_1, x_2 \dots x_t)$ where x_t denotes all the data used (returns, d/p, etc.). We can use Bayesian analysis to evaluate this concept. If we can summarize the information about parameters given the historical data as $f(\theta|x_1, x_2 \dots x_t)$, then we can find the distribution of returns by:

$$f(R_{t+1}|x_1, x_2 \dots x_t) = \int f(R_{t+1}|\theta)f(\theta|x_1, x_2 \dots x_t)d\theta$$

In turn, we can construct $f(\theta|x_1, x_2 \dots x_t)$ from a prior $f(\theta)$ and the likelihood function $f(x_1, x_2 \dots x_t|\theta)$ via the standard law for conditional probabilities:

$$f(\theta|x_1, x_2 \dots x_t) = \frac{f(x_1, x_2 \dots x_t|\theta)f(\theta)}{f(x_1, x_2 \dots x_t)}$$

$$f(x_1, x_2 \dots x_t) = \int f(x_1, x_2 \dots x_t|\theta)f(\theta)d\theta.$$

Barberis (1999), Kandel and Stambaugh (1996), Brennan, Schwartz and Lagnado (1997) use these rules to compute $f(R_{t+1}|x_1, x_2 \dots x_t)$, and solve portfolio problems with this distribution over future returns.

Fig 18.4 • How to include model uncertainty into portfolio problems

Table 18.1 • Maximum unconditional Sharpe ratios available from market timing based on regressions of value-weighted NYSE index returns on the dividend/price ratio

Horizon k (years)	R^2	Annualized Sharpe ratio
Buy&hold		0.5
1	0.17	0.71
2	0.26	0.72
3	0.38	0.78
5	0.59	0.95

unconditional Sharpe ratio is the average of the squared conditional Sharpe ratios. (The Appendix derives this result and details the calculation.) Since we take an average of *squared* conditional Sharpe ratios, volatility in conditional Sharpe ratios – time-variation in expected returns or return volatility – is good for investors who care about the unconditional Sharpe ratio. By moving into stocks in times of high Sharpe ratio and moving out of the market in times of low Sharpe ratio, investors do better than they would by buying and holding. Furthermore, *the best unconditional Sharpe ratio is directly related to the R^2 in the return-forecasting regression.*

The buy-and-hold Sharpe ratio has been about 0.5 on an annual basis in US data – stocks have earned an average return of about 8 per cent over Treasury bills, with a standard deviation of about 16 per cent. Table 18.1 presents a calculation of the increased Sharpe ratio one should be able to achieve by market timing, based on regressions of returns on dividend price ratios. (I use the regression estimates from Table 17.1 in Chapter 17.)

The table reports annualized Sharpe ratios corresponding to each R^2. The formula is $s^*/\sqrt{k} = \sqrt{0.5^2 + R^2/k/\sqrt{1-R^2}}$ and is derived in the Appendix:

As indicated by the table, market timing should be a great benefit. Holding constant the portfolio volatility, market timing should raise average returns by about two-fifths at an annual horizon, and almost double average returns at a five-year horizon.

Optimal market timing: an Euler equation approach

Brandt (1999) presents a clever way to estimate a market-timing portfolio rule without solving a model. Where standard asset pricing models fix the consumption or wealth process and estimate preference parameters, Brandt fixes the preference parameters (as one does in a portfolio question) and estimates the portfolio decision, i.e. estimates the optimal consumption or wealth process.[3] This calculation is very clever because it does not require one to specify a statistical model for the stock returns (for example, a VAR of returns and d/p), and it does not require one to solve the economic model.

Figure 18.5 presents one of Brandt's results. The figure shows the optimal allocation to stocks as a function of investment horizon and of the

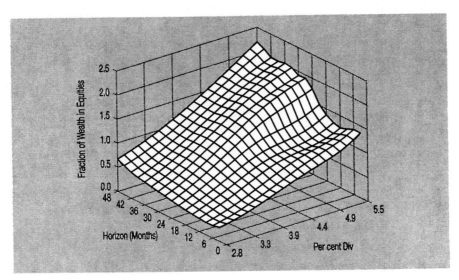

Fig 18.5 ● Optimal allocation to stocks as a function of horizon and dividend yield

Source: Brandt (1999)

dividend/price ratio, which forecasts returns. We see a mild horizon effect, about in line with Barberis' results of Figure 18.3 without parameter uncertainty: longer-term investors hold more stocks. We also see a strong market-timing effect. The fraction of wealth invested in stocks varies by about 200 percentage points for all investors. For example, long-term investors vary from about 75 per cent to 225 per cent of wealth invested in stocks.

Optimal market timing: a solution

Campbell and Vicera (1999) actually calculate a solution to the optimal market-timing question. They model investors who desire lifetime consumption[4] rather than portfolio returns at a fixed horizon, which is the right way to pose the problem. They model the time variation in expected stock returns via the simple vector autoregression (1) on dividend price ratios. Their investors live only off invested wealth, and have no labour income or labour income risk. Thus, these investors are poised to take advantage of business cycle related variation in expected returns.

As one might expect, the optimal investment strategy takes strong advantage of market-timing possibilities. Figure 18.6 reproduces Campbell and Vicera's optimal allocation to stocks as a function of the expected return, forecast from d/p ratios via (1). A risk aversion coefficient of 4 implies that investors roughly want to be fully invested in stocks at the average expected excess return of 6 per cent, so this is a sensible risk aversion value to consider. Then, as the d/p ratio ranges from minus two to plus one standard deviations from its mean, these investors range from −50 per cent in stocks to 220 per cent in stocks. This is aggressive market timing indeed!

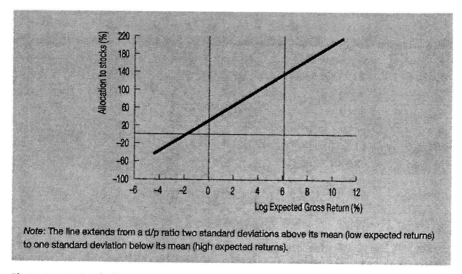

Fig 18.6 ● Optimal allocation to stocks as a function of the expected return implied from a regression that forecasts stock returns from dividend/price ratios

Source: Campbell and Vicera (1999)

Figure 18.7 presents the calculation in a different way: it gives the optimal allocation to stocks over time, based on dividend/price ratio variation over time. The high dividend/price ratios of the 1950s suggest a strong stock position, and that strong position profits from the high returns of the late 1950s to early 1960s. The low d/p ratios of the 1960s suggest a much smaller position in stocks, and this smaller position avoids the bad returns of the 1970s. The high d/p ratios of the 1970s suggest strong stock positions again, which benefit from the good return of the 1980s; current unprecedented high prices suggest the

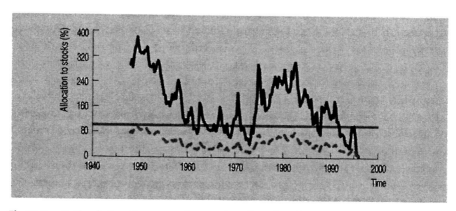

Fig 18.7 ● Optimal allocation to stocks over time, based on dividend/price ratio

Source: Campbell and Vicera (1999)

lowest stock positions ever. The optimal allocation to stocks again varies wildly, from 0 (now) to over 300 per cent.

Campbell and Vicera's calculations are, if anything, conservative compared with others in this literature. Other calculations, using other utility functions, solution techniques, and calibrations of the forecastability process often produce even more aggressive market-timing strategies. For example, Brennan, Schwartz and Lagnado (1997) make a similar calculation with two additional forecasting variables. They report (their figure 6) market-timing strategies that essentially jump back and forth between constraints at 0 per cent in stocks and 100 per cent in stocks.

Campbell and Vicera also present achieved utility calculations that mirror the lesson of Table 18.1: failing to market-time imposes a large cost.

Doubts

One may be understandably reluctant to take on quite such strong market-timing positions as indicated by Figures 18.6 and 18.7, or to believe the near doubling of five year Sharpe ratios that the strong market timing strategies give in Table 18.1. In particular, one might have trouble taking advice that would have pointed one to miss most of the dramatic runup in stock values of the late 1990s! Perhaps, rather than a failure of nerve, one's reluctance reveals that the calculations do not yet include important considerations and, therefore, overstate the desirable amount of market timing and its benefits.

First, the 'unconditional Sharpe ratio' as reported in Table 18.1 for (say) five-year horizons answers the question, 'Over very long periods, if an investor follows the best possible market-timing strategy and evaluates his or her portfolio based on five-year returns, what Sharpe ratio does he or she achieve?' This is *not* 'Given today's d/p, what is the best Sharpe ratio you can achieve for the next five years by following market-timing signals?' The latter question characterizes the return distribution conditional on today's d/p; the former does not. The answer to the latter question is harder to evaluate, it depends on the initial signal (bad right now, since p/d ratios are at all time highs), and is lower, especially for a slow-moving signal such as d/p.

To see the point, consider an extreme case that the d/p ratio is determined on day one, is constant thereafter, and indicates high or low returns in perpetuity. *Conditional* on the d/p ratio, one cannot the market-time at all. But since the investor will invest less in stocks in the low-return state and more in the high-return state, he or she will *unconditionally* market-time (i.e. adjust his or her portfolio based on day one information) and this gives the investor a better date-zero (unconditional) Sharpe ratio than he or she would obtain by fixing the allocation at date zero. This fact captures one's intuition that there is a lot more money to be made from a 50 per cent R^2 at a daily horizon than at a five-year horizon, where the calculations in Table 18.1 are not affected by the persistence of the market-timing signal. Campbell and Vicera's utility calculations are also based on the unconditional distribution, so the optimal degree and benefit of market timing might be less, conditional on the observed d/p ratio at the first date.

Second, there are good statistical reasons to think that the regressions over-state the predictability of returns. Figure 18.7 emphasizes one reason: the d/p ratio signal has only crossed its mean four times in the 50 years of postwar history. You have to be a very patient investor to profit from this trading rule! Also, we really have only four postwar data points on the phenomenon. For this reason the magnitude and nature of d/p predictability are still debated.

The natural next step is to include this uncertainty in the portfolio problem, as we did above for the case of independent returns. While this has not been done yet in a model with Campbell and Vicera's level of realism (and for good reasons – Campbell and Vicera's non-Bayesian solution is already a technical tour de force), Barberis (1999) makes such calculations in his simpler formula-tion. He uses a utility of terminal wealth and no intermediate trading, and he forces the allocation to stocks to be less than 100 per cent.

Figure 18.8 presents Barberis' results.[5] As the figure shows, uncertainty about the parameters of the regression of returns on d/p almost eliminates the usefulness of market timing.

Third, it is uncomfortable to note that funds returns still cluster around the (buy-and-hold) market Sharpe ratio (see Figure 17.9 on page 431). Here is a mechanical strategy that supposedly earns average returns twice those of the market with no increase in risk. If the strategy is real and implementable, one must argue that funds simply failed to follow it. Market timing, like value, does require patience and the willingness to suffer a portfolio that departs from the indexing crowd. For example, a market timer following Campbell and Vicera's rules in Figures 18.6 and 18.7 would have missed most of the great runup in stocks of the last few years! Fund managers who did that are now unemployed. On the other hand, if an eventual crash comes, the market timer will look wise.

Fourth, and finally, one's reluctance to take such strong market-timing advice reflects the inescapable fact that you can't get more return without taking on more, or different, kinds of risk. Market timers must buy at the bottom, when everyone else is in a panic; they must sell at the top (now) when everyone else is feeling flush. Their portfolios will have a greater mean and variance over very long horizons, but they will do well and badly at very different times from every-one else's portfolios. They will often underperform a benchmark.

Hedging demands

Hedging demands are a bit more subtle. If expected returns vary over time, investors may want to hold assets that protect them against this risk.

The easiest example is a long-term bond. Imagine an investor who wants to mini-mize the risk of his or her portfolio ten years out. If he or she invests in

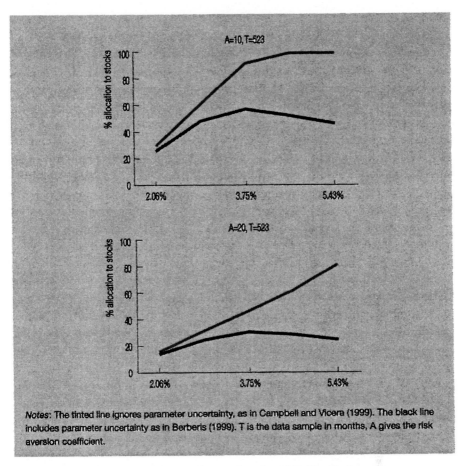

Notes: The tinted line ignores parameter uncertainty, as in Campbell and Vicera (1999). The black line includes parameter uncertainty as in Berberis (1999). T is the data sample in months, A gives the risk aversion coefficient.

Fig 18.8 ● Percentage allocation to stocks as a function of dividend/price ratio

apparently safe short-term risk-less assets like Treasury bills or a money market fund, his or her ten-year return is in fact quite risky, since interest rates can fluctuate. This investor should hold a ten-year (real, discount) bond. Its price will fluctuate a lot as interest rates go up and down, but its value in ten years never changes.

Another way of looking at this situation is that, if interest rates decline, the price of the ten-year bond will skyrocket; it will skyrocket just enough so that, reinvested at the new lower rates, it provides the same ten-year return as it would have if interest rates had not changed. Changes in the ten-year bond value *hedge* the reinvestment risk of short-term bonds. If lots of investors want to secure the ten-year value of their portfolios, this will raise demand for ten-year bonds and lower their prices.

A hedging demand is different from market timing. Market timing addresses whether you should *change* your allocation to stocks over time as a signal of subsequent returns rises or falls. Hedging demands address whether your *overall* allocation to stocks, or to specific portfolios, should be higher or lower, independent of the level of a signal, in order to protect you against reinvestment risk.

In general, the size and sign of a hedging demand depend on risk aversion and horizon and, thus, will be different for different investors. If the investor is quite risk averse – infinitely so in my bond example – he or she wants to buy assets whose prices go up when expected returns decline. But an investor who is not so risk averse might want to buy assets whose prices go up when expected returns *rise*. If the investor is sitting around waiting for a good time to invest, and is willing to pounce on good (high expected return) investments, he or she would prefer to have a lot of money to invest when the good opportunity comes around. It turns out that the dividing line in the standard (CRRA) model is logarithmic utility or a risk aversion coefficient of 1 – consumers more risk averse than this want assets whose prices go up when expected returns decline, and vice versa. Most investors are undoubtedly more risk averse than this, but not necessarily all investors. Horizon matters as well: a short horizon investor cares nothing about reinvestment risk and therefore has zero hedging demand.

In addition, the relationship between price and expected returns is not so simple for stocks as for bonds, and must be estimated statistically. The predictability evidence reviewed above suggests that high stock returns presage lower subsequent returns. High returns drive up P/D, P/E, and market/book ratios, all of which have been strong signals of lower subsequent returns. Therefore, stocks are a good hedge against their own reinvestment risk – they act like the long-term assets that they are. This consideration raises the attractiveness of stocks for typical (risk aversion greater than 1) investors. Precisely, if the two-fund analysis of Figure 18.1 suggests a certain split between stocks and short-term bonds for a given level of risk aversion and investment horizon, return predictability, a long horizon and typical risk aversion greater than one will result in a higher fraction devoted to stocks. Again, exactly how *much* more one should put into stocks in view of this consideration is a tough question.

(In this case, the hedging demand reduces to much the same logic as the horizon effects described above. The market portfolio is a good hedge against its own reinvestment risk, and so its long horizon variance is less than its short-horizon variance would suggest. More generally, hedging demands can tilt a portfolio towards stocks whose returns better predict and, hence, better hedge the expected return on the market index, but this long-studied possibility from Merton (1971a, 1971b) has not yet been implemented in practice.)

Campbell and Vicera's calculations address this hedging demand as well as market-timing demand, and Figure 18.6 also illustrates the strength of the hedging demand for stocks. Campbell and Vicera's investors want to hold almost 30 per cent of their wealth in stocks even if the expected return of stocks is no greater than that of bonds! Absent the hedging motive, of course, the optimal allocation to stocks would be zero with no expected return premium. Almost a 2 per cent *negative* stock return premium is necessary to dissuade Campbell and Vicera's investors from holding stocks. At the average (roughly 6 per cent) expected return, of the roughly 130 per cent of wealth that the risk aversion 4 investors want to allocate to stocks, nearly half is due to hedging demand. Thus, hedging demands can importantly change the allocation to stocks!

However, hedging demand works in opposition to the usual effects of risk aversion. Usually, less risk-averse people want to hold more stocks. However, less risk-averse people have lower or even negative hedging demands, as explained above. It is possible that hedging demand exactly offsets risk aversion offset, everybody holds the same mean allocation to stocks! This turns out not to be the case for Campbell and Vicera's numerical calibration; less risk-averse people still allocate more to stocks on average.

Choosing a risk-free rate

The simple analysis of Figure 18.1 describes a portfolio composed of the market portfolio and the risk-free rate. But the 'risk-free' rate is not as simple as it once was either. For a consumer or an institution[6] with a one-year horizon, one-year bonds are 'risk free', while for one with a ten-year horizon, a ten-year zero-coupon bond is 'risk free'. For a typical consumer, whose objective is lifetime consumption, an interest-only strip (or real level annuity) is in fact the 'risk-free rate', since it provides a riskless coupon that can be consumed at each date. Campbell and Vicera (1998) emphasize this point. Thus, the appropriate bond portfolio to mix with risky stocks in the logic of Figure 18.1 is no longer so simple as a short-term money market fund.

Of course, these comments refer to *real* or indexed bonds, which are only starting to become easily available. When only nominal bonds are available, the 'risk-free' investment depends additionally on how much interest rate variability is due to real rates versus nominal rates. In the extreme case, if real interest rates are constant and nominal interest rates vary with inflation, then rolling over short-term nominal bonds carries less long-term real risk than holding long-term nominal bonds. In the past, inflation was much more variable than real interest rates in the USA, so the fact that portfolio advice paid little attention to the appropriate risk-free rate may have made sense. We seem to be entering a period in which inflation is quite stable, so *real* interest rate fluctuations may dominate interest rate movements. In this case, longer-term nominal bonds become more 'risk free' for long-term investors, and inflation-indexed bonds open up the issue in any case. Once again, new facts are opening up new challenges and opportunities for portfolio formation.

WARNINGS AND DOUBTS

The advice of the new portfolio theory is alluring and can justify all sorts of interesting new investment approaches. However, there are several important qualifications that should temper one's enthusiasm and that shade portfolio advice back to the traditional view captured in Figure 18.1.

The average investor holds the market

The portfolio theory that I have surveyed so far asks, given multiple factors or time-varying investment opportunities, how should an investor *who does not care* about these extra risks profit from them? This may result from intellectual habit, as the past great successes of portfolio theory addressed such investors, or it may come from experience in the money management industry, where distressingly few investors ask about additional sources of risk that multifactor models and predictable returns suggest should be a major concern.

We must remember, however, that *the average investor must hold the market portfolio*. Thus, *multiple factors and predictability cannot have any portfolio implications for the average investor*. In addition, for every investor who should follow a value-tilt or market time taking advantage of the extra returns that exposure to those extra risks, *there must be an investor who should follow the exact opposite advice*. This investor should follow a growth tilt or sell stocks at the bottom and buy at the top, because he or she is unusually exposed to or averse to the risks of those strategies in his or her business or job. This investor knows that he or she pays a premium for not holding those risks, but rationally chooses to do so just as you pay a premium for home insurance. If not, if everyone tried to market-time or buy value stocks, the phenomena would disappear and the CAPM, random walk world would re-emerge.

Again, P/D, P/E, etc. forecast returns, if they do, *because* the average investor is unwilling to follow the market-timing strategy and buy more stocks when prices are low. The strategy can only work if it involves buying stocks when nobody else wants them; after crashes, in the depths of recessions, in times of financial panic; and selling them in booms (like now) when everyone else seems to put more and more into stocks despite very high valuations. 'Value' and 'small-cap' anomalies can only work if the average investor is leery about buying 'financially distressed' and liquid stocks. Portfolio advice to follow these strategies *must* fall on deaf ears for the average investor, and a large class of investors must want to head in exactly the other direction. If not, the strategies can't work.

You can see a social function in all this: *the stock market acts as a big insurance market*. By changing weights in, say, recession-sensitive stocks, people whose incomes are particularly hurt by recessions can purchase insurance against that loss from people whose incomes are not hurt by recessions. They pay a premium to do so, which is what gets investors to take on the recession-related risk.

The quantitative portfolio advice is all aimed at the providers of insurance, which may make sense if the providers are large wealthy investors or institutions. But for each provider there must be a purchaser of insurance, and his or her portfolio must take on the opposite characteristics. The advice to 'be a provider of insurance' cannot hold for everyone.

Are the effects real or behavioural, and will they last?

I have emphasized the view that the average returns from multifactor or market-timing strategies are earned because in following them, an investor takes on a real risk that others are anxious not to hold. This proposition is still debated for many strategies that seem to give high average returns. Roughly half of the academic studies that document such strategies interpret them as I have, while the other half interpret them as evidence that investors are systematically irrational.

For example, I have followed Fama and French's interpretation that the 'value effect' that it exposes the investor to systematic risks associated with economywide financial distress. However, authors such as Lakonishok, Shleifer and Vishny (1994) interpret the same facts as evidence for irrationality: investors flock to popular stocks and away from unpopular stocks. The prices of the unpopular stocks are depressed, and their average returns are higher as the fad slowly fades. Fama and French point out that the behavioural view cannot easily account for the comovement of value stocks; the behavioural camp points out that the fundamental risk factor is still not determined.

Similarly, the predictability of stock returns over time is interpreted as waves of irrational exuberance and pessimism as often as it is interpreted as time-varying, business cycle related risk or risk aversion. Those who advocate an economic interpretation point to the association with business cycles (Fama and French, 1989) and to some success for explicit models of this association (Campbell and Cochrane, 1999 for example); irrational interpreters point to the fact that the models are as yet imperfect.

While this academic debate is entertaining, how does it affect a practical person making a portfolio decision? At a most basic level *we don't have to take a stand on whether an average return is due to real risk or irrationality in making portfolio decisions*. If it's there, and if *you* are not exposed to the risk it represents, it does not matter whether everyone else is shying away from holding it, and thus driving up its return, due to a real risk factor or due to some irrational fear.

A portfolio problem is economically identical to the shopping problem – what should you buy at the grocery store? To answer that question, you only have to know how *you* feel about various foods and what their prices are. You don't need to know whether a sale on tomatoes represents a 'real' factor like good weather in tomato-growing areas, or whether it represents 'irrational' or 'inefficient' outcome, a sudden fad that people don't buy tomatoes anymore.

Will they last?

You do have to figure out whether an investment opportunity that did well in the past will continue to do well in the future, and the question whether a high average return comes from a real or irrational aversion to risk does bear on this question.

1　*Real.* If it is real, it is most likely to persist. If a high average return becomes exposure to risk, well understood and widely shared, that means all investors understand the opportunity but shrink from it. A horde of investment advisers advertising the opportunity will change nobody's portfolio decisions, and hence the average returns will remain.

2　*Irrational.* If it is truly irrational, or a market inefficiency, it is least likely to persist. If a high average-return strategy involves no extra exposure to risk, and is easy to implement (does not require large transaction costs), that means that the average investor will immediately want to invest when he or she hears of the opportunity. News travels quickly, investors quickly invest, and such opportunities will vanish quickly.

3　*Behavioural.* Recent work in 'behavioural' finance, I think, tries to document a way that 'irrational' phenomena can persist in the face of the above logic. If an inefficiency corresponds to a fundamental, documented, deeply formed aspect of psychology, then average investors may *not* immediately pounce on the strategy the minute they hear of it, and the phenomenon may last. DeBondt and Thaler (1985), and Daniel, Hirshleifer and Subrahmanyam (1998) emphasize this view.

For example, many people systematically overestimate the probability of aeroplanes crashing, and make systematic wrong decisions resulting from this belief, such as choosing to drive instead. No amount of statistics changes this view in fact most people readily admit that a fear of flying is 'irrational' but persist in it anyway. If an asset pricing anomaly results from such a deep-seated perceptions of risk, then it could in fact persist.

4　*Institutional; narrowly held risks.* The most likely analysis of high average return opportunities, in my opinion, is the least stressed in academic analysis, and leads to a view of moderate persistence.

The clearest example are the catastrophe insurance enhanced bonds. These bonds pay well in normal times, but either part of the principal or interest is pledged against a tranche of a property reinsurance contract. Thus, the bonds promise an average return of 10–20 per cent (depending on one's view of the chance of hurricanes); they lose money when there is a hurricane, but the risk of hurricane damage is uncorrelated with anything else. Currently, these risks are narrowly held. Before the introduction of catastrophe bonds, there was no easy way for the average investor or fund could participate in this attractive opportunity. As more and more investors and funds hold these securities, the prices will rise and average returns will fall. Once the risks are widely shared, every investor (at least those not located in hurricane-prone areas) will hold a little bit of the risk and the high average returns will have vanished.

Notice the ingredients: the risk is narrowly shared; the high average returns only disappear when the risk is widely shared (it cannot be 'arbitraged away' by a few savvy investors); and an institutional change (the introduction, packaging and marketing of catastrophe-linked bonds) is required before it all can happen.

The form of the institutional change required thought and experimentation. Catastrophe options were introduced on the CBOT long before the catastrophe bonds, but many funds and investors do not participate in options markets. While this kind of security would be useful if the anomaly were the kind that would be eliminated by savvy traders (options are very good devices for letting people trade on information), this anomaly requires a wide sharing of the risk.

This story gives a plausible interpretation of many of the anomalies I document above. Small-cap stocks were found in about 1979 to provide higher returns than the market (β) risk. Yet at that time, most funds did not invest in such stocks, and individual investors would have had a hard time forming a portfolio of small-cap stocks without losing all the benefits in the very illiquid markets for these stocks. The risks were narrowly held. After the popularization of the small-cap effect, many small-cap funds were started. These allow investors to easily hold such stocks, and most fund families now feature a small-cap style fund. As the risk has been more widely shared, the average returns seem to have fallen.

The value effect may be amenable to a similar interpretation. Before about 1990, as we have seen, few funds actually followed the strategy that gives high returns of buying really distressed stocks or shorting the popular 'growth' stocks. It would be a difficult strategy for an individual investor to follow, requiring courage and frequent trading of small illiquid stocks. Now that the effect is clear, value funds have emerged that really do follow the strategy, and the average investor can easily include a value tilt in his or her 401 (k) plan. The risk is becoming widely shared, and its average return may fall as well.

Even returns on the stock market as a whole (the 'equity premium') may follow the same story, since participation has increased a great deal through the invention of index funds, low-commission brokerages and tax-sheltered retirement plans.

This story does not mean that the average returns corresponding to such risks will vanish. They will decline however, until we have established an equilibrium as described in No. 1 above, one in which every investor has bought as much of the risk as he or she likes. In this story, one would expect a large return as investors discover each strategy and bid prices up to their equilibrium levels. This may account for some of the success of small and value stocks for the ten years or so just preceding academic publication, and for some of the stunning success of the overall market in recent years.

Inconsistent advice

Unfortunately, *the arguments that a factor will persist are inconsistent with aggressive portfolio advice.*

1 If the risk is *real*, the portfolio advice cannot apply but to half of a minuscule fraction of investors. Average investors are exposed to the risk; they know about it but choose to hold the market portfolio anyway because the extra return exactly compensates for the extra risk. For every investor who should want more of the risk, there must be another who wants less. Thus, the advice to load up on small-cap, value, or market-timing or other high return strategies can only apply to at most half of the investors. Additionally, if more than a minuscule fraction of investors (on either side) are not already at their best allocations already, then the market has not reached equilibrium and the premiums will change.

2 If the risk is *irrational*, then by the time you and I know about it, it's gone. An expected return corresponding to an irrational risk premium has the strongest portfolio implications – everyone should do it – but the shortest lifetime. Thus, this view is also inconsistent with the widespread usefulness of portfolio advice.

3 If the average return comes from a *behavioural* aversion to risk, it is just as inconsistent with widespread portfolio advice as if it were real. We can't all be less behavioural than average, just as we all can't be less exposed to a risk than average. The whole argument for behavioural persistence is that average investors would not change their portfolios, because the risk runs into fundamental ways that humans perceive risks – just as average travellers do not quickly adjust their travelling behaviour to fear the taxi ride out to the airport more than the flight.

The advice *must* again be useless to the vast majority of investors. If most people, on seeing the strategy, can be persuaded to act differently and buy, then it's an irrational risk (type 2) and will disappear. If it is behavioural and will persist, then this *necessarily* means that very few people will follow the portfolio advice! It's good salesmanship to assure each client that he or she is one of the few truly smart people who can take advantage of a strategy that everyone else is too stupid to follow, but we're not here to study the flattery of salespeople.

4 If the average return comes from a *narrowly held* risk, we have to ask what institutional barriers keep investors from sharing this risk more widely. Simple portfolio advice may help a bit – most investors still did not, and many still do not appreciate the risk/return advantages of stocks in general, small firms, value firms, market-timing strategies and aggressive liquidity trades. But by and large, a risk like this needs packaging, securitizing and marketing more than advice. Then there will be a period of high average returns to the early investors, followed by lower returns, but still commoditization of the product with fees for the intermediaries.

What's real – economic logic

The issue of why the risk gives an average return premium is also important to decide whether the opportunity is really there. Alasm stocks (and dynamic portfolio strategies) don't carry 'average return' labels quite as clearly as grocery price labels. There are many statistical anomalies that vanish quickly out of sample. The vast majority of technical trading rules, seasonal anomalies, and many too-good-to-be-true strategies spit out of black boxes fall in this category. Figuring out *why* a strategy carries a high average return is one of the best ways to ensure that the high average return is really there in the first place. Anything that is going to work has a real economic function. A story such as 'I don't care much about recessions; the average investor does; hence it makes good sense for me to buy extra amounts of recession sensitive stocks since I am selling insurance to the others at a premium' makes a strategy much more plausible.

CONCLUSION

Now, what do all these theories and facts mean for the investor, trying patiently to sort through the bewildering variety of available fund styles, claims for active management techniques, or temptations of minute by minute internet trading?

First, you have to figure out who you are. We start with, as before:

1 *What is your overall risk tolerance?*
As always, investors must first figure out to what extent they are willing to trade off volatility for extra average returns. Investors with lower risk tolerance will want portfolios more weighted to risk-free assets, and investors with greater risk tolerance will want to load up more on risky but rewarding opportunities. While this question is hard to answer in the abstract, you only need to know whether you are more or less risk tolerant than the average investor. (Honestly, now.) The overall market is about 60 per cent stocks and 40 per cent bonds, so 'average' levels of risk aversion, whatever they are, wind up at this value.

2 *What is your horizon?*

This question is first of all important for figuring out what the relevant 'risk-free' asset is, as above. Longer-term investors can hold longer-term bonds despite their poor one-year performance, especially in a low-inflation environment.

Second, the bottom line of the above analysis is that stocks are somewhat safer for 'long run' investors. They are not arbitrage opportunities – some people infer that stocks can *never* underperform bonds at a 30- or 50-year horizon, and this is not and cannot be true – they are maybe one-third less volatile than the old model of independent returns suggests.

3 *What are your risks?*

This is the first really new question. Are there times or states of the world in which you would particularly dislike poor performance of your investment portfolio, so much so that you would be willing to trade some average return in order to make sure that the portfolio does well in these particular times?

For example, an investor who owns a small company might properly be especially concerned that his or her investment portfolio does not do poorly at the same time that his or her industry suffers a downturn, that there is a recession, or a credit crunch, or that the industries he or she sells to suffer a downturn. Thus, it makes good sense for that investor to avoid stocks in the same industry or downstream industries, or stocks that are particularly sensitive to recessions or credit crunches, or even to short them if possible. This would make sense even if these stocks do 'better than they should', like the value portfolios. It would make sense for this investor to avoid an 'arbitrage' hedge fund that borrowers heavily to invest in low-grade bonds. Even if such a strategy did well on average it will lose money in a credit crunch or recession, just as the investor's business is also suffering. If the company will do poorly in response to increases in interest rates, oil prices or similar events, and if the company does not hedge these risks, then the investor should take position in interest-rate sensitive or oil-price sensitive securities to offset those risks as well.

These portfolio choices work just like buying insurance. Every investor would like his or her 'asset' portfolio to do particularly well in the event that his or her house burns down; and is willing to buy an investment with a poor financial return – home insurance, on which one loses money on average – in order to arrange this. We're just extending the principle to financial markets.

Institutions also should think about what are the risks; what are the 'bad events' for the institution, and what can be done to ensure that the investment portfolio does not do particularly badly in those events. (This advice is subject to the usual warning about why institutions should be making portfolio or hedging decisions at all.)

Thinking about one's risk exposure is a new exercise. Here are some some ways to phrase the questions. Are you particularly concerned about your portfolio going down in the following circumstances.

1 When the market goes down?

2 When the market goes down a lot?

3 In recessions?

4 In credit crunch/flight to quality/times when corporate and liquidity spreads widen?

5 At times when 'value' stocks do badly?

6 At times when small stocks do badly?

7 If different regions of the world do badly?

8 Times of low/high inflation, interest rates?

9 Do you own property in Florida?

The first question measures your concern about market beta of course. The second kind of question gets at whether you should be paying or collecting 'put premiums' or other kinds of financial catastrophe insurance premiums. Questions 3–6 get at the appropriateness of these kind of styles. The seventh question opens the door to international diversification or its opposite, in order to hedge international risks. Bond risk factors matter too, as in the eighth question. The last is not facetious. If you own a lot of property in a hurricane-prone zone though, you should be selling, not buying, catastrophe-linked bonds.

Note that this logic extends not only to the kind of 'factors' that have attracted academic attention but it applies to any identifiable movement in asset portfolios. For example, industry portfolios do not display much variation in (unconditional) average returns, and hence don't show up much in new factor models. However, shorting your industry portfolio protects you against the risks of your occupation. In fact, such 'factors' are even better opportunities than the 'priced' factors, since you can buy insurance at zero premium. This was always true; I think that the experience with multifactor models just increases our awareness of how important this issue is.

4 *What are* not *your risks?*

Next, investors may figure out what risks they do *not* face, but that give rise to an average return premium in the market because most *other* investors do face these risks. For example, investors who have no other source of income beyond their investment portfolios do not particularly care if a recession is on or not. Therefore, they should buy extra amounts of recession-sensitive stocks, 'value' stocks, or invest in a 'convergence' type hedge fund that concentrates on liquid assets, if these strategies carry a credible high average return. This action works just like selling insurance, in return for a premium.

Since this advice is rather new, too many investors (in my opinion at least) think they are in this class. The extra factors and time-varying returns would not be there (and will quickly disappear in the future) if lots of people were willing and able to take them. The presence of multiple factors wakes us up to the possibility that we, like the average investor, may be exposed to extra risks, possibly without realizing it.

5 *Apply the logic of the multifactor frontier.*

Figure 18.2 now summarizes the basic advice. After thinking through which risk factors are good to hold, and which ones you are already too exposed to, and after thinking through what extra premiums you are likely to get for taking on extra risks, you can come to a sensible decision about which risks to take and which to hedge, even if hedging them costs a substantial premium.

6 *Do not forget, the average investor holds the market.*

If you're pretty much average, you ignore everything and still hold the market index. To average investors, 'value' stocks have a high average return, but they contain some sort of risk that they are afraid of. Maybe you should be too! Right now the average investor is feeling very wealthy and risk-tolerant, therefore and stock prices have risen to unprecedented levels and expected stock returns look very low. It's tempting to sell, but if you're average, you too are feeling wealthy and risk-tolerant. Where else are you going to put the money? To rationalize anything but the market portfolio, you have to be different from the average investor in some identifiable way.

7 *Of course, avoid taxes and snake oil.*

Unfortunately, the marketing of many securities and funds is not particularly clear on the nature of the risks. It always sounds better to sell a fund as a profit opportunity with *no* risk. However, there is no return without risk. The economic reasoning in this chapter should be useful to read behind the slick marketing and to figure out exactly what type of risk a specific fund or strategy is exposed to, and then whether it is appropriate for you.

The average actively managed fund is still underperforming its style benchmark, and even the most aggressive estimates of persistence in fund performance are tiny – past performance has almost no information about future performance. Multifactor logic suggests passively managed style portfolios, but active management and black boxes are just as suspect as ever.

The most important piece in traditional portfolio advice is hidden between the lines: *avoid taxes and transaction costs.* The losses from churning a portfolio and paying needless short-term capital gain, inheritance and other taxes are large. Never take a short-term capital gain; use the inheritance that capital gains are forgiven in inheritance, delay gains, buy stocks that repurchase rather than pay dividends, watch out for funds with capital gains and so on. Tax issues are much less fun but more important to the bottom line.

Policy

An important policy theme sounds throughout this chapter, and it is worth remembering it in closing.

1 Asset markets are a big insurance market.

Though they often sure don't look like it! 'Value funds' seem to provide extra returns to their investors by buying distressed stocks on the edge of bankruptcy. LTCM was, it seems, providing 'catastrophe insurance' by intermediating liquid assets that investors want to hold into illiquid assets that were vulnerable to a liquidity crunch. Who better to provide catastrophe insurance than wildly rich investors with no other labour income or other risk exposure? Once again, we are reminded that Adam Smith's invisible hand guides apparently greedy decisions to socially useful ends, often in mysterious ways.

2 Asset market could be better insurance markets.

Surveying my portfolio advice, I am struck that the average investor should hold a stock position that is *short* his company, industry, or other easily hedgeable kinds of risk. Many managers and some senior employees must hold long positions in their own companies, for obvious incentive reasons. But there is no reason that this applies to union pension funds, for example. A little marketing should make funds that hedge industry specific risks to labour income much more attractive vehicles.

Notes

[1] To be precise, these statements refer to the conditional serial correlation of returns. It is possible for the conditional serial correlations to be non-zero, resulting in conditional variances that increase with horizon faster or slower than linearly, while the unconditional serial correlation of returns is zero. Conditional distributions drive portfolio decisions.

[2] This effort falls in a broader inquiry in economics. Once we recognize that people are unlikely to have much more data and experience than economists, we have to think about economic models in which people *learn* about the world they live in through time, rather than models in which people have so much history that they have learned all there is to know about the world. See Sargent (1993) for a review of learning in macroeconomics.

[3] The standard first-order condition for optimal consumption and portfolio choice is:

$$E((c_{t+1})^{-\gamma} Z_{t+1}) = 0 \tag{3}$$

where c denotes consumption, Z denotes an excess return, and γ is a preference parameter. We usually take data on c, Z, estimate γ, and then test whether the condition actually does hold across assets. In a portfolio problem however, we *know* the preference parameter γ, but we want to estimate the portfolio. For example, in the simplest case of a one-period investment problem, consumption equals terminal wealth $c_{t+1} = W_{t+1} = W_t \times (\alpha R^f + (1-\alpha)R^m_{t+1})$. Equation (3) then becomes

$$E[(\alpha R^f + (1-\alpha)R^m_{t+1})^{-\gamma} Z_{t+1}] = 0. \tag{4}$$

Brandt uses this condition to estimate the portfolio allocation α. He extends the technique to multiperiod problems and problems in which the allocation decision depends on a forecasting variable, i.e. market-timing problems.

[4] I.e. Campbell and Vicera model investors' objectives by a utility function $\max E \sum_n \beta^t u(c_t)$ rather than a desire for wealth at some particular date $\max Eu(W_T)$.

[5] I thank Nick Barberis for providing this figure. While it is not in Barberis 1999, it can be constructed from results given in that paper.

[6] Of course, in theory, 'institutions' as such shouldn't have preferences, as their stockholders or residual claimants can unwind any portfolio decisions they make – this is the famous Modigliani-Miller theorem. In practice, institutions often make portfolio decisions as if they were individuals, and people purveying portfolio advice will run in to many such institutions.

References

Barberis, Nicholas (1999) 'Investing for the Long Run when Returns are Predictable', forthcoming, *Journal of Finance*.

Black, Fischer and Litterman, Robert (1991) 'Global Asset Allocation with Equities, Bonds, and Currencies', *Goldman Sachs Fixed Income Research*.

Brandt, Michael W. (1999) 'Estimating Portfolio and Consumption Choice: a Conditional Euler Equations Approach', *Journal of Finance*.

Brennan, Michael J., Schwartz, Eduardo S. and Lagnado, Roland (1997) 'Strategic Asset Allocation', *Journal of Economic Dynamics and Control*, 21, 1377–1403.

Campbell, John Y. and Cochrane, John H. (1999) 'By Force of Habit: A Consumption-Based Explanation of Aggregate Stock Market Behavior', *Journal of Political Economy*, 107, 205–251.

Campbell, John Y., Lo, Andrew W. and MacKinlay, A. Craig (1996) *The Econometrics of Financial Markets*. Princeton NJ: Princeton University Press.

Campbell, John Y. and Vicera, Luis M. (1998) 'Who Should Buy Long Term Bonds?' Manuscript, Havard University.

Campbell, John Y. and Vicera, Luis M. (1999) 'Consumption and Portfolio Decisions when Expected returns are Time Varying,' forthcoming *Quarterly Journal of Economics*.

Cochrane, John H. and Sbordone, Argia M. (1988) 'Multivariate Estimates of the Permanent Components in GNP and Stock Prices', *Journal of Economic Dynamics and Control*, 12, 255–296.

Cochrane, John H. (1997) 'Where is the Market Going? Uncertain Facts and Novel Theories,' *Economic Perspectives* XXI (6), Federal Reserve Bank of Chicago.

Daniel, Kent, Hirshleifer, David and Subrahmanyam, Ananidhar (1998) 'Investor Psychology and Security Market Under- and Over-reactions,' *Journal of Finance*, LIII, 1839–1885.

DeBondt, Werner F.M. and Thaler, Richard H. (1985) 'Does the Stock Market Overract?', *Journal of Finance*, 40, 793–808.

Fama, Eugene F. (1996) 'Multifactor Portfolio Efficiency and Multifactor Asset Pricing', *Journal of Financial and Quantitative Analysis*, 31, 441–465.

Fama, Eugene F. and French, Kenneth, R. (1989) 'Business Conditions and Expected Returns on Stocks and Bonds', *Journal of Financial Economics*, 25, 23–49.

Gallant, A. Ronald, Hansen, Lars Peter and Tauchen, George (1990) 'Using Conditional Moments of Asset Payoffs to Infer the Volatility of Intertemporal Marginal Rates of Substitution', *Journal of Econometrics*, 45, 141–179.

Kandel, Schmuel and Stambaugh, Robert (1996) 'On the Predictability of Stock returns: An Asset Allocation Perspective', *Journal of Finance*, 51, 385–424.

Kim, T.S. and Omberg, E. (1996) 'Dynamic Nonmyopic Portfolio Behavior', *Review of Financial Studies*, 9, 141–161.

Lakonishok, Josef, Shleifer, Andrei and Vishny, Robert W. (1994) 'Contrarian Investment, Extrapolation and Risk', *Journal of Finance*, 49, 1541–1578.

Markowitz, H. (1952) 'Portfolio Selection', *Journal of Finance*, 7, 77–99.

Merton, Robert C. (1969) 'Lifetime Portfolio Selection Under Uncertainty: The Continuous Time Case', *Review of Economics and Statistics*, 51, 247–257.

Merton, Robert C. (1971a) 'Optimum consumption and Portfolio Rules in a Continuous Time Model', *Journal of Economic Theory*, III, 373–413.

Merton, Robert C. (1971b) 'An International Capital Asset Pricing Model', *Econometrica*, 41, 867–887.

Samuelson, Paul A. (1969) 'Lifetime Portfolio Selection by Dynamic Stochastic Programming', *Review of Economics and Statistics*, 51, 239–246.

Sargent, Thomas J. (1993) *Bounded Rationality in Macroeconomics*. Oxford: Oxford University Press.

MULTIFACTOR PORTFOLIO MATHEMATICS

This section summarizes algebra in Fama (1996). The big picture is that we still get a hyperbolic region since betas are linear just like means.

The problem is, minimize the variance of a portfolio given a value for the portfolio mean and its beta on some factor. Let:

$$
w = \begin{bmatrix} w_1 \\ w_2 \\ \vdots \\ w_N \end{bmatrix} ; R = \begin{bmatrix} R^1 \\ R^2 \\ \vdots \\ R^N \end{bmatrix} ; 1 = \begin{bmatrix} 1 \\ 1 \\ \vdots \\ 1 \end{bmatrix} ; \beta = \begin{bmatrix} \beta_{1,F} \\ \beta_{2,F} \\ \vdots \\ \beta_{N,F} \end{bmatrix} .
$$

Then the portfolio return is:

$$R^P = w'R;$$

the condition that the weights add up to 1 is:

$$1 = 1'w.$$

The mean of the portfolio return is:

$$E(R^P) = E(w'R) = w'E(R) = w'E.$$

The last equality just simplifies notation. The beta of the portfolio on the extra factor is:

$$\beta^P = w'\beta$$

The variance of the portfolio return is:

$$var(R^P) = w'Vw$$

where V is the variance-convariance matrix of returns. The problem is then:

$$\min_{w} \frac{1}{2} w'Vw \text{ s.t. } w'E = \mu; w'1 = 1; w'\beta = \beta^P$$

The Lagrangian is:

$$\mathcal{L} = \frac{1}{2} w'Vw - \lambda_0 (w'E - \mu) - \lambda_1 (w'1 - 1) - \lambda_2 (w'\beta - \beta^P)$$

The first order conditions with respect to w give:

$$w = V^{-1}(E\lambda_0 + 1\lambda_1 + \beta\lambda_2) = V^{-1}A\lambda$$
$$A'w = \delta$$

Appendix: Statistical tables

Table A-1 ● Compound (future) value factors for $1 compounded at R per cent for N periods

N	1%	2%	3%	4%	5%	6%	7%	8%	9%	10%	11%	12%	13%
1	1.01	1.02	1.03	1.04	1.05	1.06	1.07	1.08	1.09	1.1	1.11	1.12	1.13
2	1.02	1.04	1.061	1.082	1.103	1.124	1.145	1.166	1.188	1.21	1.232	1.254	1.277
3	1.03	1.061	1.093	1.125	1.158	1.191	1.225	1.26	1.295	1.331	1.368	1.405	1.443
4	1.041	1.082	1.126	1.17	1.216	1.262	1.311	1.36	1.412	1.464	1.518	1.574	1.53
5	1.051	1.104	1.159	1.217	1.276	1.338	1.403	1.469	1.539	1.611	1.685	1.762	1.842
6	1.062	1.126	1.194	1.265	1.34	1.419	1.501	1.587	1.677	1.772	1.87	1.974	2.082
7	1.072	1.149	1.23	1.316	1.407	1.504	1.606	1.714	1.828	1.949	2.076	2.211	2.353
8	1.083	1.172	1.267	1.369	1.477	1.594	1.718	1.851	1.993	2.144	2.305	2.476	2.658
9	1.094	1.195	1.305	1.423	1.551	1.689	1.838	1.999	2.172	2.358	2.558	2.773	3.004
10	1.105	1.219	1.344	1.48	1.629	1.791	1.967	2.159	2.367	2.594	2.839	3.106	3.395
11	1.116	1.243	1.384	1.539	1.71	1.898	2.105	2.332	2.58	2.853	3.152	3.479	3.836
12	1.127	1.268	1.426	1.601	1.796	2.012	2.252	2.518	2.813	3.138	3.498	3.896	4.335
13	1.138	1.294	1.469	1.665	1.886	2.133	2.41	2.72	3.066	3.452	3.883	4.363	4.898
14	1.149	1.319	1.513	1.732	1.98	2.261	2.579	2.937	3.342	3.797	4.31	4.887	5.535
15	1.161	1.346	1.558	1.801	2.079	2.397	2.759	3.172	3.642	4.177	4.785	5.474	6.254
16	1.173	1.373	1.605	1.873	2.183	2.54	2.952	3.426	3.97	4.595	5.311	6.13	7.067
17	1.184	1.4	1.653	1.948	2.292	2.693	3.159	3.7	4.328	5.054	5.895	6.866	7.986
18	1.196	1.428	1.702	2.026	2.407	2.854	3.38	3.996	4.717	5.56	6.544	7.69	9.024
19	1.208	1.457	1.754	2.107	2.527	3.026	3.617	4.316	5.142	6.116	7.263	8.613	10.197
20	1.22	1.486	1.806	2.191	2.653	3.207	3.87	4.661	5.604	6.727	8.062	9.646	11.523
21	1.232	1.516	1.86	2.279	2.786	3.4	4.141	5.034	6.109	7.4	8.949	10.804	13.021
22	1.245	1.546	1.916	2.37	2.925	3.604	4.43	5.437	6.659	8.14	9.934	12.1	14.714
23	1.257	1.577	1.974	2.465	3.072	3.82	4.741	5.871	7.258	8.954	10.026	13.552	16.627
24	1.27	1.608	2.033	2.563	3.225	4.049	5.072	6.341	7.911	9.85	12.239	15.179	18.788
25	1.282	1.641	2.094	2.666	3.386	4.292	5.427	6.848	8.623	10.835	13.585	17	21.231
30	1.348	1.811	2.427	3.243	4.322	5.743	7.612	10.063	13.268	17.449	22.892	29.96	39.116
35	1.417	2	2.814	3.946	5.516	7.686	10.677	14.785	20.414	28.102	38.575	52.8	72.069
40	1.489	2.208	3.262	4.801	7.04	10.286	14.974	21.725	31.409	45.259	65.001	93.051	132.782
45	1.565	2.438	3.782	5.841	8.985	13.765	21.002	31.92	48.327	72.89	109.53	163.98	244.641
50	1.645	2.692	4.384	7.107	11.467	18.42	29.457	46.902	74.358	117.39	184.56	289.00	450.735

Table A-1 ● Compound (future) value factors for $1 compounded at R per cent for N periods (continued)

N	14%	15%	16%	18%	20%	22%	24%	25%	30%	35%	40%	45%	50%
1	1.14	1.15	1.16	1.18	1.2	1.22	1.25	1.25	1.3	1.35	1.4	1.45	1.5
2	1.3	1.323	1.346	1.392	1.44	1.488	1.538	1.563	1.69	1.823	1.96	2.103	2.25
3	1.482	1.521	1.561	1.643	1.728	1.816	1.907	1.953	2.197	2.46	2.744	3.049	3.375
4	1.689	1.749	1.811	1.939	2.074	2.215	2.364	2.441	2.856	3.322	3.842	4.421	5.063
5	1.925	2.011	2.1	2.288	2.488	2.703	2.932	3.052	3.713	4.484	5.378	6.41	7.594
6	2.195	2.313	2.436	2.7	2.986	3.297	3.635	3.815	4.827	6.053	7.53	9.294	11.391
7	2.502	2.66	2.826	3.185	3.583	4.023	4.508	4.768	6.275	8.172	10.541	13.476	17.086
8	2.853	3.059	3.278	3.759	4.3	4.908	5.59	5.96	8.157	11.032	14.758	19.541	25.629
9	3.252	3.518	3.803	4.435	5.16	5.987	6.931	7.451	10.604	14.894	20.661	28.334	38.443
10	3.707	4.046	4.411	5.234	6.192	7.305	8.594	9.313	13.786	20.107	28.925	41.085	57.665
11	4.226	4.652	5.117	6.176	7.43	8.912	10.657	11.642	17.922	27.144	40.496	59.573	86.498
12	4.818	5.35	5.936	7.288	8.916	10.872	13.215	14.552	23.298	36.644	56.694	86.381	129.746
13	5.492	6.153	6.886	8.599	10.699	13.264	16.386	18.19	30.288	49.47	79.371	125.25	194.62
14	6.261	7.076	7.988	10.147	12.839	16.182	20.319	22.737	39.374	66.784	111.12	181.61	291.929
15	7.138	8.137	9.266	11.974	15.407	19.742	25.196	28.422	51.186	90.158	155.56	263.34	437.894
16	8.137	9.358	10.748	14.129	18.488	24.086	31.243	35.527	66.542	121.71	217.79	381.84	656.841
17	9.276	10.761	12.468	16.672	22.186	29.384	38.741	44.409	86.504	164.31	304.91	553.67	985.261
18	10.575	12.375	14.463	19.673	26.623	35.849	48.039	55.511	112.45	221.82	426.87	802.83	1477.892
19	12.056	14.232	16.777	23.214	31.948	43.736	59.568	69.389	146.19	299.46	597.63	1164.1	2216.838
20	13.743	16.367	19.461	27.393	38.338	53.358	73.864	86.736	190.05	404.27	836.68	1687.9	3325.257
21	15.668	18.822	22.574	32.324	46.005	65.096	91.592	108.42	247.06	545.76	1171.3	2447.5	4987.885
22	17.861	21.645	26.186	38.142	55.206	79.418	113.57	135.52	321.18	716.78	1639.8	3548.9	7481.828
23	20.362	24.891	30.376	45.008	66.247	96.889	140.83	169.40	417.53	994.66	2297.8	5145.9	11222.74
24	23.212	28.625	35.236	53.109	79.497	118.20	174.63	211.75	542.80	1342.7	3214.2	7461.6	16834.11
25	26.462	32.919	40.874	62.669	95.396	144.21	216.54	264.69	705.64	1812.7	4499.8	10819.	25251.17
30	50.95	66.212	85.85	143.37	237.37	389.75	634.82	807.79	2619.9	8128.5	24201.	69348.	191751.1
35	98.1	133.17	180.31	327.99	590.66	1053.4	1861.0	2465.1	9727.8	36448.	130161.	444508.	
40	188.88	267.86	378.72	750.37	1469.7	2847.0	5455.9	7523.1	36118.	163437	700037		
45	363.67	538.76	795.44	1716.6	3657.2	7694.7	15994.	22958.	134106.	732857.			
50	700.23	1083.6	1670.7	3927.3	9100.4	20796.	46890.	70064.	497929.				

Table A-2 ● Present value factors (at R per cent) for $1 received at the end of N periods

R =

N	1%	2%	3%	4%	5%	6%	7%	8%	9%	10%	11%	12%	13%
1	.990	.980	.971	.962	.952	.943	.935	.926	.917	.909	.901	.893	.885
2	.980	.961	.943	.925	.907	.890	.873	.857	.842	.826	.812	.797	.783
3	.971	.942	.915	.889	.864	.840	.816	.794	.772	.751	.731	.712	.693
4	.961	.924	.888	.855	.823	.792	.763	.735	.708	.683	.659	.636	.613
5	.951	.906	.863	.822	.784	.747	.713	.681	.650	.621	.593	.567	.543
6	.942	.888	.837	.790	.746	.705	.666	.630	.596	.564	.535	.507	.480
7	.932	.871	.813	.760	.711	.665	.623	.583	.547	.513	.482	.452	.425
8	.923	.853	.789	.731	.677	.627	.582	.540	.502	.467	.434	.404	.376
9	.914	.837	.766	.703	.645	.592	.544	.500	.460	.424	.391	.361	.333
10	.905	.820	.744	.676	.614	.558	.508	.463	.422	.386	.352	.322	.295
11	.896	.804	.722	.650	.585	.527	.475	.429	.388	.350	.317	.287	.261
12	.887	.788	.701	.625	.557	.497	.444	.397	.356	.319	.286	.257	.231
13	.879	.773	.681	.601	.530	.469	.415	.368	.326	.290	.258	.229	.204
14	.870	.758	.661	.577	.505	.442	.388	.340	.299	.263	.232	.205	.181
15	.861	.743	.642	.555	.481	.417	.362	.315	.275	.239	.209	.183	.160
16	.853	.728	.623	.534	.458	.394	.339	.292	.252	.218	.188	.163	.141
17	.844	.714	.605	.513	.436	.371	.317	.270	.231	.198	.170	.146	.125
18	.836	.700	.587	.494	.416	.350	.296	.250	.212	.180	.153	.130	.111
19	.828	.686	.570	.475	.396	.331	.277	.232	.194	.164	.138	.116	.098
20	.820	.673	.554	.456	.377	.312	.258	.215	.178	.149	.124	.104	.087
21	.811	.660	.538	.439	.359	.294	.242	.199	.164	.135	.112	.093	.077
22	.803	.647	.522	.422	.342	.278	.226	.184	.150	.123	.101	.083	.068
23	.795	.634	.507	.406	.326	.262	.211	.170	.133	.112	.091	.074	.060
24	.788	.622	.492	.390	.310	.247	.197	.158	.126	.102	.082	.066	.053
25	.780	.610	.478	.375	.295	.233	.184	.146	.116	.092	.074	.059	.047
30	.742	.552	.412	.308	.231	.174	.131	.099	.075	.057	.044	.033	.026
35	.706	.500	.355	.253	.181	.130	.094	.068	.049	.036	.026	.019	.014
40	.672	.453	.307	.208	.142	.097	.067	.046	.032	.022	.015	.011	.008
45	.639	.410	.264	.171	.111	.073	.048	.031	.021	.014	.009	.006	.004
50	.608	.372	.228	.141	.087	.054	.034	.021	.013	.009	.005	.003	.002

Table A-2 ● Present value factors (at R per cent) for $1 received at the end of N periods (continued)

$R =$

N	14%	15%	16%	18%	20%	22%	24%	25%	30%	35%	40%	45%	50%
1	.877	.870	.862	.847	.833	.820	.806	.800	.769	.741	.714	.690	.667
2	.769	.756	.743	.718	.694	.672	.650	.640	.592	.549	.510	.476	.444
3	.675	.658	.641	.609	.579	.551	.524	.512	.455	.406	.364	.328	.296
4	.592	.572	.552	.516	.482	.451	.423	.410	.350	.301	.260	.226	.198
5	.519	.497	.476	.437	.402	.370	.341	.328	.269	.223	.186	.156	.132
6	.456	.432	.410	.370	.335	.303	.275	.262	.207	.165	.133	.108	.088
7	.400	.376	.354	.314	.279	.249	.222	.210	.159	.122	.095	.074	.059
8	.351	.327	.305	.266	.233	.204	.179	.168	.123	.091	.068	.051	.039
9	.308	.284	.263	.225	.194	.167	.144	.134	.094	.067	.048	.035	.026
10	.270	.247	.227	.191	.162	.137	.116	.107	.073	.050	.035	.024	.017
11	.237	.215	.195	.162	.135	.112	.094	.086	.056	.037	.025	.017	.012
12	.208	.187	.168	.137	.112	.092	.076	.069	.043	.027	.018	.012	.008
13	.182	.163	.145	.116	.093	.075	.061	.055	.033	.020	.013	.008	.005
14	.160	.141	.125	.099	.078	.062	.049	.044	.025	.015	.009	.006	.003
15	.140	.123	.108	.084	.065	.051	.040	.035	.020	.011	.006	.004	.002
16	.123	.107	.093	.071	.054	.042	.032	.028	.015	.008	.005	.003	.002
17	.108	.093	.080	.060	.045	.034	.026	.023	.012	.006	.003	.002	.001
18	.095	.081	.069	.051	.038	.028	.021	.018	.009	.005	.002	.001	.001
19	.083	.070	.060	.043	.031	.023	.017	.014	.007	.003	.002	.001	
20	.073	.061	.051	.037	.026	.019	.014	.012	.005	.002	.001	.001	
21	.064	.053	.044	.031	.022	.015	.011	.009	.004	.002	.001		
22	.056	.046	.038	.026	.018	.013	.009	.007	.003	.001	.001		
23	.049	.040	.033	.022	.015	.010	.007	.006	.002	.001			
24	.043	.035	.028	.019	.013	.008	.006	.005	.002	.001			
25	.038	.030	.024	.016	.010	.007	.005	.004	.001	.001			
30	.020	.015	.012	.007	.004	.003	.002	.001	.001				
35	.010	.008	.006	.003	.002	.001	.001						
40	.005	.004	.003	.001	.001								
45	.003	.002	.001	.001									
50	.001	.001	.001										

Table A-3 ● Compound sum annuity factors for $1 compounded at R per cent for N periods

N	1%	2%	3%	4%	5%	6%	7%	8%	9%	10%	11%	12%	13%
1	1	1	1	1	1	1	1	1	1	1	1	1	1
2	2.01	2.02	2.03	2.04	2.05	2.06	2.07	2.08	2.09	2.1	2.11	2.12	2.13
3	3.03	3.06	3.091	3.122	3.152	3.184	3.215	3.246	3.278	3.31	3.342	3.374	3.407
4	4.06	4.122	4.184	4.246	4.31	4.375	4.44	4.506	4.573	4.641	4.71	4.779	4.85
5	5.101	5.204	5.309	5.416	5.526	5.637	5.751	5.867	5.985	6.105	6.228	6.353	6.48
6	6.152	6.308	6.468	6.633	6.802	6.975	7.153	7.336	7.523	7.716	7.913	8.115	8.232
7	7.214	7.434	7.662	7.898	8.142	8.394	8.654	8.923	9.2	9.487	9.783	10.089	10.405
8	8.286	8.583	8.892	9.214	9.549	9.897	10.26	10.637	11.028	11.436	11.859	12.3	12.757
9	9.369	9.755	10.159	10.583	11.027	11.491	11.978	12.488	13.021	13.579	14.164	14.776	15.416
10	10.462	10.95	11.464	12.006	12.578	13.181	13.816	14.487	15.193	15.937	16.722	17.549	18.42
11	11.567	12.169	12.808	13.486	14.207	14.972	15.784	16.645	17.56	18.531	19.561	20.655	21.814
12	12.683	13.412	14.192	15.026	15.917	16.87	17.888	18.977	20.141	21.384	22.713	24.133	25.65
13	13.809	14.68	15.618	16.627	17.713	18.882	20.141	21.495	22.953	24.523	26.212	28.029	29.985
14	14.947	15.971	17.086	18.292	19.599	21.015	22.55	24.215	26.019	27.975	30.095	32.393	34.883
15	16.097	17.291	18.599	20.024	21.579	23.276	25.129	27.152	29.361	31.772	34.405	37.28	40.417
16	17.258	18.639	20.157	21.825	23.657	25.673	27.888	30.324	33.003	35.95	39.19	42.753	46.672
17	18.43	20.012	21.762	23.698	25.84	28.213	30.84	33.75	36.974	40.545	44.501	48.884	53.739
18	19.615	21.412	23.414	25.645	28.132	30.906	33.999	37.45	41.301	45.599	50.396	55.75	61.725
19	20.811	22.841	25.117	27.671	30.539	33.76	37.379	41.446	46.018	51.159	56.939	63.44	70.749
20	22.019	24.297	26.87	29.778	33.066	36.786	40.995	45.762	51.16	57.275	64.203	72.052	80.947
21	23.239	25.783	28.676	31.969	35.719	39.993	44.865	50.423	56.765	64.002	72.265	81.699	92.47
22	24.472	27.299	30.537	34.248	38.505	43.392	49.006	55.457	62.873	71.403	81.214	92.503	105.491
23	25.716	28.845	32.453	36.618	41.43	46.996	53.436	60.893	69.532	79.543	91.148	104.60	120.205
24	26.973	30.422	34.426	39.083	44.502	50.816	58.177	66.765	76.79	88.497	102.17	118.15	136.831
25	28.243	32.03	36.459	41.646	47.727	54.865	63.249	73.106	84.701	98.347	114.41	133.33	155.62
30	34.785	40.568	47.575	56.085	66.439	79.058	94.461	113.28	136.30	164.49	199.02	241.33	293.199
35	41.66	49.994	60.462	73.652	90.32	111.43	138.23	172.31	215.71	271.02	341.59	431.66	546.681
40	48.886	60.402	75.401	95.026	120.8	154.76	199.63	259.05	337.88	442.59	581.82	767.09	1013.704
45	56.481	71.893	92.72	121.02	159.7	212.74	285.74	386.50	525.85	718.90	986.63	1358.2	1874.165
50	64.463	84.579	112.79	152.66	209.34	290.33	406.52	573.77	815.08	1163.9	1668.7	2400.0	3459.507

R =

Table A-3 Compound sum annuity factors for $1 compounded at R per cent for N periods (continued)

R =

N	14%	15%	16%	18%	20%	22%	24%	25%	30%	35%	40%	45%	50%
1	1	1	1	1	1	1	1	1	1	1	1	1	1
2	2.14	2.15	2.16	2.18	2.2	2.22	2.24	2.25	2.3	2.35	2.4	2.45	2.5
3	3.44	3.472	3.506	3.572	3.64	3.708	3.778	3.813	3.99	4.172	4.36	4.552	4.75
4	4.921	4.993	5.066	5.215	5.368	5.524	5.684	5.766	6.187	6.633	7.104	7.601	8.125
5	6.61	6.742	6.877	7.154	7.442	7.74	8.048	8.207	9.043	9.954	10.916	12.022	13.188
6	8.536	8.754	8.977	9.442	9.93	10.442	10.98	11.259	12.756	14.438	16.324	18.431	20.781
7	10.73	11.067	11.414	12.142	12.916	13.74	14.615	15.073	17.583	20.492	23.853	27.726	32.172
8	13.233	13.727	14.24	15.327	16.499	17.762	19.123	19.842	23.858	28.664	34.395	44.202	49.258
9	16.085	16.786	17.519	19.086	20.799	22.67	24.712	25.802	32.015	39.696	49.153	60.743	74.887
10	19.337	20.304	21.321	23.521	25.959	28.657	31.643	33.253	42.619	54.59	69.814	89.077	113.33
11	23.045	24.349	25.733	28.755	32.15	35.962	40.238	42.566	56.405	74.697	98.739	130.16	170.995
12	27.271	29.002	30.85	34.931	39.581	44.874	50.895	54.208	74.327	101.84	139.23	189.73	257.493
13	32.089	34.352	36.786	42.219	48.497	55.746	64.11	68.76	97.625	138.48	195.92	276.11	387.239
14	37.581	40.505	43.672	50.818	59.196	69.01	80.496	86.949	127.91	187.95	275.3	401.36	581.859
15	43.842	47.58	51.66	60.965	72.035	85.192	100.81	109.68	167.28	254.73	386.42	582.98	873.788
16	50.98	55.717	60.925	72.939	87.442	104.93	126.01	138.10	218.47	344.89	541.98	846.32	1311.682
17	59.118	65.075	71.673	87.068	105.93	129.02	157.25	173.63	285.01	466.61	759.78	1228.1	1968.523
18	68.394	75.836	84.141	103.74	128.11	158.40	195.99	218.04	371.51	630.92	1064.6	1781.3	2953.784
19	78.969	88.212	98.603	123.41	154.74	194.25	244.03	273.55	483.97	852.74	1491.5	2584.6	4431.676
20	91.025	102.44	115.38	146.62	186.68	237.98	303.60	342.94	630.16	1152.2	2089.2	3748.7	6648.513
21	104.76	118.81	134.84	174.02	225.02	291.34	377.46	429.68	820.21	1556.4	2925.8	5436.7	9973.77
22	120.43	137.63	157.41	206.34	271.03	356.44	469.05	538.10	1067.2	2102.2	4097.2	7884.2	14961.65
23	138.29	159.27	183.60	244.48	326.23	435.86	582.63	673.62	1388.4	2839.0	5737.1	11433.	22443.48
24	158.65	184.16	213.97	289.49	392.48	532.75	723.46	843.03	1806.0	3833.7	8032.9	16579.	33666.22
25	181.87	212.79	249.21	342.60	471.98	650.95	898.09	1054.7	2348.8	5176.5	11247	24040.	50500.34
30	356.78	434.74	530.31	790.94	1181.8	1767.0	2640.9	3227.1	8729.9	23221.	60501.	154106.	383500.1
35	693.57	881.17	1120.7	1816.6	2948.3	4783.6	7750.2	9856.7	32422.	104136.	325400.	987794.	
40	1342.0	1779.0	2360.7	4163.2	7343.8	12936.	22728.	30088.	120392.	466960.			
45	2490.5	3585.1	4965.2	9531.5	18281.	34971.	66640.	91831.	447019.				
50	4994.5	7217.7	10435.	21813.	45497.	94525.	195372.	280255.					

Appendix • Statistical tables

Table A-4 • Present value annuity factors (at R per cent per period) for $1 received per period for each of N periods

N	1%	2%	3%	4%	5%	6%	7%	8%	9%	10%	11%	12%	13%
1	0.990	0.980	0.971	0.962	0.952	0.943	0.935	0.926	0.917	0.909	0.901	0.893	0.885
2	1.970	1.942	1.913	1.886	1.859	1.833	1.808	1.783	1.759	1.736	1.713	1.690	1.668
3	2.941	2.884	2.829	2.775	2.723	2.673	2.624	2.577	2.531	2.487	2.444	2.402	2.361
4	3.902	3.808	3.717	3.630	3.546	3.465	3.387	3.312	3.240	3.170	3.102	3.037	2.974
5	4.853	4.713	4.580	4.452	4.329	4.212	4.100	3.993	3.890	3.791	3.696	3.605	3.517
6	5.795	5.601	5.417	5.242	5.076	4.917	4.767	4.623	4.486	4.355	4.231	4.111	3.998
7	6.728	6.472	6.230	6.002	5.786	5.582	5.389	5.206	5.033	4.868	4.712	4.564	4.423
8	7.652	7.325	7.020	6.733	6.463	6.210	5.971	5.747	5.535	5.335	5.146	4.968	4.799
9	8.566	8.162	7.786	7.435	7.108	6.802	6.515	6.247	5.995	5.759	5.537	5.328	5.132
10	9.471	8.983	8.530	8.111	7.722	7.360	7.024	6.710	6.418	6.145	5.889	5.650	5.426
11	10.368	9.787	9.253	8.760	8.306	7.887	7.499	7.139	6.805	6.495	6.207	5.938	5.687
12	11.255	10.575	9.954	9.385	8.863	8.384	7.943	7.536	7.161	6.814	6.492	6.194	5.918
13	12.134	11.348	10.635	9.986	9.394	8.853	8.358	7.904	7.487	7.103	6.750	6.424	6.122
14	13.004	12.106	11.296	10.563	9.899	9.295	8.745	8.244	7.786	7.367	6.982	6.628	6.302
15	13.865	12.849	11.938	11.118	10.380	9.712	9.108	8.559	8.061	7.606	7.191	6.811	6.462
16	14.718	13.578	12.561	11.652	10.838	10.106	9.447	8.851	8.313	7.824	7.379	6.974	6.604
17	15.562	14.292	13.166	12.166	11.274	10.477	9.763	9.122	8.544	8.022	7.549	7.120	6.729
18	16.398	14.992	13.754	12.659	11.690	10.828	10.059	9.372	8.756	8.201	7.702	7.250	6.840
19	17.226	15.678	14.324	13.134	12.085	11.158	10.336	9.604	8.950	8.365	7.839	7.366	6.938
20	18.046	16.351	14.877	13.590	12.462	11.470	10.594	9.818	9.129	8.514	7.963	7.469	7.025
21	18.857	17.011	15.415	14.029	12.821	11.764	10.836	10.017	9.292	8.649	8.075	7.562	7.102
22	19.660	17.658	15.937	14.451	13.163	12.042	11.061	10.201	9.442	8.772	8.176	7.654	7.170
23	20.456	18.292	16.444	14.857	13.489	12.303	11.272	10.371	9.580	8.883	8.266	7.718	7.230
24	21.243	18.914	16.936	15.247	13.799	12.550	11.469	10.529	9.707	8.985	8.348	7.784	7.283
25	22.023	19.523	17.413	15.622	14.094	12.783	11.654	10.675	9.823	9.077	8.422	7.843	7.330
30	25.808	22.396	19.600	17.292	15.372	13.765	12.409	11.258	10.274	9.427	8.694	8.055	7.496
35	29.409	24.999	21.487	18.665	16.374	14.498	12.948	11.655	10.567	9.644	8.855	8.176	7.586
40	32.835	27.355	23.115	19.793	17.159	15.046	13.332	11.925	10.757	9.779	8.951	8.244	7.634
45	36.095	29.490	24.519	20.720	17.774	15.456	13.606	12.108	10.881	9.863	9.008	8.283	7.661
50	39.196	31.424	25.730	21.482	18.256	15.762	13.801	12.233	10.962	9.915	9.042	8.304	7.675

R =

Table A-4 ● Present value annuity factors (at R per cent per period) for $1 received per period for each of N periods (continued)

N	R = 14%	15%	16%	18%	20%	22%	24%	25%	30%	35%	40%	45%	50%
1	0.877	0.870	0.862	0.847	0.833	0.820	0.806	0.800	0.769	0.741	0.714	0.690	0.667
2	1.647	1.626	1.605	1.566	1.528	1.492	1.457	1.440	1.361	1.289	1.224	1.165	1.111
3	2.322	2.283	2.246	2.174	2.106	2.042	1.981	1.952	1.816	1.696	1.589	1.493	1.407
4	2.914	2.855	2.798	2.690	2.589	2.494	2.404	2.362	2.166	1.997	1.849	1.720	1.605
5	3.433	3.352	3.274	3.127	2.991	2.864	2.745	2.689	2.436	2.220	2.035	1.876	1.737
6	3.889	3.784	3.685	3.498	3.326	3.167	3.020	2.951	2.643	2.385	2.168	1.983	1.824
7	4.288	4.160	4.039	3.812	3.605	3.416	3.242	3.161	2.802	2.508	2.263	2.057	1.883
8	4.639	4.487	4.344	4.078	3.837	3.619	3.421	3.329	2.925	2.598	2.331	2.109	1.922
9	4.946	4.772	4.607	4.303	4.031	3.786	3.566	3.463	3.019	2.665	2.379	2.144	1.948
10	5.216	5.019	4.833	4.494	4.192	3.923	3.682	3.571	3.092	2.715	2.414	2.168	1.965
11	5.453	5.234	5.029	4.656	4.327	4.035	3.776	3.656	3.147	2.752	2.438	2.185	1.977
12	5.660	5.421	5.197	4.793	4.439	4.127	3.851	3.725	3.190	2.779	2.456	2.196	1.985
13	5.842	5.583	5.342	4.910	4.533	4.203	3.912	3.780	3.223	2.799	2.469	2.204	1.990
14	6.002	5.724	5.468	5.008	4.611	4.265	3.962	3.824	3.249	2.814	2.478	2.210	1.993
15	6.142	5.847	5.575	5.092	4.675	4.315	4.001	3.859	3.268	2.825	2.484	2.214	1.995
16	6.265	5.954	5.668	5.162	4.730	4.357	4.033	3.887	3.283	2.834	2.489	2.216	1.997
17	6.373	6.047	5.749	5.222	4.775	4.391	4.059	3.910	3.295	2.840	2.492	2.218	1.998
18	6.467	6.128	5.818	5.273	4.812	4.419	4.080	3.928	3.304	2.844	2.494	2.219	1.999
19	6.550	6.198	5.877	5.316	4.843	4.442	4.097	3.942	3.311	2.848	2.496	2.220	1.999
20	6.623	6.259	5.929	5.353	4.870	4.460	4.110	3.954	3.316	2.850	2.497	2.221	1.999
21	6.687	6.312	5.973	5.384	4.891	4.476	4.121	3.963	3.320	2.852	2.498	2.221	1.999
22	6.743	6.359	6.011	5.410	4.909	4.488	4.130	3.970	3.323	2.853	2.498	2.222	2.000
23	6.792	6.399	6.044	5.432	4.925	4.499	4.137	3.976	3.325	2.854	2.499	2.222	2.000
24	6.835	6.434	6.073	5.451	4.937	4.507	4.143	3.981	3.327	2.855	2.499	2.222	2.000
25	6.873	6.464	6.097	5.467	4.948	4.514	4.147	3.985	3.329	2.856	2.499	2.222	2.000
30	7.003	6.566	6.177	5.517	4.979	4.534	4.160	3.995	3.332	2.857	2.500	2.222	2.000
35	7.070	6.617	6.215	5.539	4.992	4.541	4.164	3.998	3.333	2.857	2.500	2.222	2.000
40	7.105	6.642	6.233	5.548	4.997	4.544	4.166	3.999	3.333	2.857	2.500	2.222	2.000
45	7.123	6.654	6.242	5.552	4.999	4.545	4.166	4.000	3.333	2.857	2.500	2.222	2.000
50	7.133	6.661	6.246	5.554	4.999	4.545	4.167	4.000	3.333	2.857	2.500	2.222	2.000

REFERENCES

Ariel, R. A. (1990) 'High Stock Returns Before Holidays: Existence and Evidence on Possible Causes', *Journal of Finance*, 45, 1611–1626.

Ariel, R. A. (1987) 'A Monthly Effect on Stock Market Returns', *Journal of Financial Economics*, 18, 161–174.

Bachelier, L. (1900) 'Théorie de la Spéculation' in *Annales de l'Ecole Normale Supérieure*, 3 Paris: Gauthier-Villars. English translation in Cooter, P. H. (ed.), (1964) *The Random Character of Stock Market Prices*, Cambridge: MIT Press.

Banz, R. (1981) 'The relationship between return and Market Value of Common Stocks', *Journal of Financial Economics*, 3–18.

Bayes, T, (1763) 'An Essay Toward Solving a Problem in the Doctrine of Chances', *Philosophical Transactions*, Essay LII, 370–418.

Baxter, M. and Jermann, U. (1997) 'The International Diversification Puzzle Is Worse Than You Think', *American Economic Review*, 87, 177–180.

Benartzi, S. and Thaler, R. H. (1995) 'Myopic Loss Aversion and the Equity Premium Puzzle', *Quarterly Journal of Economics*, 110 (1), 73–92.

Black, F. (1989) 'How we came up with the option formula', *Journal of Portfolio Management*.

Black, F. (1976) 'The pricing of commodity contracts', *Journal of Financial Economics*, 3, 167–179.

Black, F., Jensen, M. C. and Scholes, M. S. (1972) 'The Capital Asset Pricing Model: Some Empirical Tests' in Jensen, M. (ed.), *Studies in the Theory of Capital Markets*, New York: Praeger.

Black, F. and Scholes, M. S. (1972) 'The Valuation of Options Contracts and a Test of Market Efficiency', *Journal of Finance*, 27, 399–417.

Black, F. and Scholes, M. S. (1973) 'The Pricing of Options and Corporate Liabilities', *Journal of Political Economy*, 81, 637–654.

Blake, D. (2000) *Financial Market Analysis*, John Wiley.

Blanchard, O. J. (1979) 'Speculative Bubbles, Crashes and Rational Expectations', *Economic Letters*, 3, 387–389.

Blanchard, O. J. and Watson, M. W. (1982) 'Bubbles, Rational Expectations and Financial Markets', in Wachtel, P. (ed.), *Crisis in the Economic and Financial System*, Lexington, MA: Lexington Books.

Bookstaber, R. M. (1982) *Option Pricing and Strategies in Investing*, Reading, MA: Addison-Wesley.

Brown, P., Kiem, D., Kleidon, A. and Marsh, T. (1983) 'Stock Return Seasonalities and the Tax Loss Selling Hypothesis: Analysis of the Arguments and Australian Evidence', *Journal of Financial Economics*.

Campbell, J. Y. and Shiller, R. (1988) 'Stock Prices Earnings and Expected Dividends', *Journal of Finance*, 43, 661–676.

Canner, N., Mankiw, N. G and Weil, D. N. (1997) 'An asset allocation puzzle', *American Economic Review*, 181–191.

Chen, N., Ross, S. A. and Roll, R. (1986) 'Economic forces and the stock market', *Journal of Business*.

Cochrane, J. (1997) 'Where is the market going? Uncertain facts and novel theories', Economic Perspectives, *Federal Reserve Bank of Chicago*, 21 (6), 3–37.

Cochrane, J. (1997) 'New facts in Finance', Economic Perspectives, *Federal Reserve Bank of Chicago*, 21 (6), 36–58.

Cochrane, J. (1999) 'Portfolio Advice For a MultiFactor World', NBER Working Paper No. 7170.

Constantinides, G. M., Donaldson, J. B. and Mehra, R. (1998) 'Junior can't borrow: a new perspective on the equity premium puzzle', NBER Working Paper No. 6617.

Cox, J. S., Ross, S. A. and Rubinstein, M. (1979) 'Option Pricing: A Simplified Approach', *Journal of Financial Economics*.

Cox, J. S. and Rubinstein, M. (1985) *Option Markets*. Englewood Cliffs, NJ: Prentice Hall.

Cox, J. S. and Rubinstein, M. (1993) 'A Survey of Alternative Option Pricing Models', in Brenner, M. (ed), *Option Pricing*, Cambridge, MA: Heath.

Cutler, D., Poterba, J. and Summers, L. (1989) 'What Moves Stock Prices?' *Journal of Portfolio Management*, 15 (3), 4–12.

DeBondt, W. F. M. and Thaler, R. H. (1985) 'Does the Stock Market Overreact?' *Journal of Finance*, 40 (3), 793–805.

DeBondt, W. F. M. and Thaler, R. H. (1987) 'Further Evidence of Investor Overreaction and Stock Market Seasonality', *Journal of Finance*, 42, 557–581.

De Long, J. B., Shleifer, A., Summers, L. H. and Waldmann, R. J. (1989) 'The Size and Incidence of the Losses from Noise Trading', *Journal of Finance*, 44 (3), 681–696.

De Long, J. B., Shleifer, A., Summers, L. H. and Waldmann, R. J. (1990) 'Noise Trader Risk in Financial Markets', *Journal of Political Economy*, 98 (4), 703–738.

Dewing, A. (1953) *The Financial Policy of Corporations*. New York: The Ronald Press.

Dumas and Solnik (1993) 'The world price of exchange rate risk, working paper, HEC School of Management.

Estes, R. (1981) *Dictionary of Accounting*. MIT (Cambridge, MA), 81–105.

Fama, E. F. (1965) 'The Behavior of Stock Market Prices', *Journal of Business*, 38, 34–105.

Fama, E. F. (1970) 'Efficient capital markets: a review of theory and empirical work', *Journal of Finance*, 25, 383–417.

Fama, E. F. (1971) 'Risk, Return and Equilibrium', *Journal of Political Economy*, 1, 30–55.

Fama, E. F. (1972) 'Components of Investment Performance', *Journal of Finance*, 27, 551–567.

Fama, E. F. (1976) 'Forward Rates as Predictors of Future Spot Rates', *Journal of Financial Economics*, 3, 361–377.

Fama, E. F. (1984) 'Forward and Spot Exchange Rates', *Journal of Monetary Economics*, 14, 319–338.

Fama, E. F. (1990) 'Term-Structure Forecasts of Interest Rates, Inflation, and Real Returns', *Journal of Monetary Economics*, 25 (1), 59–76.

Fama, E. F. (1990) 'Efficient Capital Markets: A Review of Theory and Empirical Work', *Journal of Finance*, 25 (2), 383–423.

Fama, E. F. (1991) 'Efficient capital markets II', *Journal of Finance*, 46, 1575–1617.

Fama, E. F. (1998) 'Market efficiency, long term returns, and behavioural finance', *Journal of Financial Economics*.

Fama, E. F., Fisher, L., Jensen, M. C. and Roll, R. (1969) 'The Adjustment of Stock Prices to New Information', *International Economic Review*, 10 (1), 1–21.

Fama, E. F. and MacBeth, J. D. (1974) 'Tests of the Multiperiod Two-Parameter Model', *Journal of Financial Economics*, 1 (1), 43–66.

Fama, E. F. and Bliss, R. R. (1987) 'The Information in Long-Maturity Forward Rates', *American Economic Revue*, 77 (4), 680–692.

Fama, E. F. and French, K. R. (1988a) 'Permanent and Temporary Components of Stock Prices', *Journal of Political Economy*, 96, 246–273.

Fama, E. F. and French, K. R. (1988b) 'Dividend Yields and Expected Stock Returns', *Journal of Financial Economics*, 22, 3–25.

Fama, E. F. and French, K. R. (1989) 'Business Conditions and Expected Returns on Stocks and Bonds', *Journal of Financial Economics*, 25, 23–49.

Fama, E. F. and French, K. R. (1992) 'The Cross Section of Expected Stock Returns', *Journal of Finance*, 47, 427–466.

Fama, E. F. and French, K. R. (1996) 'Multifactor Explanations of Asset Pricing Anomalies', *Journal of Finance*, 55–84.

French, K. R. (1980) 'Stock Returns and the Weekend Effect', *Journal of Financial Economics*, 8, 55–69.

French, K. R. and Poterba, J. (1991) 'International Diversification and International Equity Markets', *American Economic Review*, 81 (1), 222–226.

Fisher, I. (1896) 'Appreciation and Interest', *Publications of the American Economic Association*, 23–29, 91–92.

Fisher, I. (1907) *The Rate of Interest*. New York: Macmillan.

Fisher, I. (1930) *The Theory of Interest*. New York: Macmillan.

Garber, P. M. (1989) 'Who Put the Mania in Tulipmania?' *The Journal of Portfolio Management*, 16 (1), 53–60.

Garber, P. M. (1989) 'Tulipmania', *Journal of Political Economy*, 97 (3), 535–560.

Garber, P. M. (1990) 'Famous First Bubbles', *Journal of Economic Perspectives*, 4 (2).

Garber, P. M. (2000) *Famous First Bubbles: The Fundamentals of Early Manias*. Cambridge, MA: MIT Press.

Gibbons, M. and Hess, P. (1981) 'Day of the Week Effects and Asset Returns', *Journal of Business*, 54, 579–596.

Graham, B. and Dodd, D. (1934) *Securities Analysis*. New York: McGraw-Hill.

Greenspan, A. (1996). 'The Challenge of Central Banking in a Democratic Society.' Remarks at The Annual Dinner and Francis Boyer Lecture at the American Enterprise Institute for Public Policy Research, Washington D.C. 5 December.

Greenspan, A. (1997) 'Monetary Policy Testimony and Report to Congress'. Subcommittee on Domestic and International Monetary Policy on Banking and Financial Services, US House of Representatives, 22 July.

Hall, R. E. (2000) 'The Stock Market and Capital Accumulation' http://www.stanford.edu/~rehall/SMCA-d%205-12-00.pdf

Hardouvelis, G. A. (1988) 'Evidence on Stock Market Speculative Bubbles: Japan, United States and Great Britain', *Federal Reserve Bank of New York*, Research Paper No. 8810.

Harris, L. (1986) 'How to Profit from Intradaily Stock Returns', *Journal of Portfolio Management*, 12, 61–64.

Harris, L. (1989) 'A Day-End Transaction Price Anomaly', *Journal of Financial and Quantitative Analysis*, 24, 29–45.

Haugen, R. A. (1999) *Beast on Wall Street*. Prentice Hall.

Haugen, R. A. (1999) *The Inefficient Stock Market*. Prentice Hall.

Haugen, R. A. (1999) *The New Finance*. Prentice Hall.

Holstrom, B. and Tirole, J. (1998) 'LAPM: a liquidity-based asset pricing model', NBER Working Paper No. 6673.

Jacquillat and Solnik (1978) 'Multinationals are poor tools for diversification', *Journal of Portfolio Management*, 4, 3–12.

Jensen, M. C. (1978) 'Some Anomalous Evidence Regarding Market Efficiency', *Journal of Financial Economics*, 6, 95–101.

Jorion, P. and Goetzmann, W. N. (1999) 'Global Stock Markets in the Twentieth Century', *Journal of Finance*, 54 (3), 953–980.

Kahneman, D. and Tversky, A. (1979) 'Prospect Theory: An Analysis of Decision under Risk', *Econometica*, 47 (2), 263–291.

Kahneman, D. and Tversky, A. (1984) 'Choices, Values and Frames', *American Psychologist*, 39 (4), 342–347.

Kahneman, D., Knetsch, J. L. and Thaler, R. H. (1990) 'Experimental Tests of the Endowment Effect and the Coase Theorem', *Journal of Political Economy*, 98 (6), 1325–1348.

Keim, D. B. and Stambaugh, R. F. (1986) 'Predicting Returns in the Stock and Bond Markets', *Journal of Financial Economics*, 17, 357–390.

Kettell, B. (1998) *What Drives Financial Markets*. London: *Financial Times*, Prentice Hall.

Kettell, B. (1999) *Fed Watching*. London: *Financial Times*, Prentice Hall.

Kettell, B. (2000) *What Drives Currency Markets?* London: *Financial Times*, Prentice Hall.

Keynes, J. M. (1936) *The General Theory of Employment, Interest and Money*. New York: Harcourt, Brace and Co.

Krugman, P. (1997) 'How Fast Can the U.S. Economy Grow?' *Harvard Business Review*, 75, 123–129.

Lakonishok, J. and Smidt, S. (1988) 'Are Seasonal Anomalies Real? A Ninety-Year Perspective', *Review of Financial Studies*, 1, 403–425.

Levis, M. (1985) 'Are Small Firms Big Performers?' *The Investment Analyst*.

Lintner, J. (1965) 'Securities Prices, Risk, and Maximal Gains from Diversification', *Journal of Finance*, 20, 587–615.

Lintner, J. (1965) 'The Valuation of Risky Assets and the Selection of Risky Investments in Stock Portfolios and Capital Budgets', *Review of Economics and Statistics*, 47, 13–37.

Lintner, J. (1971) 'The Aggregation of Investors Diverse Judgements and Preferences in Purely Competitive Security Markets', *Journal of Financial and Quantitative Analysis*, 4 (4), 327–450.

Livingston, M. (1995) *Money and Capital Markets*. Blackwell Business.

Lo, A. W. and Mackinlay, A. C. (1999) *A Non-Random Walk down Wall Street*. Princeton University Press.

Malkiel, B. G. (1962) 'Expectations, Bond Prices and the Term Structure of Interest Rates', *Quarterly Journal of Economics*.

Malkiel, B. G. and Cragg, J. G. (1970) 'Expectations and the Structure of Share Prices', *American Economic Review*, September.

Malkiel, B. G. (2000) *A Random Walk down Wall Street*. 10th Edition, W.W. Norton and Company.

Mandelbrot, B. (1963) 'The Variation of Certain Speculative Prices', *Journal of Business*, 36, 394–419.

Mandelbrot, B. (1966) 'Forecasts of Future Prices, Unbiased Markets and Martingale Models', *Journal of Business*, 39, 242–255.

Mandelbrot, B. (1997) *Fractals and Scaling in Finance; Discontinuity, Concentration, Risk*. New York: Springer-Verlag.

Mackay, C. (1841) *Memoirs of Extraordinary Popular Delusions and the Madness of Crowds*. London: Bentley.

Macaulay, F. (1938) *Some Theoretical Problems Suggested by The Movements of Interest Rates, Bond Yields and Stock Prices in the United States Since 1856.* New York: National Bureau for Economic Research.

Markowitz, H. M. (1952) 'Portfolio Selection', *Journal of Finance*, 7, 13–37.

Markowitz, H. M. (1959) *Portfolio Selection.* New Haven, CT: Yale University Press.

Mehra, R. and Prescott, E. C. (1985) 'The Equity Premium Puzzle', *Journal of Monetary Economics*, 15, 145–161.

Mehra, R. and Prescott, E. C. (1988) 'The Equity Premium Puzzle', *Journal of Monetary Economics*, 22, 133–136.

Merton, R. C. (1973) 'The Theory of Rational Option Pricing', *Bell Journal of Economics and Management Science*, 4, 141–183.

Merton, R. C. (1976) 'Option Pricing When Underlying Stock Returns Are Discontinuous', *Journal of Financial Economics*, 3, 125.

Merton, R. C. (1983) 'On the role of social security as a means for efficient risk-bearing in an economy where human capital is not tradeable', in Bodie, Z. and Shoven, J.B. (eds), *Financial Aspects of the US Pension System*, Chicago: University Chicago Press.

Merton, R. C. (1990) *Continuous Time Finance.* Cambridge: Cambridge University Press.

Merton, R. C. (1995) 'Influence of Mathematical Models in Finance on Practice: Past, Present and Future', *Financial Practice and Education*, 5 (1), 7–15.

Meyer, L. H. (1997) 'Statement on Monetary Policy', Committee on Banking and Financial Services, US House of Representatives (23 July).

Modigliani, F. and Miller, M. (1958) 'The Cost Capital, Corporation Finance and the Theory of Investment', *The American Economic Review*, 48, 261–297.

Modigliani, F. and Cohn, R. A. (1979) 'Inflation, Rational Valuation, and the Market', *Financial Analysts' Journal*, 35, 22–44. Reprinted in Johnson, Simon (ed), *The Collected Papers of Franco Modigliani*, Vol. 5. Cambridge, MA: MIT Press, 1989.

Mossin, J. (1966) 'Equilibrium in a Capital Assets Market', *Econometrica*, 34, 768–783.

Nakamura, L. (1999) 'Intangibles: What Put the New in the New Economy?' *Federal Reserve Bank of Philadelphia Business Review*, July/August.

Obstfeld, M. and Rogoff, K. (2000) 'The Six Major Puzzles in International Macroeconomics: Is There a Common Cause', National Bureau of Economic Research, Working Paper 7777.

Poterba, J. and Summers, L. (1988) 'Mean Reversion in Stock Prices: Evidence and Implications', *Journal of Financial Economics*, 22, 27–59.

Ritter, J. and Warr, R. S. (1999) 'Decline of Inflation and the Bull Markets of 1982–1997', Unpublished paper, University of Florida, Gainesville.

Roberts, H. V. (1959) 'Stock Market Patterns and Financial Analysis: Methodological Suggestions', *Journal of Finance*.

Roll, R. (1977) 'A Critique of the Asset Pricing Theory's Tests: Part 1: On Past and Potential Testability of the Theory', *Journal of Financial Economics*, 129–176.

Roll, R. (1978) 'Ambiguity When Performance Is Measured by the Security Market Line', *Journal of Finance* (September).

Ross, S. A. (1976) 'The Arbitrage Theory of Capital Asset Pricing', *Journal of Economic Theory*, 13, 342–360.

Ross, S. A. (1977) 'The Capital Asset Pricing Model (CAPM), Short Sale Restrictions and Related Issues', *Journal of Finance* (March).

Ross, S. A. (1978) 'The Current Status of the Capital Asset Pricing Model (CAPM)', *Journal of Finance* (June).

Roll, R. and Ross, S. A. (1980) 'An Empirical Investigation of the Arbitrage Pricing Theory', *Journal of Finance*, 35, 1073–1103.

Rozeff, M. and Kinney, W. (1976) 'Capital Market Seasonality; The Case of Stock Returns', *Journal of Financial Economics*, 3, 379–402.

Samuelson, P. A. (1965a) 'Proof that Properly Anticipated Prices Fluctuate Randomly', *Industrial Management Review*, 6, 41–49.

Samuelson, P. A. (1965b) 'Rational Theory of Warrant Pricing', *Industrial Management Review*, 6, 13–31.

Samuelson, P. A. (1976) *Economics*. Tenth Edition. New York: McGraw-Hill.

Schiller, R. J. (1981) 'Do Stock Market Prices Move Too Much?' *American Economic Review*, 71 (3), 421–436.

Schiller, R. J. (1987) 'Investor Behaviour in the October 1987 Stock Market Crash,' National Bureau of Economic Research, Working Paper No. 2446.

Schiller, R. J. (1989) *Market Volatility*. Cambridge, MA: Cambridge University Press.

Schiller, R. J. (2000) *Irrational Exuberance*. Princeton University Press.

Schiller, R. J. (2000) 'Measuring Bubble Expectations and Investor Confidence', *Journal of Psychology and Markets*, 1 (1), 49–60.

Sharpe, W. F. (1963) 'A Simplified Model for Portfolio Analysis', *Management Science*, 9 January, 277–293.

Sharpe, W. F. (1964) 'Capital Asset Prices: A Theory of Market Equilibrium Under Condition of Risk', *Journal of Finance*, September.

Sharpe, W. F. (1965) 'Risk Aversion in the Stock Market: Some Empirical Evidence', *Journal of Finance*, September.

Sharpe, W. F. (1966) 'Mutual Fund Performance', *Journal of Business*, January.

Sharpe, W. F. (1967) 'Portfolio Analysis', *Journal of Financial and Quantitative Analysis*, 2, 425–439.

Sharpe, W. F. (1990) 'Investor Wealth Measures and Expected Return', in Sharpe, W. F. (ed.), *Quantifying the Market Risk Premium Phenomenon for Investment Decision-Making* (1990), Charlottesville, VA: The Institute of Chartered Financial Analysts.

Sharpe, W. F., Alexander, G. J. and Bailey, J. V. (1995) *Investments*. London: Prentice Hall. See Chapter 5.

Siegel, J. (1991) 'The real rate of interest from 1800–1990: A study of the US and UK', Working paper, Wharton School.

Siegel, J. (1992) 'The Equity premium: Stock and Bond returns since 1802', *Financial Analysts Journal*, XXXXVIII, 28–38.

Siegel, J. (1995) *Stocks for the Long Run: A Guide to Selecting Markets for Long-Term Growth*. Burr Ridge, IL: Irwin Professional Publishing.

Smithers, A. and Wright, S. (2000) *Valuing Wall Street: Protecting Wealth in Turbulent Markets*. McGraw Hill.

Thaler, R. H. (1987) 'The Psychology of Choice and the Assumptions of Economics.' in Thaler (1991), Ch.7, p. 139.

Thaler, R. H. (1991) *Quasi-Rational Economics*. New York: Russell Sage Foundation.

Thaler, R. H. (1992) *The Winner's Curse: Paradoxes and Anomalies of Economic Life*. New York: The Free Press.

Thaler, R. H. (1993) *Advances in Behavioural Finance*. New York: Russell Sage Foundation.

Thaler, R. H. (1995) 'Behavioural Economics', *NBER Reporter*, National Bureau of Economic Research, 9–13.

Thaler, R. H. and Shefin, H. (1981) 'An Economic Theory of Self-Control', *Journal of Political Economy*, 89 (2), 392–406.

Thaler, R. H., Tversky, D. and Knetsch, J. L. (1990) 'Experimental Tests of the Endowment Effect', *Journal of Political Economy*, 98 (6), 1325–1348.

Thaler, R. H., Tversky, D. and Knetsch, J. L. (1991) 'Endowment Effect, Loss Aversion, and Status Quo Bias', *Journal of Economic Perspectives*, 5 (1), 193–206.

Tobin, J. (1958) 'Liquidity Preference as Behaviour Toward Risk', *Review of Economic Studies*, 65–85.

Treynor, J. L. (1965) 'How to Rate Management Investment Funds', *Harvard Business Review* (January–February).

Treynor, J. L. (1989) 'Information-Based Investing', *Financial Analysts Journal*, May/June, 6–7.

Treynor, J. L. (1990) 'The 10 Most Important Questions to Ask in Selecting a Money Manager', *Financial Analysts Journal*, May/June, 4–5.

Tversky, A. and Kahneman, D. (1974) 'Judgement under Uncertainty: Heuristics and Biases', *Science*, 185, 1124–1131.

Wadhwani, S. (1999) 'The US stock and the global economic crisis', National Institute Economic Review, January, 86–105.

Zeeman, E. C. (1974) 'On the Unstable Behaviour of Stock Exchanges', *Journal of Mathematical Economics*, 1, 39–49.

INDEX